Editing Chaucer

Caxton presenting *The Receuyell of the Histories of Troye* to Margaret, Duchess of Burgundy. Reproduced by permission of The Huntington Library, San Marino, California.

Editing Chaucer

THE
GREAT
TRADITION

EDITED BY
PAUL G. RUGGIERS

PILGRIM BOOKS
NORMAN, OKLAHOMA

By Paul G. Ruggiers

Library of Congress Cataloging in Publication Data

Pilgrim Books, P.O. Box 2399, Norman, Oklahoma 73070

Library of Congress Cataloging in Publication Data

Main entry under title:

Editing Chaucer.

  Includes index.
  1. Chaucer, Geoffrey, d. 1400—Editors. 2. Chaucer, Geoffrey, d.
1400—Criticism, Textual. 3. Manuscripts, English (Middle)—
Editing. 4. Editing. I. Ruggiers, Paul G.
PR1939.E3 1984   821'.1   84-1872
ISBN 0-937664-58-8

Contents

Abbreviations and Sigils

ABBREVIATIONS OF CHAUCER'S WORKS

ABC	An ABC
Adam	Adam Scriveyn
Anel	Anelida and Arcite
Astr	A Treatise on the Astrolabe
Bal Compl	A Balade of Complaint
BD	The Book of the Duchess
Bo	Boece
Buk	The Envoy to Bukton
CkT, CkP, Rv-CkL	The Cook's Tale, The Cook's Prologue, Reeve-Cook Link
ClT, ClP, Cl-MerL	The Clerk's Tale, The Clerk's Prologue, Clerk-Merchant Link
Compl D'Am	Complaynt d'Amours
CT	The Canterbury Tales
CYT, CYP	The Canon's Yeoman's Tale, The Canon's Yeoman's Prologue
Equat	The Equatorie of the Planets
For	Fortune
Form Age	The Former Age
FranT, FranP	The Franklin's Tale, The Franklin's Prologue
FrT, FrP, Fr-SumL	The Friar's Tale, The Friar's Prologue, Friar-Summoner Link
Gent	Gentilesse
GP	The General Prologue
HF	The House of Fame
KnT, Kn-MilL	The Knight's Tale, Knight-Miller Link
Lady	A Complaint to His Lady
LGW, LGWP	The Legend of Good Women, The Legend of Good Women Prologue
ManT, ManP	The Manciple's Tale, The Manciple's Prologue
Mars	The Complaint of Mars
Mel, MelP, Mel-MkL	The Tale of Melibee, The Prologue of Melibee, Melibee-Monk Link
MercB	Merciles Beaute
MerT, MerP, MerE-SqH	The Merchant's Tale, The Merchant's Prologue, Merchant Endlink-Squire Headlink
MilT, MilP, Mil-RvL	The Miller's Tale, The Miller's Prologue, Miller-Reeve Link

MkT, MkP, Mk-NPL	The Monk's Tale, The Monk's Prologue, Monk-Nun's Priest Link
MLT, MLI, MLH, MLP, MLE	The Man of Law's Tale, The Man of Law's Introduction, Man of Law Headlink, The Man of Law's Prologue, Man of Law Endlink
NPT, NPP, NPE	The Nun's Priest's Tale, The Nun's Priest's Prologue, Nun's Priest Endlink
PardT, PardP	The Pardoner's Tale, The Pardoner's Prologue
ParsT, ParsP	The Parson's Tale, The Parson's Prologue
PF	The Parliament of Fowls
PhyT, Phy-PardL	The Physician's Tale, Physician-Pardoner Link
Pity	The Complaint unto Pity
Prov	Proverbs
PrT, PrI, PrP, Pr-ThL	The Prioress's Tale, The Prioress's Introduction, The Prioress-Thopas Link
Purse	The Complaint of Chaucer to His Purse
Ret	Chaucer's Retraction [Retractation]
Rom	The Romaunt of the Rose
Ros	To Rosemounde
RvT, RvP	The Reeve's Tale, The Reeve's Prologue
Scog	The Envoy to Scogan
ShT, Sh-PrL	The Shipman's Tale, Shipman-Prioress Link
SNT, SNP, SN-CYL	The Second Nun's Tale, The Second Nun's Prologue, Second Nun-Canon's Yeoman Link
SqT, SqP, SqH, Sq-FranL	The Squire's Tale, The Squire's Prologue, Squire Headlink, Squire-Franklin Link
Sted	Lak of Stedfastnesse
SumT, SumP	The Summoner's Tale, The Summoner's Prologue
TC	Troilus and Criseyde
Th, ThP, Th-MelL	The Tale of Sir Thopas, The Prologue of Sir Thopas, Sir Thopas-Melibee Link
Ven	The Complaint of Venus
WBT, WBP, WB-FrL	The Wife of Bath's Tale, The Wife of Bath's Prologue, Wife of Bath-Friar Link
Wom Nob	Womanly Noblesse
Wom Unc	Against Women Unconstant

Introduction

PAUL G. RUGGIERS

TEXTUAL CRITICISM of medieval English literature is nearing the end of a long debate concerning the methodology or methodologies that may be employed in the editing of various kinds of medieval texts. Consensus has it, at least since the time of Joseph Bédier, that the methods and techniques evolved by the great masters of nineteenth-century textual scholarship have become obsolete, in short, that the methods of recension cannot be applied to the editing of medieval text and that the ideal alternative would be to choose from among a number of imperfect copies (always assuming the absence of the author's autograph) a single "best" version and to edit it, in Vinaver's words, "as best he can." That there are grave temptations in the process (that as editor his sympathy and knowledge are so great that his sense of what is correct, i.e., authorial, is infallible and that he is so much in the mind of the poet that their judgments are identical) every textual editor knows. The fact is that neither of these methods taken by itself can solve the problems inherent in the search for the words the poet actually wrote.

The twentieth century has seen a goodly number of editions of the works of Geoffrey Chaucer, among them three that may be called great from special perspectives: those of Robert Kilburn Root (*Troilus and Criseyde*), of F. N. Robinson (the entire canon), and of John M. Manly and Edith Rickert (*The Canterbury Tales*, with text, description and classification of manuscripts, and *Corpus of Variants*). Taken together, they mark the end of a long tradition of editing Chaucer, their varying methodologies evincing a reaction to the techniques of their nineteenth-century predecessors but in the main reaching for sounder methods of making text, providing commentary, and generally throwing light upon the ever-present uncertainties that characterize both the manuscript tradition and that of the printed editions.

We are inclined, somewhat carelessly, in looking back at the succession of editors of Chaucer, to assume that Caxton's shadow is cast forward, gradually diminishing in density up to the time of Tyrwhitt; then Tyrwhitt shines more brightly than all other editors until Skeat's great edition; next

1

Skeat holds sway until Robinson's production of 1933. This view is in part correct, but in its gross simplicity it falsifies the evidence of a succession of editors and publishers who gradually accumulated most of what is known in the way of canon, language, text, and cultural range. The accumulated commentary, presented to us so economically by the modern editors, has been made possible, of course, by the work of their predecessors, as well as the bit-by-bit accretions of periodical scholarship. This volume is an attempt to provide an overview of the evolution of the editions of Chaucer; not only can we thus fill in the gaps of the history of Chaucer's reputation among the publishers and editors, but also we can pay tribute to the devotion, the practicality, the general good sense of those editors who have made their contributions to what we know today.

William Caxton, the first English printer, produced the first edition of *The Canterbury Tales* in 1478, less than a year after he established his printing shop at Westminster. Later, in the famous Preface to his edition of 1483, to a gentleman critic who had seen a good manuscript of Chaucer's *Tales* and had criticized Caxton's first edition in the light of it, averred that he had in no way varied from the materials present in his copy text. The difficulty, we now know, of course, is that Caxton relied in his first edition upon a manuscript of an inferior line. In his second edition, with access to a better manuscript, perhaps the very one referred to by his critic, he made the error of not making a complete transcription of the manuscript and printing from that. Although he did not collate the two manuscripts, he made an attempt to correct omissions and to eliminate spurious lines and a considerable number of inferior readings.

Whatever the deficiencies inherent in being the first of a line of publishers and editors of Chaucer (in his second edition he dropped four lines of genuine authority, whether by carelessness or by editorial prerogative), Caxton is in a sense the father of the editing of Chaucer. He was surely not an editor in the modern sense, nor would his immediate successors be, but he produced seven Chaucers in his lifetime. Their differences from what we believe to be Chaucer's own language can be explained by the enormous change in the pronunciation of English in the fifteenth century, as well as by the freedom exercised by his compositors, who, like the scribes working with the manuscripts, made adjustments in their texts for a great variety of reasons but in the main to bring them into conformity with the linguistic usage of their time. We can always defend him, if we need to, on the ground that the fifteenth-century scribes tampered with the manuscripts as a fairly common practice, editing them in the direction of modernization, and that this editing quite naturally found its way into Caxton's printed Chaucers.

Caxton was not, as we have said, an editor in the modern sense. We wish that he had paid more scrupulous attention to his copy texts or that he had made his copy editors and compositors do so; we remember his poems, his prologues, and his epilogues, in one of which he writes felicitously of Chaucer: ". . . in alle hys werkys he excellyth in my oppynyon alle other wryters in our Englyssh / For he wrytteth no voyde wordes / but all hys mater is ful of hye and quycke sentence."

Caxton, his successor Wynkyn de Worde, and Pynson were all publishers primarily; that is to say, they earned their living printing and selling books. Chaucer was, in spite of protestations to the contrary, one among several business ventures. With the edition of William Thynne, an official in the household of Henry VIII, we see the first serious attempts at correcting Chaucer's work by collation with the available manuscripts. If Francis Thynne is an accurate reporter of his father's activities, William Thynne owned twenty-two manuscripts of Chaucer's works, which he used in making his various texts of the poetry. In his *Animadversions*, Francis reports that his father was commissioned to search out in all the libraries of England the works of the poet. William's purpose was to correct the errors in the texts of Chaucer's poetry and, further, to add to the Chaucer canon. To his enormous credit he was the first to print *The Romaunt of the Rose, The Legend of Good Women, The Book of the Duchess, A Treatise on the Astrolabe*, and some of the minor poems. As for the correction of Chaucer's texts, it is difficult to tell whether he collated in any systematic way. He apparently relied heavily upon a variety of copy texts, namely, Caxton's first edition, Pynson, the manuscript Longleat 258 and the manuscript Tanner 638, and he varies from them only for occasional punctuation or spelling modification, some-times resorting to a manuscript for a specific series of lines or stanzas. In difficult cases, where there were few sources, his method tended to be statistical, opting for majority-favored readings. For *The Canterbury Tales* there is some evidence that Thynne used a manuscript of the *cd* line to collate against his base text, perhaps one of the Caxton texts. And although Tyrwhitt thought that generally Thynne's text was worse than that of preceding editions, Root much later was to offer the opinion that the *Troilus* was well edited, having been collated against several manuscript authori-ties. In general Thynne's editing is spotty, his knowledge of Chaucer's language is limited, and his modernizations mingled with archaisms are somewhat bizarre. He bequeathed to subsequent editions by others his notion of the Chaucer canon, leaving Stow and Speght with a view of Chaucer's output that they did not correct and that was not in fact corrected until much later, in the nineteenth century.

A man of wide learning and interests, better known to us as a historian and antiquarian, John Stow derived his edition of Chaucer mainly from that of the 1550(?) edition of William Thynne. He thus perpetuated errors in ascription of works to Chaucer and repeated the general editorial mis-information about the function of Middle English final *−e* upon which

Chaucer's metrics depends. His claim that he was making "divers additions, whiche were neuer in printe before" has to be evaluated against the
fever of the profitable publication of compendia in the sixteenth century. It
is clear that he collated a text of Thynne with a manuscript (for *A Balade of
Good Conseile*, which he correctly ascribed to Lydgate). More important, to
the Chaucer canon he added *Gentilesse, A Complaint to His Lady*, and *Adam
Scriveyn*, along with the doubtful *Proverbs* and *Against Women Unconstant*. Of
the twenty-three poems that Stow attempted to add to the Chaucer canon
fourteen are to be found in the manuscript Trinity College, Cambridge,
R.3.18, though their presence there is not proof that Stow garnered them
from that source. And he knew the Manuscripts Fairfax 16 and Gg.4.27.

With Thomas Speght the word *editor* begins to take on a more modern
connotation. A contemporary of Francis Beaumont, who urged him to take
up the edition of Chaucer, Speght may also have received assistance from
John Stow as he worked on his edition of Chaucer of 1598. The edition, in
fact a reprint, was already in press when Speght came into the project
solicited by Beaumont and Stow, among others, to whom he deferred.
Although this first edition is dominated by Stow's earlier edition, Speght
deals intelligently in his introduction with meanings of various of the tales,
recognizes the Chaucer of *The General Prologue* as a "comprehensive" poet,
and produces a "Life" of Chaucer based upon documents, providing materials about Chaucer's travels, his pensions, his work as controller of pensions,
his parentage, and so on, much of the information gleaned from Robert
Glover and from Stow. The "Life" has given way to extensive correction in
modern times, though Speght is the first to report that Chaucer's name was
on the records of the Inner Temple and that he was fined two shillings for
beating a Franciscan friar in Fleet Street. The story is still with us.

   His editorial work consists of some emendations to the text of *The General
Prologue*. He added to the canon *The Floure and the Leafe* and *The Isle of Ladies*,
which he titled *Chaucer's Dreame*, the name earlier editors had assigned to
The Book of the Duchess. He also created a glossary of about two thousand
difficult words with simple glosses. His edition is, in its hurried style, of
dubious value, but it is a first in editions of Chaucer. In general his
annotations and corrections show a more self-conscious and conscientious
quasi-scholarly bent.

   His second edition (1602) marks an advance in Speght's ability to "edit"
Chaucer. Noteworthy in it are his explanation and defense of Chaucer's
metrics and the emphasis upon Chaucer's seriousness. Of special importance for us is the revision of the text of *The Canterbury Tales* with
numerous new readings, some influenced by Francis Thynne. We do not
know what manuscript or manuscripts Speght used as the bases for his
corrections, but he deserves commendation for the improvement, however
unsystematic, of his text. In the canon he introduced the genuine *ABC* from

manuscript Gg.4127, which he transcribed faithfully, and *Jack Upland*. He expanded his Glossary to include some etymologies, evidencing here, too, the influence of Francis Thynne. It was a popular edition, and even after the appearance of Urry's edition in 1721, Speght's edition continued for some time to be the reigning collection of the poet's work.

When on March 19, 1715, John Urry died of fever, he left largely undone much of the work on his edition of Chaucer. John Dart was commissioned to write a "Life," and Timothy and Dwight Thomas took up the task of the Glossary, the prefatory matter, and the preparation of the book for press. The book finally appeared in 1721; unfortunately from that time to this the work has come under severe criticism, some critics naming it the worst edition of Chaucer ever produced. These criticisms, it should be said, were lodged against the text; time has tended to vindicate other aspects of the edition.

On the credit side it should be said that the edition contained, along with the spurious works that had accrued to previous editions, the entire accepted canon of Chaucer's works. And with the Glossary and "Life" the work was standard for almost the entire century.

Urry's method is good by the standards of the time: he claimed that he had compared earlier and later printed editions and had collated "many rare and ancient Manuscripts [some fourteen], not hitherto consulted" and, further, that he had identified some pieces ascribed to Chaucer as apocryphal, had augmented the canon, and had even restored hitherto omitted lines. When he died, he left behind confusion and uncertainty and a major part of the edition incomplete, but we recognize that he was on the right track. There was a method, and although it may seem to us somewhat primitive, it was the not uncommon method of noting manuscript readings in the margins of his own copies of earlier printed editions. From these readings he selected those to be transferred to a copy text, in all likelihood the Speght of 1602.

In spite of the protestations that he intended to clear up the difficulties of establishing the Chaucer canon Urry continued the tradition of the miscellany, including in his table of contents the non-Chaucerian pieces inherited from previous printed editions. But the Preface of 1721, by combining the list of manuscripts consulted by Urry (and Thomas), brings a large number of manuscripts for the first time into an available resource pool. The manuscripts, moreover, are described with remarkable accuracy as regards form, condition, contents, and location. Illumination, orthography, and spurious links are noted.

On the debit side the freedom with which Urry emended his text, often without manuscript authority, and the steps he took to bring Chaucer's verse into metrical regularity, based upon unresolved assumptions about

Middle English fifteenth-century scribal habits, have brought the edition into disrepute.

With Thomas Tyrwhitt the making of a Chaucer edition was finally submitted to the workings of a truly learned mind and freed from the taint of dilettantism.. What Urry had groped toward came to be more fully realized in Tyrwhitt's attempt to make a Chaucer text on sound principles. Beginning with the conviction that the making of a text should be preceded by the selection of genuine readings from collated manuscripts, Tyrwhitt worked hard toward eliminating subjectivity from the process, and although his methods have long been superseded, they represent a giant step in the direction of a reliable methodology. In retrospect his edition seems everywhere instinct with intelligence and humility, as evidenced by his resistance to the impulse to uniformize spelling practices or to tamper with the text by imposing in the manner of Speght typographical signals to indicate pronunciation.

Of the approximately twenty-four manuscripts he had to hand, Tyrwhitt's reliance upon such manuscripts as Harley 7334, Harley 7335, Dd.4.24, Egerton 2726, and Additional 5140 demonstrates his ability to discern the soundest manuscripts among those available to him. His copy text, if we may call it that, was Speght (1687), but the printed pages interleaved with blank sheets were used only to have something to work with. Readings were selected, it would seem, from concurrence of readings from the best manuscripts, though in many instances he has the good sense and humility to admit that none of the readings in his manuscripts is satisfactory. His respect for the readings of even inferior manuscripts is evidenced by his choice, on occasion, of readings from these lesser sources.

Departing from the practice of the earlier printed editions, Tyrwhitt adopts an order for *The Canterbury Tales* based upon the manuscripts mentioned earlier. He was sensitive to the ways in which scribes distort a text, and as a result of careful examination he was able to correct individual words and phrases and could explain his thinking on the matter judiciously. Occasionally he regularizes a line to accord with his sense of the meter, a habit that tended to vitiate his usual respect for the manuscripts.

His commentary on Chaucer's *Canterbury Tales* is a reservoir of learned discourse and intelligently discursive information. Being conversant with a wide variety of writing from the Middle Ages—Froissart, Boccaccio, *Le Roman de la Rose*, Dante—he is able to adduce these as instructive of our reading of particular lines and passages. Although his methods of making text and his views of Chaucer's metrics are not entirely sound, still with him it must be said the story of modern textual editing of Chaucer begins.

Thomas Wright, whose edition of Chaucer has fared ill in the history of Chaucer textual criticism, stumbled, perhaps in ignorance, upon the best-text method. To his credit it must be said that many of the notes that came to be incorporated into his commentary found their way into Skeat's annotations. Wright was a kind of professional scholar-editor who made his living by editing medieval English and Latin works, the two volumes of Chaucer being in a sense a culmination of a remarkable succession of publications for the Percy, Camden, and Shakespeare societies. When he came to the editing of *The Canterbury Tales*, he was convinced from his review of Tyrwhitt's work that a reliance upon readings from manuscripts copied over a stretch of time was "absurd." He preferred to rely upon a single manuscript, Harley 7334, as "best . . . in regard to antiquity and correctness," claiming collations of a small number of manuscripts with his favored one and utilizing Tyrwhitt's text as a kind of monitor.

Wright was, to put it simply, insufficiently grounded in textual criticism to recognize the now obvious defects of what Skeat called the "faulty and treacherous Harleian MS." If he had chosen Ellesmere or Hengwrt, indeed, if Tyrwhitt had chosen a single "best" manuscript of their type, the history of Chaucer editions would have been a remarkably different story. As it is, although the edition was badly received, it exerted a strong influence upon later nineteenth-century editions of Chaucer, including Skeat's edition of 1878.

Frederick James Furnivall may be considered in one sense to be the midwife of nineteenth-century Chaucer scholarship. In an amazing life he brought into existence a host of literary societies and, not least among his brilliant ideas, *The New English Dictionary*. Although not an editor in the modern sense of the word he engendered for the Chaucer Society a steady succession of Chaucer texts, a body of transcriptions that constitute from one perspective the greatest single contribution to the study of Chaucer's text. Their appearance and availability have expedited immeasurably the work of later scholars up to and including those of our own century.

His judgments were, though sometimes hasty and impulsive, accurate: he recognized the supremacy of Ellesmere and Hengwrt. He was taken with Harley 7334 (though it is not included in the Six-Text edition), Cambridge Gg.4.27, Cambridge Dd.4.24, and Lansdowne, Corpus, and Petworth. On the question of tale order he follows Bradshaw's suggestion, moving the tales of the Shipman through the Nun's Priest to follow that of the Man of Law. Resisting Bradshaw, who scorned the idea of parallel texts for the Six-Text edition, Furnivall went ahead with the idea; since their appearance posterity has breathed a grateful thanks for his sound judgment. Following the advice of Bradshaw, who badgered him to do so, he read Tyrwhitt carefully.

His claim upon our gratitude is strong: although he seems never to have conquered an impulsive and feisty spirit, often riding roughshod over the opinions of others, he chose a life devoted to facilitating the labors of others by bringing a knowledge of Chaucer to greater and greater numbers of readers. One wishes, in spite of the plenty he provided, for more: British Library Additional 35286 and Christ Church 152. But we are forced to remember that he provided much for later scholarship, including transcriptions of the minor poems, the vision poems, and *Troilus and Criseyde*, to which modern scholarship turns casually as if they had always been there. One stands in awe before the virtually ceaseless flow of energy into his determination to do "good work."

With Walter W. Skeat textual criticism and the editing of Chaucer come of age. A mathematician by training, in 1864, the year in which Furnivall established the Early English Text Society, Skeat returned to Christ College to lecture. Furnivall invited the twenty-eight-year-old Skeat to edit *Lancelot of the Lake*, blithely averring that he could learn to edit a manuscript. Skeat took to the process well enough to be invited eventually, upon Bradshaw's death in 1886, to be editor of the Clarendon Chaucer, and when that edition appeared in 1895, it was rightly hailed as a landmark, the finest edition since Tyrwhitt's edition of 1775–78.

Skeat's scholarly prowess had been aided and abetted by that of scholars whom he regarded as his betters, among them Richard Morris, Henry Bradshaw, and Furnivall. Henry Bradshaw's support was a constant in Skeat's career; with Furnivall he accepted Bradshaw's placement of fragment VII (B^2) immediately after fragment II (B^1) and the placement of B 1163–90 as the *Man of Law Endlink*. (Skeat called it *The Shipman's Prologue*). He could not accept Furnivall's placement of fragment VI (C) immediately after fragment VII, though he printed it there for reasons mainly of general convenience.

Skeat's reliance upon the Six-Text edition, along with Harley 7334, has earned his method of making a text the general disapproval of subsequent scholarship as too limited in its perspectives. His recording of variants is spotty, and his justification of emendation of substantives is somewhat quixotic, being arrived at, in Eleanor Hammond's word, "intuitively." With Ellesmere as his base text he felt free to modernize the spelling, generally smoothing the text in pursuit of some notion of regularity of forms not demonstrable in the manuscript. In this he was bolstered by the greatest of all temptations, the yielding to the conviction that one understands fully the mind of the fifteenth-century scribe or, more dangerous still, that of the poet himself. Thus he felt free to make changes on grounds of meter, phonetics, and orthography that were unjustified by the manuscripts themselves.

Skeat's greatest contribution lies in his commentary; in the series of decisions leading to the establishment, finally, of a Chaucer canon; and in the full Glossary. The notes, in the main gathered from earlier editions and included in the Clarendon edition of 1895, are still of great value to students of Chaucer. Even if they occasionally block our view of previous periodical contributions by a wide variety of scholars and general commentators, we would be less than truthful if we did not say unconditionally that Skeat is one of the great milestones in the editing of Chaucer, standing with Tyrwhitt as the greatest of their respective centuries.

With the work of Robert Kilburn Root twentieth-century textual criticism of Chaucer (and English vernacular literature generally) faces up to problems that have not yet been resolved in the making of the Chaucer text. That major step in the right direction has now been taken: all the variants of a particular work have been gathered for the first time. But how to find absolutely reliable evidence leading to original readings?

Root inherited from Sir William S. McCormick the unresolved manuscript tradition of *Troilus and Criseyde*. Unable to group the manuscripts genetically, McCormick thought that he saw past the confusion of scribal intervention to the possibility that differences of the manuscripts were the result of differing versions of the poem: an alpha version of unrevised text and a beta version of revised text. To these McCormick subsequently added a gamma version that he later recanted. From here on study of the variants could be presumed to yield evidence of revision. The notion is exciting, but it does not eliminate the problem of all textual editing, the settling of a method leading to the identification and elimination of unoriginal variants within the several stages of revision.

Having accepted these conclusions Root could have opted to produce a "best" text or, after the gathering of a corpus of variants, could have chosen to make a fully eclectic text (not necessarily one that Chaucer wrote but an adequate version of the poem). Both of these choices he rejected. In fact, the theory of differing stages of revision is based on a surprisingly sparse body of evidence; what is sure evidence in one place is unsure elsewhere. And among the variants, which ones are signs of authorial revision, and which ones are signs of scribal interference? Root thought to solve the problem by minimizing the occurrence of scribal interference, elevating variants to the status of authorial changes within revision states. The method is seductive and hypnotic. It led Root into the construction of an elaborate apparatus that overwhelms by sheer bulk but fails to do much more than demonstrate the McCormick-Root theory. Unfortunately the arguments for clearly defined states of revision in three subsequent layers of development remain unproved. What he produced in his edition is a text that fits the theory well enough but produces in fact a text that the author could certainly not have written. In the absence of an autograph let the textual editor beware.

The collations, selected carefully to support the theory of successive layers of an evolving text, unfortunately exclude the readings deemed scribal, readings that subsequent students of the text would have found invaluable. The collecting of evidence therefore remains to be done in a form similar to that of Manly and Rickert's Corpus of Variants for *The Canterbury Tales*, so that the full evidence of all the manuscripts can be seen in one place. Root's real contribution, like Skeat's, is in the wide-ranging literary and historical commentary to the student's edition of *Troilus and Criseyde*. He remains an indispensable aid to the understanding of the poem.

The publication of John M. Manly and Edith Rickert's *The Text of the Canterbury Tales* in eight volumes in 1940 (the project was undertaken in 1924) was the product of Manly's and Rickert's mature years; it occupied them both until death. In its detailed description of all the known manuscripts, a volume on classification of the manuscripts, two volumes of text, and four volumes recording the Corpus of Variants, it is an impressive achievement indeed.

Their plan, summarized in the subtitle ("Studied on the Basis of All the Known Manuscripts") is grand: for the first time the manuscripts were to be examined and put into genetically related groups; the variants would be scrutinized with an eye to the elimination of unoriginal readings; the intelligent application of conjecture necessary to the recovery of an archetype would enable them to make a text close to Chaucer's intentions. In the process they would discriminate between evidence of "editing" and authorial revision.

There have been problems in the critical reception of the edition: the classification system and that of the constant groups are complicated; the case for lines of transmission of tales and parts of tales is only partly demonstrated; the text, although it may be the finest text of *The Canterbury Tales* ever produced, is purportedly derived by the processes of recension but is not clearly demonstrated to be so. There may be a flaw in logic in the reasoning-through to the notion of an archetype.

On several occasions in volume 2, Manly and Rickert come close to facing the central problem arising out of their trust in the regular operations of the laws of probability. "In spite of the vast amount of fluctuating variation" (p. 23), Root in 1941 asked the crucial question: Has Manly reconstructed "with rigorous adherence to scientific procedure the original copy . . . from which the existing MSS are ultimately derived"? Unfortunately not, thought Root. Perhaps equally unfortunate is that the resemblance of the text to that of the Hengwrt manuscript has tended to create a false polarity between Hengwrt and Ellesmere.

But nothing can change the fact that Manly and Rickert occupy the highest place in the pantheon of textual scholars. The description of the manuscripts, the Corpus of Variants, even with its severe policy of exclusions, affords us information virtually impossible to come by otherwise. The stalwart text, although it has not become the text for citation, gives us glimpses of a sturdy poetics not available elsewhere. Flawed though their edition may be, it is the greatest single contribution to our knowledge of the text of *The Canterbury Tales* in our time. Even now, Manly and Rickert's disciples are debating the merits of their work, a sign of the continuing quest for a methodology at the end of which may be the elusive text such as we suppose came from the hand of Geoffrey Chaucer.

F. N. Robinson's edition of Chaucer needs little introduction. Although the task had been undertaken in 1904 as part of the Cambridge Poets series, it was from 1933 on the foremost edition of Chaucer in the world. Even with the appearance in 1940 of John M. Manly and Edith Rickert's monumental edition of *The Canterbury Tales*, which addresses itself to only one part of the Chaucer canon, Robinson's edition has continued to supply the needs of students and scholars alike. And for good reasons: in spite of the demurrals of a relatively few reviews that appeared between 1935 and 1938 in Germany, England, and the United States, in its scope the edition has occupied a place in scholarship akin to that of the Skeat of 1895.

Robinson's *Chaucer*, it has been repeatedly pointed out, is not a full critical edition. The textual notes are sparse; there is no full critical apparatus. The Glossary is sometimes misleading or excessively restricted in range of meanings; the grammar is oversimplified. More important for the integrity of the text, the addition or subtraction of final -e and the mending of dialectal spellings is inconsistently practiced. Evaluation of the work has generally been biased in the direction of regarding it as a definitive text of Chaucer's poetry and prose. Robinson himself was not so sanguine. His presentation of the texts is that of a mature, highly competent scholar, without pretensions to definitiveness; subsequent scholarship has perhaps inadvertently given status to the text beyond its intentions or deserts.

Robinson's method was generally as follows: he relied upon ElHgDd.4.24Gg.4.27 with a strong preference for El. Where his historical judgment dictated otherwise, he accepted readings from some inferior manuscripts and normalized spellings to avoid eccentricities. He always recognized the difficulties of separating scribal intervention from authorial intention and had sufficient conviction to depart from tradition and from accepted opinion where necessary (from R. K. Root's determinations for *Troilus*, for example).

There is, nonetheless, some ambiguity in the editorial procedures. The "editorial principles" averred lend themselves to some misunderstanding, and his rough-draft statement that he "has not always adopted the readings which strict critical process would yield" opens the door to a plaguing eclecticism and subjectivity. The reliability of the text is thus called into question, even when we know that such readings have been decided on grounds of language, meter, and usage. And we are always aware that in conjectural emendation there is inevitably a subjective element, however informed by knowledge. Even so it is Robinson's great achievement that in a lifetime of sparse output he gave us two editions of Chaucer (1933 and 1957) that have dominated scholarly thinking for half a century.

1. William Caxton
(1422?–1491)

BEVERLY BOYD

THE FIRST editor to leave more than a few headings as commentary on the text of *The Canterbury Tales* was William Caxton, the first English printer.[1] His commentary is contained in the preface to his second edition of Chaucer's unfinished masterpiece (1483), printed after he had discovered that his first edition (1478) had been taken from a poor source. The preface to the second edition is an account of textual problems that awaited the fifteenth-century editor of Chaucer, as well as an encomium upon the poet.[2] Caxton offers it as an apology for having done a disservice to a great poet, though some have seen his motives for bringing out the new edition as chiefly commercial.[3] Since Caxton also printed Chaucer's *Boece* and *Troilus and Criseyde* and three volumes containing the minor poems, his editions have an important place in the textual history of Chaucer's works.

The man who was the first to print Chaucer was neither a professional scholar nor a printer by career but a mercer. He served his apprenticeship under Robert Large, who became lord mayor of London in 1439. Little definite information is known about Caxton's earlier life and education except that he was born on the Weald of Kent. Several sites claim to be his birthplace, including Long Barn, in the village of Weald (near Sevenoaks), owned in much later times by Vita Sackville-West. While the name Caxton, or Causton, was once common in those parts, no ordinary man had money to pay for a son's apprenticeship to a prominent London mercer and alderman.

Caxton spent most of his adult life abroad, chiefly in the service of the Merchant Adventurers in Bruges, which was then part of Burgundy. The Merchant Adventurers were overseas guildsmen, mostly mercers; they were known in Bruges as the English Nation. Caxton eventually became governor (head) of the English Nation, a position that had important political implications, for England was then in the throes of civil war, both Yorkist and Lancastrian factions competing for Continental backing. Caxton is believed to have been involved in the politics leading to Duke Charles's marriage to Margaret of York (1468), who became Caxton's patroness.

Caxton's retirement from the governorship of the English Nation was probably related to a brief return to power of the Lancastrians (October, 1470–March, 1471). Whether or not he then entered Margaret's service, as scholars have assumed, or merely received a stipend for some kind of advisory duties,[4] in 1471 he went to Cologne and there learned the new art of printing with movable type. For the circumstances involved, Caxton is his own chief witness. In the prologue he later wrote for his *Recuyell of the Histories of Troie* (Bruges, 1475), he tells how he had begun a translation of a Troy book rendered into French from Latin by Raoul Lefevre, chaplain to Duke Charles's father, and how he had given up the project, finding his linguistic ability inadequate, until Duchess Margaret commanded him to finish it. Having done so, he says in the epilogue to book 3, he had found himself unable to supply by traditional methods all the copies requested, and he had set about learning to print for that reason.[5] The *Recuyell* thus became the first book printed in English.

There is evidence, based on the quiring and on the paper, that the *Recuyell* (and after it all of Caxton's large books) was printed on three presses and also that the *Recuyell* was followed immediately by another of his translations, *The Game of Chess*.[6] Caxton may have done some of the presswork and set some of the formes of type. But pulling the lever that worked the press was physically demanding, and Caxton was by then middle-aged, though in learning to print he doubtless learned presswork. It is now thought that his role in the production of books was rather that of a publisher in the modern sense than that of a printer.

Caxton published four other books in Bruges. Since he was still involved in politics, and since he traveled a great deal, his personal activity in their production, if any, is less than clear. Especially unclear is his business relationship with the printer Colard Mansion, whose own career is connected with the press in Bruges from which the *Recuyell* was issued. Painter thinks that he was Caxton's business partner.[7] It was once believed that Mansion had taught Caxton to print, but in Cologne Caxton had worked on the edition of Bartolomaeus Anglicus now attributed to Johann Veldener, who moved from Cologne to Louvain in 1473 and who suppled Caxton's types. Veldener became the leading typefounder in the Low Countries, and it is thought that he set up presses for other printers, possibly including Caxton. Current opinion makes Veldener Caxton's teacher.[8]

That Caxton moved to England in 1476 may have been a coincidence of an apparent end to the Wars of the Roses and an old dream of an Englishman abroad to return home. But other political events may have turned opportunity into necessity, for by 1475 Charles of Burgundy was surrounded by enemies; his army was beaten by the Swiss in both March and June of the following year. Caxton paid rent to the abbot of Westminster for a shop in the abbey precincts in September, 1476.

At Westminster, Caxton printed more than one hundred items, the first believed to have been an indulgence of Pope Sixtus IV in aid of a war against the Turks, printed before December 13, 1476. Caxton afterward printed works by all the English authors who were well known, and also translations by him and others.[9] He did no creative writing of his own, though he wrote prefaces and epilogues, none of them very original, for many of his books. It was formerly thought that he also wrote a chapter for John Trevisa's translation of Higden's *Polychronicon* (1482), bringing it up to date, but Painter has disproved that.[10] Besides literary works Caxton printed advertisements, pamphlets, and Latin service books. His actual influence upon English literature at the time is hard to assess, since it is a matter of controversy whether he catered to literary taste or created it. The influence that his press had upon English spelling has been greatly exaggerated. Far from standardizing it, as has been thought, his pages show the chaotic spelling characteristic of Middle English manuscripts, the same word appearing in multiple spellings as often as not. Nor is there evidence that mass production of books by printing caused a sudden upsurge of literacy among the English; it is now known that the extent of literacy was much greater in fifteenth-century England than was once supposed.[11] What Caxton actually did was to set up a successful press that specialized in vernacular books at a moment when humanism was taking hold in England, both creating and answering a demand for books.[12] The success of his endeavor is the more interesting because many Continental printers, including Gutenberg, went bankrupt.

The quincentennial of Caxton's press at Westminster (1476–1976) occasioned new interest in the printer's life, in his books, and in the methods used by his press. After five hundred years the appearance of his rag paper is still a creamy white, while classics printed in the nineteenth century yellow upon library shelves. His early books resemble manuscripts very closely, having their lines of type uneven at the outer margins, though printers already knew how to set type with even (justified) lines. It is fair enough to assume that Caxton was not merely stodgy and old-fashioned but determined to avoid any appearance of novelty so that his books would sell. On the other hand, his long career in Bruges connected him with a milieu noted for handsome manuscript books, and Caxton evidently tried to make his printed books resemble fine manuscripts as closely as possible.

This chapter is concerned with Caxton chiefly as an editor of Chaucer, though the editing of his Chaucers for publication cannot be divorced from the methods of his compositors and the technology of his press. Since these books came out in two groups, or came out around two dates separated by at least five years, it is not surprising to find them also separated by different types. But more than smaller type separates the first and second groups of books. Between one and the other Caxton had gained experience. He had also acquired potential competition as other printers moved to England, though, as it turned out, they were not to threaten his own market for vernacular books.

It is impossible for scholars interested in Caxton's dealings with Chaucer to approach his seven Chaucers unconditioned by Caxton's *Morte Darthur* (1485) and by the crisis precipitated by the discovery in 1934 of the Winchester manuscript of Malory's Arthurian romances. Eugène Vinaver's studies proved that Caxton had edited his source significantly by removing the explicits marking the separation of the individual romances, thus presenting the whole series as if Malory had meant the book as a continuous narrative under Caxton's ill-fitting but venerated title based on Malory's final explicit.[13] The text, moreover, has been modernized. Caxton thus came to be known in this later day as one who took irresponsible liberties with his texts. Vinaver denied that the Winchester manuscript could have been Caxton's copy-text, and this was the consensus among scholars until recently, when an investigation of ink smudges, leading to the discovery of offsets of Caxton's types on some of the pages, reopened the matter for further investigation.[14]

The widespread view of Caxton as a rather unscrupulous editor clouds the approach to his Chaucers. These are listed below, under the titles now customary for Chaucer's works. Caxton did not use title pages. Among these seven books only *Boece* and *The House of Fame* have printed titles. Bibliographers have retained Caxton's references to his Chaucers as titles. The books are as follows:

The Parliament of Fowls (The Temple of Brass, 1477 or 1478) 4°, Type no. 2: Duff 93, De Ricci 25, *STC* 5091; 24 leaves. Contains also (2) a treatise by Scogan that quotes Chaucer's *Gentilesse* (3) an anonymous stanza beginning "Wyth empty honde men may no hawkes lure," (4) Chaucer's *Truth*, (5) Chaucer's *Fortune*, and (6) three stanzas of Chaucer's *Envoy to Scogan*, after which the book breaks off, lacking a quire at the end.

Anelida and Arcite (Queen Anelida and the False Arcite, 1477 or 1478), 4°, Type no. 2: Duff 92, DeR. 24, *STC* 5090; 10 leaves. Contains also (after an explicit) (2) Chaucer's *Complaint to His Purse*, followed by an explicit, and (3) an anonymous poem beginning "Whan feyth failleth in prestes sawes," followed by an explicit (*"Et sic est finis"*).

The Canterbury Tales (1478), folio, Type no. 2: Duff 87, DeR. 22, Goff C-431, *STC* 5082; 374 leaves.

Boece (Boecius de Consolacione Philosophie, 1478), folio, Type nos. 2, 3: Duff 47, DeR. 8, Goff B-813, *STC* 3199; 94 leaves.

The Canterbury Tales, 2d ed. (1483), folio, Type nos. 2*, 4*: Duff 88, DeR. 23, Goff C-432, *STC* 5083; 312 leaves.

The House of Fame (The Book of Fame, 1483), folio, Type no. 4*; Duff 86,
    DeR. 21, *STC* 5087; 30 leaves.
Troilus and Crisyede (1483), folio, Type no. 4*: Duff 94, DeR. 26, *STC*
    5094; 120 leaves. [15]

The longest of these books is the first edition of *The Canterbury Tales,* 374
leaves, or 748 pages. Some scholars consider it the most handsome of the
Caxton incunabula. Since the two editions of *The Canterbury Tales* have
drawn the most attention, the present study of Caxton as an editor of
Chaucer will begin with these. Such a study, however, requires some
preliminary information about fifteenth-century printing. Because there is
no manual of printing from the fifteenth century, modern knowledge of the
subject is derived from the appearance of incunabula and from sixteenth-
century woodcuts showing printers at work.

In Caxton's time, some twenty years after Gutenberg's now famous
forty-two-line Bible, printing presses were made of wood. The press was a
gallowslike structure that housed a screw worked by a lever pulled by hand.
Descent of the screw caused a wooden platen to lower. In printing, the
essentials were the platen, an inked forme of type, and paper. From the
front of the press projected a plank supported by a prop. Attached to this
plank were rails upon which a carriage was mounted, and upon that a
bottomless box (coffin) containing a press stone, on which was set a forme of
type. Ink was beaten onto the forme with wooden balls (with handles)
covered with leather and stuffed with wool. To the end of the coffin away
from the press was attached a hinged frame (tympan), covered with parchment. Paper was fastened to the tympan, which had points. Hinged above
the tympan was the frisket, a light frame covered with parchment, cut away
to expose the surface of the paper to be printed. The frisket was folded down
over the tympan; then tympan and frisket together were folded down over
the inked forme. The carriage was cranked under the platen, which, when
lowered, exerted pressure on the paper, thus creating an impression.
Caxton's press or presses would have had most, if not all, of these features.

Caxton had to import paper. The first paper mill in England was that of
John Tate, first noted in the 1490s. [16] When producing books, printers
(like scribes) worked under a concept of folded paper, usually several sheets
folded and inserted into each other to form gatherings (quires), which could
then be sewn onto bands for binding. Paper folded once, in half, produced
quires in folio; a second fold produced quires in quarto; and third fold
produced quires in octavo. Caxton's Chaucers are all in folio or in quarto.
Their quires are mostly quaternions (gatherings composed of four sheets of
folded paper), though they are filled out variously. Printers kept track of the
quires by signing them with letters followed by numbers. The signatures
were often cut off, especially during binding. Caxton's later Chaucers have
printed signatures; the earlier ones are without signatures, presumably

because they were added by hand and afterward trimmed off. Mistakes could get into a printed book if the copy editor or compositor failed to recognized misplaced leaves or quires in his exemplar, or if he did the misplacing himself. Mistakes could also get into a book during binding or rebinding. Textual problems can sometimes be solved by working back to the original quiring.

Printing from movable type depended upon the forme, as well as upon the paper, the ink, and the press with its platen. To produce a forme of type, the compositor picked pieces of type from a case (a container filled with compartments) and assembled them into words and lines on a tray to be enclosed within an iron frame (chase), which was then tightened (locked up) by means of blocks (furniture) and wedges (quoins) hammered in with a mallet. An important advance, the composing stick, enabled the compositor to set several properly spaced lines of type in a tray held in the hand before sliding the contents into a tray (galley) to be locked up by the chase. Another fifteenth-century advance was the two-pull press, by which a forme of type, set to accommodate two folio pages, could be slid further under the platen after the first page had been printed, by raising the screw slightly; the lever could then be pulled again to print the second page. Pages printed in this manner would be correctly aligned; if the printer proceeded one printed page at a time, the impressions set separately on the same side of the same sheet of paper were often crooked, as is the case with Caxton's early Chaucers. Printing could be further expedited by the employment of more than one compositor to set type, and also by using more than one press, so that a book could be portioned out to two or more teams of compositors and pressmen. While all these procedures seem cumbersome in retrospect, printing remained essentially the same into the eighteenth century. Sixteenth-century woodcuts show pressmen with muscles bulging from the physically demanding work.[17]

The success of the forme itself depended on the availability of pieces of movable type of exactly uniform height, which, when assembled into lines and locked into place, presented an absolutely flat surface of letters in relief to be inked and printed. This absolutely flat surface was the result of a laterally adjustable mold for casting type, perfected by Gutenberg, who was a goldsmith. The shape of a particular letter came from a matrix, made by punching the desired shape in reverse onto a piece of metal, such as brass; this matrix was placed in the mold, after which molten lead, with antimony for hardening, was poured into it from a crucible.

Letters were designed from handwriting of the time. Caxton's Type no. 1, used only for the books he printed in Bruges, was designed by Colard Mansion, apparently from his own book hand (Mansion had been a professional scribe), which was of a style then practiced in Burgundy combining cursive features with features proper to Gothic, whence the name Flemish Bâtarde now applied to type of this style. All the types in which

Caxton printed his Chaucers are Flemish Bâtarde, except his Type no. 3 (Gothic), used for the headings of *Boece*, which are in Latin.[18] Gothic writing was traditionally used for Latin, especially for liturgical books, though by Caxton's time the distinction was not observed strictly, if indeed it ever had been. Like scribal handwriting, Caxton's types have brevigraphs, but in his Flemish Bâtarde types there are no special sorts (letters) for the thorn and the yogh, which were still used in English vernacular manuscripts, though Caxton does have brevigraphs for *the, that*, and *thou* that use the thorn in combination. His brevigraphs present problems to scholars interested in textual matters, because consistent expansions are difficult to achieve owing to the fact that the orthography involved is not the work of a scribe copying a source but the work of a series of involved persons from author to compositor, the compositor being heavily influenced by the mechanical aspects of printing. Some have evaded editorial questions through facsimile editions with little or no *apparatus criticus*.[19]

To set type for printing, the compositor required a copy-text, which was prepared by marking a manuscript for the purpose or by making a transcript. If the one procedure defaced the manuscript that was to be printed, the other took time and expense, though it is not necessary to assume that manuscripts used as copy-text were as a matter of course battered in the process. Copy editing involved adapting the pages of manuscript books to the rigid limitations of the forme. In setting type, the compositor did not have the same flexibility as scribes had, though he could use brevigraphs, substitute a similar letter for one actually needed, alter spellings, change grammar and syntax, and make minor deletions. Such accommodations are most common at the ends of pages, where shortages were most likely to occur.[20]

Fifteenth-century printers did not always correct typographical errors, though they could and did unlock the forme for corrections, often making other errors in the process. Incunabula are sprinkled with errors that a good scribe would have deleted, such as turned letters and failures of letters to print, as well as with the same kinds of errors that scribes made. But Caxton's books were indeed proofread. Corrections in *The Parliament of Fowls* show up on waste sheets discovered in the bindings of a dilapidated copy of *Boece*, and other corrections can been seen in the books extant in multiple copies.[21]

The kinds of errors here discussed are only part of the problem of separating characteristics of fifteenth-century printing from Caxton's own editorial work. Another dimension is the difficulty presented by rapid changes in the English language between Chaucer's time and Caxton's. The Great Vowel Shift had altered the pronunciation of long vowels; leveling, largely responsible for the schwa vowel (unstressed final -*e*) at the ends of words that had provided Chaucer with a vital part of his verse technique, had so far disappeared from English pronunciation that the principles for a correct reading of Chaucer's poetic line had been forgotten; words and phrases that Chaucer had written had fallen out of usage. Thus the scribes who wrote the fifteenth-century manuscripts edited Chaucer's orthography, grammar, syntax, and vocabulary to suit those who employed them, if not to suit themselves, so that few of the manuscripts that have come down to modern times present reliable texts of Chaucer's works. Chaucer had realized only too well what might be in store for his works at the hands of posterity, for he had written at the end of *Troilus and Criseyde* (lines 1793–98):

> And for ther is so gret diversite
> In Englissh and in writyng of oure tonge,
> So prey I God that non myswrite the,
> Ne the mysmetre for defaute of tonge.
> And red wherso thow be, or elles songe
> That thow be understonde, God I biseche![22]

And yet that is exactly what had happened by 1478. Since in no case do we possess Caxton's copy-text for his Chaucers, or any of the source manuscripts from which transcripts may have been made for his printed editions of Chaucer, we must realize that scribes were accustomed to editing English vernacular manuscripts, including works by Chaucer, toward modernization and that Caxton's sources probably already contained some of this editing. It is also to be expected that Caxton's shop routinely did some of this kind of editing. Blake has shown that fifteenth-century compositors modernized as they set type, without necessarily writing such changes on their copy-texts and without necessarily being methodical.[23] As noted earlier (n. 14) Lotte Hellinga has presented a discussion of the possible use in this manner of the Winchester manuscript by Caxton's shop. In any case, either his source manuscript or his own shop, if not both, did precisely this to Malory's book, not out of stupidity but out of custom; the modernizing done to Caxton's Chaucers need not have been his own handwork at all.

Caxton doubtless left all of the work of printing to others once he had assembled a staff (there were not, of course, any other printers in England when he returned there in 1476). Wynkyn de Worde, who was Alsatian, is believed to have joined him soon after his arrival, presumably as his foreman. Without competent help Caxton would not have been able to bring out so many books or do so much translating and writing of prefaces. That he chose the manuscripts for printing is obvious, even if the choice consisted of agreeing to print for a patron. Caxton had influential patrons, including the queen's brother, Anthony Woodville (Lord Rivers), who was tutor to the royal children. *Boece* was printed at the request of a friend, whom Caxton does not name, thought to have been William Pratt, a prominent London mercer.

Caxton's patrons were doubtless involved in the printing of *The Canterbury Tales*. As noted earlier, Caxton leased his Westminster shop in September, 1476. Since he had already used his Type no. 2 in the *Cordyale*, printed in Bruges, he had this type with him when he moved to England. The first edition of *The Canterbury Tales* is a huge work to have been printed little more than a year after the printer had established a new press. There is a slim piece of external evidence that he issued short books before major productions at his Westminster press. This is reported by the printer Robert Copeland, who worked for Wynkyn de Worde; if true, Caxton may have printed the two quarto Chaucers before either *Boece* or the first *Canterbury Tales* was issued.[24] Allan H. Stevenson's studies of watermarks appear to confirm this, for two Lydgate quartos (*The Horse, the Goose, and the Sheep* and *The Churl and the Bird*), which Stevenson dates late in 1476, have the same paper as the first running paper of Caxton's first edition of *The Canterbury Tales*, which was evidently interrupted by the *Jason* and the *Dicts or Sayings of the Philosophers* for the compelling reason that both were commissioned by Lord Rivers.[25] Also Caxton may have imported more help than we know of, and he may have prepared to print a certain list of books before he left Bruges. This possibility eliminates the need for supposing an entirely insular origin for the first printed *Canterbury Tales*: even the source manuscript may have been obtained on the Continent. In Bruges, of course, Caxton had had influence with the Burgundian court through Duchess Margaret, and probably also with the Seigneurs de Gruthuyse, rich beer barons who had curried favor with the English Yorkists by protecting Edward IV during his Flemish exile. Caxton says that the book had been brought to him, though he does not say where or by whom. In short, the book may have been planned under Burgundian patronage and published after Caxton had moved his press. As for the manuscript that was Caxton's source, neither its owner nor its printer was much of a Chaucer scholar, or its shortcomings would have been perceived before it was printed. But then, Caxton was a mercer, an administrator of foreign trade, and a diplomat turned printer, not a professional scholar.

The first printed edition of *The Canterbury Tales* is exactly as Caxton describes it in the preface to the second edition. The passage is so famous that it is best given in his own words:

> For I fynde many of the sayd bookes / whyche wryters haue abrydgyd it and many thynges left out / And in somme place haue sette certayn versys / that he neuer made ne sette in hys booke / of whyche bookes so incorrecte was one brought to me vj yere passyd / whyche I supposed had ben veray true & correcte / And accordyng to the same I dyde do enprynte a certayn nombre of them / whyche anon were sold to many and dyuerse gentyl men / of whome one gentylman cam to me / and said that this book was not accordyng in many places vnto the book that Gefferey chaucer had made / To whom I answerd that I had made it accordyng to my copye / and by me was nothyng added ne mynusshyd / [26]

Caxton's insistence that he had followed his copy is supported by manuscript evidence. He had simply printed a manuscript of the *b* text of *The Canterbury Tales*. The *b* text is one of four textual traditions (*a*, *b*, *c*, *d*), besides the text as it appears in several prestigious single manuscripts, such as the famous Hengwrt and Ellesmere manuscripts, all representing Chaucer's unfinished work as defined by unknown authorities after the poet's death in 1400. The *b* text has many omissions and spurious lines, as well as numerous other poor readings. It also has a characteristic order, involving both the clusters of tales as they appear in the Ellesmere manuscript (known as fragments I–X), and the groups of tales classified by the Chaucer Society in connection with the "Bradshaw shift" (which corrects geographical discrepancies in the Ellesmere order of the tales). In the *b* text order, fragment VIII (group G) has a different location, and the tales of fragments IV and V are run in, two before and two after, fragment III (group D), producing the order A B F^1 E^2 D E^1 F^2 G C B^2 H I.[27] The *b* text compares very badly with the text of *The Canterbury Tales* as now known from the identification of the best manuscripts and their careful screening to establish the correct readings.

Caxton was neither a knave nor a fool for printing a *b*-text manuscript, since the *b* text was very influential in the fifteenth century, though the printer did not have a present-day scholar's knowledge concerning the text of *The Canterbury Tales*. Besides his printed edition there are extant three manuscript copies of the *b* text: Helmingham (Princeton University Library), consisting of a vellum core (1420–30) filled out front and back with text written on paper (1450–60), which is greatly edited and cut but still of textual type *b*; D 314, New College, Oxford (1450–70); and R.3.15, Trinity College, Cambridge (1480–1500).[28] These manuscripts are all acephalous; only Caxton's edition shows the beginning of *The General Prologue* according to the *b* text. Current opinion holds that the Trinity College manuscript was copied from Caxton's exemplar after it had become dilapidated, but that is not my opinion, as will appear shortly; the remarks that follow do not apply to the Trinity College manuscript for that reason.

A number of other manuscripts follow the *b* text only in part, forming what Manly and Rickert called the *b** group.[29] Despite its antiquity, the vellum core of Helmingham is not the archetype of the *b* text. In a study of its editing, Virginia Everett Leland has shown that its scribe did a fairly conventional job of editing his source, through modernization of the grammar, syntax, and vocabulary. She cites one line, H 316 (*The Manciple's Tale*), as evidence that he did not scruple to substitute a line of his own making for one that he did not understand.[30] But in the other extant manuscripts of the *b* text the line, which is the second member of a rhymed couplet, does not appear; it is simply omitted, as it is from Caxton's edition. Upon looking further at random examples of spurious and omitted lines, we find other interesting cases in Caxton's edition. In the case of B 1807 (*The Prioress's Tale*) a spurious line occurs only in Caxton's edition, and it is likewise the second member of a rhymed couplet; in other manuscripts the line is Out. In the case of A 2195 (*The Knight's Tale*) a spurious line, with slightly different wording, appears in all the *b*-text manuscripts as well as in Caxton's edition. In the case of A 2212 (*The Knight's Tale*) a line is Out in both Helmingham and New College; Caxton shares a spurious line, the second member of a rhymed couplet, with manuscript Lansdowne 851 (1410–20), British Library, which is of a different textual tradition.

To turn to spurious lines and omitted lines in other situations, in the case of A 197–98 both members of a rhymed couplet are Out in Caxton's edition only. In the case of A 305 the first member of a rhymed couplet is Out in Caxton and in three other manuscripts: Ii.3.26, University Library, Cambridge (1430–50), Laud 600, Bodleian Library (1430–50), and Northumberland, privately owned (1450–70); all four have a spurious line with slight differences in wording before A 309—Ld, Ii, and Nl being *b** texts. Another first line of a rhymed couplet, A 403, is a spurious line in Cx^1 and in these same *b** manuscripts. Line B 985 is spurious in Cx^1, Out in both He and Ne, and Out also in one other manuscript, Laud 739, Bodleian Library (1470–90), by reason of losses; the line is the second member of a pair of lines that should rhyme.

The whole situation regarding omissions and spurious lines is very complicated and probably has no one explanation. The matter becomes the more interesting when it is seen that manuscript Ii, one of the principal manuscripts of the *b** group, leaves spaces for many of the missing lines, some of which have been filled in with correct or spurious lines. While Ii is not one of the better manuscripts of *The Canterbury Tales*, it follows the *b* text in a large part of its contents. It certainly gives an idea how some of the spurious lines got into the *b* text. As for omissions, there is no single factor to account for them all. The most obvious explanation, not necessarily the correct one but one that is certainly plausible, is that at least parts of the *b* text were copied from drafts of work still under revision that Chaucer had lent or given to acquaintances, as Boccaccio and Petrarch had done before him, with constant risk of plagiarism.[31] In that case plagiarism may figure in the peculiarities of the *b* text. Plagiarized work was notorious for inaccuracy.

Did Caxton invent any of the spurious lines that infest the *b* text? Not according to this point of view. He certainly did not invent lines that appear in older manuscripts. But the Trinity College manuscript (Tc^2) is a problem. It is very close to Cx^1 through E 375 (disarranged), when it changes affiliation. While with Cx^1, it has all the spurious lines and omissions, so that Manly and Rickert concluded that it had been copied from Caxton's exemplar after it had been shattered by his shop during printing and that the text of missing parts was on that account supplied from another manuscript.[32] If this were true, hardly any spurious lines, or missing lines, where the two are together, could be Caxton's responsibility. Unfortunately, the case for this relationship is not well founded. One piece of evidence that Manly and Rickert offer is agreement of some of the paper with paper Caxton was using ca. 1484, but that evidence is circumstantial: all paper used in England was imported. Their case for similarities of readings argues exactly the opposite of their opinion here. In A 1493, *fity Phebus* certainly entered Caxton's text through a wrong letter, *t*, used by the compositor instead of an *r* which it resembles in Caxton's Type no. 2. In A 3150, *Mylward* got into Caxton's text as a *b*-text reading, found also in line 3120. In short, it is more likely that Tc^2 was copied from a shattered copy of Cx^1; nor would that be unusual, for other manuscripts are known to have been copied from incunabula, as was *The Monk's Tale* as found in manuscript R.3.19, Trinity College, Cambridge, copied into that manuscript after 1478 from Cx^1.[33]

This still leaves unanswered the question of Caxton's authorship of unique spurious lines, such as B 1807. Textually, there is no proof at all that he did not write them. If he had done so, however, the likelihood is that he would have completed all or most of the rhyming couplets, which is not the case. A stronger argument comes from his press in Bruges. Whatever his role was in the printing of the *Recuyell*, five other books came from that press while Caxton was frequently away and otherwise busy with politics. Aside from *The Game of Chess*, which he had translated and which was printed immediately after the *Recuyell*, these other books (all in French) were printed at a time when it is virtually impossible that Caxton had opportunity to do more than contract for their publication, or that he would have worked on them if he had indeed possessed the time. Painter sees him as a gentleman printer who had compositors to do his work.[34] From this perspective the preface to the second edition of *The Canterbury Tales* has nothing to hide: Caxton had merely handed over to his staff a book for printing. He himself had edited it not at all. When he disclaims adding or subtracting from the text, he may as well be taken at his word.

Nothing is known of the identity of the person who told Caxton about the shortcomings of the text of his first edition. When Caxton uses the term "gentleman," he doubtless refers to a member of the aristocracy. This individual had a father who possessed a good manuscript of *The Canterbury Tales*. The interview referred to in the prologue of Caxton's second edition occurred about six years before the publication of the second edition. The person, moreover, knew enough about the text to be sure that his father's book had a better one, implying both that he had the education to study it and that his father's copy carried some kind of authority, perhaps by tradition or perhaps by an inscription. This is not an impossibility, for William Thynne owned a copy of a work by Chaucer inscribed "Examinatur Chaucer."[35] The whole incident is important witness that some of Caxton's contemporaries were interested in the text of *The Canterbury Tales*. As for the new manuscript, it was of the *a* text. Scholars have long assumed that the owner's reluctance to lend it to Caxton implies that it was a luxury manuscript, though there are other reasons for cherishing a book.

If Caxton had really suffered embarrassment because of textual problems in his first edition of *The Canterbury Tales*, he would surely have approached the prospect of another edition with some personal involvement in its preparation, and that indeed was the case. Thomas F. Dunn proved conclusively that the new edition was made by correcting a copy of the old edition against the new manuscript, neither collating it nor making a new transcript.[36] What Caxton did, presumably in person, was write corrections on the pages of a copy of the first edition and then turn over the result to his staff as copy-text. His compositor appears to have enjoyed full authority over his own work, for Caxton did not require extensive corrections as far as can be ascertained from the extant copies. Dunn shows several instances in which the editor wrote corrections in the margins at the beginnings of lines, which were then mislocated by the compositor because Caxton had not indicated clearly enough where they were to go. To cite but one example, Cx^1 reads (A 3299), "A clerk had *lowdly* biset . . .," whereas a large number of manuscripts read, "A clerk had *litherly* biset . . ."; the reading appears in Cx^2 as "*Lytherly* a clerk had biset . . . ."[37] That Caxton was himself the editor this time is clear from his preface, for he says, "I have corrected my book."

It has been widely assumed from the text of the second edition that Caxton's corrections were merely random, but that is not completely true. What he did was go after the spurious lines in the first edition and the lines that had been omitted from his source, precisely the faults of which his work had been accused. He did this systematically, though not perfectly. As Dunn has shown, 277 lines appear in Cx^2 that are not in Cx^1, Cx^1 having spurious lines in place of 62. There are 27 other spurious lines in Cx^1 that do not appear in Cx^2. Thus a total of 89 spurious lines of Cx^1 were removed in editing the text for the new edition, leaving 15 that Caxton, whether through reasons of his own or through carelessness, retained. In the process he also dropped four genuine lines.[38]

Cx^1 contains many other bad readings besides spurious lines and lines omitted. These appear in the *Corpus of Variants* published by Manly and Rickert. Some are modernizations, but some are real boners, so bad as to be laughable in terms of the text of *The Canterbury Tales* as known now. In Caxton's version of *The General Prologue* alone appear the following examples (italics added):

A	12	Than *longing* folk to gon on pilgremage
A	14	To *serue* halowis couthe in sondry londis
A	66	Agayn another *hethen man* in Turkye
A	187	As austyn *dide*, but hou shal the worlde be serued
A	217	And with worthy *yemen* of the toun
A	292	But al that he mighte of his frendis *haue help*
A	307	Sownyng moral vertu was his *prudence*

None of these readings, however strange, is unique to Caxton's edition. The most bizarre is *serue* (A 14), but the blunder is easily explained as a scribal misreading, first of *s* for long *f*, then (consequently) of *u* for *n* (*ferne*). In A 217 someone may have misread *y* for *w*, unless Chaucer really wrote that first and then revised it with a subtle dig at the Friar's circle of acquaintances. Another possible explanation is that the text was censored to get rid of exactly this innuendo, but not by Caxton, since the same reading appears in three manuscripts of the *b** group: Ii, Ld, and Nl, as well as in two other manuscripts (Paris Anglais 399, Bibliothèque National, Paris, 1422–36?; and Trinity College, Cambridge, R.3.3., 1450–60; manuscript CLII, Christ Church, Oxford, 1460–1500, originally read *men*, though the scribe corrected the reading). Leland found evidence that the scribes of Ii and Nl did some censoring as they edited,[39] but the readings of the earliest *b*-text manuscripts, He and Ne, cannot be ascertained because these manuscripts have lost leaves from their beginnings and with them this particular line. Thus there is some possibility that *yemen* was a *b*-text reading, though this cannot now be proved. In any event, Caxton did not invent the change.

Dunn has shown that in many cases Caxton's editorial changes conflate the text. To illustrate (italics added):

E 828   in *high nobles and honourey* Cx^1
        in *honour and nobleye*   33 manuscripts, none *b* text
        in *high honour and nobleye* Cx^2
E 948   sely *poure creature the Marquesse* Cx^1
        sely *povre Grisildis*   39 manuscripts, none *b* text
        sely *poure creature Grisildis* Cx^2 [40]

From these examples and from others it appears that Caxton was seriously attempting to save the text of his first edition by correcting it without trying to rewrite entire lines, for if he had been going to rewrite lines, he might as well have made a completely new transcription, which would have required more time and expense. The prose tales he corrected hardly at all. Nor is any of this editing necessarily the product of the kind of haste that Dunn and others have assumed, as, for example, that Caxton was not allowed to have the manuscript either as a copy-text or long enough to make a transcription of it as a copy-text, logical as this defense may seem.[41] Caxton made many corrections in the text, and they must have taken time as well as thought. What he was trying to do was enable his shop to produce the new *Canterbury Tales* from a printed copy text and to do it efficiently by cutting the book into portions for production on three presses, a procedure that he actually carried out, as Blake has shown from the quiring and signatures.[42] Contrary to what has been supposed, it may not have been even desirable to Caxton to have the new manuscript for a copy-text.

There is another major change in Cx^2, invariably attributed to Caxton's editing though the evidence for that is circumstantial: in Cx^2 the link between *The Franklin's Tale* and *The Squire's Tale* appears, and F^1 and F^2

are united and placed after E^2, producing the unique order A B^1 E^2 F D E^1 G^1 C B^2 H I. Unfortunately, the whole editorial procedure for the second edition, while indeed producing many better readings, also produced a hybrid text that originated in Caxton's shop. It rests on a colossal mistake in judgment, made when Caxton decided to correct his old book instead of making a completely new transcription. The result was a famous book, but one with a text so weak that it encouraged editorial tinkering for centuries until it was finally realized that the only way to obtain a good text was to begin with an entirely new transcription made from the most reliable manuscript of *The Canterbury Tales* as the base text.

The second edition of *The Canterbury Tales*, famous despite all its textual shortcomings, contains a well-known series of twenty-six woodcuts representing the Canterbury pilgrims. Woodcut art in books was intended to be painted, in the same manner as other miniatures. Like the invention of printing, woodcut art had an earlier origin in the Orient, though it was not until the sixteenth century that it became an important art form in its own right in Europe, reaching its best expression in the work of Albrecht Dürer. It had long been used, however, to stamp textiles for embroidery, and this may have been the route through which Caxton, a mercer, became aware of printing in the first place.[43] The portraits of the Canterbury pilgrims are by the same artist who was responsible for the woodcuts in the second edition of *The Game of Chess* (1482).[44] Indeed, the woodcut showing the Canterbury pilgrims at table dining upon boar's head had already been used in the *Chess* book. It is assumed that the portraits were copied from a series in the manuscript Caxton had used to correct his first edition, but there is no proof that this was indeed the case. As woodcut art they are not very good, but they have acquired fame from Caxton's book, certainly one of the most renowned ever printed in English. Only the Kelmscott Chaucer shares its position among editions of Chaucer noted as specimens of the printer's art. Caxton's book was reprinted in 1492 by Richard Pynson, in 1498 by Wynkyn de Worde, and again by Pynson in 1526.

Caxton produced another work by Chaucer late in the period of Type no. 2 (revised after the end of 1478): the poet's translation of *The Consolation of Philosophy*, written in prison by the Roman patrician and philosopher Anicius Manlius Severinus Boethius early in the sixth century A.D. Boethius, who had offended the emperor Theodoric's political faction, passed the time by writing his celebrated dialogue in which Lady Philosophy teaches him to leave off blaming Fortune for his problems. Chaucer's was the second notable English translation of the *Consolatio*, the earlier one attributed to King Alfred, though it is unlikely that either Chaucer or Caxton knew of the Alfredian version. Chaucer's sources were some medieval version of the work itself, a French translation attributed to Jean de Meun, and a commentary by Nicholas Trivet. A vulgate text of the *Consolatio* was current in the later Middle Ages in which numerous errors had become stereotyped as

proper to the work along with the characteristics of medieval Latin grammar, syntax, and orthography.[45] Since this has not been clearly understood,
Chaucer has been accused of being a poor Latinist.[46] Unfortunately, his
translation cannot be evaluated properly without a scholarly edition of the
vulgate text, which has yet to appear.[47]

An interesting characteristic of the manuscript copies of Chaucer's *Boece*
is that they usually give quotations from the Latin text at the head of each
prosa and metrum into which the five books of the *Consolatio* are divided.
Some Latin headings are a word or two; some are quite long. One manuscript (Ii.3.21, University Library, Cambridge, 1430–50) alternates the
complete Latin text with Chaucer's translation; only Caxton's edition
approaches its generosity with Latin headings. Chaucer's translation,
however, does not match the Latin of the headings, and it does not do so in
Caxton's edition.[48] Whether the printer took his copious headings from the
same manuscript that was his source for the translation it is impossible to
say on the basis of textual evidence. His dealings with the text of the first
edition of *The Canterbury Tales* suggest that he did, though his patron—
assuming that he had one, since he says in his epilogue that *Boece* is printed
at the request of an unnamed friend—may have wanted the headings from
some other source agreed upon in advance. But that Caxton would have
done this sort of thing on his own during the period of his early Chaucers
appears unlikely. Caxton's edition is still important in the editing of *Boece*.
It belongs to the first of two textual traditions, alpha and beta, which do not
differ greatly. Scholars have wavered between one and the other as the better
text, and the case is not yet closed.[49] The second printing of Chaucer's *Boece*
was by William Thynne (1532), who included it in the first collected
edition of the poet's works.

The text of the *Consolatio* properly contains many quotations from Greek
writers in the original language. Although most were dropped from the
vulgate text, Caxton's Latin heading for book 3, prosa 6, preserves the
vestiges of a quotation from Euripides (*Andromache* 319–20), undoubtedly
garbled by some scribe before Caxton came to print its opening as " . . . cros.
azosa. myplocia etc." It was evidently becoming fashionable to display an
attempt at Greek. This blunder does not occur in the Middle English,
either because Chaucer was intelligent enough to leave it out or because he
was spared that decision by his Latin and French sources. The passage in its
correct context is quoted in *Troilus and Criseyde* (1.731–35), when Pandarus
says to his heartsick friend:

> Or artow lik an asse to the harpe,
> That hereth sown whan men the strynges plye,
> But in his mynde of that no melodie
> May sinken hym to gladen, for that he
> So dul ys of his bestialite?

Either Caxton or his exemplar found more pseudo-Greek in the source manuscript, judging from "etc.," which is followed by the end of Caxton's line of type, a short one, and then by the beginning of a new sentence in the (Latin) heading. In the present context it seems likely that Caxton printed exactly what he saw in his exemplar and that he thought the quotation correct since he knew no Greek.

At the end of *Boece*, Caxton printed an epilogue that he had written, followed by an epitaph for Chaucer by Stephanus Surigonus, an Italian humanist who made several journeys to England, including one in 1475–76, when he was at Cambridge; he had also visited the court of Charles the Bold of Burgundy, presumably when Caxton was still in Bruges as governor of the English Nation. The printer could have met Surigonis, and it is likely, as Painter believes, that he commissioned Surigonis to write the epitaph, the idea for which may have come from one of the many epitaphs for Boethius found in manuscripts of the *Consolatio*. Caxton not only printed it but had it placed on a tablet that hung on a pillar near Chaucer's tomb in Westminster Abbey. The tomb was moved in 1556 to its present location, and there is now no trace of such a tablet.[50] It is evident that by 1478 Caxton had become an admirer of Chaucer. This has some importance because it indicates that the praise of Chaucer in the preface to the second edition of *The Canterbury Tales* was not merely rhetoric.

In the same period (before the end of 1478) Caxton also published the two quartos containing Chaucer's minor poems and other short pieces.[51] The testimony of Copeland, already noted, says that Caxton printed small works, including stories, before printing long ones, which sounds as if both *The Parliament of Fowls* and *Anelida and Arcite* may have been produced before the first edition of *The Canterbury Tales* and before *Boece*, possibly as early as 1476. That Caxton himself did the typesetting and presswork is doubtful though not impossible. Both quartos were discovered bound together with other short pieces from Caxton's press in a volume from Archbishop Parker's library acquired by Cambridge University through a bequest of books from George I. Since manuscripts were often small libraries (miscellanies), Caxton may have printed a number of short items for inclusion in miscellanies. The particular contents of the two quartos besides their major works were probably not of Caxton's own arranging, since manuscripts of *The Canterbury Tales* frequently contain also short works by Chaucer and by others. Caxton does not offer any of the non-Chaucerian pieces as Chaucer's. The two quartos were thought to be unique until 1858, when some leaves of the *Parliament* quarto, which were waste sheets from Caxton's press, were found in the bindings of a water-damaged copy of *Boece*. There is no known explanation of the fact that both the fragment and the Cambridge copy end at folio 24b. A quire is missing from the Cambridge copy, so that it ends before the conclusion of Chaucer's *Envoy to Scogan*; it is not known what the other contents may have been.

That Caxton printed the two quartos according to his source or sources is evident from textual situations. First, he reports only the first line of the song at the end of Chaucer's *Parliament of Fowls*: "Que bien aime / tarde oublie," thus agreeing with three manuscripts: R.3.19, Trinity College, Cambridge (written at various dates of the fifteenth and sixteenth centuries; the minor poems are sixteenth century); Fairfax 16, Bodleian Library (mid-fifteenth century); and Bodley 638 (third quarter, fifteenth century). Since there are several songs with the same first line, specific identification of Caxton's reference is unlikely. Robinson's edition of Chaucer's works gives as lines 630–92 the entire text of a rondel or triolet in English, "Now welcome, somer, with thy sonne softe." His authority is manuscript Gg.4.27, University Library, Cambridge (1420–40), the only manuscript of the several that cite it to give the whole text. Robinson thinks that Caxton's title refers to the melody of a song rather than to the words.[52] In any case, the difference between Caxton's text and the now-familiar one rests on manuscript authority, not on Caxton's editing.

Likewise with manuscript precedent, Caxton omits lines, as in *Fortune* 76, also Out in all manuscripts except Ii; and in *Anelida and Arcite* 290–98, the stanza also being Out in manuscripts Pepys 2006, Magdalene College, Cambridge (1470–1500), and Harley 7333, British Library (begun ca. 1450–60 and continued for a long time). Although Caxton has been thought involved in contaminating texts of the Minor Poems by crossing textual traditions in the course of editing, the Harleian manuscript is itself of precisely such origins, and Caxton is more likely to have found such editing in his sources than to have done it personally.[53] There is, however, a case where portions of the text have been transposed in Caxton's edition. Lines 41–80 of Scogan's treatise in all manuscript copies have been transposed with lines 86–125 in Caxton's edition. Since the error does not appear elsewhere, and since Caxton's source is not known, the reason for the shift may reside in an error made in his shop, not in the printing but in the ordering of loose leaves in the source manuscript.

The hand of Caxton's compositor is more visible than his own in the two quartos. The books are so short that typographical errors and errors in interpreting the scribal handwriting show up clearly. Typical errors in the *Parliament* quarto are: inexpert use of *wh* (PF 40, *whas*; 208, *wom*); confusion of manuscript brevigraphs involving *th* (PF 114, *thou* for *the*; line 263, *that* for *the*). There are also typical compositor's errors, such as errors in letters composed of minims (PF 178, *holin* for *holm*); metathesis (PF 135, *mrotal* for *mortal*); wrong letters (PF 310 and *Anel* 78, *te* for *to*); confusion of long *s*, *l*, and long *f* (*Anel* 51, *susfille* for *fulfille*). Some of these present textual cruces, as *Anel* 322, where Caxton's edition has *marred* (double-*r* ligature) whereas the manuscripts have *mased*; the compositor evidently meant to print *matted*, and it is impossible to know what was in the lost manuscript source.

The *Anelida* quarto is much shorter than the *Parliament* quarto, having only ten leaves, and it is also complete, since the book ends folio 10 and since folio 10b is blank. The last item, an anonymous stanza beginning "Whan feyth failleth in prestes sawes," is plainly not offered as Chaucer's, though some manuscripts call it a prophecy by the poet. The *Parliament* quarto begins with neither a guide letter nor a printed capital. Space has been left for a one-line initial, which has been added in brown ink. *Anelida and Arcite* has a guide letter only. Since both quartos borrow a capital *T* from Type no. 3, as does another quarto, *The Book of Courtesy*, Painter thinks that they were printed together.[54]

The remaining Chaucers belong, with the second edition of *The Canterbury Tales*, to the later group of Chaucers printed by Caxton: *The House of Fame* and *Troilus and Criseyde*. Neither contains woodcut illustrations. Current opinion is that Caxton used woodcuts only in works that were usually illustrated.[55] All three of the later Chaucers have been dated 1483, though there is at present no evidence that they were printed together.

The House of Fame, unlike the earlier books containing minor poems, is printed in folio. According to his epilogue, Caxton did not know that the lead poem was unfinished, though his source lacked the entire ending after line 2094. After searching in vain for a copy containing the rest of the poem, which in fact has sixty-three more lines, he concluded that Chaucer had left the poem unfinished, and he composed a conclusion himself, signed and echoing that of *The Parliament of Fowls*:

> And wyth the noyse of themwo   Caxton
> I Sodeynly awoke anon tho
> And remembryd what I had seen
> And how hye and ferre I had been
> In my ghoost / and had grete wonder
> Of that the god of thonder
> Had lete me knowen / and began to wryte
> Lyke as ye haue herd me endyte
> Wherfor to studye and rede alway
> I purpose to doo day by day
> Thus in dremyng and in game
> Endeth thys lytyl book of Fame.

While the patch is not the way of present-day editing, it was the way with fifteenth-century scribes, who invented spurious lines to plug gaps in Chaucer's text, as well as spurious links for some of *The Canterbury Tales*, and did so anonymously. But the printer had evidently learned something from his experience with the text of *The Canterbury Tales*: his own authorship is clearly marked. He concluded his book, possibly under the spell of his preface to the second edition of *The Canterbury Tales*, with an epilogue, which is partly, like the preface, an encomium upon Chaucer:

> I fynde nomore of this werke to fore sayd / For as fer as I can vnderstonde / This noble man Gefferey Chaucer fynysshyd at the / sayd conclusion of the metyng of lesyng and sothsawe / where as yet they ben chekked and maye not

departe / whyche werke as me semeth is craftyly made / and dygne to be
wreton & knowen / For he towchyth in it ryght grete wysedom & subtyll
vnderstondyng / And so in alle hys werkys he excellyth in myn oppynyon alle
other wryters in our Englyssh / For he wrytteth no voyde wordes / but alle
hys mater is ful of hye and quycke sentence / to whom ought to be gyuen
laude and preysyng for hys noble makyng and wrytyng / For of hym alle other
haue borowed / syth and taken / in alle theyr wel sayeng and wrytyng / And
I humbly beseche & praye yow / emonge your prayers to remembre hys
soule / on whyche and on alle crysten soulis I beseche almyghty god to haue
mercy   Amen[56]

The text of Caxton's edition of Chaucer's poem came from a manuscript
now lost; indeed, there are extant only three manuscripts and one fragment
of the poem. They show two versions of the text, now known as "alpha" (of
which the head manuscript is Bodley 638) and "beta" (of which the only
manuscript copy is Pepys 2006). The two versions witness a work still
under composition. Both Heath and Brusendorff favored the beta text of the
poem, to which Caxton's edition belongs,[57] but editors since have preferred
alpha, although both texts are bad, and both have to be used together to
produce an edition.[58] Blake wrongly implies that Caxton is to blame for
printing a bad text; there is in fact no good one.[59] Some of the standard
readings come from Caxton's edition: as *Devyne* (line 14), and *dystinctions*
(line 18). Between Caxton and Thynne (1532) there was no real study of the
texts of the minor poems. The second printing of *The House of Fame* is in a
volume of short pieces published in 1526 by Pynson; this follows *The House
of Fame* with *The Parliament of Fowls* and five non-Chaucerian items, the first
(*La bell Dame sauns mercy*) incorrectly ascribed to Chaucer's translating.
Pynson removed Caxton's signature from *The House of Fame* patch, corrected
the first line to read *hem two* instead of *themwo*, which may have been a
typographical error even though in the printer's own line, and substituted
two new lines at the beginning of Caxton's epilogue. Wynkyn de Worde
also published a *Parliament of Fowls* (1530), with a prefatory address and an
envoy by Copeland, who edited it for de Worde under the title *The Assemble
of Foules*. John Rastell had also printed it in 1525. It is interesting that these
printers did not reproduce the quartos successively with the same contents
and the same order that Caxton had used. While the manuscripts themselves had introduced apocryphal writings into the Chaucer canon, it was
through other early printers, not through Caxton, that apocryphal works
entered the canon of the minor poems authoritatively.

Painter believes that *The House of Fame* followed the second *Canterbury
Tales* and that *Troilus and Criseyde* came last, all three being printed between
July and September, 1483, the date being supported by the use of Type no.
4* and by the absence of printed initials and paragraph marks from Caxton's
books before December, 1483.[60] Caxton's *Troilus* is considered a handsome
book. It preserves one of only two copies of Chaucer's poem that consistently follow the beta text, the other being manuscript Rawlinson Poetry

163 (Bodleian Library, written by four fifteenth-century hands). There are three texts of *Troilus and Criseyde*, known as "alpha," "beta," and "gamma," of which alpha is the unrevised poem. But beta and gamma are problems in textual criticism, long dominated by Robert K. Root's essay on the manuscripts and their texts, which holds that beta is Chaucer's revision, though most manuscripts, including the famous Campsall manuscript in the Pierpont Morgan Library, follow the gamma text. According to Root, gamma was derived from a copy made before the revision (beta) was finished.[61] Robinson and others believe that gamma, not beta, is the final revision.[62]

The limitations of Caxton's knowledge of the text of the *Troilus* are similar to those revealed by his two editions of *The Canterbury Tales*. His edition is still useful in textual scholarship as a witness of the beta text, but his source manuscript was not a good copy of that text, which had been cut and otherwise corrupted through editing, though some of the modernization could have been done in Caxton's shop. A complete list of major defects is given by Root, including differences in line positions characteristic of the beta text, which are not really defects. Apart from the corrupt lines, and apart from differences that are characteristic of the beta text, the faults are as follows: transposed lines (1.111–12; 2.328–29; 3.1266–67; 4.137–38, 153–54; 5.70–71; lines 4–5 of a Latin argument from Statius found in some manuscripts); lines otherwise mislocated (5.1829 after 1832, 1831 after 1828); omissions (1.449–504, 890–96 [one stanza]; 2.246–301 [eight stanzas]); 3.442–76 [five stanzas], 1114–69 [eight stanzas]; reversed leaves in the source manuscript (1.785–812 after 840; 904–31 after 959).[63] The principal typographical flaw in Caxton's book is that some of the copies have errors on the outside sheet of sig. m, the sheet being corrected in others.[64] Both Wynkyn de Worde (1517) and Pynson (1526) reprinted the book, though their work made no contribution to the study of the text. The *Troilus* was afterward edited by Thynne (1532).

From this description of Caxton's printed Chaucers, some aspects of Caxton as an editor of Chaucer are clear. His knowledge of the texts of Chaucer's works was not that of an exegete of his own time, much less that of a present-day editor of Chaucer, though the printer himself never claimed such skill. In no case do we have copies or precise records of Caxton's sources for these books. Within these limitations the evidence is strong that he followed his texts closely except in the second edition of *The Canterbury Tales*, where he can be faulted for a serious mistake in judgment when he tried to correct the first edition from a manuscript obviously of a different textual tradition, though the circumstances were not altogether his fault. Having followed his sources elsewhere may not, however, be entirely to his credit, for the evidence is that in most of the Chaucers he did little or nothing in the way of editing but turned over the exemplars to his staff for copy editing and printing. In that case his staff is mainly responsible for what actually appears on the printed pages, all of which contain routine modernization of the grammar, syntax, vocabulary, and orthography. Definite evidence of his own editing resides only in his second edition of *The Canterbury Tales* and in his *House of Fame*.

2. William Thynne (d. 1546)

JAMES E. BLODGETT

THE PREFACE that dedicates William Thynne's edition of Chaucer of 1532 to Henry VIII is a wonderfully energetic, if stylistically overwrought, expression of Renaissance attitudes toward language and vernacular literature.[1] It begins with the conventional observation that language helps distinguish mankind from "brute beests" and is an "outwarde declaration of reason or resonablenesse / wherein consysteth the symylitude of man vnto aungels." A brief history of writing follows, along with a paean to the Greek and Latin tongues and a description of the development of various languages from Greek and Latin. The preface then notes the recent efforts by some speakers of French and German to amend their respective languages and observes that there have been Englishmen too working to beautify and better the English language. William Thynne includes himself among those men, saying that he was "moued by a certayne inclynacion & zele / whiche I haue to here of any thyng soundyng to the laude and honour of this your noble realme" to read and hear, as time and leisure allowed,

> the bokes of that noble & famous clerke Geffray Chaucer / in whose workes is so manyfest comprobacion of his excellent lernyng in all kyndes of doctrynes and sciences / suche frutefulnesse in wordes / wel accordynge to the mater and purpose / so swete and plesaunt sentences / suche perfectyon in metre / the composycion so adapted / suche fresshnesse of invencion / compendyousnesse in narration / suche sensyble and open style / lackyng neither maieste ne mediocrite conuenable in disposycion / and suche sharpnesse or quycknesse in conclusyon / that it is moche to be marueyled / howe in his tyme / whan doutlesse all good letters were layde a slepe thoughout yᵉ worlde . . . [that] suche an excellent poete in our tonge / shulde as it were (nature repugnyng) spryng and a ryse.

The "compendyousnesse" of the excellences ascribed to Chaucer's works catalogues qualities valued by Renaissance rhetoricians. The direct associa-

35

tion of a poet's glory with that of his native country further reflects Renaissance humanism, as does the low regard for the state of learning in the fourteenth century. Especially striking is Thynne's readiness to measure Chaucer most favorably against classical standards:

> For though it had ben in Demosthenes or Homerus tymes / whan all lernyng and excellency of sciences florisshed amonges the Grekes / or in the season y^t Cicero prince of eloque*n*ce amonges latyns lyued / yet had it ben a thyng right rare & strau*n*ge and worthy perpetuall laude / y^t any clerke by lernyng or wytte coulde than haue framed a tonge before so rude and imperfite / to suche a swete ornature and co*m*posycion.

Had Chaucer been fortunate enough to live in the present, "bei*n*g good letters so restored & reuyued as they be," he might have been able to bring the English language to "a full and fynall perfection."

Thynne's adulation of Chaucer does not stop with high-sounding praise: the germ for his edition was the discovery, as he read previous editions of Chaucer, of

> many errours / falsyties / and deprauacio*n*s . . . wherby I was moued and styred to make dilygent sertch / where I might fynde or recouer any trewe copies or exemplaries of the sayd bookes / whervnto in processe of tyme / nat without coste and payne I attayned / and nat onely vnto such as seme to be very trewe copies of those workes of Geffray Chaucer / whiche before had ben put in printe / but also to dyuers other neuer tyll nowe imprinted / but remaynyng almost vnknowen and in oblyuion.

In other words, Thynne was prepared to accord to the works of Chaucer the same respectful treatment that humanist scholars had been according to classical Greek and Latin writings since the fourteenth century, when Petrarch established the practice of collecting and collating as many manuscripts of classical works as possible.[2] It was not unprecedented to so treat the works of a major author writing in the vernacular: in fourteenth-century Italy the *Divine Comedy* enjoyed such treatment as is exemplified by the extensive commentaries in some early manuscripts and by the teaching of the *Comedy* in Italian universities alongside the classics.[3] Such scholarly approaches to vernacular literature were still unusual, however. A contemporary and more modest example perhaps known to Thynne before 1532 was Clément Marot's edition of 1526 of the *Roman de la Rose*, which, while primarily a reprint of an earlier edition, did draw on a manuscript source for some emendations.[4]

It is seriously questionable, however, whether a bureaucrat in the king's household would have the time and the capability to edit Chaucer's works with humanist rigor. Would Thynne's duties have left him much time for such work? How might the early Tudor royal household have encouraged him to pursue such editorial efforts? What precedents had earlier and contemporary English printers and editors set for editing Chaucer's works?

Fittingly enough, William Thynne, like his poet, was a functionary in the royal household. Surviving records trace his rise through the bureaucratic ranks. In a document from 1524, the earliest containing a definite reference to Thynne, he is called second clerk of the kitchen.[5] By 1526 he had become the chief clerk of the kitchen, his title in household records dating through 1533 as well as in the preface to the edition of 1532.[6] In documents from 1536 and 1538, Thynne is referred to as clerk controller of the king's household.[7] By the end of 1540 he was one of the masters of the household, a position that he retained until his death in August, 1546.[8]

It is not known how Thynne became attached to the king's household, but one possibly relevant fact is that his father-in-law, William Bond, was a clerk of the Green Cloth.[9] Thynne's early association with the household coincided with Cardinal Wolsey's reorganization of the household in an effort to pare away hangers-on and to increase efficiency. Wolsey's efforts assured that Thynne would have to work hard in his various positions, for they were not to be sinecures.[10]

Wolsey's Statutes of Eltham, dating from 1526, set out the main responsibilities of the clerks of the kitchen: to assure that only the best food was obtained for the king and his household, that it was on hand in ample time for preparation, that it was cooked well, and that none of it was stolen.[11] Surviving records give us glimpses of some of Thynne's specific duties. In one six-month period he received seventy-four pounds just to apparel what must have been a small army of turnspits.[12] Thynne's agreement with a John Wylkynson for the latter to scour the sinks of the king's kitchens at Windsor, Richmond, Hampton Court, and four other royal residences reminds us that Thynne's responsibilities extended to all the king's residences at the time he was editing Chaucer.[13]

Beyond performing his kitchen duties, Thynne would have been called upon in times of crisis, as were other officers of the household, to help with state affairs.[14] Sometimes Thynne was required to travel in the king's train. In 1532 he was one of a group that journeyed to Boulogne on government business.[15] In addition, from July, 1529, until his death Thynne held a position in the Exchequer, that of second collector of custom and subsidy of wool, leather, and fells in the Port of London.[16] This office makes another fitting parallel for Thynne with Chaucer, who was for several years controller of the wool custom in London, but the combined duties of both positions must have minimized the time that Thynne could devote to editing Chaucer.

That Thynne performed his duties well is attested not only by his series of promotions but also by various royal grants. As early as 1526 he received an annuity of ten pounds, and in the next seven years he was made a bailiff, the keeper of two parks, a cograntee for the presentation of a church, and receiver-general of the Earldom of March.[17] In 1532 and 1533 the king granted Thynne some oaks from the royal forests.[18] Such perquisites might be typical for all members of the household, but one honor suggests strongly that Henry VIII held Thynne in special favor: in 1533 he was one of two household officers who waited on Anne Boleyn at her coronation dinner.[19]

The royal favor implied by the official documents is explicitly asserted by William Thynne's son, Francis Thynne. In his *Animadversions*, a defense of his father against slighting remarks in the Preface to Thomas Speght's edition of Chaucer of 1598, the younger Thynne gives a spirited account of his father.[20] Written more than half a century after William's death by a son no more than two years old at the time of that death, the account is flagrantly mistaken in some details. However, there is no reason to doubt Francis Thynne's claim that his sources of information included persons who knew and worked with his father.[21]

Francis Thynne relates how the elder Thynne made a long-term enemy of Cardinal Wolsey by sheltering John Skelton in his house at Erith, in Kent, while Skelton was writing *Colin Clout*.[22] William Thynne did not lease the house in Erith until 1531, but, as has been pointed out, that error need not invalidate the whole story.[23] *Colin Clout* was published in 1522, so that early on Thynne was involved in court politics.

Francis Thynne illustrates the good relationship between his father and the king with an anecdote about how the king shielded William from Cardinal Wolsey's wrath at Thynne's inclusion of the virulently anti-episcopal *Pilgrim's Tale* in his supposed first, single-column edition of Chaucer. As the king had predicted after reading the tale, Thynne was called in by the bishops and "heaved at" by Cardinal Wolsey. Because of the king's favor Thynne was spared bodily harm, but Wolsey succeeded in convincing the king that the edition of Chaucer had to be reprinted with the *Pilgrim's Tale* omitted.[24]

Many problems are raised by the anecdote, not the least of which is the reference to an edition of Chaucer by Thynne that predates the edition of 1532 while including a poem that, at least in its surviving version, refers to the Pilgrimage of Grace, which occurred in 1536 (that is, six years after Wolsey's death), and cites a passage from the *Romaunt of the Rose* in terms of where it appears in Thynne's edition of 1532.[25] The younger Thynne has almost certainly taken liberties with the anecdote, but if the underlying premise of Wolsey's enmity toward William Thynne is true, that in itself would have strengthened Thynne's relationship with his monarch in the late 1520s.

However much the court was caught up in politics, it also nurtured a thriving interest in Chaucer. It was his poetry, especially *Troilus and Criseyde*, the most popular of his poems in the sixteenth century,[26] that provided the inspiration and diction for much of the poetry being written at court, including Sir Thomas Wyatt's.[27] The court in the 1520s and 1530s might even be considered an unofficial center for Chaucer studies. Certainly

John Skelton, John Leland, Sir Brian Tuke, and Thynne, all of whom had a strong interest in Chaucer, were at the court for several years after 1522. Many years earlier, as tutor to Prince Henry, Skelton would have had opportunity to infuse the future king with his own enthusiasm for Chaucer.[28] The gift of royal oaks and the honor of serving Anne Boleyn her coronation meal may have stemmed partly from Thynne's editing of Chaucer.

In defending his father's edition against Thomas Speght's aspersions, Francis Thynne asserts that William Thynne, at his death, owned about twenty-five Chaucer manuscripts, including one supposedly with the repeated marginal notation "examinatur Chaucer."[29] Purportedly an important source of many of these manuscripts was a commission his father received "to serche all the liberaries of Englande for Chaucers Workes, so that oute of all the Abbies of this Realme . . . he was fully furnished with multitude of Bookes."[30] Whatever their sources, five manuscripts are still extant, as well as a Caxton print, that can be identified with varying degrees of certainty as having been at least briefly in William Thynne's possession. In addition, there are at least four hypothetical manuscripts that Thynne used.[31]

Two manuscripts associated not only with William Thynne but with his edition of Chaucer of 1532 (hereafter Th) are Hunterian V.3.7 (hereafter Gl), University of Glasgow Library, and 258 (hereafter Lg), in the Library of Longleat House.[32] Also, the Longleat copy of Caxton's edition of Chaucer's *Boece* (hereafter Cx) is associated directly with Th.[33] Gl is the only manuscript extant of *The Romaunt of the Rose*. Lg is an anthology of love poetry, mostly complaints and debates, including six pieces printed in Th: four of Chaucer's poems—*The Parliament of Fowls, Anelida and Arcite, The Complaint of Mars,* and *The Complaint unto Pity*—as well as *La Belle Dame sans Merci* and *The Assembly of Ladies.*

All of Gl, parts of Lg, and all of Cx are counted off in marks characteristically used by Tudor printers to prepare copy.[34] The marks reflect the layout of the columns in Th. Numbers in a series from one to twelve correspond to the twelve pages within each signature of folios in sixes that, with the exception of one folio in fours and one in nines, make up Th. The book is printed two columns to a page; thus between each number in the series there is also the notation "coll" to indicate the first line of the second column on each page in Th. The relationship between these printer's marks and the corresponding texts in Th proves that Thomas Godfrey, the printer of Th, used Gl as his copy for the *Romaunt*, Lg as his copy for *The Assembly of Ladies* and for the concluding six stanzas of *La Belle Dame sans Merci*, and Cx as his copy for many sections of *Boece*.[35]

In addition to the printer's marks in Lg, there appears on folio 147v, beneath a Latin table of contents, a faded inscription in secretary hand: "Maister Willm͛ thyne / clerke of the kechin / to our soueraigne lorde / King

henry the viii[th] / [some squiggle] Thomas / Godfray."[36] Rather tantalizing-
ly, there appears in Gl on 150r, below the conclusion of the *Romaunt*, a large
smudge, the remnant of perhaps four or five lines of writing, a note, one
would like to think, similar to the one at the end of Lg. Unfortunately, even
ultraviolet light reveals nothing more than that there once was writing
there, perhaps in secretary hand.

Two other manuscripts at Longleat include some of Chaucer's works.
Manuscript 257 includes *The Knight's Tale* (entitled "Arcite and Palamon")
and *The Clerk's Tale* (entitled "Grisild") among several other items, mostly
longer narratives, including Lydgate's *Siege of Thebes*, a prose *Ipomedon*, and
verse paraphrases of several of the narrative books in the Old Testament.
Manuscript 29 contains religious tracts and expositions in English and
Latin, including *The Parson's Tale*. Only the presence of these two manuscripts at Longleat House, built by William's nephew John Thynne,
suggests that William Thynne ever owned or had access to them.[37]

Manuscript HM 144, now at the Huntington Library, passed through
the hands of John Stow, but Manly and Rickert suggest that William
Thynne had access to it earlier. They tentatively ascribe to Thynne a note at
the top of folio 81r that correctly identifies the work starting on that page as
"Chausers talle of melebe."[38] The history of the manuscript certainly
invites a plausible hypothesis about how Thynne might have gained at least
temporary access to many Chaucer manuscripts such as HM 144. In the
sixteenth century the manuscript probably belonged to a John Skinner of a
wealthy family in Surrey.[39] One John Skinner is included in a 1531 grant of
commissions of peace in Surrey. Many of the other names in the same grant
are those of members of the king's household, including Sir Brian Tuke.[40]
The extensive network among officers in the king's household and reaching
out to other courtiers and the country gentry must have provided Thynne
frequent opportunities, perhaps here through Tuke if not directly, to
borrow Chaucer manuscripts.

Chaucerians have long had fantasies about the manuscript mentioned
above, in which, by Francis Thynne's report, the marginal notation "examinatur Chaucer" recurred. Manly and Rickert have suggested that either
Egerton 2726 or the Cardigan manuscript might actually be the manuscript
to which the younger Thynne refers, but neither has the exact notation
given by Francis Thynne, only "*ex'.*"[41] The possibility is intriguing, but
there is no reason to associate either manuscript with William Thynne.

There is also evidence to hypothesize several manuscripts no longer
extant that Thynne used. Analysis of Th's text of many of the minor poems
indicates that Thynne used a manuscript closely related to the Oxford group
and especially close to Tanner 346 (hereafter T). The text of Thynne's
manuscript (hereafter *T) seems to have been at least one copy closer to the
common exemplar for the Oxford group than any of the surviving manuscripts in that group. When the contents of the three central manuscripts

in the group—T, Fairfax 16 (hereafter F), and Bodley 638 (hereafter B)—are compared, of the fourteen works found in T, twelve also appear in F and B, and thus were probably also in *T.[42] Eleven of these twelve are printed in Th. As discussed below, *T was used by Thynne to help establish his texts of *Anelida* and *The Complaint of Mars*. In addition, F. N. Robinson places Th's text closest to T's for *The Legend of Good Women* and closest to that of the manuscript group including T for *The Complaint of Venus*.[43] A modern editor of *The Complaint of the Black Knight* places Th's text of that poem in the same subgroup as T's, and two editors of *The Book of Cupid* conclude independently that Th's text of that poem is closest—and very close indeed—to T's.[44]

Further textual analyses indicate that Thynne used a manuscript unrelated to the Oxford group to help establish his text for *The Parliament of Fowls*. To emend his base text of *The Canterbury Tales*, Thynne used a manuscript affiliated with Manly and Rickert's manuscript family cd*. Th's text of *Boece* was printed in irregularly alternating sections from Caxton's edition and from a manuscript whose text most closely, although not particularly closely, resembles that of Bodley 797.

Thus there seems little reason to doubt the claims of father and son that William Thynne gathered manuscripts with the intention of restoring the original texts of Chaucer's poems previously printed and of searching for works by Chaucer not yet in print. How Thynne carried out his first purpose needs to be discussed at some length, but his success in the second endeavor is easily documented. Of works genuinely by Chaucer, Thynne was the first to print *The Romaunt of the Rose* (generally agreed to be at least partly Chaucer's), *The Legend of Good Women, The Book of the Duchess, The Complaint unto Pity, Lak of Stedfastnesse,* and *A Treatise on the Astrolabe*. Thynne's efforts to rescue neglected works of Chaucer paid off handsomely.

Thynne has been berated, however, for having introduced many spurious works into Chaucer's canon. Richard Pynson set the precedent by including five non-Chaucerian pieces in the second part of his tripartite edition of Chaucer of 1526. These poems illustrate that, though Thynne added many works to the canon, he did exercise some choice, not simply printing whatever fell into his hands. He reprints from Pynson's edition only two of the non-Chaucerian pieces: *La Belle Dame sans Merci* and *The Lamentation of Mary Magdalene*. Thynne's additions show him especially susceptible to love poetry (even the *Lamentation* is basically a lover's complaint in which Mary Magdalene laments that Christ, of the "noble dalyaunce," has forsaken his "louer iust & trew"), for he prints for the first time Robert Henryson's *Testament of Cresseid, The Flower of Courtesy, The Assembly of Ladies, A Praise of Women, The Remedy of Love,* Thomas Hoccleve's *Letter of Cupid, The Book of Cupide,* and a few ballades. He also, however, prints for the first time some nonamatory pieces, including the prefatory poems "Eight Goodly Questions" and Hoccleve's "To the King's Most Noble

Grace," Thomas Usk's *Testament of Love*, and John Gower's *In Praise of Peace*. For many of the works that Thynne first printed manuscripts or prints survive with texts superior to those in Th, but for some works Th provides important texts: Th's text for *The Testament of Love* is the only one surviving, and its text of *The Testament of Cresseid*, for all its corruptions, is the earliest one extant.[45]

Although Thynne clearly used his manuscripts as sources for works never before printed, there remains the more difficult question of whether he collated them in the effort to improve a text. The identification of Gl, Lg, and Cx as printer's copy helps us determine with certitude how Thynne prepared his texts. A comparison of the printer's copy with the corresponding text in Th reveals what substantial changes have been introduced. Such a comparison gives no reason to hypothesize that any manuscript was collated against Gl or Cx, though it uncovers other interesting changes, discussed below. A comparison of Th's texts with Lg's does indicate, however, that Thynne used collation.

In Lg printer's marks are found throughout *The Assembly of Ladies*, through more than half of *Anelida and Arcite*, and in the last seven stanzas of *La Belle Dame sans Merci*. In the marks for the *Assembly* an initial set of numbers has been crossed out and replaced. The second set corresponds exactly to the layout of the *Assembly* in Th; probably the poem had been originally intended for some other place in Th than where it does appear. A comparison of Th's and Lg's texts provides no evidence that Thynne collated any other text against Lg's. Of the poem's 756 lines Th varies from Lg's text in only 104 places. Almost all these variants can be explained as compositorial errors, self-evident corrections of errors or seeming errors in Lg, or changes of the sort that the compositors introduced on their own and at general instructions from Thynne.[46]

Pynson's text of *La Belle Dame sans Merci* of 1526 undoubtedly was Thynne's copy text.[47] In line after line Th's text varies from Pynson's by only a punctuation mark or an insignificant spelling change; in more than 150 lines the accord is perfect, letter for letter. For the final six stanzas, however, Thynne abandoned Pynson's text and had Thomas Godfrey print from Lg; thus we find the printer's marks appearing in the final seven stanzas of Lg's text. The shift is easily explained. Entirely different from the conclusion found in all the complete manuscript copies, Pynson's final six stanzas disapprove of the lover in the poem, asserting that the beautiful lady rightfully spurns him because he shams misery over her coldness solely for selfish desires. Finding such a gloss on the poem unacceptable, Thynne substituted from Lg the much more sympathetic conclusion that urges ladies not to emulate the merciless lady of the poem.

Although Pynson's edition was clearly Godfrey's copy text for the first 812 lines of the poem, Thynne could have readily emended Pynson's text with Lg. However, most of the 34 readings in the first 812 lines where Th and Lg agree against Pynson's text can be explained otherwise. Still, 6 of these readings that cluster together between lines 189 and 206 suggest just by their relative density that Thynne may have emended that section of Pynson's text with Lg: line 189, Th and Lg's *this* for Pynson's *his*; line 197, *wonder* for *very*; line 198, *more* for *nere*; line 202, *sore* for *so*; line 206, *strayned* for *constrayned* and *for payne* for *payne*. None of the other 77 readings in the first 812 lines where Th's text varies from Pynson's suggests collation with any other manuscript, nor, in the final six stanzas, does any of Th's 8 readings that vary from Lg's.

Although Lg's text of *Anelida and Arcite* was marked off as printer's copy, it does not seem to have been Godfrey's copy. The marks do not correspond to the layout of the poem in Th, nor are they corrected as are those found in Lg's text of the *Assembly*. Furthermore, an analysis of Th's text indicates that Lg could not have been Thynne's copy text. The analysis does suggest, however, that Thynne established his text by collating Lg, another manuscript of the poem, and Caxton's edition of the poem (hereafter Cx^1).[48]

Although Th and Cx^1 share only three readings against all the extant manuscripts, one of these shared readings leaves little doubt that Thynne used Cx^1. In line 193 Th's *meate or syp* must be taken directly from Cx^1's *mete or sype*: all the manuscripts read *fee or shippe* (from Old English *scipe*, "stipend") except for one, which reads *mete or shepe*.

Th and Lg agree about 180 times against Cx^1. However, only five of these readings cannot be duplicated in one or more of the other manuscripts of *Anelida*; but, taken with the evidence that Thynne had Lg in hand, these five indicate that Thynne used Lg. For example, in line 13, Th and Lg read *And* against *As* in all the other authorities, and in line 17 they read *Cirsa* against *Cirrea* in all the other texts except for one with *Circa*. In line 336, Th and Lg's *neuermore* destroys the internal rhyme preserved with *neuermo* in all the other texts. The most convincing agreement is in line 357, where Th and Lg read *as ye may plainly here* against *as ye shall aftyr here* in the three other manuscripts, including T, that contain the so-called continuation stanza, which is not found in Cx^1. In this stanza Thynne did have a choice between these two readings since in the same stanza his text agrees three times against Lg with the other three manuscripts: *Whan that* against Lg's *whan*, *she gan* against *began*, and *sorouful* against *woful*.[49]

Of the 59 readings in Th found in neither Cx^1 nor Lg, 43 can be duplicated in at least one of the other manuscripts. T duplicates 35 of these readings, more than any of the others. Some of the readings that T does not share with Th can be assumed for a manuscript such as *T hypothesized above. For example, in lines 274, 286, and 310, where Th reads, respectively, *ben* against T's *be*, *bethe* against *be*, and *maken* against *make*, Th's readings are found in manuscript Ff.1.6 at Cambridge University Library, closest to T of all the extant manuscripts. Th's readings of *or* in line 197, *her better* in line 296, and *and mercy* in line 332 can all be duplicated in other manuscripts also closely affiliated with T. Further evidence for the proximity of Thynne's second manuscript to T occurs in line 48, where T's *Partinope* is the only reading that duplicates Th's *Partynope*. The other texts provide such testimonies to scribal difficulties as *pertynolope* (Lg), *parthonope* (Cx[1]), *Prothonolope, partonope*, and *Parathone*. Three other, minor variant readings are found only in T and Th.

Because we have two of the texts that Thynne used, Lg and Cx[1], as well as T, which is very close to his third one, *T, we can readily detect one of Thynne's editorial practices. Quite simply, he usually selects the reading given numerical support by his three textual witnesses; that is, he usually keeps a reading found in all three texts, and, for readings where two of the texts agree against the third, he most often selects the reading supported by two. In the latter situation, however, Thynne is less likely to abandon his base text *T even when Lg and Cx[1] agree against it. Thus Th prints 163 of the 187 readings where Lg and T agree against Cx[1] and 66 of the 73 readings where T and Cx[1] agree against Lg, whereas Th prints only 26 of the 51 readings that Lg and Cx[1] share against T. Editing by show of hands is a simplistic but certainly defensible technique; at the very least it prevented Thynne from printing most of the many bad readings unique to Lg or to Cx[1].

William Thynne clearly devoted much effort to establishing his text for *Anelida*. Initially he seems to have chosen Lg as his copy text; otherwise, it would not have been marked off as was Thomas Godfrey's copy. Yet even after Lg was presumably in Godfrey's shop, Thynne reconsidered his choice, making *T his base text and then emending it extensively from Cx[1] and Lg. Indeed, since *Anelida* is relatively short and the text in Th is heavily emended, Thynne might even have resorted to making a new copy that incorporated all his emendations for Godfrey to print from.

Although both *The Complaint unto Pity* and *The Complaint of Mars* are found in Lg, neither text has been marked for printing, and an analysis of Th's text of the two poems indicates that again *T was probably the base text for each. It is possible that two or three minor emendations were included from Lg to establish Th's text of *Pity*. For *The Complaint of Mars*, Th's text is is especially close to *T's; of almost three hundred lines there are only 35 readings in Th that cannot be found in either F or T and 10 readings in Th found elsewhere only in T. Although Lg's text for the poem was at hand, there are only two readings in Th otherwise unique to Lg; the more significant one is their shared reading of *sparcles* in line 96, where all the other texts read *sparkys*.[50]

Thynne's text of *The Parliament of Fowls* raises many questions in its details, but clearly Thynne established his text through extensive collation. He apparently used Caxton's edition of the poem as his base text for the first 140 lines of the poem and Pynson's edition for the rest of the poem.[51] Thynne emended most of the poem extensively with readings from a manuscript closely related to those in a textual subgroup comprised of manuscripts Pepys 2006, Magdalene College, Cambridge; Laud 416, Bodleian; and St. John's College, Oxford, LVII.[52] After line 600, Thynne emended Pynson's text more heavily than before, perhaps as a result of his shifting his trust more toward his source for the words to the roundel; neither Pynson's nor Caxton's text includes the roundel. Thynne may also have drawn on a manuscript related to the Oxford group for his text after line 600.

The apparent shift at line 141 of base text from Caxton's edition to Pynson's does not coincide with a signature break or a page break in either of those two editions, but line 141 starts a new page (sig. Ccc fol. 4r) in Th. Theoretically, expediency might have encouraged the shift, since it would permit two compositors to set type simultaneously for this poem, but it is difficult to see the actual benefits, since each base text was extensively emended.

A similar question is raised on a much larger scale by Th's text of *Boece*. The printer's marks found throughout Cx and their relationship to the layout of *Boece* in Th leave no doubt that Godfrey used Cx as copy. A comparison of Th's text and Cx's makes it equally clear that Thynne also resorted to at least one manuscript. Not counting mere spelling differences, there are roughly 1,300 readings in Th that vary from Cx's text, a large number of which cannot be ascribed to compositorial interference. For example, there are in Th 137 additions to Cx's text that range in length from one to twenty words. Most of these additions can be duplicated in at least one of the extant manuscripts of *Boece* and usually in several or all of the complete ones.

The distribution of variant readings in Th is highly uneven, however. On the one hand, there is, for example, sig. Vv, fol. 3r with no significant variants on the whole page, only spelling differences on the order of Th's *father* for Cx's *fader*. On the other hand, there is sig. Zz, fol. 3r with 72 variant readings, many minor, but also including twelve added words or phrases. These additions and many of the other variants are well attested in the *Boece* manuscripts. When 72 such variants occur on a single page, coincidental variation does not seem a likely explanation, nor, since there are no signs of changes in Cx, does emendation of Cx. The page must have been set from Thynne's manuscript.

Clearly sig. Vv, fol. 3r and sig. Zz, fol. 3r are extreme examples, but the contrast they make can be found in almost as sharp definition throughout Th's text of *Boece*. One can argue that two compositors set type for *Boece*, one using Cx as copy and the other using Thynne's manuscript.

Such an argument would be based on the distribution of two different spellings of the negative particle, *not* and *nat*. Throughout Th these two spellings occur in alternating clusters that are of irregular and widely varying lengths, sometimes several signatures long and sometimes less than a page. These different spellings do not seem to reflect the spelling in the printer's copy. For example, the alternation can be observed in Th's text of *The Romaunt of the Rose*, for which Gl was the sole printer's copy and whose spelling favors *not* to the total exclusion of *nat*. There are some passages in Th in which the two spellings become intermixed, and one cannot argue for a 100 percent consistency in the compositors' spellings, but the evidence for a general correlation is strong.

There certainly is a pattern in Th's *Boece* of the *not* sections seemingly having been set from Cx and the *nat* sections from Thynne's manuscript. To illustrate, on Aaa 1r, with six *not*'s and no *nat*'s, there are only nine readings that vary from Cx, mostly in a minor way, such as *haue* for Cx's *han* or *byrdes* for Cx's *briddes* (a standard accidental throughout Th). On the next five pages of signature Aaa, which have 54 *nat*'s among which are scattered four *not*'s, the readings that vary from Cx number, respectively, 54, 44, 59, 63, and 47. Many of these variants, which include some extensive additions, can be found in the *Boece* manuscripts. There are exceptions, but generally the correlation between compositor and copy holds throughout *Boece*. Again, composition from two texts should expedite printing, but the actual distribution of work between the two compositors weakens that explanation.[53] Whatever questions Th's text of *Boece* raises concerning early Tudor printing-house practices, it provides a clear example of Thynne's failure to collate a manuscript at hand against his base text.

All the information necessary for a full understanding of how William Thynne established his text for *The Canterbury Tales* is not yet available, but at the very least Thynne collated one manuscript against his base text for parts of the *Tales*. A comparison of the data in W. W. Greg's exploratory attempt to trace the textual sources of the first six printed editions of the *Tales* with the manuscript variants in Manly and Rickert's edition indicates that Thynne did emend his base text with a manuscript related to Manly and Rickert's manuscript family cd*.[54] Greg's small sample, the first 116 lines of *The Knight's Tale*, allows only tentative conclusions, but an analysis of the entire text in Th for *The Canon's Yeoman's Prologue* and *Tale* leads to the same conclusion. There are 389 readings in Th's text that do not occur in any of the preceding five editions of the *Tales*. The fifteen manuscripts in cd* that include *The Canon's Yeoman's Prologue* and *Tale* duplicate from 66 to 76 percent of these readings. Only one manuscript from outside that group duplicates more than 66 percent, and that only 68 percent. A thorough analysis needs to move beyond simple statistics, but the figures are significant: Thynne did emend his base text with readings from a manuscript and at a fairly impressive rate of about one emendation for every four lines of text.

The consensus is that Thynne's choice of a base text for *The Canterbury Tales* was one of the previous printed editions, but there is disagreement about which one: Tyrwhitt identifies Thynne's base text as Caxton's second edition; Skeat, as Caxton's first edition; and Greg, as de Worde's edition, whereas the evidence for *The Canon's Yeoman's Tale* indicates that the base was one or the other of Pynson's two editions.[55] Two explanations that are not necessarily mutually exclusive suggest themselves for this uncertainty. One is that, to facilitate Godfrey's work, Thynne might have used, for a work as long as *The Canterbury Tales*, two or more base texts, so that different sections of the *Tales* might be based on different printed editions. The other is that Thynne might have emended whichever edition was his base with readings from one or more of the other editions (in spite of the dismay about their texts that he expresses in his Preface) as well as from at least one manuscript.

There can be no doubt that William Thynne used several manuscripts as well as earlier editions in preparing his edition of 1532. Occasionally some of the uses that he made of these materials seem to have been determined, as with *Boece*, by the needs of the printer more than modern editors would consider appropriate, but Thynne also collated different textual authorities of a work to help establish his texts, as with *Anelida and Arcite*, *The Parliament of Fowls*, and at least parts of *The Canterbury Tales*. In addition, Robert K. Root attests that Thynne's text of *Troilus and Criseyde*, unlike that of any of the other early editions, was based on the collation of several texts.[56] Thynne, however, also knew of other means to improve a text: emendations can be based on an editor's knowledge of a writer's language and cultural environment and on a consultation of the original work when the work being edited is a translation.

Thynne recognized some of the details of Chaucer's language that had become archaic by the early sixteenth century. He made some emendations apparently intended to restore more archaic, and thus, presumably, more authentically Chaucerian, readings to the texts in Th. The most common of these emendations is the restoration of *hem* and *her* wherever the copy text has the originally Northern forms, *them* or *their*. The consistency with which this change occurs suggests that Thynne gave the printer general instructions always to make the change. Certainly the Southern forms occur with greater frequency in Th than in editions by Caxton, de Worde, and Pynson. The exceptions in Th stand out as unusual and, where the printer's copy is known, often can be duplicated in that copy.

Another archaization that Thynne used sporadically is the -(e)n infinitive ending. For example, in Thynne's text of *Anelida*, the -(e)n ending is chosen several times even when two of Thynne's three textual authorities have the -(e) ending. In passages in the *Romaunt* in which Thynne almost certainly emended Gl's text, he repeatedly introduces verbs with that form, as in line 1063, where Th reads *Han hyndered / and ydon to dye* for Gl's *An hundred haue do to dye*. The *y*- prefix in this line is another archaic touch that Thynne adds to his text. Not found at all in Gl, the prefix occurs twenty-two times in Th, mostly in the first part of the poem; it appears twenty times by line 1610.

Thynne occasionally substituted for one word another that he might have thought archaic. For example, in line 123 of *La Belle Dame*, with one of the few emendations that he draws from Lg, he replaces Pynson's *soude* with *sowne*. A similar motivation may explain Th's *Iolyfe* for Gl's *ioly* in line 109 of the *Romaunt*. On the whole, however, such substitutions were not favored by Thynne.

Thynne's knowledge about differences between Chaucer's language and his own was limited in general to the very common points cited above. About other differences, even ones repeatedly illustrated in Chaucer's works, he can be obtuse. For example, in line 1065 of the *Romaunt*, Th's *And maketh* for Gl's *Haue maad* betrays a faulty grasp of Chaucer's grammar, which would have required *maken* for the plural subject in the preceding line. In the twenty-five passages in which Chaucer uses the strong preterit *wepe*, Th prints it as *wept(e)* in twenty-one instances and *wepeth* in two.[57] Occasionally some of the manuscripts or earlier printed editions make the same change, but frequently the change is unique to Th. In line 138 of *Anelida and Arcite*, as well as in line 1732 of *The Legend of Good Women*, the form *wepe* must be retained to preserve the rhyme. In both places Thynne changes *wepe* to infinitive by placing an auxiliary verb before it, *dothe* in *Anelida* and *gan* in the *Legend*; both readings are unique. Thynne's emendation in *Anelida* also reveals his ignorance about Chaucer's use of *do* as a periphrastic auxiliary only in questions, and even then very rarely.

Along with archaization, Thynne practiced classicization, a direct but wrongheaded result of Thynne's wish to accord Chaucer's text the respect that the humanists showed Latin and Greek texts. One rather trivial manifestation of Thynne's classicizing is the respelling of proper names to reflect more closely and sometimes exactly the classical Latin spelling. Thus Th's restoration of the *mn* consonant cluster to *Polymnia* in line 15 of *Anelida* brings that word closer to its classical spelling *Polyhymnia* than do any of the other authorities. In the *Romaunt*, Th prints *Pythagoras* for Gl's *Pictigoras* in line 5649 and replaces the *J* in Gl's *Jerusalem* in line 554 with *H*. The largest number of such respellings occurs in *Boece*: *Agamemnon* for *Agamenon*, *Pythagoras* for *pictagoras*, *Alcibiades* for *Altibiadis*, *Tityus* for *Tycius*, *Epicurus* for *epicurius*, *Coribantes* for *Coribandes*, and so on. For these instances and others, neither Cx nor any of the surviving manuscripts has the more learned spelling.

A more rigorous and sustained display of learning appears in Cx, where, throughout the first three books and for part of the fourth, someone has edited the Latin rubrics that precede each meter and prose. These rubrics, simply the opening lines in Latin of the section that follows, are frequently very lengthy in Cx. The editing is detailed, involving changes such as making lower case letters upper case and vice versa, correcting spellings, writing out abbreviations, changing and adding punctuation, and correcting faulty spacing.[58] The editing also includes more substantial changes, such as correcting grammatical forms, changing word order, substituting one word for another, and adding new words. The length of the rubrics is reduced in Th, but they incorporate almost all the corrections made in the corresponding lines in Cx.

A particularly interesting learned emendation is found in Th's text of *The Physician's Tale*. The perjurer Claudius is called a *churl* eight times in the course of the tale. At least that is the reading in most of the manuscripts and in all five editions of *The Canterbury Tales* previous to Th. The only variant reading recorded by Manly and Rickert is *clerk*. Yet in Th, Claudius is called a *client* eight times. Thynne or a learned colleague must have turned to the source for the tale cited in the opening line (*as telleth vs Tytus Liuius*), come across the following line, *M. Claudio clienti negotium dedit* [*Appius*], and corrected the text accordingly.[59]

Th's text of *The Romaunt of the Rose* offers further evidence that Thynne consulted a source in another language to emend his copy text. Nine lines scattered through Th's text are completely omitted from Gl, and 4 others differ entirely from the corresponding lines in Gl. Otherwise, there are 685 readings in Th that vary from Gl. The great majority of these variants can be explained as compositors' errors, self-suggesting improvements of obviously faulty readings in Gl, and the results of archaizing changes similar to those mentioned above. What remain are some 40 or 50 variants, plus the 13 complete lines.

Except for the complete lines, most of the significant variants appear before line 1700, and even in that section of the poem they are unevenly distributed. Editing selectively rather than thoroughly, Thynne seems to have emended Gl by referring to a copy of the *Roman de la Rose* rather than to another manuscript of the *Romaunt*. The case cannot be argued at length here, but a few examples can be cited for which Th's text reflects the French original more closely than does Gl's, even though by itself Gl's text makes sense. In line 286, Th's *one eye* is a closer translation than Gl's *eien* for the French *.i. oil*; in line 421, Th's *symple* is closer than Gl's *semely* to the variant *simple* found in some of the French manuscripts; in line 673, Th's *whan I hem herde* is closer than Gl's *that I hem herde* to the French *quant je l'oi*; and in line 1068, Th's *aryued* is closer than Gl's *achyued* to the French *ariué*.[60] Again, in these, as well as other, instances, Gl's readings make sense; Thynne's working assumption seems to have been that Chaucer would have translated with scholarly accuracy rather than poetic license. Some of the other small variants might have been self-suggesting emendations, but most of them arguably result from Thynne's consulting the French text.

Five of the nine lines in Th that Gl omits translate more or less directly the equivalent lines in the *Roman*. For example:

> Line 892: Ypaynted all with amorettes
>   Peintes par fines amoreites [line 880]
> Line 3136: His eyes reed sparclyng as the fyre glow
>   S'ot les eulz roges come feus [line 2923]

In addition there are lines 1553, 4856, and 6205. The *Ypaynted* in line 892 is exactly the archaizing touch to be expected from Thynne, and the metrical awkwardness of line 3136 at least hints at editorial fabrication. The sixth line that Thynne supplies (line 6318), *That al to late cometh knowyng*, could translate a French source that reads *tart* for *fort* in *Que trop est (fort) l'aperceuance*; unfortunately, Ernest Langlois records no such variant.[61] The remaining three lines omitted from Gl occur in a passage muddled by a transposition of leaves in a manuscript anterior to Gl.[62] Thynne apparently fell back on his own resources to make good the seeming omission in Gl. It has been suggested that the four lines in Gl for which Th prints entirely different lines may have been blank at the time Thynne prepared his edition and that the versions in Th can best be understood as Thynne's translations of the French equivalent.[63] On the whole there is little evidence that Thynne collated another manuscript of the *Romaunt* against Gl, but he seems to have emended selectively from a copy of the *Roman*.

Thus, overall, we find William Thynne working to recover Chaucer's works and to purge the printed editions of their corruptions. The effort was uneven. If there are the heavily emended texts of *Anelida* and the *Parliament* on the one hand, there is also the patchwork text of *Boece*, along with the spottily edited *Romaunt* on the other. It would thus be easy to write off Thynne as a dilettante, but I would rather believe that his duties in the king's household left him with too little time. At any rate, his achievement, for its time, is impressive, and the results of his work had long-term results.

William Thynne's influence on the subsequent editing of Chaucer is almost glaringly evident in one regard. All the poems, Chaucer's and otherwise, printed in the edition of 1532, survived through several subsequent editions. In his own edition of 1542 Thynne dropped nothing and added *The Plowman's Tale* at the end of *The Canterbury Tales*.[64] The only change in his undated third edition was the placement of *The Plowman's Tale* before *The Parson's Tale*. John Stow adopted for his edition of 1561 the canon as conflated by Thynne, and, maintaining the tradition begun by Pynson, Stow made some major additions. Stow's edition became in turn the basis for Thomas Speght's two editions of 1598 and 1602. Finally, Speght's second edition became the basis for the print of 1687.[65] Thus Thynne's edition stands at the head of a long line of single-volume black-letter editions of the works of Chaucer (and many others) from which several generations of sixteenth-, seventeenth- and early-eighteenth-century readers learned their Chaucer. This tradition also set one of the major tasks for Chaucerian Scholarship from the eighteenth century into the twentieth: to identify those works that are authentically Chaucer's.

In his own century Thynne exercised another influence, more difficult to document today, but one by which he helped raise standards for editing earlier works of English literature. Thynne's three major predecessors,

Caxton, de Worde, and Pynson, were all businessmen whose livelihood was the printing and selling of books. There are differences among them on how closely and intelligently they followed their copy (de Worde being especially nonchalant and Pynson especially careful), but the time necessary to edit a text thoroughly, collating it thoughtfully against other authorities, was probably not available to all of them.[66]

A contemporary of Thynne who was concerned with printing good texts is Thomas Berthelet, the king's printer from 1530 until 1547. In the Preface to his edition of 1532 of John Gower's *Confessio Amantis*, Berthelet voices his dissatisfaction with Caxton's edition of the same because it had so many errors and omissions that "this moste pleasant and easy auctour coude not well be perceived."[67] Berthelet acted on his dissatisfaction to the extent that he printed his edition from a manuscript, even though his task would have been much easier if he had used Caxton's edition as copy text. A modern editor of John Lydgate's *Temple of Glas* praises Berthelet's extensive and effective revisions of the many errors in his copy text, de Worde's third edition of the poem.[68] In the *Preface* to his edition of 1535 of the English translation of Bartholomaeus Anglicus's *De proprietatibus rerum*, for which his copy text was de Worde's edition of 1495, Berthelet claims that "many places therein [are] amended by the latyne exemplare."[69]

It seems likely that Berthelet and Thynne, sharing similar concerns about the texts of older literary works in English and resorting to similar editorial practices, knew each other personally. At the very least there was contact between Berthelet and Thomas Godfrey: the frame on the title page of Th was printed from a woodcut owned by Berthelet that he apparently lent to Godfrey.[70] In addition, John Leland's mistaken identification of Berthelet as the printer of Thynne's edition could reflect Leland's knowledge of friendship between the two men.[71] Berthelet himself praises Thynne in the Preface to the *Confessio Amantis* of 1532: "The . . . noble warke *Troilus and Criseyde*, and many other of the sayde Chausers, that neuer were before imprinted, & those that very fewe men knewe, and fewer hadde them, be nowe of late put forthe together in a fayre volume."[72] Whether or not the two influenced each other directly, we do find in the early 1530s two editors who acted on their perceived need to restore the texts of older works in English from the corruption of earlier editions.

By the 1550s publishers expected to help sales by claiming that a book had been emended. On the title page of his edition of 1554 of John Lydgate's *Fall of Princes*, Richard Tottel asserts that the book is "nowe newly inprynted, corrected, and augmented out of diuerse and sundry olde writen copies in parchment," a claim confirmed by a modern editor of that poem.[73] John Wayland explains in the Preface to his edition of Lydgate's *Fall of Princes* (1554?) that he "caused the copy to be red over & amended in dyvers places wher it was before, eyther through the wryters or Prynters fault, corrupted."[74] It may seem farfetched to suggest a connection between

Thynne's editorial efforts in 1532 and such expressions of editorial concern from the 1550s. Still, Robert Braham, in his epistle to the reader in his edition of Lydgate's *Troy Book* (published 1555 by Thomas Marsh) singles out Thynne for special praise after a laudatory account of the valuable work that an editor does, work that involves not only use of one's "inuencion & wytt," along with "ripenes of iudgement," but also study of many exemplars. Braham claims that "Chaucers workes had vtterly peryshed, or at ye lest bin so depraued by corrupcion of copies, that at the laste, there shoulde no parte of hys meaning haue ben founde in any of them" except for "the dylygence of one willyam Thime [sic]."[75] This is strong praise, which is seconded in the same decade when John Leland writes of the edition of William Thynne, who "employed much labor, zeal, and care in searching diligently for ancient copies, and added many things."[76]

William Thynne was, of course, to receive the full and detailed praise of his son in 1598, but after that his reputation declined. In 1727 he earns a paragraph in Thomas Cox's *Magna Brittania et Hibernia, Antiqua & Nova*.[77] About fifty years later he attracts the scorn of Thomas Tyrwhitt, who believed that in Thynne's text of *The Canterbury Tales* "its material variations from Caxton's *second* edition are all . . . for the worse."[78] Through the work mentioned above by Walter W. Skeat, W. W. Greg, and Robert K. Root, Thynne's reputation has been qualifiedly improved, but as recently as 1963 Charles Muscatine seriously doubted whether Thynne used his manuscripts to collate.[79]

William Thynne's edition of Chaucer of 1532 was a remarkable achievement for a household officer kept busy in service to his king. Its value to modern editors of Chaucer is limited because Thynne's editorial abilities did not match his aspirations (one has only to read his son's *Animadversions* with its pedantic but impressive displays of textual criticism to become aware of Thynne's limitations). His emendations frequently were based on a limited and flawed understanding of Chaucer's language and a misguided attribution of humanist practices to Chaucer. Yet modern editors cannot afford to ignore Thynne's edition because Thynne did have access to manuscripts no longer available. Less ambivalent is the value of Thynne's edition to literary and cultural historians. As primarily a monument to the courtly literature of pre–War of the Roses England turned out with some of the appurtenances of the New Learning, it epitomizes the late-medieval traditions of Henry VIII's reign as they were just beginning to be quickened and transformed by Renaissance humanism. The edition of 1532 is a landmark in the long history of Chaucer's successful accommodation to changing literary and social values, and it is a testimony to William Thynne's enthusiasm and the valuable service that he rendered to his poet.

3. John Stow
(1525?–1605)

ANNE HUDSON

T O INCLUDE John Stow in a volume entitled *Editing Chaucer: The Great Tradition* may seem to require justification. Stow's edition of Chaucer, produced in 1561, has been regarded, in large measure correctly, as a mere reprint of Thynne's edition with a supplement, that supplement containing poems the large majority of which have been rejected from the Chaucer canon.[1] Impatience with Stow's work is clearly seen in Tyrwhitt's rejection of the "heap of rubbish" added by Stow, a rejection that biased Tyrwhitt into rejecting apparently genuine work of Chaucer because it was first printed in 1561.[2] Yet anyone concerned with the textual tradition of Chaucer's writings can hardly ignore Stow: even if the edition is an imperfect production, it is plain that a number of important Chaucer manuscripts passed through his hands and that Stow came to a knowledge of Chaucer's works that far outreached the limited grasp of that early edition. Equally, it seems highly probable that many Elizabethan authors, including Spenser and Shakespeare, knew Chaucer through the medium of this imperfect edition.[3]

Much is known of Stow's life, but little that is relevant to the 1561 edition.[4] He appears to have been born in London in 1525, and lived there for the whole of his life until his death in 1605. His grandfather and father were tallow chandlers, but John was apprenticed as a tailor, was admitted as a freeman of the Merchant Taylors' Company on November 25, 1547, and continued as a working tailor for some thirty years. His interest in earlier English poetry must have begun at least by the 1550s. C. L. Kingsford, whose biography of Stow prefixed to the modern edition of *A Survey of London* remains the best guide to his life, thought that Stow's first publication was the edition of 1561. More recently it has been suggested that Stow was the initiator of the edition of 1559 of John Lydgate's *Serpent of Division*.[5] The opening colophon claims that the text was "set forth after the Auctours old copy by I.S.," but, although Lydgate's name was added, the text appears to be simply a reprint of the earlier anonymous edition put out about 1535.[6] After the edition of Chaucer, and that of the Lydgate poem, if indeed it is his, Stow's attention was more fully directed toward history than literature. He obviously gained some renown as an investigator of records, and was induced to put together a history of Britain, a work in rivalry to Richard Grafton's chronicles.[7] The first edition of Stow's *Summarie of Englyshe Chronicles* appeared in 1565, and was enlarged through a series of subsequent editions.[8] An abridgment first came out in 1566, and this too was reprinted a number of times.[9] The larger *Chronicles of England* appeared in 1580, and the even bigger *Annales of England* in 1592, with subsequent reprintings and updatings up to and beyond Stow's death.[10] In the *Summarie, Chronicles*, and *Annales* appears an ever lengthening list of records, documents, and chronicles that Stow had consulted. While Stow may be faulted in some details, and did not always correct errors that had crept into the various editions of his work, such investigation of his handling of these sources as has been done indicates the care with which Stow scrutinized his material and the memory he had for trivial pieces of information.[11] It appears that Stow for some time before his death had been working toward a history in more sophisticated form than the annals of his published material, but he found difficulty in finding a publisher, and little trace of his drafts has survived.[12] The best known of Stow's productions is, of course, his *Survey of London*, three editions of which, published in 1598, 1599, and, revised, in 1603, appeared during its author's lifetime.[13] Here Stow combined his unrivaled knowledge of documentary sources with his own detailed observations from a lifetime in London and from a number of special perambulations.

Because of his interests and wide learning Stow came into contact with many of the Elizabethan antiquaries. He participated in Matthew Parker's editions of the *Flores Historiarum* (1567), of Matthew Paris's *Chronicles* (1571) and of Thomas Walsingham's *Chronicles* (1574), "all which he [the archbishop] receiued of my hands," Stow later claimed.[14] If the "I. S." of the *Serpent of Division* was Stow, then two more editions of English poetry were his responsibility: a collection of poems attributed to Skelton that appeared in 1568 and a group of three anonymous fifteenth-century poems, produced in 1597 and interestingly dedicated to Spenser.[15] Stow was certainly acquainted with William Lambarde, Henry Savile, William Camden, and John Dee; to these and many others he supplied information and with them exchanged books and documents. It is plain too that Stow acted many times as an unofficial searcher and archivist in the city of London.[16]

An immense amount of information is available on Stow's life and his methods of work both in the many books for which he was responsible and in the notebooks that survive.[17] The notebooks vary from complete drafts in Stow's own hand for the first version of the *Summarie* or for the *Survey of*

London to collections of scraps, some in Stow's hand, some in other hands, of uncertain date and chaotic order. Although many scholars have picked out small bits of information from these collections, no one has yet undertaken the herculean task of describing and sorting their evidence—a task not made simpler by the execrable writing of many of the scraps. In default of such a catalogue it is rash to claim that these notebooks contain nothing of use for those interested in Stow's edition of Chaucer of 1561. But two hasty searches for widely different purposes, separated by nearly twenty years, lead me to suggest that most of the notebooks come from a period too late to shed light on Stow's activities before 1561. The reason for this may lie in the investigation for suspected favoring of the papacy that Stow underwent in 1569; the evidence apparently consisted largely of Stow's possession of "olde phantasticall popishe bokes." Unfortunately, although the document mentions "folishe fabulous bokes of olde prynte as of Sir Degorye, Tryamour &c," and books "written in olde Englishe in parchement," the only possessions that are listed in detail are post-Reformation theological editions or tracts.[18] Stow was acquitted of papistry, but apparently did not retrieve all his confiscated books. As a result, all that we know about Stow's aims and methods in his edition of Chaucer must be gleaned from that edition itself, with the problematical addition of some indications from manuscripts that at some time passed through his hands.

Something should be said here of the problems of these manuscripts. It is well known that a number of medieval manuscripts survive in which Stow's distinctive, if unattractive, hand appears.[19] The larger number of such manuscripts, and those relevant to the present purpose, contain poetry by Chaucer, Lydgate, or one of their fifteenth-century imitators. It has sometimes been assumed that the annotations imply that Stow owned the manuscript, but this is not a necessary deduction; all that the annotations prove is that at some time Stow scrutinized the book. There is no reason to mistrust inscriptions such as that in Trinity College, Cambridge, R.3.21, "John Stowes boke" (folio 320v), or a similar one in Bodleian Laud Misc. 557, folio ir; but the very fact that Stow made such a claim and elsewhere recorded the date of his transcription of poems may lead to the suspicion that where the annotation is slight and there is no claim of ownership the volume was only briefly in Stow's hands. Leaving aside this suspicion, most of the annotations are undated; they may well (as will be argued below concerning manuscript Bodleian Fairfax 16) date from later than 1561 and thus cast no light on that edition. Furthermore, even if it were possible to prove that annotation dated from before 1561, this would not necessarily be of interest for Stow's edition. An interesting case is *The Siege [Story] of Thebes*, which Stow appended to his edition of Chaucer, though stating it to be by Lydgate.[20] In manuscript British Library Additional 29729 is a copy of the poem described on its last page (folio 288v): "This boke perteynythe to John Stowe, and was by hym wryten in þe yere of owr Lord M.d.lviij";

the same claim, "wretyn by John Stowe," appears immediately after the end of the poem (folio 83r).[21] Yet the modern editors of *The Siege of Thebes* concluded that the print of the poem that Stow produced only three years later was textually entirely unrelated to this copy; while the manuscript, though not copied directly from Wynkyn de Worde's edition, is allied to it, Stow's print derives from a completely different branch of the stemma.[22] Why Stow should have gone to the trouble of copying the poem and then have abandoned that copy and its exemplar in favor of another exemplar within such a short time is entirely obscure. It is clear from the constant revisions that Stow made to his historical writings that Stow was not one to adhere sentimentally to what he had previously written. Presumably he thought his new exemplar for some reason preferable. But this instance conveniently points up the danger of assuming that annotation, or even transcription, by Stow carries any implication for the sources of his printed editions.

Although his commitments to historical writing prevented Stow from producing a revised version of his Chaucer edition, it is plain that his interest in Chaucer continued. In his *Survey of London*, Stow briefly reviewed the printing of Chaucer's works:

> . . . his workes were partly published in Print by *William Caxton* in the raigne of *Henry* the sixt, increased by *William Thinne* Esquier, in the raigne of *Henry* the eight: corrected and twise encreased through mine owne paynefull labors, in the raigne of Queene *Elizabeth*, to witte in the yeare 1561, and againe, beautified with notes by me collected out of diuers Recordes and Monuments, which I deliuered to my louing friend *Thomas Speight*, and hee hauing drawne the same into a good forme and Methode, as also explayned the olde and obscure wordes, &c. hath published them in *Anno* 1597.[23]

Speght in his edition of 1598 in fact claims as his own the collections on which his life of Chaucer were based.[24] He acknowledged, however, the use of books owned by Stow: he refers to "a booke of *Iohn Stowes* called Little Iohn," mentions "a written copy" of Chaucer's *Complaint to His Purse* "which I had of Iohn Stow (whose library hath helped many writers)," and justifies his inclusion of *The Plowman's Tale* by stating, "I haue seene it in written hand in Iohn Stowes Library in a booke of such antiquity, as seemeth to haue beene written neare to Chaucers time."[25] The last of these would be the most interesting, since no medieval manuscript of *The Plowman's Tale* is now known. Also in the *Survey*, Stow speaks of John Shirley and records his epitaph; he observes:

> This Gentleman, a great traueller in diuers countries, amongest other his labours, painefully collected the workes of *Geffrey Chaucer, Iohn Lidgate* and other learned writers, which workes hee wrote in sundry volumes to remayne for posterity. I haue seene them, and partly do possesse them.[26]

Stow annotated one manuscript written by Shirley, now Trinity College,

Cambridge, R.3.20, and three further manuscripts that seem to derive from Shirley's workshop, Trinity College, Cambridge, R.3.19; British Library Harley 2251; and British Library Additional 34360. Stow's own transcriptions in British Library Additional 29729 are claimed by him to have been partly from a Shirley manuscript.[27] Beyond these Stow annotated a number of manuscripts containing early English poetry: among them are Trinity College, Cambridge, R.3.21 and R.3.22; British Library Stowe 952, Bodleian Laud Misc. 557; Fairfax 16; Lambeth Palace 306; and Huntington HM 144. Further pieces appear in his collections, as in Harley 78 and Harley 367.[28] Aage Brusendorff claimed also that Stow was the first to identify the main characters in *The Book of the Duchess*: in Fairfax 16, folio 130, appears the annotation "made by Geffrey Chawcyer at ye request of ye duke of Lancastar: pitiously complaynynge the deathe of ye sayd dutchesse blanche," which Brusendorff took to be in Stow's hand.[29]

The edition of Chaucer's works that appeared in 1561 did not mention Stow on the title page. Stow's part in the book becomes apparent only on sig. Ppp.2 with the heading "Here foloweth certaine woorkes of Geffray Chauser, whiche hath not here tofore been printed, and are gathered and added to this booke by Jhon Stowe." The edition survives in two issues, one dated 1561 and both printed by John Kyngston for John Wight (*STC* 5075 and 5076).[30] The chief difference between the two lies in the first substantive item, *The General Prologue* to *The Canterbury Tales*. *STC* 5075 has a more elaborate title page and the date 1561; *STC* 5076 lacks this date, but otherwise both issues have the same preliminary material taken over without alteration from Thynne's edition.[31] In the *Prologue*, however, *STC* 5075 includes woodcuts of each pilgrim before the description, while *STC* 5076 lacks these woodcuts. Consequently, the *Prologue* in *STC* 5075 extends to eighteen sides, in the other to only nine. From the beginning of the quire marked "B.i" the two issues are identical, and both have the woodcut of the Knight that stands at the head of his tale.[32] It has generally been assumed that the edition without woodcuts is the later of the two issues, but there is little evidence so far available to prove or disprove this assumption.[33] There is, as is usual with books produced at this date, some variation between individual copies of each issue (minor corrections of error and inadvertent new mistakes), and laborious scrutiny of all surviving copies in these points would be the only way in which an informed judgment could be reached.[34] In the issue with woodcuts there is a strange error in the *Prologue*, not corrected in any of the copies I have seen. This is the displacement of the woodcut and description (A 285–308) of the Clerk of Oxenford from its rightful place after the Merchant (A 284) to a position after the Doctor (A 444) and before the Wife of Bath. The woodcuts are numbered, and the Clerk has the expected number 8, but as the text stands, the numbering runs from 7 to 9 and then has 8 after 14. The account of the Merchant ends at the foot of sig. *iv^v, and the catchword is unhelpfully *The*; but after the description of the Doctor on sig. *vi^v appears the heading "The Clerke of Oxenforde. viii," and the catchwords *A clerke*. The transposition cannot therefore be a simple error of placing, an error that should in any case have been avoidable from the numbering of the woodcuts.[35] The issue without woodcuts does not have this displacement, and I have not found it in any previous edition.

Of the twenty-two woodcuts in the *Prologue* of *STC* 5075, fourteen derive from Pynson's edition of 1526, though they were not always used for the same character. Thus Stow's illustration for the Yeoman was in Pynson's edition prefixed to *The Canon's Yeoman's Tale*, Stow's picture of the Cook was in Pynson before *The Reeve's Tale*, and Stow's Merchant was, in Pynson, Chaucer himself, appearing before *The Tale of Sir Thopas* and *The Tale of Melibee*.[36] Only the first of these transpositions can be explained by the fact that Pynson's woodcuts were placed not in the *Prologue* but before the individual tales. Pynson's reprint of Caxton's second edition, produced about 1492, contributed five woodcuts to Stow's edition: the Knight in the *Prologue*, the Ploughman, the Reeve, and the Pardoner are taken over for the same persons, while the Chaucer of the earlier edition was used for the Franklin of 1561.[37] Caxton's own second edition provided the woodcut for the Haberdasher.[38] So far untraced is the woodcut of the Summoner. The strangest is the picture of the Wife of Bath. Instead of the traditional picture of the Wife, with hat "as brood as is a bokeler or a targe," that appears in Pynson's and Thynne's editions,[39] the edition of 1561 used the same portrait as that for the Prioress; consequently the Wife has a wimple and habit. The woodcut at the opening of *The Knight's Tale* that appears in both issues (sig. B.1) derives from the (1550?) reprint of Thynne's edition (sig. B.1).

An examination of Stow's edition may conveniently be divided into two parts: the material that Stow derived from Thynne and the poems that Stow added to Thynne's edition.

Material Adopted from Thynne

Critics have been right to regard Stow's edition as largely derivative and, for that derivative material, as inferior to its source, the edition of William Thynne. The first nine-tenths or more of Stow's edition is directly taken from the earlier edition, and there is, with one exception, no evidence that Stow compared his predecessor's work with any manuscript or with any other edition. The only additions to the material of 1532 occurring before the colophon that mentions Stow's name are *The Plowman's Tale*, which had been added by Thynne in his reprint of 1542,[40] and two short poems (numbers 1 to 3 in the table below) added in the middle of the collection of miscellaneous material toward the end of Thynne's edition.[41] Two further poems, present in the edition of 1532 but there anonymous, *The Floure of Curtesye* (*IMEV* 1487) and *A balade of good counseile* (*IMEV* 653), are by Stow attributed to Lydgate, an attribution accepted by modern critics.[42] Furthermore, the order in which the items occur, an order that is completely arbitrary, is exactly the same as Thynne's. After the major works, *The Canterbury Tales, The Romaunt of the Rose, Troilus* with the *Testament of Crisseid* and *The Legend of Good Women*, Chaucerian and non-Chaucerian items, long poems such as *The House of Fame* and short such as *The Complaint unto Pity*, poetry and prose are mingled haphazardly together. In all of this Stow follows Thynne precisely.

Granted the derivative nature of Stow's edition, certain questions nonetheless arise. The first is the version of Thynne's edition from which Stow worked: the second, closely related to this, is the care with which Stow handled his predecessor's material. Thynne's edition of 1532 was reprinted in 1542 in two issues; this reprint differed from the edition of 1532 in major matters only by the addition of *The Plowman's Tale* at the end of *The Canterbury Tales*. A second reprint, with four different imprints, came out some years later, probably in about 1550 but without any date on the title page; here *The Plowman's Tale* was placed within *The Canterbury Tales* before *The Parson's Tale* and with an appropriate adjustment to the text of *The Parson's Prologue*.[43] Since Stow's edition of the *Tales* agrees with this last reprint, it is inherently likely that Stow worked from a copy of it.

It is a slow and not very certain task to establish textually that Stow's edition is for all its texts entirely dependent upon the (1550) reprint of Thynne. The slowness arises from the laboriousness of collating the text of 1561 against seven other printed texts (one of 1532, two of 1542, and four of [1550], to allow for possible divergencies among issues), since it is necessary to establish the point negatively (that Stow could not be from 1532 or 1542) as well as positively. The uncertainty derives from the closeness of all these eight texts, even though there were clearly four distinct typesettings. A superficial glance might suggest that differences are legion. But it is clear that most of the evidence is of no significance. Differences of spelling, including some that no medieval scribe would be likely to regard as interchangeable, must be ignored. More seriously, it is plain that none of the printers or editors here involved understood the function of Middle English final -*e* or grasped that its presence or absence could affect the meter. Along with this went complete ignorance of the principles of Middle English elision. Printers inserted or omitted final -*e* arbitrarily, and variants between editions involving it can afford no help in tracing affiliations. A typical example is the case in *Troilus and Criseyde* 2.1704, where final -*e* must be metrically silent: the edition of 1532 reads *outwarde*, the two issues of 1542 *outward*, the four (1550) issues *outwarde*, and the two Stow prints *outward*.[44] The two forms were to the printers precise equivalents, and evidence such as this reveals nothing about textual relations.[45]

To assess the relationship of Stow's text, specimen collation of between 50 and 150 lines from each work, and from the normal subdivisions within

The Canterbury Tales and *Troilus*, or the whole poem when this was shorter than 50 lines, was done using all eight texts between 1532 and 1561. Inevitably there emerged instances where Stow's reading could not be found in any antecedent version. Many of such readings are new errors, for instance, *CT* A 487, *oft* for *of*; *BD* 481, *yeleth* for *eyleth*; *PF* 571, *better* for *better for the*; *HF* 922, *winge* for *wynges*. In a few cases the versions of 1542 and (1550) agreed with Stow against Thynne's original edition; such is the position in *CT* B 39 *ieo*, against 1532 *iche*, or *CT* B 66 *Dieanire* correcting the 1532 error *Dyane*. But in most instances where any significant variants among the eight texts were found, Stow's text agreed with the (1550) issues and against the versions of 1532 and 1542; there was no instance in a material reading where Stow's text agreed with 1532 or 1542 or both and against (1550). Thus in *CT* A 3856 the (1550) edition and Stow read *hynd*, 1532 and 1542, *hende*; the same distribution is found in *CT* A 3918, *kreke* against *breke*; *CT* 325, *mortal* against *moral*; *CT* D 569, *bostaunce* against *bobaunce*; *PF* 602, *se* against *nat se*; *HF* 876, *it* against *yet*; *HF* 926, *place* against *space*. At *HF* 911–12 the couplet in the modern accepted text reads:

> And seyde, "Seest thou any toun
> Or ought thou knowest yonder doun?"

Thynne in 1532 and 1542 has in place of this:

> And sayd: Seest thou any token
> Or aught / that in this worlde is of spoken.

The (1550) edition and Stow omit *is* in the second line. Metrically this last version is preferable to that of 1532 and 1542, but for the sense *is* must be present; the metrical felicity is entirely fortuitous. Stow, then, used the most recent version of Thynne's edition for his own work.[46] It seems, unfortunately, impossible to go further and distinguish among the four issues of the (1550) reprint; in none of the cases that came to light did there appear to be any discrepancy among the four issues.

During the investigation of the eight versions, however, one poem was found in which Stow did not simply adopt without conscious alteration the material in Thynne's edition. That this one exception came to light actually does much to confirm the derivativeness of the majority. This instance is the final poem adopted from Thynne, *A balade of good counseile* (*IMEV* 653) to which Stow's edition added the name of Lydgate, an attribution now generally accepted. Stow's alterations to this poem were strangely over-looked by Skeat, who printed it among the Chaucerian apocrypha. Skeat heads the poem with Stow's title and attribution but appears not to have looked further at Stow's text. Skeat says that two extra stanzas "occur in the MSS. only" and that he is printing them for the first time.[47] In fact, Stow had included these stanzas in his edition of 1561. Furthermore, in addition to adding these two stanzas, after the tenth and fourteenth stanzas as the text appears in all versions of Thynne's edition,[48] Stow considerably modified the text of the rest of the poem. It is plain that Stow collated Thynne's text against some other exemplar in this poem alone. There are seven manuscripts of this poem now surviving.[49] Comparison suggests that Stow's other exemplar was either Trinity College, Cambridge, R.3.20 (T), a Shirley manuscript in which some of Stow's annotations appear, or British Library Additional 29729 (A), the manuscript that Stow possessed by 1558. There are about sixty readings (excluding for the usual reasons spelling variants and variants involving final -e) where Stow's print agreed with T and A against Thynne's text. Most significant of these is the second half of line 68, where Stow and T A have the erroneous *some loue in clothes white*, against Thynne and the other manuscripts' *some laugh in clothes whyte*; the contrast with *mourne* in the first half line makes the verb *laugh* preferable. The evidence is, however, more interesting than it would be if it appeared that Stow had simply substituted a manuscript for Thynne as his sole exemplar. But it is plain that he collated the text of Thynne with a manuscript and made selection between the variant readings. There are seventeen instances where Stow and Thynne agree against both T and A. Stow accepted Thynne's better readings at line 100, *sugred eloquence*, rather than T A, *swete eloquence*, and at line 127, *princes*, rather than T, *pryncesses* or A, *pryncesse*. On the other hand, he was ill-advised to accept Thynne's unmetrical line 96, *With al Alixaunders dominacioun*, rather than the T A version, which omitted the adjective *al*. In four instances of the refrain line Stow combined elements of Thynne's versions with others from T A (lines 63, 70, 98, 105), producing the more regular *A wicked tonge wol alway deme amis* where Thynne had the verb *say* and T A, largely by inversions, varied in the wording. There are only nine cases where Stow's readings are not accounted for by either Thynne or T and A, and apart from the refrains mentioned all are trivial; the most serious is an obvious error of *him* for *hem* in line 62. The differences between T and A are very few; Stow's edition seems marginally closer to T than to A, but the discrepancies of Stow from A could in every instance be explained equally from Thynne's text.[50] It is a pity for Stow's reputation that this care was lavished on a short poem rejected from the Chaucer canon. Stow's handling of it makes a difference to a correct assessment of Stow as editor, for it is the one case in which he can be shown to be critically aware of an editor's task. He may not reveal himself as particularly expert in performing that task, but he clearly perceived the possibility of collation and selection of variants.

Material Added by Stow

Stow has been much criticized for his additions to Thynne's material. *The Siege of Thebes* was stated on the title page to be by Lydgate, and its status as an appendix is clear from the preceding colophon "Thus endeth the workes of Geffray Chaucer." The appendix below gives certain basic information about the remaining twenty-three poems that Stow added. Of these, three, number 5, the balade *Gentilesse*, number 20, *A Complaint to His Lady*, and number 23, Chaucer's address to Adam Scriveyn, have been accepted as genuine Chaucer. Two further poems, number 6, *Proverbs*, and number 7, the balade *Against Women Unconstant*, were included by Robinson in the standard edition under the heading "Short Poems of Doubtful Author-ship," and are accepted with some reservations by Pace and David (1982). The rest have been rejected from the canon with varying degrees of vehemence. It is not, however, entirely clear that Stow himself regarded all the poems as of equal authenticity. He headed the section in which all but the first four appeared "Here foloweth certaine woorkes of Geffray Chauser, whiche hath not here tofore been printed, and are gathered and added to this booke by Jhon Stowe." Chaucer is mentioned again in the headings to numbers 5, 7, 8, 9, 20, and 23, but no specific attribution is given to the remainder. It is noteworthy that four of the five poems now associated with Chaucer appear in the attributed group. Stow was well aware that Thynne's Chaucer had included apocryphal material: Thynne had himself acknowl-edged one poem to be by Gower and another by Scogan, and Stow had added the attribution of two poems to Lydgate.[51] It is possible that the hostility to Stow shown by such critics as Tyrwhitt has been too raucous.

The source of Stow's added material has been the subject of a detailed, largely reliable article by Bradford Y. Fletcher.[52] He endorses the earlier suggestion of Skeat, Greg, Brusendorff,[53] and others that Stow's main source was Trinity College, Cambridge, R.3.19, a manuscript in which Stow's distinctive hand is found. Fletcher argues that this manuscript provided copy for fourteen of the twenty-three items.[54] Having checked through the evidence from the manuscripts, I find this a reasonable argument,[55] though it should be acknowledged that in eight instances the Trinity manuscript is the sole surviving text. Fletcher adds that "with reasonable certainty" four more poems came from Trinity College, Cam-bridge, R.3.20, and "with less certainty" one from each of Bodleian Fairfax 16, British Library Cotton Cleopatra D.VII and Harley 78. The first and second of these four passed through Stow's hands, but whether before or after 1561 is uncertain. In two instances, poems 7 and 8, Fletcher regards Stow's text as of independent value, not descended from any extant man-uscript.[56]

Interesting and generally convincing though Fletcher's article is, it does not attempt to answer any question beyond that of the relation of Stow's text to the extant manuscripts. The most important question that is neither answered nor even raised is the reason for Stow's decision to print this particular selection of twenty-three poems. The question obtrudes when Trinity College, Cambridge, R.3.19, Stow's main alleged source, is con-sidered: that manuscript contains a large number of items that Stow did not choose to print.[57] As the manuscript was originally written, all the poems were anonymous. A later hand has attributed a number to Chaucer, three to Lydgate and one to George Ashby.[58] Skeat thought that the hand was that of Stow, but Greg disputed this responsibility and urged that the squarish hand of the vast majority was that of the seventeenth-century Beaupré Bell and that the attributions derived from a knowledge of Stow's edition.[59] Greg accepted only one of the instances of "Chaucer" as in Stow's hand, this beside the last stanza of the *Craft of Lovers* (no. 9). In the Trinity manuscript the date of the poem is given as 1448 (in the other two extant manuscripts it is 1459),[60] and Stow noted against this that Chaucer died in 1400; presumably Stow intended the note to show not Chaucer's authorship but the impossibility of this. Puzzlingly, in his edition Stow explicitly attributes the poem to Chaucer and has the date 1348 in the final stanza. If Greg's argument is correct, it would explain why there is complete correspondence between the annotation and the poems printed in Stow's edition; equally, the manuscript then reveals nothing about Stow's choice of material from it. Some of the poetry that Stow did not print is now ascribed to Lydgate, and Stow himself may well have known of his authorship. This would explain the rejection of portions of Lydgate's *Fall of Princes* that occupy folios 170v–202 and of the *Tale of the Churl and the Bird* on folios 9–11v, both of which had been printed, the first with Lydgate's name.[61] Similarly, Stow could have recognized the authorship of the four fables on folios 12–16, a collection that Stow supplemented by two more on folios 236–37. Equally, Stow could well have spotted that the poem headed *Lady of pite* on folio 160v (attributed in the squarish hand to Chaucer) contained four stanzas from the *Craft of Lovers*, and ignored it for this reason.[62] But there remains a group of poems where no obvious reason for Stow's rejection is apparent. Most inexplicable are three items: an untitled balade on folio 157 (*IMEV* 2311) and a poem *Honour and Ioy* on folio 159v (*IMEV* 1238), of which this is the sole surviving manuscript, and *Of God and Kynde* (folio 206) found in several other manuscripts, now ascribed to Lydgate but not attributed in this manuscript.[63] All three are of a type and in a meter that are represented among the material that Stow did adopt.

A possible answer to the question of Stow's acceptance or rejection of poems from manuscript R.3.19 is that, although this manuscript formed the basis for his *texts* of the fourteen poems, another manuscript was the source of his attribution of the material to Chaucer. This may be the correct solution, but it cannot now be demonstrated to be so; if another manuscript contained those poems attributed, that manuscript is now lost. None of the fourteen poems taken from R.3.19 is ascribed in any other surviving manuscript, though, as has been noted, for eight of the poems no other text is now known. For some of the poems that did not derive from R.3.19 more positive evidence of authorship survives. *Gentilesse* (no. 5) is attributed to Chaucer in the original scribes' hands in Bodleian Ashmole 59 and British

Library Harley 7333; the *Proverbe agaynst couitise* (no. 6) is similarly attributed in Bodleian Fairfax 16 and British Library Harley 7578. The first
manuscript in each case may have gone though Stow's hands at some time,
though Fletcher did not consider that the text of number 5 came from
Ashmole 59.[64] In British Library Additional 34360, Stow added the note
"dan Chaucer" to the copy of number 20, though Fletcher thought that
Stow derived his printed text of the poem from the only other surviving
manuscript, Harley 78.[65] Stow's note may date from a time later than his
edition. Even when an ascribed text is known to have been available to Stow
before 1561, he apparently did not make use of it for his printed version. As
has been described, Additional 29729 was owned by Stow in 1558; this
manuscript contains copies of poems 1–3, the first two of which are ascribed
to Lydgate. But Stow did not give the printer his own copy as exemplar:
number 1 in his copy lacks line 5; line 7 in number 3 reads in the manuscript
in for the correct *The* of the edition and the other manuscript.

The problem of Stow's selection of poems brings us back to the question
of those manuscripts that are known to have been in the antiquary's
possession at some time. The most interesting case is Bodleian Fairfax 16, a
manuscript which Fletcher argued formed the exemplar for the edition's
poem number 6. If this is right, Stow's inclusion would be explicable since
the original scribe headed the poem *Proverbe of Chaucer*.[66] Why, however,
did Stow not take his text of numbers 7 and 8 from this same source?
Admittedly, in Fairfax both are anonymous, but Fletcher has to argue that
Stow's text of each poem is independent of this and of the two and three
manuscripts, respectively, in which these poems survive elsewhere.[67] In the
recent facsimile of Fairfax, John Norton-Smith has argued that Stow did not
encounter the manuscript until the 1590s. The reference to Holland that
Norton-Smith quotes seems incontrovertible, but his observation that
Stow's failure to correct Thynne's text of *The Book of the Duchess* from this
manuscript shows that his acquaintance with it was later than 1561
overestimates the degree to which Stow interfered in his reprint.[68] In
support of Norton-Smith's view it may be noted that against the entry in
the list of contents on folio 2 "A.devoute balette to oure lady" a fifteenth-
century annotator has entered "A.b.c. per Chaucer." Yet Stow did not
include this poem in his edition; it was first printed by Speght in 1602.[69]
On the other hand, the editors of Lydgate's *Reson and Sensuallyte* observe that
the copy in BL Additional 29729, Stow's anthology of Lydgate material
dated 1558, derives from Fairfax. To reconcile these two points it seems
necessary to assume that Stow borrowed Fairfax only briefly and for the sole
purpose of making the copy of the Lydgate poem, and that at that stage he
looked no further.[70] If this is correct, then Fairfax 16 testifies to Stow's
continuing researches into Chaucer's works, but offers no elucidation of his
print. It follows that Pace's view that Stow's text of the *Proverbe* has
independent value should be accepted.[71]

Another of the manuscripts known to have been through Stow's hands, Harley 2251, also contains a text of the *ABC to the Virgin* (folios 49–51v), here anonymous and with no annotation from the antiquary. It also contains texts of numbers 5, 9, and 19, all anonymous and none of them apparently used by Stow as printer's copy.[72] The case of Stow's note in British Library Additional 34360 against number 20 has already been mentioned; the manuscript also contains an unascribed version of number 9, but this equally did not form copy for the 1561 edition. Trinity College Cambridge R.3.20, a manuscript in Shirley's hand that Stow annotated, also offers problems. It contains copies of five poems that Stow printed; three of them, numbers 1, 2, and 3, are all anonymous, though they seem to have formed Stow's exemplars; number 5 is attributed to Chaucer but was not used by Stow; and only in the case of number 23, *Adam Scriveyn*, do manuscript attribution and Stow's exemplar coincide.[73] Harley 78, from which Fletcher thought Stow took the text of number 20, is a collection of material put together by Stow from a number of sources though at uncertain date.[74] The poem was there originally anonymous, and the evidence for Stow's use of it for his text is not very convincing, being largely negative in that the only other surviving manuscript could not have formed the copy.[75] Cotton Cleopatra D.VII, the putative source for the text of number 5 and containing also number 7, both unattributed, is not known to have been in Stow's hands.[76]

Returning, however, to the small and uncertain amount of evidence that survives, it remains to ask how reliably Stow reproduced his alleged exemplars. It is, of course, impossible to assess reliability in regard to numbers 7 and 8; for reasons already given, it is perhaps better to ignore numbers 5, 6, and 20. The brevity of poems 1–3 and 23 means that they afford little help. This means that, in making an assessment, we are in fact dealing with only one manuscript, Trinity R.3.19. G. Bone pointed to marks in that manuscript that indicated that it had been in a printer's workshop and had been used to set up type.[77] If this is so, it must be recognized that many of the comments that follow reflect in the first place upon the compositor and not upon Stow himself. In the absence of marks in the manuscript Stow's part (if Bone's supposition is correct) must have been limited to proof corrections; it seems unlikely, given Stow's fondness for annotating manuscripts, that he would have supplied the printer with a separate sheet of alterations.

In the first place, all the divergencies noted between printed editions (see above) reappear in this case of the reproduction of a manuscript and must be ignored. There are also some instances of modernization of the language (e.g., poems 11/33, 18/21, and 22/186, *you* for T *ye* nom.; 20/101, *gentelnes* for T *gentilesse*), but attempted archaization is also found (22/184, *hath*, inappropriately since the subject is *ye*; 22/186, *mote* for *moste*). There are also a number of errors in transcription, some relatively minor (9/150, *your* for T *yow*; 9/151, *her* for T *hert*; 11/27, edition omits T *theym*; 11/55, *Ty* for T *To*; 22/285, *Or* for T *of*, etc.), others more serious (e.g., 9/16, *intenuate* for T *intemerate*; 9/160, *portent* for T *prepotent*; [78] 12/29, *Logeans* for T *trogeans*; 19/32, *a* for T *haue a*; 22/479, *waie* for T *alway*). More interesting are the cases in which correction of a faulty reading in the manuscript has been made in Stow's edition. Some of these are fairly self-evident modifications that might have been made by an attentive compositor (e.g., 9/51, *this* for T *hys*; 9/99, print adds *of*; 9/144, *creatures* for T *creature*; 11/14, *your* for T *oure*; 15/3, print adds *and*; 17/15, *her* for T *hys*; 18/18, *is* for T *hit*; 19/41, *thei* for T *then*; 22/111, *aged* for T *a god*; 22/389, *then* for T *thou*).

Other modifications, however, would seem to require more attention to the sense of the stanza or poem as a whole than would be likely in one whose primary task concentrated on individual letters and words. They are more likely to originate with Stow. Examples are 9/46, *not disdein* for T *dedeyn*;[79] 11/75, *langage* for T *langyng*; 12/27, *benignite* for T *beauteuous benygnyte*; 17/35, *that prudence* for T *than prudent*; 21/58, *tyranyes* for T *tyranny*; 22/97, *descrie* for T *discrive*; 22/495–96 and 640–41, reversal of lines; 22/747, *thanke* for T *think*; 22/874, *you* for T *lyon*; reordering of 22/901–903; 22/928, *greuen* for T *growen*; 22/1324, *shrine* for T *shyne*; 22/1327, *brake* for T *blak*; 22/1335, *thanken* for *taken*. There are also a number of instances in which, though certainty of error is less clear, Stow's edition diverges from the claimed base-manuscript. In three poems a stanza has been omitted in the edition: in poem 15, after line 56; in poem 18, after line 7; and in poem 21, after line 63. All these poems are peculiar to T, and there are rough crosses in the manuscript against the first and last of the stanzas mentioned. That these marks were Stow's indication to the printer to omit the stanzas must, however, be uncertain in the absence of such a mark in the second case; they could, like the attributions in the squarish hand, derive from a later reader's comparison of T with Stow's edition. If T was the exemplar, Stow's certain intrusion must be responsible for the extra line supplied in a stanza of poem 22; the added line *But now we dare not shew our selfe in place* is necessary for the rhyme scheme.[80] It could have been Stow's invention or the result of comparison with another copy. The possibility of such comparison also arises in a few other instances: 11/82, *lace* for T *brace*; 12/41, *p^t blood had thursted* for T *and take no thurst*; 15/27, *neuer* for T *noon*; 15/59, *Pitie* for T *haue pyte on*; 19/20, *but* for manuscripts *full*. For none of these changes or the corrections mentioned before is there any indication in T, save for the two stanzas marked with crosses.

Can anything be concluded from this mass of confusing detail? It seems to me that the evidence of the last section calls into question the view that T was the printer's copy for fourteen of the added poems. T may well be the manuscript that, in default of Stow's actual copy, stands nearest to the edition of 1561. But I find it hard to envisage, if T was given to the printer, how the changes outlined above can have come about; there are no instructions for alteration, no clear indications of what the printer should include or omit. Changes such as the addition of a line or the rearrangement of two or three lines might conceivably have been made in proof, but they go far beyond anything that Stow attempted in regard to the material he adopted from Thynne. To see T as related to Stow's edition only indirectly would, of course, involve ignoring Bone's contention that there are smudges of printer's ink and some printer's marks in the manuscript; the former are capable of other explanation, and the latter are very few and far between and of uncertain meaning.[81]

Putting the textual evidence just described along with the problem of Stow's choice of material, I believe that the only safe conclusion is that the vital evidence for both selection and text has disappeared. It is tempting to conjecture that Stow possessed, or made for himself, an anthology of poetry in which relevant items were attributed to Chaucer. We may recall the confiscation of Stow's books in 1569, the library to which Speght referred, and the several Shirley manuscripts that Stow claimed he owned. But this may be unreasonable, as it is certainly unprovable. As Stow's historical writings reveal, he picked up information constantly, read new material voraciously, and often recorded his knowledge on scraps of paper. The only assembly of Chaucer material before Stow gave his printer copy may have been in his own memory; the copy could well have been Thynne's (1550) edition with a few extra leaves and a text of *The Siege of Thebes*; that copy the printer would have had no reason to preserve after his task was complete. This may seem a negative conclusion, disappointing after the apparent certainty offered by Fletcher. But it seems to me that Fletcher's certainty was the result of his concentration solely upon minutiae of text. Had he considered the larger question of Stow's choice of material, this, along with the contrary textual evidence that he has to set aside, would have led to a more doubtful assessment.

In the course of investigating Stow's edition of 1561, a good deal has been said of Stow's other Chaucerian observations. It is plain that his interest in Chaucer and in other late Middle English poetry continued after his preoccupation with more historical matters. He maintained his concern with details of the poet's life and writings and went on collecting and annotating manuscripts of Chaucer, Lydgate, and others. In *A Survey of London*, as well as mentioning Shirley and the various editions of Chaucer's works, he printed part of another poem that he by then regarded as by Chaucer. This is a seven line stanza whose title is given in the margin "Chaucer. chance of dice."[82] This Stow probably derived from Fairfax 16, folio 149; although the poem is not there ascribed to Chaucer, either in the list of contents or in any rubric, Stow had noted against the reference to the *shafte of Corneylle* in the manuscript "S. andrew vndarshafte," and it is in his description of that church that the lines are quoted.[83] Much has been made here, and by previous critics, of those manuscripts in which Stow's handwriting is proof that they passed beneath his scrutiny. But Stow did not annotate all the books that he must have seen. A note in Fairfax 16 makes it plain that he had looked with some attention at the manuscript of Chaucer's poems, then in the possession of Joseph Holland, now Cambridge University Library Gg.4.27.[84] Equally, another quotation in the same Fairfax manuscript seems to indicate Stow's acquaintance with the manuscript of Lydgate's *Temple of Glas* that is now Pepys 2006 in Magdalene College, Cambridge.[85] In neither of these is Stow's hand found.

The amount that Stow contributed to Speght's edition of Chaucer, and particularly to the prefatory material in that edition, is not entirely clear. Stow, as the quotations given before indicate, seems to imply a more considerable involvement than Speght's own words specify. Francis Thynne, in his *Animadversions* on Speght's edition, does not allude to Stow's part in that edition, though it is usually thought that his disparaging sentence "I will here shewe suche thinges as, in mye opynione, may seme to be touched, not medlinge withe the seconde editione to one inferior personne then my fathers editione was" refers to Stow's edition of 1561.[86] Stow seems, indeed, to have gained scant appreciation from either his contemporaries or later critics for his pains in regard to Chaucer. Certainly his edition added little to knowledge of the canon and offered no improvement in the texts already published by Thynne. Equally, his annotations of manuscripts are often cryptic, sometimes misguided, and almost invariably infuriatingly abbreviated or fragmentary. But the chief emotion that this attempt to review Stow's work has left in me is one of regret—regret that Stow was diverted from his study of medieval literary manuscripts and that he did not find the time or opportunity to produce an edition of Chaucer forty years later.

Appendix

The material that Stow added to Thynne's edition is listed below. In the first column is given the heading provided by Stow, the quire signature(s) and folio(s) on which the poem occurs, and the *IMEV* number; the second column lists the manuscript(s) in which the poem is preserved with an asterisk before that which Fletcher considered the exemplar.

1. A saiyng of dan Jhon (sig. Ooo,   *TCC R.3.20, p. 8
   fol. 2v), *IMEV* 3523   BL Add. 29729, fol. 132r

2. Yet of the same[1] (sig. Ooo, fol.   *TCC R.3.20, p. 9
   2v), *IMEV* 3521   BL Add. 29729, fol. 132r

3. Balade de bon consail[2] (sig. Ooo,   *TCC R.3.20, p. 48
   fol. 2v), *IMEV* 1419   BL Add. 29729, fol. 132v

4. A balade in the praise and commendacion of master Geffray Chauser for his golden eloquence[3] (sig. Ppp, fol. 1v), *IMEV* 2128

*TCC R.3.19, fol. 25
BL Harley 7333, fol. 132v

5. A balade made by Chaucer, teching what is gentilnes, or whom is worthy to be caled gentil[4] (sig. Ppp, fol. 2r), *IMEV* 3348

*BL Cotton Cleopatra D.VII, fol. 188v
BL Harley 2251, fol. 48v
BL Harley 7333, fol. 147v
BL Harley 7578, fol. 17r
BL Add. 22139, fol. 138r
TCC R.3.20, p. 358
TCC R. 14.51, fol. 1v
Bodley Ashmole 59, fol. 27r
CUL Gg.4.27, fol. 1v
Coventry Corporation Record
    Office, fol. 76v
Nottingham University Mellish LM1[5]

6. A Prouerbe agaynst couitise and negligence[6] (sig. Ppp, fol. 2r), *IMEV* 3914

*Bodley Fairfax 16, fol. 195v
Harley 7578, fol. 20r
BL Add. 16165, fol. 246v
BL Add. 10392, fol. 185^{r7}

7. A balade whiche Chaucer made agaynst women vnconstaunt[8] (sig. Ppp, fol. 2r), *IMEV* 2029

Bodley Fairfax 16, fol. 194v[9]
BL Cotton Cleopatra D. VII, fol. 189v
BL Harley 7578, fol. 17v

8. Here foloweth a balade whiche Chaucer made in ye praise, or rather dispraise, of women for ther doublenes[10] (sig. Ppp, fols. 2r–2v), *IMEV* 3656

Bodley Fairfax 16, fol. 199r
Bodley Ashmole 59, fol. 47v
BL Harley 7578, fol. 17v
BL Add. 16165, fol. 252r

9. This werke folowinge was compiled by Chaucer and is caled the craft of louers[11] (sig. Ppp, fols. 3r–3v), *IMEV* 3761

*TCC R.3.19, fol. 154v
BL Harley 2251, fol. 52r
BL Add. 34360, fol. 73v

10. A Balade[12] (sig. Ppp, fols. 3v–4r), *IMEV* 2661

*TCC R.3.19, fol. 156v

11. The.x.Commaundementes of Loue[13] (sig. Ppp, fols. 4r 4v), *IMEV* 590

*TCC R.3.19, fol. 109r
Bodleian Fairfax 16, fol. 184r

12. The ix.Ladies worthie[14] (sig. Ppp, fols. 4v–5r), *IMEV* 2767

*TCC R.3.19, fol. 110v

13. [untitled, inc.Alone walkyng][15] (sig. Ppp, fol. 5^r), *IMEV* 267

*TCC R.3.19, fol. 160r

14. A Ballade[16] (sig. Ppp, fols. 5r–5v), *IMEV* 1562

*TCC R.3.19, fol. 160r

15. A Ballade[17] (sig. Ppp, fols. 5v–6r), *IMEV* 2510

*TCC R.3.19, fol. 161r

16. Here foloweth how Mercurie with Pallas, Venus and Minarua, appered to Paris of Troie, he slepyng by a fountain.[18] (sig. Ppp, fol. 6r), *IMEV* 3197

*TCC R.3.19, fol. 161v
Leiden Vossius 9, fol. iii^{v19}

17. A balade pleasaunte[20] (sig. Ppp 6r–6v), *IMEV* 1300

*TCC R.3.19, fol. 205^r
Leiden Vossius 9, fol. 110v

19. A balade, warnyng men to beware of deceitptfull women.[22] (sig. Ppp, fol. 6v), *IMEV* 1944

*TCC R.3.19, fol. 207r
TCC O.9.38, fol. 28r
BL Harley 2251, fol. 149v
Rome English College 1405, fol. 75v

20. These verses next folowing were compiled by Geffray Chauser and in the writen copies foloweth at the ende of the complainte of petee[23] (sig. Qqq, fols. 1r–1v), *IMEV* 3414

*BL Harley 78, fol. 82r
BL Add. 34360, fol. 51r[24]

21. A balade declaring that wemens chastite Doeth moche excel all treasure worldly[25] (sig. Qqq, fols. 1v–2r), *IMEV* 1592

*TCC R.3.19, fol. 2v

22. The Court of Loue[26] (sig. Qqq fol. 2r–sig Rrr, fol. 3^r), *IMEV* 4205

*TCC R.3.19, fol. 218^r

23. Chaucers woordes vnto his owne Scriuener[27] (sig. Rrr, fol. 3v), *IMEV* 120

*TCC R.3.20, p. 367
CUL Gg.4.27, 1b, fol. 35r
(from the 1598 edition)

4. Thomas Speght
(ca. 1550–?)

DEREK PEARSALL

THE BOOKSELLERS' reprints in the sixteenth century of William Thynne's edition of Chaucer's works are not in any sense "editions." They are set up, line by line, from their predecessor, diverging from it only insofar as the text undergoes the usual mechanical degeneration at the hands of the compositor. The only claim to novelty is in the augmentation of the canon, which had indeed been a primary claim of Thynne himself, as he announces on his title page: "The Workes of Geffray Chaucer newly printed, with dyvers workes whiche were never in print before."[1] So the edition of 1542 adds *The Plowman's Tale*, the edition of 1545 moves it, and the edition of 1561 has the following at the end of the reprinted matter of Thynne: "Here foloweth certaine woorkes of Geffray Chaucer, whiche hath not here tofore been printed, and are gathered and added to this booke, by Iohn Stowe." Stow added a number of "Chaucerian" poems from Trinity College, Cambridge, manuscript R.3.19 and also Lydgate's *Siege of Thebes*, which he clearly declared to be by John Lydgate and which he evidently included because of its association with *The Canterbury Tales*. Like Thynne, who named Gower, Lydgate, and Scogan as the authors of poems in his table of contents, Stow was very content to include in Chaucer's works poems by other named authors who had an association of some kind with Chaucer; he was equally content to attribute to Chaucer any anonymous verse of Chaucerian appearance that came into his hands. The first "edition" for which Thomas Speght was responsible, that of 1598, is firmly within this tradition of reprint-with-augmentation, though the added matter now includes the beginnings of an editorial apparatus.

Thomas Speght, as we find in the *Dictionary of National Biography*, was born of a Yorkshire family about 1550 and entered Peterhouse, Cambridge, in 1566. As a sizar, or poor scholar, he would have been accustomed to eke

out the yearly scholarship he received from Sir William Cecil, Lord Burgh-
ley (the father of the Sir Robert Cecil to whom he dedicates the volume of
1598, with part-time work as a college servant. He graduated, B.A.,
1569–70, and M.A., 1573, having acquired at Peterhouse an enthusiasm
for Chaucer that he shared with his fellow student at the college, Francis
Beaumont (as Beaumont tells us in his prefatory epistle to the Chaucer of
1598), and perhaps too with other Peterhouse men of his time, such as Peter
Ashton and Peter Betham, whose subsequent writings, on diverse subjects,
show knowledge and appreciation of the old poet.[2] Spenser, it is worth
remembering, was a young student at Pembroke College at this time
(1569–76). Thomas Speght became a schoolmaster, and he was, according
to the epitaph on the tomb of his son Lawrence (who had a distinguished
career as a civil servant) at Clopton, Northamptonshire, a "paragon" of the
profession, who sent to Oxford and Cambridge and the Inns of Court "nere a
thousand youths of good report." He was probably the Speght reported in
1572 as a minor canon of Ely and headmaster of the grammar school
attached to the cathedral there. He contributed commendatory Latin verses
to Abraham Fleming's *Panoplie of Epistles* (1576) and John Baret's *Alvearie*
(1580). The Rachel Speght who in 1617 got herself involved in a pamphlet
war with Joseph Swetnam, that "cynicall baiter and foulmouthed barker
against Evah's sex," was perhaps his daughter. He was clearly a man on the
fringes of the literary and antiquarian and book-collecting circles of London, not in the first rank, with Robert Bruce Cotton, William Camden,
Joseph Holland, and Henry Savile, or even in the second, with John Stow
and Francis Thynne, both of whom boasted membership in the Society of
Antiquaries, but he was well known to these last two, who gave him
assistance of various kinds with his work on Chaucer.

Speght was not brought into the plans for a reprint of Chaucer's works
until a late date. The book was first entered in the *Stationer's Register* on
October 6, 1592, under the hands of "master Bisshop and master Stirrop,"
to be printed by Abell Jeffes.[3] But Abell Jeffes fell on hard times, and was
suppressed on December 3, 1595, for printing "a lewde booke called *the
most strange prophecie of Doctor Cipriano.*" Meanwhile, the title for the print of
"Chawcers *Workes*" was transferred to Adam Islip on December 20, 1594.
Islip eventually brought out the book in the early months of 1598, in three
impressions, for George Bishop, Bonham Norton, and Thomas Wight,
respectively; the first has a slightly different title page, but otherwise the
three are the same.[4] Speght explains how he became involved in the project
in his address "To the Readers": he had long spent his study in the
gathering of materials for the understanding of Chaucer's life and poetry
and the reparation of the text, and he had communicated thus much to his
friends:

> But so it fell out of late, that Chaucers Works being in the Presse, and three
> parts therof alreadie printed, not only these friends did by their Letters sollicit

> me, but certaine also of the best in the Companie of Stationers hearing of these Collections, came vnto me, and for better or worse would have something done in this Impression.

Speght goes on to apologize for the imperfections of the work so hurriedly set forth, particularly for "putting diverse things in the end of the booke, whiche els taken in time might have bene bestowed in more fit place" (this refers to the "Annotations and Corrections," which were indeed so bestowed in the edition of 1602), and expresses the hope that he may one day, with the help of his friends, do something better. At the very end of the volume, in a note added to the "Annotations and Corrections," Speght expresses his regret that the corrections were not incorporated in the text, which he would have done, he says, if time had served: "Whereas now no more then the Prologues only, are in that sort corrected: which fell out so, because they were last printed." He concludes with the comment, "Sentences also, which are many and excellent in this Poet, might have ben noted in the margent with some marke, which now must be left to the research of the Reader." This defect, again, was to be supplied in 1602.

The "best in the Company of Stationers" to whom Speght refers are no doubt George Bishop, for many years Master of the Company, and Bonham Norton, one of the wealthiest stationers of the day.[5] The friends who solicited him with their letters certainly include Francis Beaumont,[6] his old college mate, whose letter to "his very louing friend, T. S.," dated June 30, 1597, is printed in the prefatory matter to the edition. Beaumont exhorts his friend to publish "those good obseruations and collections you have written of him," and not to be deterred by objections that Speght has mentioned to him as commonly alleged against the poet, namely, that his words are grown "too hard and vnpleasant" and that he is "somewhat too broad in some of his speeches." Beaumont defends Chaucer against these objections and praises him for the vigor of his satire in *The Canterbury Tales* ("His drift is to touch all sortes of men, and to discouer all vices of that Age") and for the eloquence and sententiousness of his *Troilus*. He compares Chaucer with classical poets and concludes by reminding his friend of the high opinion of Chaucer held by their teachers, "those auncient learned men of our time in Cambridge," as well as by "that worthy man of learning, your good friend in Oxford" (Dr. Thomas Allen, whom we shall meet later), and of the unjust neglect to which Chaucer is condemned if he does not have his "interpretours," as have the Greek and Latin poets, as well as more recent French and Italian poets such as Du Bartas, Petrarch and Ariosto.

Another friend who was probably of more practical help to Speght was John Stow, the ubiquitous Elizabethan bibliophile and antiquary. Speght seems to acknowledge Stow as the source of his own additions to the canon in the advertisement at folio 340r, which marks the point of transition from the Thynne matter of 1532 to the Stow additions of 1561 and which may be compared with the original 1561 heading cited above:

> Here followeth certaine workes of Geffray
> Chaucer, annexed to the impression printed
> in the yeare 1561: with an adition of some thinges
> of Chaucer's writing, neuer before this time
> printed, 1597. All collected and adioined to his former
> workes by Iohn Stowe.

This looks like something inserted at Stow's express requirement. In his "Argument" to *The Plowman's Tale* (added in 1542), Speght comments: "made no doubt by Chaucer with the rest of the Tales. For I haue seene it in written hand in Iohn Stowes Library in a booke of such antiquity, as seemeth to haue beene written neare to Chaucers time." Speght's "no doubt" seems to imply a reservation, and the impression one gets is that Speght's caution was overwhelmed by Stow's enthusiasm, knowledge, and access to manuscripts. Further, in offering a list of works attributed to Chaucer but not known to be extant (in the section on "His Bookes" in the "Life of Chaucer"), Speght comments: "Others I haue seene without any Authours name, which for the inuention I would verily iudge to be Chaucers, were it not that wordes and phrases carry not euery where Chaucers antiquitie." In 1602, Speght inserted between "Authours name" and "which" the addition "in the hands of M. Stow that painefull Antiquarie." Whether he did this because he was conscious, or was made conscious, of not having given Stow sufficient credit or whether the reference to Stow is intended to substantiate Speght's doubts it is hard to say. But certainly Speght's comparative reticence about Stow's part in his edition is not shared by Stow himself. In the edition of 1600 of his *Annales of England* he adds the following to his earlier remarks about his edition of 1561: " . . . and againe in the yeere 1597. further increased with other his workes, as also his life, preferment, issue and death, collected out of records in the towre and else where by my selfe, and giuen to *Thomas Spight* to be published, and was performed."[7] Again, in the same vein, in his *Survey of London*, commenting on the editions of Chaucer by Caxton and Thynne, he goes on to describe his own part:

> corrected and twise encreased through mine owne paynefull labors, in the raigne of Queene *Elizabeth*, to witte in the yeare 1561. and again, beautified with notes by me collected out of diuers Recordes and Monuments, which I deliuered to my louing friend *Thomas Speight*, and hee hauing drawne the same into a good forme and Methode, as also explayned the olde and obscure wordes, &c. hath published them in *Anno* 1597.[8]

Stow was thus clearly an important informant and collector of material for Speght, especially for the "Life."[9]

Whatever Speght's reservations about the imperfections of the volume of 1598—and we may assume that they were as genuine as they were proper—it was put out with a deal of pomp. The title page is done in a woodcut border designed as a portal with columns, and reads as follows:

The / Workes of our Antient and Learned / English Poet, Geffrey Chavcer, / newly Printed. / In this Impression you shall find these Additions. /
1   His Portraiture and Progenie shewed.
2   His Life Collected.
3   Arguments to euery Booke gathered.
4   Old and obscure words explaned.
5   Authors by him cited, declared.
6   Difficulties opened.
7   Two Bookes of his, neuer before Printed.
London, / Printed by Adam Islip, at the charges of / Bonham Norton. Anno 1598. /[10]

"Antient and Learned" are epithets newly applied to Chaucer, and the whole emphasis of the title page, as of the volume as a whole, is to present Chaucer as a "classic,"[11] a writer of established reputation, a man of learning, whose writings deserve the interpretative apparatus appropriate to his stature. The "Portrait" page, showing "The Progenie of Geffrey Chaucer," has Hoccleve's picture of the poet in the center, with the tomb of Thomas Chaucer and Maud Burghersh portrayed below, and at the sides medallions and coats of arms showing, in parallel, his own descendants and those of his wife's brother-in-law (John of Gaunt), that is, the royal house of England. The "Life" has appended to it a list of commendations, "the iudgments and reports of some learned men, of this worthy and famous Poet," such as were habitually attached to the published work of reputable writers.[12] The "Arguments" too are a direct imitation of editorial practice with classical writers, as is the list of authors cited. All add to the dignity of the poet, and of the book, as also do its decorative features. The title page and the portrait page are both elaborate new production features, and the volume contains also some of the decorations of 1561, including the title-page coat of arms (relegated to the leaf after *The General Prologue*); the large genealogical design that frames the division titles of *The Canterbury Tales, The Romance of the Rose*, and the *Siege of Thebes*; and the woodcut of a knight on horseback that introduces the Knight's Tale.[13] Black-letter type, by now archaic in itself yet seemingly integral to the sixteenth-century view of Chaucer, is used for all the old matter taken from Thynne and Stow; roman is used for the apparatus, except for quotations from the text, which remain in black letter. The combined effect is not unhandsome.

A tabulation of the contents of the volume is useful at this point, so that it can be used for reference in the discussion that follows (reprinted matter is inset):

[Title page]
[Dedication] To . . . Sir Robert Cecil
To the Readers
F. B. to his very louing friend T. S.
The Reader to Geffrey Chaucer [a short dialogue, by "H. B.," in which

Chaucer expresses his gratitude to the editor who has brought him forth
from obscurity]

(Portrait) The Progenie of Geffrey Chaucer[14]

The Life of our learned English Poet, Geffray Chaucer

Arguments to euery Tale and Booke

Epistle of William Thinne to King Henry the eight

A Table of all the names of the workes, contained in this volume [two titles
added]

[a group of short poems, beginning with "Eight Goodly Questions"][15]

[The Works, page-reprinted from Stow 1561, including errors in
foliation][16]

[Stow's additions of 1561, with new heading]

Chaucers dreame [i.e., *The Isle of Ladies*]

The Floure and the Leafe

Chaucers Words vnto his owne Scriuener

[*Adam Scriveyn*, detached from Stow's additions and placed last, with
"Thus endeth the workes of Geffray Chaucer"]

[Lydgate, *Siege of Thebes*, from Stow 1561, with new heading]

[List of Lydgate's works, from Stow 1561, with new heading]

The old and obscure words of Chaucer explaned

The French in Chaucer translated

Most of the Authours cited by G. Chaucer in his workes, by name declared

Corrections of some faults and Annotations vpon some places

Faults Escaped [and final note]

The introductory matter has already been treated in part, though it may
be worth commenting that the "Arguments" convey some excellent insights into Speght's understanding of Chaucer. Short, pithy, and accurate
for the most part, they occasionally introduce some interpretative comment. "Sentence" is clearly favored in *The Nun's Priest's Tale*: "the morall
whereof is to embrace true friends, and to beware of flatterers." The
comment on *The Tale of Sir Thopas* shows thought and careful reading: "A
Northren tale of an outlandish Knight purposely vttered by Chaucer, in a
differing rime and stile from the other tales, as though he himselfe were not
the authour, but only the reporter of the rest." This is perhaps the first overt
recognition of the existence of "Chaucer the narrator." The longest "Argument" is that to "The Prologues" (i.e., *The General Prologue*), where Speght
describes the two purposes of the portraits as, first, "that the Reader seeing
the qualitie of the person, may iudge of his speech accordingly" and,
second, that he may understand that description may be as well done in
English as in Greek or Latin poetry. He commends the comprehensiveness
of Chaucer's picture of society, describing it as done "with such Arte and
cunning, that although none could deny himselfe to be touched, yet none
durst complaine that he was wronged." He concludes: "Who so shall read
these his works without preiudice, shall find that he was a man of rare
conceit and of great reading." Dryden, in his preface to the Fables, clearly
took a lead from Speght's generous and measured words.

But the introductory matter is dominated by the "Life" of Chaucer, which introduces new material from documentary sources and which remains the basis for the standard biography of Chaucer until the 1840s.[17] It is the first life of Chaucer in English, and the records gathered by Stow are used intelligently by Speght to give some account of Chaucer's "official" life—his controllership of customs, his foreign journeys, and his pensions. Speght's own additions are probably confined to the details of Chaucer's presumed life drawn from the writings ascribed to him. He uses *The Testament of Love* as evidence that Chaucer was born in London (rather than Oxfordshire or Berkshire, as stated by Leland) and that Chaucer got into trouble about 1379 "by fauouring some rash attempt of the common people" and was obliged to go into exile "in Holland, Zeland, and France, where he wrote most of his bookes." Speght also uses *The Court of Love* as evidence that Chaucer attended the University of Cambridge—as well as Oxford, where he was traditionally supposed to have been a student. This new discovery fitted well with the emphasis on Chaucer's learning.

Less to his taste was the evidence, presumably turned up by Stow, that Chaucer was a vintner's son. Speght is not the man to conceal an unpalatable fact, but he declares stoutly his belief that the family was no doubt wealthy "and of good account in the common wealth" and probably descended from some ancient but decayed noble line. Fortunately there was evidence available concerning Chaucer's marriage and descendants that redounded much more to his credit and was much more appropriate to what was expected of a great poet. Speght prints a pedigree devised, as he explains in the "Life," by Robert Glover, Somerset herald, 1571–88, in which for the first time Chaucer is shown as having married a daughter (unnamed) of Sir Payne Roet and as the father, by this marriage, of Thomas Chaucer. At a stroke the vintner's son is equipped with a very respectable set of descendants (Thomas's daughter Alice married the future Duke of Suffolk) and a spectacular collateral line through his relationship, ambiguous as it may have been initially, with John of Gaunt (whose mistress, later wife, Katherine Swynford, was the elder Roet daughter). Speght expounds these matters with some circumstance and satisfaction and has the Glover pedigree incorporated also in the decorative "Progeny" page drawn up at his request (as he explains in the "Life"), with appropriate coats of arms displayed, by John Speed. Speght probably took all his information on these genealogical matters from Glover and Stow, and can have had no part in any contrivance, happy as he may have been with the outcome. But Glover, though a reputable herald,[18] seems to have deduced rather than discovered a pedigree for Chaucer's descendants, since none of the recorded heraldic evidence makes any explicit association between Chaucer and Roet. The nearest approach is on the tomb of Thomas Chaucer at Ewelme, where Roet is found quartering Burghersh (Maud Burghersh was Thomas's wife). This is an odd substitute for what might have been expected (Chaucer-Roet).

Glover, or Stow, may have had access to evidence that is now lost, though they might have been expected to mention the source of such a significant discovery. Whatever the case, the Glover pedigree is now generally accepted, except for those who maintain that Thomas "Chaucer" was John of Gaunt's bastard son by Chaucer's wife.[19]

Respectably scholarly as it was for its time, Speght's "Life" has been almost entirely superseded by later scholarship, with the exception of one intriguing and enigmatic allusion. In speaking of the friendship of Chaucer and Gower, Speght makes the following remark: "It seemeth that both these learned men were of the inner Temple: for not many yeeres since, Master *Buckley* did see a Record in the same house, where *Geoffrey Chaucer* was fined two shillings for beating a Franciscane fryer in Fleetstreete." For a long time this "record" was regarded with skepticism, as by Lounsbury,[20] who recounts Chatterton's embroidery of it—where the occasion of the beating is said to be Chaucer's annoyance at the friar's lampooning of his (Chaucer's) "Tale of Piers Plowman"—as demanding little more in the way of credulity. But later scholars[21] discovered that a master William Buckley did indeed exist at the time and that he was a bencher of the Inner Temple and butler of his house. As Manly puts it (pp. 11–12): "Master Buckley turned out to be the one man in England whose business it was to have seen such a record, if it existed. He was not only a member of the Society of the Temple but the official whose duties included the preservation and care of the Temple Records."

The records themselves have disappeared, but the records of Lincoln's Inn, which survive from 1422, can be shown to be broadly similar to what has been lost, and there fines for fighting and other disorderly conduct regularly appear, with fines ranging from 1*s*. 3*d*. to 3*s*. 8*d*. Fleet Street bounds the Temple on the north. All the fifteenth-century evidence makes it clear that the Inns of Court at that time were a kind of "university" where students were equipped not only for the law but also with a liberal education more amenable to the generality than the predominantly ecclesiastical education of Oxford and Cambridge. Whether the Inner Temple existed in precisely this form in the period 1360–67 (the vacant years in Chaucer's career) is more debatable, but there is nothing to prove that it was not so.[22] Master Buckley could conceivably have made a mistake, or invented the story, not unaware of the prestige that would accrue to his society from Chaucer's alleged association with it, but suspicion in this case strains the evidence, so proper and plausible in itself, more than belief. Speght was certainly not a man whom one would suspect of any kind of fabrication, and some endorsement of his story is forthcoming from Joseph Holland, a man in the first rank of the antiquaries of his day. Holland owned the famous Cambridge manuscript Gg.4.27, and was later to let Speght take his copy of Chaucer's *ABC* from it. But meanwhile he was supplying the many lacunae in the manuscript (caused by the cutting out of folios containing miniatures) with text copied, on added leaves, from Speght's Chaucer of 1598. He also took over in abridged form much of Speght's prefatory matter and other apparatus, including portions of the "Life," reporting the Inner Temple reference thus: "There is a record in the same howse [the Inner Temple] where Geffrey Chavcer was fined at two shillinges, for beatinge a franciscane fryer in fletestrete."[23] Holland's change in wording substitutes affirmation for hearsay and suggests that he had seen the record of which he speaks, as he could well have done, being himself a member of the Inner Temple, interested in records and in Chaucer.

Before we turn to Speght's additions to the works and his concluding apparatus, it is necessary to comment briefly on his handling of the texts he inherited from Stow. Brief comment is all that is necessary since Speght's own hopes, as he expressed them in his address "To the Readers," for the reformation of the text by old written copies were not, for the reasons he explains, realized. The inherited matter is page-reprinted from Stow, the only changes being the sporadic minor substitutions, additions, and omissions that are endemic to the work of the compositor, whether provoked by momentary carelessness or momentary interest. The evidence of my own collation, on different occasions, of the 1561 and 1598 texts of *The Nun's Priest's Tale* and of *The Assembly of Ladies* is conclusive on this point.[24] On the other hand, Lounsbury[25] reports sporadic changes in the text of *The General Prologue* that are clearly the product of deliberate editorial intervention, and this fits well with Speght's own remarks, quoted earlier, about the little that he had the time to do. The changes are not the product of any systematic collation with a good manuscript, some of them are mistakes, and all could be in the nature of on-sight "corrections."[26]

Speght, however, did his best to carry out his editorial responsibilities as an augmentor, and the two additions he made to the canon survived unchallenged until the late nineteenth century.[27] *The Floure and the Leafe* is indeed a gracious little poem, and Speght must have been pleased to light on it. How he did so is a mystery, though some circumstantial speculation is possible.[28] A manuscript of ca. 1500 at Longleat House, manuscript 258, has a contemporary list of contents on the last leaf (folio 147v), in which the fourth item is "De folio et flore." At the point in the manuscript where the poem should appear, a whole quire (folios 33–48) is missing, just sufficient to contain *The Floure and the Leafe* and the six stanzas missing from the beginning of the next piece, *The Complaint of Mars*, as Henry Bradshaw explains in a note inserted in the manuscript. Longleat 258 passed through the hands of Thomas Godfray, the printer responsible for William Thynne's edition of 1532, and *The Assembly of Ladies* was printed from it. From William the manuscript passed to his nephew Sir John Thynne, who built Longleat House. It is hard to see why William would not have taken in *The Floure and the Leafe* from Longleat 258 if the missing quire had been present when the manuscript was in his hands. If, on the other hand, the missing quire came to Speght by a roundabout route, one would have expected the spelling and other peculiarities of his text of *The Floure and the Leafe* to resemble in some measure those of the Longleat 258 texts of *The Assembly of Ladies* and other poems. This is not the case. In fact the corruption of text and meter and modernization of language in *The Floure* is of a degree so advanced as to argue for an extended chain of transmission in the sixteenth century. One would have to presume that the quire was removed from Longleat 258 at an early date in its history, perhaps for independent circulation or to serve some printing venture all trace of which has been lost, and that it was some careless copy of the poem that eventually reached Speght.

Another Longleat manuscript plays an equally mysterious background role in the story of Speght's other addition of 1598, *The Isle of Ladies*.[29] Two manuscripts of the work survive, Longleat 256 (mid-sixteenth century) and British Library Additional 10303 (second half of the sixteenth century), each of which contains *The Isle of Ladies* alone. Both contain the added lines (a 6-line stanza, three 7-line stanzas with envoy, and a couplet added in a different hand), which Jenkins prints as an "envoy" and which Speght has too, but neither manuscript appears to be Speght's direct source for his copy of the poem.[30] Again it seems that manuscript "pamphlets" of old poems were in lively circulation in the sixteenth century, ready to be picked up by collectors such as Stow and put into print.[31] Whatever the channels through which the poem came to Speght, he caused inordinate confusion by the title he gave to it, "Chaucers dreame." This was the title given in previous editions of the works to *The Book of the Duchess*, which Speght therefore has to retitle, in his "Arguments," "The booke of the Duchesse, or the death of Blanch; mistermed heretofore, Chaucers Dreame." Unfortunately, his "Argument" to the new "dreame" included an interpretation of part of it as an allegory of the presumed death of Blanche, and with this the way was clear to an almost inextricable confusion.

In the "Life," Speght himself seems to have lost track of what happened, when he comments on the second of his new additions: "*In obitum Blanchiae Ducissae*, neuer before published: which seemeth rather to be his Dreame: and that other called his Dreame, The complaint for Blanch: as after the perusing of them both, any meane Reader will iudge." Francis Thynne, meanwhile, was on hand to make things even more confused. In his "Animadversions" of 1599 he took Speght to task for his rashness and argued that the old "Dreame" should keep its title (p. 30): "That whiche you will haue 'the Dreame of Chaucer,' is his 'Temple of Glasse,' as I haue seene the title therof noted, and the thinge yt selfe confirmethe." Sure enough, on a flyleaf in Longleat 256 is scribbled, in an untidy sixteenth-century hand (possibly the same hand that wrote in the added couplet at the end), "The Temple of glasse / Compiled by geoffray / Chaucer."[32] It is conceivable that Francis wrote this in himself, to provide good manuscript authority for his opinion, but clearly Longleat 256 had been through his hands. Stow too may have had an interest in the newly discovered poem. Certainly, Speght's "Argument" to the new "Dreame," whereby he interprets it as "a couert report of the mariage of Iohn of Gaunt the kings sonne with Blanch the daughter of Henry Duke of Lancaster" and of Chaucer's own match with "a certaine Gentlewoman," has the "gossipy" quality that Stow might well have caught from his extensive acquaintance with such headings in the manuscripts of John Shirley. There is, of course, no basis whatsoever for such an allegorical interpretation, though it no doubt helped to fortify, or was fortified by, the new revelations in the "Life" concerning Chaucer's relationship with John of Gaunt.

Apart from the "Life" and the two new poems, the most striking feature of Speght's edition of 1598 is the concluding matter, which includes for the first time a list of "hard words." Chaucer's language was growing increasingly difficult to understand in the sixteenth century, as is evidenced by the comments of writers such as Skelton and Berthelet, the misreadings of editors, and the occasional glosses introduced in manuscripts by sixteenth-century readers.[33] Beaumont, in his prefatory letter, had referred to Speght's own reservations on this score. The answer was clearly some kind of glossary. "E. K." had provided some glosses for the "old words" in Spenser's *Shepherds Calendar* in 1579, and a small *Vocabula Chauceriana* had appeared in a grammatical textbook in 1594. The vocabulary consisted of single synonyms for about 120 words, a third drawn from E. K.[34] But Speght's glossary is on a completely new scale, and, with the revisions of 1602, it remained the standard Chaucer glossary until Urry's edition of 1721 and influential still after that. For its time it is quite an ambitious project, and it is likely to have been largely Speght's own work. It contains about 2,000 words, with explanations mostly in the form of single-word synonyms. There is no attempt at parsing or etymology, no record of grammatical variants or inflected forms, no citation of line references, and no discussion[35] or support provided from context or contemporary writings. The alphabetization is very erratic, rather as if the list had been hurriedly thrown together at the last moment. The meanings supplied are mostly guesswork from context and common sense: most of the guesses are good, but some are completely off target. *Blackeburied*, for instance (*The Pardoner's Tale* C 406) is defined, simply, "Hell." A single line in *The Assembly of Ladies* (line 61), in a description of a quiet arbor and its flowers, "Ne m'oublie-mies and sovenez also," having deteriorated in the printed texts to the unintelligible "Ne momblishnesse and sonenesse also," produced two guesses in Speght (*momblishnesse*, "taulke"; *sonenesse*, "noyse") that survived as ghost words in the dictionaries until the eighteenth century.[36] Speght evidently thought of his glossary as a simple, practical aid to understanding, not as a place to store learned observations. He was to be taught better, as we shall see, but for the moment his ambitions are confined within the limits set by common sense, a decent education, and no great desire to put himself to a lot of work. The same is true of the translations of Chaucer's Latin and the list of authors cited, which are no more than could have been put together by any man with a reasonable education. For the latter, access to a modest encyclopedia would have provided the dates of *floruit* that are sometimes added, though even these are lacking in the more airy declarations: "*Avicen*, a Physician of Ciuill, wrote a multitude of bookes," or "*Damascenus presbiter* did write many things in the Greeke tongue."

It is in the "Annotations and Corrections," however, that we find the most vivid evidence of Speght's personal presence, of the range and nature of his interest in Chaucer. Some of the contents of this section are indeed corrections of the text such as we have already seen him explaining, including the omission of a whole passage from *Sir Thopas*, but much is the product of Speght's own "observations." In his notes on *The General Prologue*, for instance, we find him commenting, at not inordinate length, on palmers (line 13), the knights of Prussia (line 53), the siege of Alexandria (line 51), the four orders of friars (line 210), the Merchant's "shildes" (line 278), vigils (line 377), astronomy and natural magic (lines 414, 416), and the vernicle (line 685). Occasionally he gives us the source of his information, as in his note on *Anticlaudianus*, where the reference to the author as Alanus de Insulis is acknowledged to be "Gesner"; this is certainly Conrad Gesner, a Swiss scholar and scientist whose *Bibliotheca universalis* appeared in 1545.[37] The reference was dropped, though the information kept, in 1602, as if Francis Thynne had spoken scornfully to Speght about this amateurish habit of disclosing obvious and readily available secondary sources. Another source is acknowledged in the note to *Valerie and Theophrast*: "This Valerie wrote a booke *De non ducenda uxore*, with a Paraphrase vpon it, which I haue seene in the studie of Master Allen of Oxford, a man of as rare learning as he is stored with rare bookes." This is almost certainly Thomas Allen, fellow of Trinity College, Oxford; a renowned mathematician, philosopher, and antiquary; a great collector of manuscripts; and a correspondent of Bodley, Camden, Cotton, and Selden.[38] Occasionally an unnamed source can be identified, as with Speght's note on *Gawayn*, where the account of the discovery of Gawain's bones, those of a man fourteen feet tall, in Wales in 1082 can be traced directly to H. Lloyd's *Historie of Cambria*, published in 1584.[39] Often, however, Speght needs no more than general knowledge or common report to supply him with the matter of his annotation. So, in his note on the *Tabard* inn, he records its decay since Chaucer's time, but adds, with the air of someone who knows, that "it is now by Master *I. Preston* . . . newly repaired, and with conuenient roomes much encreased, for the receipt of many guests." Concerning Henry II's mistress *Rosamond*, he speaks of a recent disinterment: "Not long since her graue was digged, were some of her bones were found, and her teeth so white (as the dwellers there report) that the beholders did much wonder at them." This same generous spirit of wonderment at the beauty and nobility of the lives of the past is present too in Speght's note on the "madness" of Troilus (*TC* 1.499): "This madnesse counted by some an *indecorum* in such a valiant man, for as much as it proceeded of earnest loue, doth nothing to disgrace *Troylus*." Speght allows too a touch of humor, quoting as his illustration of *Aposiopesis* (annotating *WBP* D200) a verse that Chaucer "is said to haue written with his Diamond somtime in glassewindowes, expounded by his man Wat":

> A maried man and yet, qd Chaucer.
> A merry man, qd. Wat.
> He is a knaue that wrote me that, qd. Chaucer.

Speght's most famous annotation, however, is his nonannotation of the reference to "Wades bote" (in *MerT* E1424): "Concerning *Wade* and his bote called Guingelot, as also his strange exploits in the same, because the matter is long and fabulous, I passe it ouer." Says Tyrwhitt, "Mr. Speght probably did not foresee that Posterity would be as much obliged to him for a little of this *fabulous matter* concerning *Wade* and his *bote*, as for the gravest of his annotations."[40] But the point is worth making that Speght, for all his earnest attempt to present Chaucer as an "ancient and learned" poet, is here, as on other occasions, intimate with Chaucer's poetry in a way that we, across many more centuries, can never be.

In the volume of 1598 Speght had already hinted, as we have seen, at a revision that might follow, in which better leisure might allow things to be more orderly bestowed. The revised edition was put out, in fact, with extraordinary dispatch only four years later, in 1602. We can attribute the speed and energy with which Speght moved, without much doubt, to the influence of Francis Thynne, who sent him a long letter containing his "Animadversions" on the edition of 1598 on December 20, 1599.[41] As the son of William Thynne, Francis (1545–1608), born the year before his father's death, felt himself to have a position of privilege in relation to the editing of Chaucer. He was zealous for his father's reputation and perhaps nettled at being forestalled in his own plans for an edition, though there is no evidence that he had made any plans or indeed that he ever did more than point out the defects, real or supposed, in what others had done. The pattern of his whole life, in fact, was repeated here with what must have been to him painful familiarity. He never went to university or the Inns of Court, and his reputation as a scholar was built entirely on his own passion for antiquarian studies, particularly the more arcane studies such as heraldry and alchemy. He made a disastrous marriage and spent two years in prison (1574–76) at the instigation of his wife's relatives. He lived for some time after this at Longleat but seems to have been turned out when his cousin Sir

John died in 1580. He was commissioned to contribute part of the continuation of Holinshed's *Chronicles* in 1587, but many of his long-winded additions (he was inordinately fond of lists, of earls, archbishops, etc., and would throw them in at the slightest provocation) were cut from the book after printing and before publication.[42] His life's ambition was to become a member of the College of Heralds, but his continued solicitations, begun in 1588, met with no response until Egerton finally recommended him to the position of Lancaster herald in 1602, a few years before his death. He published nothing of note, and his whole life was a history of being put upon.

Francis Thynne was a professional scholar, and to that extent in a different class from Speght, with kinds of knowledge and access to sources that Speght could in no way claim. But to speak of Francis as "at least potentially, and for his day, a really great Chaucerian scholar,"[43] is too much. Even for his day he is not a very good scholar, and certainly no Chaucerian. His judgment is poor, his understanding of context unsound, and he lacks all sense of the difference between important and trivial matters. He is, in fact, the perfect pattern of the pedant, and the tone of his letter, which ranges from the patronizing to the irascible, is in accord. He begins by complimenting Speght upon his edition but soon proceeds to elaborate on its deficiencies, expressing his regret that Speght did not consult him, as the inheritor of the Thynne wisdom. He bears no malice: "This whiche I write ys not nowe vppon selfe will . . . but in frendlye sorte to bringe truthe to lighte" (p. 5). He takes issue first with Speght's claim to have corrected the text by "written copies," not so much with the claim itself, which he would have done well to question, as with the implication that the text handed down from Thynne was incorrect. It is his zeal here for his father's reputation that is his undoing, for in many of his comments on Speght's "Annotations and Corrections" his obvious desire is to assert the correctness of the form in the text, which of course derives from his father's edition. Thus he argues against Speght's correction of the name Campaneus to Capaneus (*KnT* A 932); in 1602, Speght therefore kept Campaneus, which is wrong. He argues likewise against the correction of the form *unseriall* to *cerriall* (*KnT* A 2290); again he is wrong, and again Speght kept the wrong form in 1602, without comment. Francis also makes extensive criticism of Speght's glossary and picks on some details in the "Life" and the "Arguments" for comment. He tends to a preoccupation with side issues such as whether Gower's family came from Yorkshire, or the question of the title of *The Isle of Ladies*. On many occasions, of course, his comments are well justified, especially where questions of ascertainable historical fact are concerned, and he is able to offer corrections, as of *Mertenrike* to *Mercenrike* (in *NPT* B 4302), which even Chaucer might have been grateful for. But he is wrong nearly as often as he is right, wrong where Speght is right, right where Speght is wrong, and sometimes, to make utter confusion, wrong where Speght is wrong, but in a different way. At the end he hopes that Speght will accept his criticisms in good part,

> to the ende Chawcers Woorkes by muche conference and manye judgmentes mighte at lenghe obteyne their true perfectione and glorye,—as I truste they shall, yf yt please godde to lende me tyme and leysure to reprinte, correcte, and comente the same, after the manner of the Italians, who have largely comented Petrarche. [p. 75]

Time and leisure were not, however, forthcoming, and Francis's influence is exerted solely through Speght's edition of 1602.

Speght did indeed take everything in extraordinarily good part. He perhaps realized that he was outgunned by the more professional scholar, and a natural and likable modesty and generosity made him receive all Thynne's criticisms "with such tact as to turn away all the latter's irritation."[44] He speaks with the profoundest deference of the Thynnes, father and son, introducing special tributes to William's "praise-worthy labours" in a rewritten dedication to Cecil and an added commendation of the early editor ("whose iudgement we are the rather to approve, for that he had further insight into him then many others") in the revised "Life," while thanking Francis profusely in a rewritten address "To the Readers" for his help in correcting and improving the text, glossary, and notes. He even persuaded Francis to contribute to the prefatory material a short poem praising Chaucer: it is not a very good one.

The new edition was completely reset and was again printed by Adam Islip, partly under his own imprint, with a new border for the title page, and partly shared with George Bishop, the copies printed for the latter having the old border as found in Bishop's copies of 1598.[45] The wording on the title page is new, and reads as follows:

> The / Workes of Ovr / Ancient and learned English / Poet, Geffrey Chavcer, / newly Printed, / To that which was done in the former Impression, / thus much is now added. /
>
> 1 In the Life of Chaucer many things inserted.
> 2 The whole worke by old Copies reformed.
> 3 Sentences and Prouerbes noted.
> 4 The Signification of the old and obscure words prooued: also Caracters showing from what Tongue or Dialect they be deriued.
> 5 The Latine and French, not Englished by Chaucer, translated.
> 6 The Treatise called Jacke Vpland, against Friers: and Chaucers A.B.C. called La Priere de nostre Dame, at this Impression added.

The layout of the new edition is substantially that of 1598, but with the addition of two short poems in praise of Chaucer, one by Francis Thynne, before the "Life"; the omission of some of the decorative features; the addition of *Jack Upland* and the *ABC* poem between *The Floure and the Leafe*

and *Adam Scriveyn*; the addition of the translations from the Latin; and the
absorption of the "Annotations and Corrections" into the text (where
appropriate) and glossary. However, although the layout is substantially
the same, the whole edition has been subjected to revision and completely
reset, and it could be said with some truth that this 1602 volume is indeed
Speght's "edition" of Chaucer's works. The dedication to Cecil is rewritten,
as we have seen, so as to incorporate a proper acknowledgment of William
Thynne's editorial labors.

The address "To the Readers" is much expanded and includes now a
generous tribute to Francis Thynne for the help he has given toward this
new edition, as well as Speght's answer to those who conceive of Chaucer as
unlearned or unserious, his judicious defense of the regularity of Chaucer's
versification (his views here inspire many of his textual emendations, and
were what Dryden took issue with, nearly a hundred years later), and his
refutation of the charge that many of his interpretations of meaning, in the
glossary, are "conjectural": "such as understand the Dialects of our Tongue,
especially in the *North*, and have knowledge in some other Languages, will
judge otherwise." The letter of Beaumont is slightly altered here and there,
one notable change being the newly emphatic assertion that Spenser's
"much frequenting of Chaucers auncient words, with his excellent imitation of diuerse places in him," is one of the sources of his excellence as a poet.
The "Life" is also subjected to minor revision, with some added acknowledgment of the help of John Stow and Francis Thynne, a discussion of
the lost *Pilgrim's Tale* (for which see below), and a frank admission that his
"geometrical" explanation of Chaucer's coat of arms, which Francis had
dismissed fairly scornfully (p. 15), was perhaps a little fanciful. Further
examples of the care Speght took in this revision are the distribution of the
"Arguments" so that they stand at the head of the tale or poem to which
they refer and the provision of little marginal fists with pointing finger to
mark aphoristic statements of general truth. This latter feature, duly noted
among the attractions of this new edition announced on the title page,
clearly indicates the value still placed, as by fifteenth-century admirers of
Chaucer, on his sententiousness as a poet. No great sophistication is
involved in the selection of lines to be dignified in this way (in *The Nun's
Priest's Tale*, for instance, it is lines 3991, 4103, 4243, 4353, 4395, 4446,
4515, 4621, 4623, 4633), but it is all part of the plan to present Chaucer as
a "serious" poet. One final small pointer to the care with which this image is
sustained, as well as to the attention to detail in the revision, is the
alteration in the attribution of *The Complaint of Chaucer to His Purse*, which is
now assigned to Hoccleve. The reason for this is not far to seek: a learned and
serious poet does not write comically self-deprecating appeals for money.
Hoccleve, on the other hand, did little else.

Speght's claim, now advanced to the title page, to have reformed the text
by "old Copies" is, for once, partly true. The text of the new edition was

reset from Stow's edition of 1561, which probably represents a gesture, however misguided, in the direction of greater authenticity, and the exemplar was sporadically and unsystematically "improved." The instigation for this had come, as we have seen, from Francis Thynne, whose "Animadversions" were based, certainly in part, on access to "written copyes." There is good reason to believe that Francis communicated further readings to Speght or otherwise provided him with access to manuscripts. Speght did not, of course, engage in any systematic collation, and he was able to revise only those texts for which manuscript evidence was available. From my own collation of *The Floure and the Leafe* and *The Assembly of Ladies* it is clear that Speght did no more, in these texts, than make occasional on-sight "corrections."[46] But in *The Canterbury Tales*, at least, he proceeded to a revision of the text that was for its day remarkable. In *The Nun's Priest's Tale*, for example, he introduced more than fifty new readings, most of which are corrections or at least improvements, and many of which defy the whole tradition of the printed texts up to his day. The influence of Francis's erudition is clearly at work, from the evidence of the *Animadversions*, in lines 4302 (*Mercenrike*), 4380 (*thritty* for *twenty*), and 4385 (*Twenty* for *Fourty*)[47]—Francis's knowledge of astronomy was particularly valuable in the latter two cases—and Speght may also have got *Andromacha* (line 4331), after its many bizarre peregrinations (*Andromeda* in 1598), privately from Francis. On the other hand, Speght, in whom good sense is always likely to break out, did not follow Francis's eloquent and completely erroneous defense of the reading of 1598 for line 4146 (*Where the sonne . . .*) and he incorporated in his text the correction (*Ware the sonne . . .*) he had proposed in his "Annotations and Corrections."

There seems no distinctive pattern in the selection of readings for correction, except for the direct and known influence of the *Animadversions*, and they follow exclusively no known manuscript. Many of them are obvious and straightforward—replacing of single words that have slipped out of the text, removal of single words that have crept in, simple substitutions—and could have been introduced independently by an intelligent editor with an ear for Chaucer's verse. Meter indeed seems to be a factor in a number of the emendations, as Speght may have been hinting in the address "To the Readers." But it is inconceivable that the corrections, including as they do the restoration of authentic lines previously omitted, could have been made without the use, direct or indirect, of written copies. Whether this extends much or at all beyond *The Canterbury Tales* is a question that will await the results of a complete collation. Whatever the case, some considerable credit attaches to Speght for the care and interest, however sporadic and inconsistent by modern standards, he showed in the task of revising the text. Unfortunately, the tradition of the printed texts was by now so degenerate that no attempt to improve a text set up from a printed copy could do more than tinker with its defects. Inevitably, too, more errors were introduced, whether or not in the form of misguided "improvements," and the punctuation of the edition of 1602, on the whole heavier than that of 1598, is on the whole worse.[48]

Speght's efforts with his new edition did not end with the improvement of the old. Augmentation of the canon was still clearly an editorial desideratum, and he introduces two new works in 1602. One is the genuine *ABC* poem to the Virgin, translated from Deguilleville, to which is affixed this heading:

> Chaucers A.B.C. called La Priere de nostre Dame made, as some say, at the request of Blanch, Duchesse of Lancaster, as a praier for her priuat vse, being a woman in her religion very deuout.

It is known that Speght took this poem from Cambridge University Library manuscript Gg.4.27, which was owned by Joseph Holland and into which Holland had inserted text and other matter derived from the edition of 1598.[49] The existence of a known manuscript exemplar puts us in the fortunate position of seeing Speght at work on an *editio princeps*: the sight is reassuring, for, apart from some obvious corrections and the inevitable modernizations of language, Speght keeps close to his original. It is not known where he got his French title and heading, for Gg.4.27 begins with the text of *ABC*, with only Holland's brief title, after loss of four leaves. It may once have had the French title, which appears in a sister manuscript, Pepys 2006. The "gossipy" heading may also have been there and may go back to an authentic tradition but may go back no further than Stow (imitating Shirley), and it certainly fits suspiciously well with the increased emphasis on Chaucer's aristocratic connections in the Speght "Life."

Jack Upland answers to a different conception of Chaucer, this time as the earnest critic of the old abuses of the Church, and Protestant by premonition. Speght prints the original "Complaint" only (which is extant in two manuscripts, British Library, Harley 6641 and Cambridge University Library Ff.6.2), not the sequels, *Friar Daw's Reply* and *Upland's Rejoinder*, which appear only in Bodleian manuscript Digby 41.[50] His text is taken not from a manuscript but from the text printed in the second edition of John Foxe's *Actes and Monumentes* (1570), which in turn is taken from a small octavo print of 1536 by John Gough. Both Gough and Foxe attribute the work to Chaucer, and Speght found added support for the attribution in his identification of the work as the Plowman's *Creed* alluded to in *The Plowman's Tale* (lines 1065–68, which he quotes in his headnote), which of course had long been accepted as Chaucer's. "And al was fals."

Speght had hopes of yet a third addition to the works, in the form of the long-lost *Pilgrim's Tale*, but he has to acknowledge temporary failure on this score. In an addition to the "Life" he speaks of the original printing of the *Tale* by William Thynne: "The argument of which tale, as also the occasion thereof, and the cause why it was left out of Chaucers Workes, shall

hereafter be shewed, if God permit, in M.Fran. Thyns coment vpon
Chaucer: & the Tale it selfe published if possibly it can be found." All this is
due to the inspiration of Francis Thynne, who in his *Animadversions* had told
a cock-and-bull story of his father's attempt to print *The Pilgrim's Tale*, "a
thinge more odious to the Clergye, then the speche of the plowmanne"
(i.e., *The Plowman's Tale*). William asked Henry VIII how he felt about it,
whereupon the king replied, "Williame Thynne! I dobte this will not be
allowed; for I suspecte the Byshoppes will call the in questione for yt" (ed.
cit., p.9). So the first edition, containing the tale, had to be canceled, and
the second edition (that is, the edition of 1532) brought out without it.
Bradshaw points out that Tyrwhitt proves that the tale could not possibly
have been written before 1536–40[51] and that the reference is probably to
the Douce printed fragment (ca. 1540) of *The Court of Love*, including *The
Pilgrim's Tale*,[52] confused word of which had reached Francis, perhaps
through his uncle Sir John.

Speght's revision of his concluding matter is the most striking evidence
of Francis Thynne's influence. The section of the apparatus headed "Most of
the Authours cited by G. Chaucer in his workes, by name declared," which
Francis had acidly described as aptly entitled since so many were left out
(ed. cit., p. 71), is retitled "The Authors cited . . .," and revised to include
many more names. They are thrown in, without regard to alphabetization,
in chunks at the beginning or end of each letter. Some of them are
desperately uninformative ("*Helowis, Maximinian, Livian, Aurora, Zansis,*
and diuers others alledged by Chaucer, haue none or few of their workes
extant"), though occasionally Speght turns up some fresh source of biographical information, as for "*Vergilius*, the most famous Poet of Mantua,
whose life *Petrus Crinitus* hath set downe at large in Lib. 3 *de Poetis
Latinis*."[53] The apparatus of translations from the French is expanded to
take in a few omissions, and a new list of translations from the Latin is
introduced. It includes, for good measure and no good reason, a list of the
arguments to the twelve books of Statius's *Thebaid*, a piece of information
that Speght, like Pandarus, clearly thought too good to pass by.

The main changes, however, are in the Glossary, where etymologies, of a
fairly primitive kind, are introduced, new material added, some of it
directly from Thynne, and the whole of the "Annotations" of 1598 transferred into more or less appropriate alphabetical slots. This last move,
though prepared for in the 1598 apologies,[54] is a piece of pure pedantry in
which Francis must have had some part. It means that annotations which do
not refer to some single word have to be slotted in arbitrarily (and confusion
increased in an already disordered alphabetization), so that, for example,
the note on the knights of Prussia comes under *Bourd begon*, and that on
aposiopesis under *Yee knowe what I meane*. As is often the case, mechanical
systematization ensures that the information is irretrievable. Elsewhere
Francis's influence is explicitly in evidence. A long note on *Harrolds* (i.e.,

"harlots") ends "But more hereof when time shall serue in M. F. Thins comment," and Speght concludes his long note on *Eros*, (i.e., "Hereos") with the respectful admission that those who read *Heroes* (namely, Francis) may be right: "I cannot dislike their opinion, for it may fitly stand with the sense of the place" (but it is nevertheless quite wrong). The explanations of *orfrayes* and *anelace* are much expanded under Francis's guidance, with citation of chapter and verse from Matthew Paris; likewise *besant*, with citation from William of Malmesbury, and *Valerie and Theophrast*, with citation from John of Salisbury, for the translation of whose writings Speght, presumably at Francis's incitement, makes an eloquent plea. Francis also provides material, in his "Animadversions," for new or expanded notes on *nowell, bigin, heroner, porpheri, vernacle, trepeget, autentike* (not "of antiquitie" but "of awthoritie"—"which I muse that you did not remember," comments Francis with unwonted placidity; p. 42). Sometimes Francis's knowledge of heraldry comes in useful, as in his correction of *owndy* from "sliked," to "wauing," or his new comment on *Wiuer* ("You expounde not wherefor I will tell you," he says, imperturbably; p. 41), at other times his knowledge of alchemy, as in the explanations of *citrination, fermentation* and *resagor*.[55]

Speght, as we have seen, has a mind of his own, and he does not always accept Francis's offerings. He keeps unaltered his definitions of *haketon, sendall*, and *hipe*, despite Francis's advice, and he does not mention, perhaps wisely, Francis's Hebrew derivation for *nowell*. At other times he seems to be having a shot of his own, as with *barbicans*, "watch toures, in the Saxon tongue, borough kennings"; *Lollar*, "a breaker of fasting daies"; *herawdes*, "furious partes in a play" (i.e., Herod, in *The Millers Tale*: could this be completely unmischievous in relation to Francis's prized profession?); *gossomor*, "things that flie in the aire in sommer time like copwebs." He adds too a supposedly humorous poem, apparently taken from Bodleian manuscript Rawlinson Poet. 149, in his explanation of *iape*, a word now "growen odious."[56] The disappearance of the generous comment on Troilus's passion, quoted above, may have something to do with Francis's tart rebuke to the "furye" of Arcite's love, though it may be lost because Speght could find nowhere to put it in his new scheme. The replacement of *blankemanger*, "a meat of Rise and Almon milke: brawne of capons and sugar"(1598), with, simply, "custard," may be an acknowledgment that explanations of such trivialities have no place in the interpretation of an ancient and learned poet.

Speght's edition of 1602 brought to an end what may be called a spate of Chaucerian publication, with six editions of the poet's complete works in seventy years (1532–1602). Whether because Speght had done his work to the satisfaction of seventeenth-century readers or because Chaucer was growing increasingly distant and hard to understand, there was no further edition until 1687, and this publication, it has been suggested, was not so much a response to public demand as an attempt to preserve the title to the work in the hands of a particular group of publishers.[57] The copyright to the Speght edition of 1602 had been transferred in 1611 by the widow of George Bishop to Thomas Adams, who had succeeded to her husband's business. At Adams's death in 1620 the title passed to his wife, but there is no record of it thereafter. The reprint of 1687 was put out by a small printer, John Harefinch, who seems to have been acting at the behest of an influential group of publishers: "The 1687 edition of Chaucer may, then, be viewed as a publisher's venture, one which took advantage of a steady though limited public demand for a printed edition of the whole corpus of his poetry and which also had the practical effect of asserting copyright in a respectable older text."[58]

The work is a page reprint of the edition of 1602, carefully done, in the now-venerable black letter, with only slight further deterioration at the hands of the compositor. The title page is new:

> The / Works / of our / Ancient, Learned, & Excellent /
> English Poet, / Jeffrey Chaucer. / As they have
> lately been Compar'd with the best Manuscripts, /
> and several things added, never before in Print . . . .

The claim to have consulted manuscripts is false, though it is an interesting sign of the times, and of the interest in antiquity, that it should have been made, while the "several things added" consist of spurious endings, of twelve and ten lines, respectively, to *The Cook's Tale* and *The Squire's Tale*, which are added at the end of the volume. An accompanying "Advertisement" says that the endings were found in a manuscript,[59] but too late to insert in the body of the text. Another "Advertisement," by "J. H.," at the beginning of the volume speaks inevitably of the many solicitations to reprint the works of "this Ancient Poet" that have been received and explains the absence of "any new Preface or Letters Commendatory" as being a choice based on the conviction that "his own Works are his best Encomium." A desperate search has been made, it is added, for the lost *Pilgrim's Tale*, but to no avail. Such is the new matter of 1687.

And so ends the story of Speght's contribution to the Chaucerian editorial tradition. His edition held sway for well over a hundred years, far longer than any other. It was the text read and owned by Milton, Junius, Pepys, Dryden, and Pope, and by a multitude of seventeenth- and eighteenth-century gentlemen with respectable tastes and sturdy bookshelves.[60] It retained its popularity among Chaucer readers long after the appearance of Urry's more "modern" edition in 1721 and achieved a notable posthumous existence in being used by Tyrwhitt as the base-copy for his great edition of *The Canterbury Tales* in 1775.[61] Such a distinction in posterity may not have been deserved, but it can hardly be begrudged to an editor so sensible of the merits of his author, so generous in his acknowledgment of the labor of others, and so modest in his claims for himself.

5. John Urry
(1666–1715)

WILLIAM L. ALDERSON*

ARLY IN February, 1721, Bernard Lintot proudly announced the imminent publication of *The Works of Geoffrey Chaucer, Compared with the Former Editions, and many valuable MSS . . . By John Urry, Student of Christ-Church, Oxon. Deceased.* The title page of the sumptuous folio that shortly appeared specified further that the volume contained a glossary "By a Student of the same College," the life of Chaucer "newly written," and a preface "giving an Account of this Edition." The work was conceived on a grand scale. Long in preparation, it had engaged, directly or indirectly, the interest of a number of scholars—several of them more than ordinarily competent antiquaries—and hopes for it ran high. Its publisher did not stint himself in providing it with a format appropriate to a major edition of an English classic, and he had confidently assured one of the collaborating editors that the planned printing of 1,250 copies would "go off,"[1] even though the subscription price (30 shillings for copies on fine demi, 50 shillings for those on Royal paper) must have placed the work beyond the means of many potential buyers. The edition was, furthermore, fortunate in its temporal context, for it was preceded and accompanied by a discernible quickening of interest in Chaucer and his works. A series of published modernizations, imitations, and varied celebrations of Chaucer created an atmosphere extremely favorable to a new edition of his poetry. The stage was set. Enter Chaucer, in new dress.

Despite happy auguries, the performance failed to please. Even before the actual appearance of the edition, Richard Rawlinson, editing John Aubrey's *Natural History and Antiquities of Surrey* (1719), had raised, by implication

*Excerpted by permission from William L. Alderson and Arnold C. Henderson, *Chaucer and Augustan Scholarship*, University of California Publications, English Studies, no. 35 (Berkeley: University of California Press, 1970).

at least, a question about Urry's textual changes in *The General Prologue* to *The Canterbury Tales*: he offered his readers parallel passages from the Urry text and from the Thynne edition of 1542, "there being much Differences in the Orthography." In 1723, John Dart, who had contributed the biography of Chaucer printed in Urry's edition, proclaimed that he was not "willing to buy it, when my old one, with my own written Notes, serv'd me as well."[2] By 1730 the scholarly dissatisfaction with Urry's work had even sifted down to the relatively popular level of the periodical press, for in July of that year a letter in the *Grub-Street Journal* (no. 26) compares a passage from Urry's *House of Fame* with Caxton's edition and makes Rawlinson's unstated doubt explicit with the query, "Who can make sense of the following passage . . . as it stands in Mr. URRY's edition?"[3] In 1734–35 Hearne, devoted though he was to the memory of his friend Urry, reluctantly observed that "Curious men begin to esteem the old editions more than the new one."[4] William Brome, as Urry's executor, had received one-third of the copies printed by Lintot, and a plaintive letter from him to a London friend indicates that, twelve years after the publication of the edition, his copies still "lie upon hand."[5] In 1736, Thomas Morell flatly characterized Urry's text as one "of no Authority" and "the worst that is extant,"[6] while in the Preface to his *Canterbury Tales* of 1737 (pp. xxiii–xxvi) he criticized Urry's views on meter and his erratic use of manuscript authority. Tyrwhitt pronounced Urry's text "by far the worst that was ever published,"[7] and later scholars have been almost unanimous in their contempt for it. In the Chiswick Chaucer (1822), for example, Singer speaks of it as an "edition of little value," for Skeat (*The Chaucer Canon*, 1900, p. 143) it is "the worst of the set" of printed editions, in E. Irving Carlyle's *DNB* article on Urry (1909) it is "probably the worst [edition] ever prepared," and Spurgeon echoes these judgments ("the worst ever issued").

Such triumphant obloquy should not, however, be allowed to obscure two historically significant facts about the postpublication history of Urry's Chaucer. First, the criticism to which it was subjected was almost entirely directed at its Chaucerian text. Other features of the edition—because of the anonymity of their contributors sometimes identified as Urry's by hasty readers—had a better reception. In a letter of 1722 the aging William Wotton announced his delight with the Glossary: "whoever writ it was a very able Man. He seems to me to understand Welsh; he quotes Welsh words every now and then, & always to the purpose."[8] Morell's use of the 1721 Glossary is apparent in the "Annotations" of his *Canterbury Tales*, and Tyrwhitt later acknowledged that his own glossary (1778) was "built upon his [the Urry glossarist's] foundations, and often with his materials."[9] Dart's life of Chaucer, too, influenced most of the later eighteenth-century biographical treatments of the poet. Morell, concluding that it was done "more fully and accurately" than the earlier accounts by Leland, Pits, and Speght, simply summarized Dart's information of his volume of 1737

(pp. xv–xx). Tyrwhitt also limited himself to "An Abstract of the Historical Passages of the Life of Chaucer" (Appendix to Preface, 1798 ed.,
1:xvii–xxv), remarking that he "coud add few *facts* to those, which have
already appeared in several lives" and did not care to repeat their "in-
ventions" (p. iii). Although he does not single out Dart's life for explicit
praise, his citations of the "Life of Ch. Urr." are sufficient proof of his
dependence on it for several of his "authentic evidences" of Chaucer's life.
Morell and Tyrwhitt abridge and abstract from Dart; other biographers of
the century show less restraint and produce elaborate composites of Dart,
Speght, Leland, and other obvious sources. . . .

Of the later history of Urry's Chaucer we must also observe that the
much-abused Chaucerian text itself was used widely, even by those who
were harshest in their criticism of its quality. Between 1721 and 1810, in
fact, Urry's remained the "standard" text for a large part of Chaucer's
poetry. Morell and Tyrwhitt attempted to deal only with *The Canterbury
Tales*, and while Tyrwhitt's text of the *Tales* became the generally accepted
one after 1775, for the remainder of the Chaucerian canon readers were
obliged to consult Urry. Paradoxically, such scholars as Morell and Warton
actually contributed to the continued life of Urry by making the Urry text
the basis for their citations of Chaucer's works other than *The Canterbury
Tales*. In John Bell's *Poets of Great Britain* (Edinburgh, 1782) the Tyrwhitt
text of the *Tales* is, not illogically, combined with the Urry text of the other
poems, and Robert Anderson's *British Poets* (Edinburgh, 1793) adopted the
same scheme.[10] Even in the nineteenth century Urry does not pass wholly
from the scene. Henry John Todd regarded the Urry text of *The Flour and the
Leaf* as worth collating in his *Illustrations of the Lives and Writings of Gower
and Chaucer* (1810), and as late as 1841 the headnote to the 1721 *Friar's Tale*
is approvingly quoted—presumably by Leigh Hunt, the modernizer—
from "the old commentator, Urry" in the *Poems of Geoffrey Chaucer, Modernized* (p. 195). (The attribution to Urry incidentally reveals the writer's
ignorance of Speght's edition; in this note Urry merely reproduces Speght's
"argument" to the tale.)

Both the virtues and the failings of the 1721 Chaucer are largely
explicable in terms of the prepublication history of the edition. Its story is a
chapter of accidents and misunderstandings—the tale of an editor who did
not realize the enormity of his task soon enough to delegate parts of it to
other scholars, of the flat defection of one of the later undertakers, and of a
radical lack of sympathy with Urry's guiding principles on the part of the
young men who finally saw the work through the press. No less than five
men contributed directly to the preparation of the volume which finally
emerged from Lintot's shop: John Urry, Thomas Ainsworth, John Dart,
Timothy Thomas, and William Thomas. If to this company we add the
names of Francis Atterbury, who was responsible for setting the whole
project in motion; of Thomas Hearne, George Hickes, and William Brome,

who advised or aided Urry in various ways; and of Anthony Hall, who at one point undertook to supply a glossary to the work, it is clear that the group "interested" in this edition of Chaucer lacked neither learning nor wit. Their association unfortunately was not that of true collaborators, however. . . . The labor of those who prepared the 1721 Chaucer was discontinuous, unorganized, and marked by basic differences of mind about matters of historical fact and even about the objectives of the edition. Except for the Thomas brothers, it is doubtful that any single member of the group wholly understood what any other was about, and the tone of the publication, set by Timothy Thomas's Preface, was not calculated to do more than mouth-honor to Urry and his concept of Chaucer's text. . . .

As an undergraduate at Christ Church in the eighties John Urry had been the contemporary of a number of men whose names have already figured in this account. Francis Atterbury was there at the same time, and it is to be presumed that their acquaintance dated from this period. . . . He matriculated at Christ Church on June 30, 1682, and proceeded B.A. in 1686. His strong Stuart sympathies are evident from the active part he took in the suppression of Monmouth's rebellion in 1685. A corporal in the company of foot raised from Christ Church and Jesus colleges, Urry retained a sentimental attachment both for the Jacobite cause and for his former comrades-in-arms, and according to Hearne, he "kept one of ye Halberds by him to his dying Day."[11] In 1688 he became a nonjuror. "For this reason," says Hearne, "tho' he had the Degree of A.M. yet he was not presented . . ." Henceforth he appears to have led the quiet life of an antiquary who, because of his politics, could not hope for academic preferment. He moves modestly in and out of Hearne's voluminous record of the scholarly world of early-eighteenth-century Oxford, "a stout, lusty Man" preoccupied with antiquarian documents and the owner of at least one old manuscript.[12] That his interest in Chaucer dates from a period before he received Atterbury's injunction is borne out both by Timothy Thomas's statement and by Hearne's diary, from which we learn that Urry had sometime before April 28, 1711, transcribed portions of Kinaston's manuscript commentary on *Troilus and Criseyde*.[13] However, he does not seem to have thought in terms of a new edition until Atterbury suggested it, and he undertook the labor with a show of humility rare among Augustan scholars, confessing that "he had not the least thought of publishing his private Diversions" (Preface, sig. i2r).

Atterbury's wisdom in selecting Urry has been questioned from 1721 down to Spurgeon's time. Damned with faint praise in the printed Preface to the edition, Urry is in one of Timothy Thomas's manuscript notes explicitly condemned as a man "not qualified for a work of this nature."[14] Thomas, however, did not know Urry, and his scorn for Urry's editorial methods embraces features which we should regard as good (the concept of Chaucer's metrical regularity, for example) as well as his questionable addition of words and syllables not found in the manuscripts. Men who knew Urry—contemporary scholars of the stature of Hearne and Hickes—respected his talents. . . .

Urry entered upon his task energetically. By December 5, 1711, he had written to Hickes for advice. He spent some time in the Bodleian with the Junius manuscripts, discovering perhaps the fallacy of Hickes's belief "that an Edition of Chaucer was there in great measure done to his Hands."[15] He set vigorously to work assembling manuscripts and early printed texts of his poet. He showed Hearne many of his finds, and Hearne's diary for the next few years is an eloquent witness to the number of Chaucerian texts which passed through Urry's hands. Through the good offices of Atterbury, Urry procured two manuscripts and a 1542 printed text from Harley's fine library. Hans Sloane provided two manuscripts and an imperfect Caxton. Bagford lent his Caxton, Thomas Rawlinson a manuscript, and other collections, private and semi-private, were laid under contribution. There is little doubt that the list of fourteen manuscripts which Timothy Thomas found among Urry's papers and printed in the 1721 Preface represents only a part of those which Urry actually consulted in the course of his study of the text.[16]

By the end of November, 1712, Urry's letter to Harley indicates that he has made distinct progress in his collation, even though it is slow work: "I transcribe every line, so that I, that am not a swift penman, find I have set myself a tedious task. I am advanced a great way in the Tales . . ."[17] There is later evidence that Urry had not, as he professed, prepared a "compleat" copy of his text by the time he applied for a license to print in July, 1714, but the basic labor of collation was probably substantially finished by that time. Moves preparatory to publication follow shortly thereafter. Lintot's memorandum book records the bookseller's agreement with Urry, dated December 17, 1714:

> To publish the Works of Chaucer. Himself [i.e., Urry] to have One Third; the college of Christ Church at Oxford One Third; and Bernard Lintot One Third (and he the said Lintot to pay for paper, print, copper-plates, and all incidental expences) of all the moneys arising by the Subscription for the said Book.[18]

(Urry's copyright was assigned to Lintot at this time.) On January 27 and again on January 29, 1715, the *Daily Courant* advertised Urry's Chaucer as a work for which subscriptions were being taken by Lintot and "most Booksellers in London and in the County." In these proposals the claims of the Urry license are echoed, and we learn further that each tale is to be illustrated with plates "from the best Gravers" and that "a new black letter, Accented, has been cast on purpose for this Work, for the Ease of the Reader."[19] The choice of a typeface for the edition brings us near the end of Urry's story. . . .

It was on March 19 that Hearne sadly reported, "Yesterday about 3 Clock in the Afternoon died of a Feaver my great and good Friend M.ʳ John Urry, Student of Christ Church." The Latin epitaph upon himself which was found in his pocket after his death was incomplete. The edition of Chaucer upon which he had labored for more than three years was also far from completion, despite the confidence with which plans had been going forward to publish the work. He had apparently determined on the readings which his text would contain. According to Thomas, he "had prepared a fair Copy for the Press, written partly in his own hand, and partly by Mr. [Thomas] *Ainsworth*, to the end of the *Frankelein's* Tale," and the remainder was left in a state of sufficient clarity so that Ainsworth, a Christ Church man, was supposedly able to carry on with the transcription. Aside from the text proper, however, Urry died with the apparatus for his edition still in his head. In a "short Sketch of a Preface" which he left behind, he spoke of "writing out Indexes" and "looking over a great many Dictionaries for words I could not find, as well as for words I could,"[20] but beyond a few notations ("of very little service to anybody except himself," observed Thomas) he had made no headway on the Glossary. The notes which were to accompany the text and, incidentally, demonstrate the influence of Greek or Latin poets on Chaucer, had not proceeded further than a single reference to Ausonius, and for the biography of Chaucer—if indeed Urry planned to write it himself—the materials he had assembled were limited to a few extracts from the records. He had not, furthermore, set down any description of his principles and procedures in working with the Chaucerian text, and while it appears that he meant to provide his text with a corpus of variant readings and some typographical indication of his conjectural emendations, neither scheme was carried through. All in all, the edition which he had hoped would be his scholarly monument was left in a parlous state.

Urry's death was followed by a period of confusion. It was at first presumed that he had died intestate, and the disposition of his books and papers—including a number of manuscripts which he had borrowed to prosecute his edition of Chaucer—thus presented legal problems. . . . Whatever the difficulties were, they must have been satisfactorily resolved by August 26, for on that date Lintot entered into a fresh agreement with the authorities of the college and with Brome, as Urry's executor. . . .

. . . On June 30, 1716, Lintot issued a new *Proposals* which advertised the work "very near compleated" by Urry as "now finish'd from his Papers by a Member of the same College." The *Proposals* also announced that the glossary would be done by Anthony Hall and that publication would be swift: "This Work will be put into the Press on *Michaelmas Day* next, and is intended to be published the *Lady Day* following." Lintot, at least, was carrying out his part of the agreement with good will.

The collegiate authorities, on their part, were unfortunate in their choice of Hall as glossarist, and they do not appear to have found anyone immediately who would assume the responsibility of seeing to the edition as a whole. Until October, 1717, in fact, it is impossible to determine who, if anyone, was actively at work on the project, and even after Dr. Smalridge assigned Timothy Thomas the task of preparing a glossary and taking general charge of the edition, progress was slow.[21]

. . . several men at different times made contributions of varying degrees of importance to the volume which finally appeared in 1721. . . .

. . . William Brome—the "learned" Brome of Philips' *Cider*—had been a close friend of the editor, and according to some rather late evidence, Urry "consulted him much in the progress of his work."[22] A man of leisurely antiquarian habits, Brome spent a good part of his life bringing together materials for a history of Herefordshire which was never written. After Urry's death, in concert with Dr. Terry, subdean of the college, Brome valiantly strove to deal with Urry's accumulation of books and manuscripts, and he appears to have found it an onerous chore. . . . Brome does not seem to have taken a direct or effective part in prosecuting Urry's Chaucer, and if he was privy to Urry's plans and procedures, he notably failed to communicate information about them to those who later took over the edition.

Another possible bond of continuity existed in the person of Thomas Ainsworth, to whom Urry had in the later stages of his work on the text turned over the task of making a clean copy for the printer. While Urry was alive, of course, Ainsworth could always apply to him when problems arose, and Ainsworth's status was scarcely more than that of editor's amanuensis. After Urry's death, however, his role was somewhat altered. Over four-fifths of the text which the edition was to contain had not been transcribed at that time, and Ainsworth was asked to continue the work which he had begun under Urry's direction. Ainsworth is very probably the anonymous "Member of the same College" who, according to the 1716 *Proposals*, "finish'd" the work from Urry's papers. But from what we know of Urry's method of proceeding, "finishing" the work involved no small expense of time and mind. Urry, like later eighteenth-century editors, appears to have carried out his collation by noting various manuscript readings in the margin of his own copies of earlier printed texts. A 1561 Stow is extant in which Urry's collation of that text with several manuscripts is identifiable.[23] From such records of variants Urry presumably selected the readings which satisfied him, perhaps transferring them along with his own emendations to a single printed copy (conceivably a 1602 Speght, since Speght's "arguments" and headnotes are frequently reproduced without change in the 1721 edition).[24] Whether Ainsworth transcribed from a single copy or whether he was obliged to shift, and even coordinate, exemplars as he passed from *The Canterbury Tales* into the other works we do not know,[25] but it is almost inevitable that he should, from time to time at least, have been called on to make judgments of an editorial kind. Not until very late in the edition, however, does Ainsworth actually emerge in his own person, and even then he does so reluctantly. In a headnote to the *Prologue* and *History of Beryn*, apocryphal works printed for the first time in this edition, Ainsworth points out that Urry had found them in only one manuscript, "so that if the sense and measure of the Verse are not so perfect here as in the other Tales, it must be attributed to the want of MSS. upon the authority of which all the other corrections are chiefly grounded" (p. 594). He identifies the metrical scheme, properly enough, with that of *Gamelyn*, and professes that he offers only "a faithful Transcript" of the works from the unique manuscript. That is to say, he has not carried Urry's special devices of spelling and accentuation into these pieces.

In addition to this transcription of the text, Ainsworth served the edition by conveying some of Urry's views about Chaucer's text to Timothy Thomas. Thomas makes clear in the Preface that his fragmentary information about Urry's ideas and methods is largely due to Ainsworth. Ainsworth's death in August, 1719, "soon after the whole Text of *Chaucer* was printed off," left the edition devoid of any sponsor who had detailed knowledge of how Urry had arrived at his text.

Before turning to the culminating activity of Timothy and William Thomas, we must deal with two other figures whose names have already been mentioned in connection with the Urry edition. In the 1716 *Proposals* the prominence given Anthony Hall (who was to compile a "Useful and Copious" Glossary) was undoubtedly calculated to add another recommendation to the edition. Widely known as an antiquarian, Hall, Fellow of Queen's College, had already edited Leland and contributed to an edition of Camden. Whether he made any real effort on the glossary we do not know. He did not, in any event, produce one. In Thomas's Preface, Hall's defection is treated with heavy irony: " . . . as we are deprived of the Benefit of his Labours in this Kind (for what reasons I am not at this time satisfied) I would not have his Reputation suffer by the imperfection of this Performance, and therefore am bound to acquit him of having any hand in compiling this *Glossary*." Not only did Hall fail to contribute, he served to delay the publication date by the several years required by the Thomas brothers to compile the Glossary which finally appeared in 1721.

The biography of Chaucer included in the 1721 edition was, as we have noted, the work of John Dart. Dart's own life is a good deal less well attested than that of the poet he studied. Of his origin and education we know nothing. . . . Dart does not appear in Foster's *Alumni Oxoniensis*, and our first reliable evidence of his association with the Christ Church Chaucer comes from Timothy Thomas's rather unflattering description of an anonymous "Gentleman who had made some Collections" toward a life of Chaucer being employed, after Urry's death, "to draw up the account of our Author's Life" (Preface, sig. i2v). The "Collections" which Dart had made may have been the result of an earlier request that he do the biography for the edition; our evidence is uncertain.[26] But if that was the case, it constitutes the only instance of Urry's voluntary resignation of any part of his planned work to other hands. . . .

Dart's relationship with the 1721 Chaucer was not a happy one. The Thomases did not approve of the biography which he submitted. William Thomas, in a note in his personal copy of the 1721 edition, remarked that it "was very uncorrectly drawn up," and required corrections and additions.[27] Dart testified, with some passion, that "upon the Queries mark'd, I submitted to such corrections as they thought proper," only to discover that in the printed work further cutting had omitted his evidence for asserting that Chaucer did not write *The Plowman's Tale.* "The Life," he added, "was in other Places alter'd, as concerning Mr. *Packer's* Estate at *Donington*, and some few other Places, which I cannot now remember. . . .This Usage, I think undeserv'd, having spar'd no Pains, and was at a very extraordinary Expense to collect Records, and write as particular and full a Life as possible, of a Name I ever reverenc'd . . . ."[28]

Timothy and William Thomas will complete the roll of contributors to the 1721 edition. In justice to them it must be admitted that the task of completing another man's work was not a grateful one, especially so since they were radically opposed to some of Urry's controlling ideas. Consciously or not, the brothers did much to assure that those who had preceded them in the work should have dubious fame. Timothy Thomas's Preface is a triumph of oblique criticism of Urry's aims and methods, and the notes and memoranda which they carefully preserved have played no little part in posterity's judgment of the scholarly reliability of the several contributors to the edition. Morell, knowing only the printed Preface, was convinced that Timothy Thomas "would have done it much better, had he never seen Mr. *Urry's* Design at all."[29] and after the Thomases' more outspoken criticism of Urry and Dart was given the dignity of print by Tyrwhitt, few men have felt it necessary to study the edition before condemning it out of hand.

Brothers though they were, both in blood and in antiquarian tastes, Timothy and William Thomas pursued very different careers. Timothy's is of the more usual kind. Born in Llandovery, he entered Christ Church in 1712 at the age of eighteen, received his B.A. in 1716, and proceeded M.A. in 1719. Evidently he remained at Oxford for some time thereafter. . . . Later he returned to Wales, becoming rector of Presteign, Radnorshire, in 1727, and it was there that he died in 1751.[30] . . .

William Thomas is much more difficult to trace and place than his brother. Even after meeting him twice, Hearne was still in doubt about his status. On November 26, 1717, he noted: "M.ʳ William Thomas, who belongs to the Earl of Oxford, is now in Town, . . . He never had any Academical Education. . . . Some say he is my Lord's Gentleman. . . . He pretends to Learning, and to be particularly nice in the British Language."[31] In later entries it becomes increasingly clear that "Lᵈ Oxford's

Man" carried out a variety of commissions for his employer, some of them of a personal nature requiring much tact . . ., others calling for a wide knowledge of books and manuscripts. Despite his lack of university training, Thomas seems to have been a scholar by temperament. . . .

These, then, were the men who collaborated in finishing Urry's Chaucer and seeing it through the press—the one representing the common Augustan combination of university scholar, cleric, and antiquary, the other that more unusual development, the antiquary and bibliographer who served one of the period's important private collections of rare books and manuscripts. Hearne gives no details of their progress on the edition, but his diary shows that William Thomas repeatedly shuttled between London and Oxford from 1717 to 1721 and that the brothers were in continuous contact with one another. Humphrey Wanley's record (October 14, 1720) that "Mr. William Thomas sent in 3 of the four MSS. of Chaucer borrowed lately by him . . ." suggests that the Thomases may still have been at work on the Glossary at that date.[32] Their obligation was, of course, discharged with the final publication of the edition four months later, but both brothers seem to have retained their interest in Chaucer long afterward. William is known to have borrowed Harley 1758 (Atterbury's gift) late in 1722, presumably to collate with a printed Urry, and years later we catch a glimpse of Timothy Thomas tendering a copy of the Urry edition to his friend Sneyd Davies.[33]

Recognizing that the 1721 Chaucer did not perfectly reflect the plans or desires of any of those who took part in its preparation, we have still to examine the volume which emerged from Lintot's press. It is true that a closely observant Augustan reader might have perceived a clash of contradictory judgments and points of view as he passed from Dart's biography to William Thomas's account of Chaucer's works and thence into Timothy Thomas's Preface and the Urry text proper—with frequent application, we must assume, to the Thomas Glossary. Some of the inconsistencies were minor: Dart's expressed doubt of the Chaucerian authorship of *The Plowman's Tale* and of *Jack Upland* (sig. CI), for example, was tacitly refuted by their inclusion in William Thomas's list of Chaucer's works (sig. f2), upon the authority of Leland and Foxe. Other jars, however, were more fundamental. In the biography it was maintained that "those nice discerning Persons" who regarded Chaucer's metrics as regular "would find it difficult, with all their straining and working, to spin out some of his Verses into a measure of ten Syllables" (sig. fl), and yet from the prefatory explanation of Urry's method it is obvious that Urry's overriding concern as editor was to restore Chaucer "to his feet again" (sig. i2v). Both in the Preface and in the glossary, furthermore, the Thomas brothers revealed that they had discovered many better, or fuller, readings in manuscripts which were either unknown to Urry or little used by him, and thus, by implication at least, they cast doubt on the reliability of the whole of Urry's text. But in spite of such discords the 1721 volume had a certain total effect, and it is of some interest to consider what it accomplished, as a whole, toward (1) the establishment of a canon and text, (2) the glossarial explanation of Chaucer's language, and (3) the documentation and interpretation of Chaucer's biography.

In canon the Urry Chaucer betrays a mixture of motives. The original editor professed, in the language of the royal license, to have "remarked many Pieces in [former editions] falsely ascribed to *Chaucer*," but there is no evidence that he actually intended to exclude such works from his edition, and indeed, in the volume which finally saw print, of all the non-Chaucerian matter which had accumulated in the vulgate editions between Thynne and Speght, only *The Siege of Thebes* is omitted. For the rest, although Chaucer's authorship of a number of items is flatly denied or seriously questioned in the headnotes, the life, the Preface, or other parts of the volume's apparatus, the edition, in its gross contents, partakes of the "miscellany" character of the earlier tradition.

Urry's own principal concern, reflected both in the 1714 license and in the 1721 title-page announcement of "Three Tales . . . never before Printed," seems to have been to add rather than to subtract matter, and he may well have been affected by Hearne's expressed conviction that from the contents of known manuscript collections "we might, in all likelyhood, make another intire Volume of *Chaucer* in *Folio*."[34]

As we have seen, Urry began his editorial work by collecting and comparing manuscripts, and though we may doubt that the list of manuscripts which was transmitted to Timothy Thomas represents all the texts which Urry knew and made use of,[35] it nevertheless remains our best direct evidence for the kinds of interest Urry took in his manuscript sources, and supplemented by Thomas's additions to Urry's numbered manuscripts, it stands as the earliest printed record of the location and contents of a series of Chaucerian manuscripts. Furnivall, Hammond, and Manly and Rickert have all taken an interest in identifying the manuscripts listed in the 1721 preface. Miss Hammond was able to equate nine of Urry's fourteen with presently known manuscripts, and Furnivall's inquiries elicited one further identification (Hammond, p. 130). Aided by the descriptions and collations made available in Manly and Rickert's *Text of the Canterbury Tales* (Chicago, 1940), we can now go further and identify all but one of Urry's list with certainty and offer a judicious guess even in this doubtful case. A brief survey of the 1721 list will serve both as an indication of the particular points of interest which the manuscripts had for Urry and Thomas and as a means of estimating, from the standpoint of recent study, the textual value of manuscripts with which these Augustans worked (the manuscripts are, in each case, identified by their present-day designations, followed by Manly and Rickert's sigils. The Roman numerals are Urry's).

[Following is a condensed account of the list of manuscripts used by Urry and Thomas.]

   I. Harley 1758 (Ha^2) . . . (MR, 1.206), "worthless as a text."
  II. Harley 1239 (Ha^1) . . . MR judge the text of CT "very bad" (1.190).
 III. Sloane 1685 (Sl^1). An early representative of group d.
  IV. Sloane 1686 (Sl^2). A member of group c.
   V. Egerton 2726 (En^1). Together with the Devonshire MS (Urry's XIV) making up an important subgroup (MR, I.135) Dd.
  VI. The only MS in the group described in the 1721 preface which cannot now be identified certainly, or probably, with extant MSS. . . . Harley 7335 and Christ Church CLII come closest to fulfilling the several requirements, though neither does so perfectly.
 VII. Royal 18C.2 (Ry^2). "Of no individual textual authority" (MR, 1.487).
VIII. Royal 17D.15 (Ry^1). A late, much edited text from many sources, but one whose exemplars represented "good tradition" (MR, 1.479).
  IX. Phillips 8136 (Ph^2). "Corrupt and much edited" (MR, 1.423).
   X. Egerton 2963 (En^2). A member of one of MR's constant group d, which also includes Urry's I, III, VII, and XII, and the Cholmondeley (now Delamere) MS used by Timothy Thomas.
  XI. Cambridge University Gg.4.27 (Gg). According to MR (1.176), "a MS of the highest importance," representing "the El tradition without the El editing."
 XII. Cambridge University Mm.2.5 (Mm). One of the constant group noticed above under X.
XIII. Northumberland (N1). As a text "very corrupt" (MR, 1.390).
 XIV. Devonshire (Ds). Textually related to and perhaps a copy of IV above.

Timothy Thomas ekes out Urry's list with seven other manuscripts (the order of listing is Thomas's):

  1. Delamere (Dl). A "badly contaminated" member (MR, 1.111) of a constant group referred to above under Urry X.
  2. Huntington Library HM 114 (formerly Phillipps 8252, . . . A TC MS belonging to Root's best group (Introduction, pp. lviii–lix).
  3. Another TC MS identified only as belonging to Harley.
  4. Harley 78.
  5. Arundel 140 (Ar). The text of Mel, its sole Chaucerian item, is "late, and, though much corrected, still corrupt" (MR, 1.53).
  6. Selden Arch. B.14 (Se).
  7. Harley 6641. . . .

Promising though the prefatory list of manuscripts is, the canon and text of the 1721 volume are still dependent in many ways on the earlier vulgate tradition of printed Chaucerian texts. Comparison with the 1687 Speght shows that while Urry operated very freely in revising and emending his texts, especially that of *The Canterbury Tales*, on the level of word and phrase, there are surprisingly few changes in the number and order of the works included, or even in the headnotes which, in 1602 and 1687, served to introduce each of the individual tales and a majority of the other works.

Though the items are not listed in the table of contents of either edition, Urry, like Speght, opens with four short apocryphal bits: *Eight godely*

Questions, To the Kinges most noble grace, Chaucer's Prophecie, and eight untitled lines beginning "It falleth for a gentelman." The reference to Ausonius which Timothy Thomas pointed out (Preface, sig. i2v) as the sole product of Urry's scheme to annotate his author makes its appearance here, in connection with the first item, and presumably Urry is also responsible for the note which reveals that the title *Chaucer's Prophecie,* here attached to the crude sestet for the first time in print, was from "a Book in the Ashmolean Museum."[36]

In both editions, the main pagination of the volume begins with *The Canterbury Tales.* Here Urry drops the whole of Speght's broadly introductory "Argument to the Prologues" and in his brief subtitle instead emphasizes the new concern for textual authority by specifying the "prologues" as drawn "from the MSS." Manuscript authority, however, does not seem to play a decisive role in determining the general contents of the new edition. As we noted earlier, *The Siege of Thebes* is omitted, and "Three Tales are added," but for the rest, the several blocks of *The Canterbury Tales, The Romaunt of the Rose, Troilus and Criseyde, The Legend of Good Women,* and the Minor Poems, both authentic and apocryphal, follow each other in the order in which they appeared in Speght. The single exception to this statement consists of a shift of *The Flour and the Leaf*—which stood between *Chaucer's Dream* (i.e., *The Isle of Ledies*) and *An ABC* in Speght (pp. 609–14)—to a place between *The House of Fame* and *The Testament of Love* in 1721 (pp. 473–78). The order of tales within *The Canterbury Tales* which Urry takes over from Speght, it should be noted, is not duplicated in any of the manuscripts in Urry's list.[37] The Urry text, further, does not reject any of the spurious or canceled links (e.g., the Host's Stanza, the *Pardoner's Tale–Shipman's Tale* link, the *Canon's Yeoman's Tale–Physician's Tale* link)[38] which regularly appear in the earlier vulgate texts, and even the refusal to admit the conclusions to *The Cook's Tale* and *The Squire's Tale* which had been first printed in the publisher's "Advertisement" at the end of the 1687 edition probably springs, in part at least, from the difficulty of reconciling one of the passages with the new material which Urry was adding. In sum, Urry's edition is conservative and cumulative in its general contents. It rejects scarcely any of the matter which had appeared in the vulgate editions of Chaucer. While manuscript authority is sometimes cited, such attention is occasional and casual rather than consistent and methodical. There is no evidence that the works included are continuously subjected to any clearly definable tests of authenticity.

In the matter of canon the importance of the Urry volume lies primarily in the additions which it introduces into the Chaucerian text and in its new or significantly altered headnotes to certain of the works. Neglecting for the moment the frequent but very limited additions of word or phrase which mark Urry's attempt to regularize Chaucer's metrics, we find the first introduction of new matter at the end of the incomplete *Cook's Tale*, where the editor remarks (p. 35):

In some of the MSS is the History of Gamelyn under the Title of the Cooke's Tale; but it is not the Cooke's Tale that Lidgate saw, for that was, as he says, of Ribaldrie, as the abovesaid Tale savours of, and which in the MSS is joined to his by these verses.

> But hereof, Siris, I woll pass as now,
> And of yong Gamèlyn I wol tell you. Q𝑦 the Cook.

The headnote to *Gamelyn,* which follows immediately, is certainly Urry's since Thomas refers the reader to "the Note before" the new tale for "Mr. Urry's Sentiments concerning it" (Preface, sig. k2). As the first extant example of Urry's own thinking about a particular problem of canon the note deserves quotation *in extenso*:

> So many of the MSS have this Tale, that I can hardly think it could be unknown to the former Editors of this Poet's Works. Nor can I think of a Reason why they neglected to publish it. Possibly they met only with those MSS that had not this Tale in them, and contented themselves with the Number of Tales they found in those MSS. If they had any of those MSS in which it is, I cannot give a Reason why they did not give it a Place amongst the rest, unless they doubted of its being genuine. But because I find it in so many MSS, I have no doubt of it, and therefore make it publick, and call it the Fifth Tale. In all the MSS it is called the Cooke's Tale, and therefore I call it so in like manner: But had I found it without an Inscription, and had been left to my Fancy to have bestow'd it on which of the Pilgrims I had pleas'd, I should certainly have adjudg'd it to the Squire's Yeoman; who tho as minutely describ'd by Chaucer, and characteriz'd in the third Place, yet I find no Tale of his in any of the MSS. And because I think there is not any one that would fit him so well as this, I have ventur'd to place his Picture before this Tale, tho' I leave the Cook in Possession of the Title. [P. 36]

In the light of the numerous later expressions of a similar view we may take a historical interest in the priority of Urry's "fancy" that the tale would be more appropriate to the Yeoman than to the Cook. The most striking feature of the statement, however, is the respect shown for manuscript authority. The references to "the MSS" or to "so many MSS" are vague, it is true. Actually *Gamelyn* is to be found in seven of the manuscripts in Urry's list, as well as in five Oxford manuscripts which he probably knew, in Rawlinson Poetry 149, and perhaps in his "Worsely MS," if it is identified as Christ Church 152. Though the headnote implies that other grounds may exist for determining the genuineness of a work, Urry clearly bases his acceptance of *Gamelyn* on the frequency with which it occurs in manuscripts of *The Canterbury Tales*.[39]

Other additions in the *Tales,* whether in text or in comment, are less substantial. At the end of *The Squire's Tale,* Urry emphasizes the finality of Speght's remark that "there can no more be found of this TALE, which hath been sought for in diverse places" by adding "say all the Printed Books that I have seen, and also MSS" (p. 64). Two new seven-line stanzas, spurious in the eyes of more recent editors, are introduced at the end of *The Clerk's Tale* as a link between the Host's Stanza and *The Friar's Tale*. The "Earl of Oxford's MS" is in this instance cited as authority.[40] Another particular manuscript, one which we have identified as Thomas I, is named as the source of a spurious quatrain added to the *Sir Thopas–Melibee Link* (p. 146); and in a headnote to *The Plowman's Prologue* (p. 178) Urry (or Thomas, for at this point it may well be the younger man) again alludes to manuscripts, this time to explain why a possibly genuine work should have no manuscript versions:

> *This and the Tale is in none of the MSS that I have seen, nor in any of the first Printed Books*; Caxton *and* Pynsent, *I presume, durst not publish it: The former printed his Poet's Works in* Westminster-Abbey, *and both before the Abolition of Popery; and the MSS being before that, I fancy the Scriveners were prohibited transcribing it, and injoyn'd to subscribe an Instrument at the end of the Canterbury Tales, call'd his Retraction. So that if this Tale had not been carefully collected and preserv'd in Master* Stowe's *Library, as the Editor of* Islip's 1602 *Book says he has seen it, in a hand of near to* Chaucer's *time for Antiquity, in all likelyhood it had been lost.*

In due course the *Retraction* makes its appearance (p. 214). Missing from all printed texts of Chaucer from Thynne (1532) through Speght, it had been an object of interest to Hearne in 1709,[41] and Urry appears to have taken particular pains to specify its presence in the manuscripts of his list. Just what the older editor thought of it cannot be determined, for the 1721 text is the work of Timothy Thomas, whose introductory note only points out that his textual basis is the Cholmondeley manuscript (Thomas I) "with some amendments out of other MSS where the sense required it." The headnote to *The Plowman's Tale*, whether it be the work of Urry or of Thomas, echoes Hearne's view that this revocation is a monkish forgery and would undoubtedly have led an Augustan reader to conclude that it was not authentically Chaucerian.

In the remainder of the works included in the volume major changes, whether in text or in headnotes, are even less frequent. Urry's devices for regularizing Chaucer's prosody—particularly his respelling of *-ed* and *-en* endings—are continued, but the texts and the introductory comments do not reveal the solicitude for manuscript authority which is earlier apparent in *The Canterbury Tales*. As noted previously in connection with Ainsworth's contribution to the edition, the *Prologue*, "the merry adventure of the Pardonere and Tapstere at the Inn at Canterbury," and the *Merchant's Second Tale (The History of Beryn)*, when finally introduced (pp. 594–626), are frankly offered as transcripts from "the MS. borrowed from the honourable Lady Thinn's" (i.e., Urry XIII). This instance of outright abandonment of Urry's general critical scheme, combined with Thomas's handling of the *Retraction* and his prefatory recommendation that the *Jack Upland* text of Harley 6641 (Thomas's 7 above) be reprinted as it stands might suggest that the 1721 editors at least adumbrate the notion of a "diplomatic" edition of a Chaucerian text. The example, however, seems to have been wholly lost upon the later eighteenth century, and when the Chaucer Society finally reasserts and demonstrates the usefulness of literal reproductions of important Chaucerian manuscripts, the context and issues of Chaucerian textual scholarship have so altered that the Urry edition's precedent, limited in practice and unformulated in principle, is not recognized.

That a number of the shorter poems included in the Speght editions were designated, in title or headnote, as the products of writers other than Chaucer we have already observed. The Urry edition scrupulously follows Speght in all of these non-Chaucerian attributions,[42] and in two instances new evidence of the apocryphal character of particular works. In the headnote to *The Testament of Cressida* (p. 333) the authorship of the piece is, for the first time in printed editions of Chaucer's works, assigned to a later poet:

> The Author . . . I have been informed by Sir *James Eriskin*, late Earl of *Kelly*, and diverse aged Scholars of the Scottish Nation, was one Mr. *Robert Henderson*, chief Schoolmaster of *Dumferlin*, a little time before *Chaucer* was first printed, and dedicated to King *Henry* VIII, by Mr. *Thynne*, which was near the end of his Reign.

Earlier expressions of a conviction that the poem was not genuinely Chaucerian had been confined to manuscript. Francis Thynne's *Animadversions* (p. 69) had singled it out as one of the "adulterat" pieces which should be distinguished from "Chaucers proper woorkes," while Sir Francis Kynaston, in the manuscript notes to his Latin translation of *Troilus and Criseyde*, apparently presented almost verbatim the information contained in the Urry headnote.[43] The practical force of Urry's published note was effectively to remove the poem from the Chaucer canon, and it is not treated or alluded to as Chaucer's work by later Augustans.

In introducing the *Letter of Cupid*, furthermore, the 1721 headnote goes beyond any previous edition through its reference to internal evidence that the piece is not Chaucerian. Speght had already pointed out that the epistle was "made by *Thomas Occleve*, . . . *Chaucers* Scholar" (p. 552). To this ascription the Augustan editor makes a significant addition: "the Author telling us at the Conclusion it was made *Anno Dom.* 1402. it can't be *Chaucer's*, who dy'd *A.D.* 1400" (p. 534).[44]

The evidence of the effect of the 1721 edition on the Chaucer canon which has been presented thus far has been drawn largely from the text proper or from notes and headings closely connected with that text. Here, in part at least, the attitude of the original editor, John Urry, is represented or reflected. Other evidence as to canon is more clearly the product of later contributors to the edition. Dart's "Life of Chaucer" tacitly assumes the authenticity of such works as *The Testament of Love* and *The Court of Love* by its extensive use of the autobiographical references contained in these poems.

In his treatment of Chaucer's relationships with other poets and "men of learning" Dart refers to "Occleve" as author of the *Letter of Cupid*, citing the 1402 date as evidence that its ascription to Chaucer is a "mistake" (sig. eI^r), and he incidentally clarifies the relationship between Lydgate's *Siege of Thebes* and Chaucer's *Canterbury Tales*. Dart expressly denies the Chaucerian authorship of *The Plowman's Tale* and *Jack Upland* (fol. cIr),[45] but as we have previously noted, these items are still included in the "account of his Works, in the order wherein they were written" with which this life concludes. This chronological list, attributed to William Thomas, goes a good deal further than Speght's very brief and unorganized remarks on canon in the earlier edition's biography of the poet. Here all the major works, together with a number of the shorter lyrics, are surveyed. Chaucer's own references to his works in the *Retraction* and in *LGW*, and Lydgate's comments in the Prologue to *The Fall of Princes* are repeatedly cited as evidence of authenticity, but the lack of such evidence does not lead the compiler to doubt Chaucerian ascriptions in most instances. For *The Testament of Creseide*, the reader is referred to the note prefixed to that poem, and certain "ballads" are "justly suspected not to have been written by him; as that beginning, *O mossie Quince*, &c. and that beginning *I have a Ladie*, &c. which must needs be written long after his time: for the Marriage of Queen *Jane* with King *Henry* IV. which is therin mentioned, did not happen till after *Chaucer's* Death" (fol. f2r). In Timothy Thomas's glossary only one entry specifically raises a question about canon. There, under *Crede*, evidence of relationship between *Piers Plowman's Crede* and *The Plowman's Tale* is briefly presented, but the glossarist declines to draw a conclusion as to authorship.

If the view of Chaucerian canon reflected in the Urry edition is, on the whole, a conservative one, that edition's handling of text on the level of word, phrase, and line represents a radical departure from the procedures of previous editors. As Thomas pointed out in his Preface, Urry's "chief business was to make the Text more correct and compleat than before" (fol. i2^v). In a letter to Harley late in 1712 Urry already indicates his principal aim and the basic assumption upon which his text of Chaucer will be erected:

> I am advanced a great way in the Tales, and have taken as great care of the versification as I can, being persuaded Chaucer made them exact metre, but the transcribers have much injured them. . . . So that if I, by the help of MSS. and several printed editions can restore him to his feet again, I shall have done, though no great matter, as much as I am able to do, and that in a good measure I think I shall do (Spurgeon, 1.325).

In the printed *Proposals* of 1716, a "restored and perfected" text is emphasized, while the final and fullest statement of the methods which Urry employed in "correcting" his author makes its appearance in the Thomas Preface.

Although Thomas sees Urry's textual changes as falling into two large classes—devices to augment and devices to diminish the number of syllables in a line—Urry's procedures may, for our purposes, be conveniently considered under four heads, two of which involve no more than the use of diacritical marks or spelling devices to indicate pronunciation.

1. Convinced that Chaucer was metrically regular, Urry has resort to a grave accent to distinguish those medial or final -*e*'s which should be pronounced in a Chaucerian line. Of the most important instances of this Thomas remarks:

> Whether the assistance of this Final *è* be not here too frequently, and sometimes unnecessarily, called in, is not my business at present to enquire into: But it seems beyond contradiction that it was anciently pronounced; and I have seen a Note of Mr. *Urry*'s, wherein he affirms that in some parts of *England* it is still used, and instances in the words *pipè, buttonè, don't finè*, &c. wherein the Final *è* is pronounced in *Dorsetshire* at this day.

2. To distinguish those instances of -*ed*, -*es*, -*est*, and -*eth* endings which were to be given full syllabic value, Urry arbitrarily respells them -*id*, -*is*, -*ist*, and -*ith* when they are to be so pronounced, leaving them unaltered otherwise. (Although the consistent respelling, as opposed to the *addition*, in *any* person of -*en* [-*in*] as a verb ending is not distinguished in the Preface, it too should possibly fall under this heading.)

3. In filling out lines which might otherwise appear to be metrically deficient, Urry resorts to the addition of entire prefixes and suffixes which he seems to have regarded as free counters in his metrical game. Thomas defines these "Initial Syllables" as consisting "chiefly" of *a, i*, and *y* and notes that the "discreet use" of -*en* (-*in*) as an ending of verbs, nouns, and adverbs was another of Urry's arts.

4. Last of all, Urry adds or omits whole words when none of his other devices will serve his metrical purpose. Of the omissions the Preface takes no account, but Thomas is obviously critical of Urry's freedom in emending his text by arbitrary additions of words.

> Mr. Urry had observed particularly, that the word *which* was sometimes written *whiche*, and very frequently followed by *that*, and that without the one or the other, or sometimes both, the Verse was lame, but that with one or both it would have its just number of Feet; and therefore he added them accordingly as he found it requisite. And in short I find it acknowledged by him, "That whenever he could by no other way help a Verse to a Foot, which he was perswaded it had when it came from the Maker's hands, but lost by the Ignorance of Transcribers, or Negligence of Printers, he made no scruple to supply it with some Word or Syllable that serv'd for an Expletive": But I find at the same time that he had once a design of enclosing such words in hooks thus [ ] to distinguish them from what he found justified by the authority of MSS. but how it came to pass that so just, useful and necessary a Design was not executed, I cannot satisfy the curious Reader (fol. kI[r]).[46]

The opening lines of the 1721 text will serve to illustrate Urry's textual procedures:

> When that Aprilis with his Shouris sote,
> The drought of March had percid to the rote,
> And bathid every veyn in such licour,
> Of which vertue engendrid is the flour.
> When Zephyrus eke, with his swetè breth   5
> Enspirid hath, in every holt and heth
> The tender croppis; and that the yong Sunn
> Hath in the Ramm his halvè cours yrunn:
> And smalè foulis makin melodye,
> That slepin allè night with opin eye,   10
> (So prickith them nature in ther corage)
> Then longin folk to go on pilgrimage:
> And Palmers for to sekin strangè strondes,
> To servin Hallowes couth in sondry londes:
> And specially fro every shir'is end   15
> Of England, to Canterbury they wend,
> The holy blisfull Martyr for to seke,
> That them hath holpin, whan that they were seke.
>   Befell that in that seson on a day
> In Southwerk at the Tabberd as I lay;   20
> Redy to wendin on my Pilgrimage
> To Canterbury, with devote corage,
> At night wer come into that Hostery[47]
> Wele nine and twenty in a cumpany
> Of sundrie folk, by aventure yfall   25
> In felaship; and Pilgrimes wer they all;
> That toward Canterbury wouldin ride.
>   The Chambers and the Stablis werin wide,
> And well we werin esid at the best:
> And shortly whan the Sunnè was to rest,   30
> So had I spokin with them everychone,
> That I was of ther felaship anone;
> And madè forward erli for to rise,
> To take our weye, ther as I did devise.

The passage already indicates that Urry's concept of metrical regularity was essentially a matter of syllable count. Every line in the passage shows ten syllables, though in several instances (e.g., in lines 7, 15, and 16) the pattern of rhetorical accent which results is tortured and unnatural. Unlike Thomas, we are struck by Urry's relatively infrequent use of the sounded final -*e*. He seems never to have considered that it might exist at the line end, and in consequence Chaucer's verse is made to appear overpoweringly masculine in the final foot. This particular oversight, we should note, persists among later eighteenth-century editors. Morell, for example, argues (Preface, p. xxvii) that the final -*e* is "never used"—i.e., pro-

nounced—in a final position in the Chaucerian line, and even Tyrwhitt
seems to have been initially disposed to discount the final -*e* at a line end. In
concluding his analysis of the first eighteen lines of *The General Prologue*, he
confesses, "I have hitherto considered these verses as consisting of *ten*
syllables only; but it is impossible not to observe that . . . all of them, except
the 3d and 4th, consist really of *eleven* syllables" (1798 ed., 1.bb).

In this passage Urry's diacritical marking of sounded final -*e*'s and his
methodical respelling of syllabic -*en*, -*ed*, -*es*, and -*eth* endings make obvious
contributions to the syllabic regularity which he has imposed upon the text.
His other editorial changes can perhaps best be estimated by comparing this
text with the corresponding passage in the Speght of 1687 and considering
the degree to which the manuscripts available to him might justify the
readings which he adopts. First we must note that the *Aprilis* of line 1, like
them and *ther* throughout (lines 11, 18, 31, 32), is an arbitrary change
wholly lacking in manuscript authority. The sole virtue of *Aprilis* lies in its
service to the decasyllabic pattern, but the form is not Chaucerian. In the
1721 Glossary entry under *Averel*, Timothy Thomas points out:

> I should chuse to read *Averel* or *Apparaile* (as *MS. Sp.* hath it for *Aprilis, Tr. L.*
> 1. 156.) in the first Verse of the Prologues; thus, *Whanne Averal*, or
>
> *Whanne Apparaile had with his shouris sote*
> *The drought of March ypercid to the rote.*

(It is disconcerting to observe that in the very process of appealing to
manuscript for the correction of one of Urry's forms the glossarist introduces
two other wholly unjustifiable changes into the text.) The non-Chaucerian
forms *them* and *ther* spring, clearly, from Urry's lack of understanding of ME
pronominal inflection.

Urry's other innovations in the course of thirty-four lines are, however,
much more respectable. His *enspirid* for *espired* (line 6), the much improved
order of *his halvè cours* (line 8), the addition of *for* (line 13) and *that* (line 18),
the superior *Befell that* (line 19), *on* for *in* (line 21), *At* and *wer* (line 23), the
reading *well we werin* (line 29), *to* for *at* (line 30), and even *did* for *you* (line
34) all could be supported by manuscripts known to the editor. True, only a
single manuscript offers evidence for *did* (line 34) or *wer* (line 23), and we
may suspect that the added *that* of line 18, like the elaboration of syllabic -*en*
(-*in*) in *servin* (line 14), *wendin* (line 21), *wouldin* (line 27), might as easily be
the result of free emendation as of rigorous manuscript collation. But a
surprising number of Urry's changes represent real improvements of the
Speght text, improvements, furthermore, for which manuscript authority
could be cited. Even the reading *slepin allè night* (line 10) makes the best of
language in which the majority of the manuscripts available to him agreed
with Speght's version, while the form *Hostery* of line 23, though corrected to
Hostelry by the Thomases in the "Errata" on the last leaf of the volume, may
conceivably represent Urry's real intention since it exists in at least three of
Urry's manuscripts.

The choice of the opening of *The General Prologue* for our test of Urry's editorial method may not be entirely fair to his detractors. Though Urry's ignorance of Chaucerian pronominal forms is evident in it, it does not reveal the full extent of Urry's misinformation about Middle English morphology. Lounsbury, for example, was especially irritated by Urry's use of an -*en* (-*in*) ending in singular forms of the verb, though he could produce only three examples from *The General Prologue*.[48] Urry, furthermore, to a degree not evident in our test passage, adds words—typically *that* or *tho*—when there is no possibility of appeal to manuscript authority.

Any final judgment of Urry's handling of the Chaucerian text and of the effect of the 1721 text upon Augustan readers and later editors must take into account both Urry's general assumption about Chaucer's metrical regularity and the particular devices by which such regularity is, by and large, achieved throughout the text. We should recall, too, that there was little in either earlier printed editions of Chaucer or in . . . seventeenth-century antiquarian works which would have served Urry's textual purposes very directly. Only the Douglas of 1710 offers an earlier counterpart for Urry's assumptions and procedures, and here, as we have seen some of the prefatory contentions—e.g., that verb endings were "promiscuously" used in earlier English and that "words and syllables" had been omitted by manuscript copyists—were mistaken or potentially misleading.

To Urry's general view of Chaucer's metrics and to several of his particular textual devices even Lounsbury, harshly unsympathetic though he is to printed editions earlier than Tyrwhitt's, had no objection: "Every student of Chaucer will see at a glance that Urry had hit upon some of the most approved modern methods of regulating the metre and rectifying the text of the poet."[49] The consistency and ingenuity with which Urry carries out his regulation of the metrical pattern is, indisputably, the salient characteristic of his text. Even Timothy Thomas's glossary adds weight to the edition's testimony for metrical regularity. While the glossarist is critical of Urry's textual procedures and does not wholly agree with the older man's view of Chaucerian verse, he can offer a variant manuscript reading with a recommendation (s.v. Gest) that "the Sense and Numbers are easier in MS. Sp." Under *Misse-metre* his entry expands into a short essay on Chaucerian versification in which, after citing *HF* 1098, as evidence that Chaucer sometimes consciously wrote lines which were one syllable short, he comments:

> It seems plain from this Passage, as well as his words to *Adam Scrivenere* at the end of the Book, and his care about Pointing, *RR*. 2157, 2161. that he was not so loose in his Metre, as some may imagine; for by collating any part of his works with MSS. or old Editions, it will appear, that Verses, which in one Copy or Edition are defective, may out of others be made compleat; and that very often without the use of *i* or *y* prefixt to Verbs, the distinct pronunciation of the final *in* or *é*, or useless Expletives.[50]

Despite the doubts expressed in Dart's life, it would be almost impossible for an Augustan reader to emerge from the Urry volume with any other conclusion than that Chaucer's verse was recognizably regular in its syllabic pattern. Argument about Chaucer's metrics will continue, certainly. One late Augustan editor will, in a moment of exasperation, rashly offer to defend either Dryden's or Urry's position. But with the Urry edition the orientation of the argument has been forever altered, and the issues which will be of the most serious concern hereafter involve the nature and placement of accent and the degree to which, within a recognizable metrical system, Chaucer's verse admits hypermetrical or catalectic lines.[51]

As for Urry's particular devices to achieve metrical regularity, the great Tyrwhitt himself was to acknowledge that Urry had anticipated him in recognizing both the syllabic value of the final -e and the pronunciation of -es and -ed endings in Chaucer's verse. (These instances, it should be observed, constitute two of the three categories under which Tyrwhitt disposes of apparent irregularities in Chaucer's metrics.) Urry's use of a diacritical mark to distinguish pronounced final -e's is not in itself objectionable, though Tyrwhitt complained that it might lead an "ignorant reader" to put stress on a syllable which was "always to be pronounced with an obscure evanescent sound" (1798 ed., 1.57n). The respelling of syllabic -ed, -es, -en, -est, and -eth endings is perhaps less defensible, for even where distinction can be maintained—certainly not the case with -est or -eth, and rarely so with -en—the device has the unfortunate effect of giving Chaucer's language a Northern character which is conspicuously absent from any manuscript known to Urry. The most serious objection to Urry's procedures, both in his own time and subsequently, is directed at the freedom with which he emends the text by adding syllabic affixes or whole words. In justice to Urry we must recall that the process of tacit, and probably unconscious, modernization of spelling and forms which marks the succession of vulgate printings of Chaucer had, in fact, frequently obscured entire prefixes and inflectional endings and, further, that Urry's addition of short words to fill out metrically deficient lines is a practice which was employed by fifteenth-century scribes as well as by editors much more recent, and reputable, than Urry.[52] Tyrwhitt, for example, confesses that he has supplied both syllables (2.410, 421) and words (2.406, 422, 423) "for the sake of the verse." But, as we have noted, Urry's plan to bracket his emendations and provide a corpus of variant readings was not carried out. Only the intial poem (*Eight godely Questions*, fol. nI^v) employs brackets to distinguish Urry's changes, and it is the absence of a clarifying textual apparatus which constitutes the greatest weakness of the 1721 edition. In a 1734 letter to Richard Rawlinson, Hearne lamented the edition's lack of "various lections, which would have been of great satisfaction to critical men" and professed his belief that "Mr. Urry would (what I used often to tell him to do) have accounted for the alterations with a particular nicety, had he lived to have printed the book himself."[53]

The edition as it appeared, however, did not account for Urry's alterations, with the result that a future editor must face almost as baffling a problem in determining the manuscript authority behind a reading in Urry's text as he would in accounting for a textual variant in Speght, Stow, or Thynne . . . .

6. Thomas Tyrwhitt (1730–1786)

B. A. WINDEATT

THOMAS TYRWHITT was born on March 27, 1730, the oldest son of Robert Tyrwhitt, rector of Saint James's, Westminster, and later archdeacon of London and canon of Windsor. His maternal grandfather was Edmund Gibson (1669–1748), bishop of London. Educated at Eton and Queen's College, Oxford, Tyrwhitt was elected a fellow of Merton College in 1755, in which year he was also called to the bar at the Middle Temple, but did not practice ("his health was visibly unequal to the fatigues of the profession," obituary, *Gentleman's Magazine* 1(1787):219). He combined the office of deputy secretary at war with his fellowship until his appointment in 1762 as clerk of the House of Commons, and his obituary speculated on his achievements "if the too constant fatigues and late hours of that office had not proved too much for his constitution" (ibid.). In 1768 "he retired to his beloved books, and the remainder of his life was devoted entirely to literary pursuits" (ibid.). Indeed, as another obituary commented, he "was naturally of a calm and contemplative disposition. . . . Even when he sustained a public character, his vacant hours were appropriated to the closest study of the dead and living languages" (*Gentleman's Magazine* 2(1786):718). Moreover, "besides a knowledge of almost every European tongue, Mr. Tyrwhitt was deeply conversant with the learning of Greece and Rome" (ibid., p. 717). He was elected a fellow of the Royal Society in 1771 and a trustee of the British Museum in 1784. He died on August 15, 1786, and was buried in his family's vault in Saint George's Chapel, Windsor.

By the time of his death Tyrwhitt was esteemed as a scholar in a number of fields, as the obituaries make clear: "The profundity and acuteness of his remarks on Euripides, Babrius, Chaucer, Shakspeare and the Pseudo-Rowley, bear sufficient witness to the diligence of his researches and the

117

force of his understanding" (ibid., p. 718). Apart from a stream of publications on classical subjects, Tyrwhitt made contributions to Shakespeare studies and in his edition of the Rowley poems exposed Chatterton's forgeries, as well as producing his edition of *The Canterbury Tales* in four volumes in 1775, with a fifth volume containing a Glossary in 1778.[1] This range of scholarly endeavor illustrates the breadth of experience that Tyrwhitt brought to the task of editing Chaucer. Apart from the learning he could command in the general annotation of the poems, Tyrwhitt also combined the textual training of a classical scholar with that exceptional knowledge of Middle English that he brought to bear on the Rowley controversy.

Tyrwhitt deserves to be considered the founder of modern Chaucer editing, and his contribution is described below in the following sections: "Editorial Principles," "Sources," "Emendation: Editorial Practices," "Commentary," and "Achievements."

Editorial Principles

"The first object of this publication was to give the text of *The Canterbury Tales* as correct as the Mss. within the reach of the Editor would enable him to make it." With these words Tyrwhitt opens the Preface to his edition, and they fairly describe the principle which governs his practice as an editor of *The Canterbury Tales*. In forming his text, Tyrwhitt consults a certain body of manuscripts available to him, and from these he is concerned to select what he feels is the best reading in any crux. Tyrwhitt's editing—as his notes bear witness—is characterized by great respect for the manuscripts as the best available evidence. Accordingly, he goes on in his Preface: "The Editor therefore has proceeded as if his author had never been published before. He has formed the text throughout from the Mss. and has paid little regard to the readings of any edition, except the two by Caxton, each of which may now be considered as a Manuscript."

In this way Tyrwhitt's editorial principles and practices mark a new departure in Chaucer editing. The Urry edition had consulted manuscripts, but with a very cavalier attitude toward their authority. The partial Morell edition is much closer to Tyrwhitt's in its governing principles, and Tyrwhitt's commendation of Morell's work reflects his own ideas in editing: "[Morell] appears to have set out upon the only rational plan of publishing Chaucer, by collating the best Mss. and selecting from them the genuine readings; and accordingly his edition, as far as it goes, is infinitely preferable to any of those which preceded it" (1.xxi). By extension Tyrwhitt's attitude to those earlier editions is determined by their use of the manuscripts. To Caxton Tyrwhitt is generous: despite his inaccuracies he has the honor of being first, and "it is still more to the honour of Caxton, that when he was informed of the imperfections of his edition, he very readily undertook a second" (p. vi). But for the other early editions Tyrwhitt has censures founded on their failure to respect the manuscripts. Of Thynne's edition he remarks: "With respect to the Canterbury Tales . . .they received no advantage from the edition of 1532. Its material variations from Caxton's *second* edition are all, I think, for the worse" (p. xvii). Speght's edition he feels draws heavily on Thynne's and ignores the improvements in Caxton's second edition, "nor have I observed any such verbal varieties as would induce one to believe that he had consulted any good Ms." (p. xix). As for Urry: "The strange licence, in which Mr. Urry appears to have indulged himself, of lengthening and shortening Chaucer's words according to his own fancy, and of even adding words of his own, without giving his readers the least notice, has made the text of Chaucer in his Edition by far the worst that was ever published" (p. xx), and even more damningly in the "Advertisement" to the glossary volume: "Mr. Urry's edition should never be opened by any one for the purpose of reading Chaucer."

Tyrwhitt's censures of Urry's practice reveal what he holds to be the editor's proper procedure: all editorial contribution to the text should be signaled to the reader. Tyrwhitt "does not recollect to have deviated from the Mss. (except, perhaps, by adding the final *n* to a very few words) in any one instance, of which the reader is not advertised in the notes" (1.v). In his own editorial comments Tyrwhitt characteristically casts himself as working with the manuscripts rather than imposing himself upon them. His Preface states that his list of errata is owing "partly to his having imprudently adopted some less authorized readings, and even conjectures, instead of the readings of the best Mss." (p. v).

Such scholarly responsibility, and relative deference to the medieval documents themselves, makes Tyrwhitt the founder of modern traditions of Chaucer editing, for his attitude to his manuscripts makes their evidence naturally and rationally seem the best means of access to Chaucer's text (e.g., "As this line is not only in all the best Mss. but also in [Caxton's second edition] it seems very extraordinary that the later Editions should have exchanged it for the following"; 4:285). This is not to suggest that Tyrwhitt is an uncritical reader of the manuscripts, for he has a clear eye for their range of authority: he gives in his notes a bungled scribal conclusion to *The Summoner's Tale*, adding, "I only mention this to shew what liberties some Copyists have taken with our author" (p. 277). Yet Tyrwhitt's notes also reflect a recurrent scholarly modesty in the face of the manuscript evidence, as in the note: "O stronge lady store]   As all the best Mss. support this reading, I have not departed from it, for fear *store* should have some signification that I am not aware of " (p. 289). In another place he observes the weight of manuscript authority for a variant: "After this verse, the two following are found in so many Mss. that perhaps they ought to have been inserted in the text" (p. 237). Similarly, Tyrwhitt notes of certain lines in the prologue to *The Second Nun's Tale*: "I should have been glad to have met with any authority for leaving out this parenthesis of fourteen lines, which interrupts the narration so aukwardly, and to so little purpose" (3.296). But failing any such manuscript authority, then Tyrwhitt allows the extant manuscripts their authority over his own critical dislike for the passage. Again, Tyrwhitt quotes one of Urry's emendations, commenting "which I should have preferred to the common reading, if I had found it in any copy of better authority" (3.300). In short, Tyrwhitt's editing is formed on a critical yet sympathetic assessment of the nature of the manuscript evidence. This is nowhere seen more clearly in operation than in Tyrwhitt's note to the *Retractions*: "what follows being found, with some small variations, in all complete Mss. (I believe) of the Canterbury Tales, and in both Caxton's Editions, which were undoubtedly printed from Mss., there was no pretence to leave it out in this Edition, however difficult it may be to give any satisfactory account of it" (3.308).

But Tyrwhitt's concern for manuscript evidence (beyond the elimination of observable corruption) does rest on an attempt to understand the manuscript evidence for the original nature of Chaucer's language, and for the meter and versification that govern his use of this language:

> In order to make the proper use of these Mss., to unravel the confusions of their orthography, and to judge between a great number of various readings, it was necessary to enquire into the state of our language and versification at the time when Chaucer wrote, and also, as much as was possible, into the peculiarities of his style and manner of composition. [Preface 1.i]

Tyrwhitt's inclusion in his edition of the substantial "Essay on the Language and Versification of Chaucer" is accordingly very much part of his work as an editor, for in the "Essay" Tyrwhitt establishes the background to those metrical principles on which he edits.

It is with his characteristic combination of wide and scholarly reading in the period with a reasoning, commonsensical approach that Tyrwhitt here sets Chaucer in his context, disposing of the earlier exaggerated and unhistorical praise or blame of Chaucer in his use of English and Romance vocabulary and of his role in the use of rhyme in England: "The Metrical part of our Poetry was capable of more improvement, by the polishing of the measures already in use as well as by the introducing of new modes of versification," (4.75). Morell had interpreted the line in *The House of Fame* ("Though som vers fayle in a sillable," line 1098) as indicating Chaucer's "own confession that he did not write in equal measure," but Tyrwhitt objects that "it proves also, that he knew well what the laws of measure were, and that he thought that any deviation from them required an apology" (p. 81n.). But where Morell would defend Chaucer's meter even when irregular, Tyrwhitt has a firmer idea of a regular meter ("I have no conception myself that an heroic verse, which wants a syllable of its complement, can be musical, or even tolerable"; p. 82n.). And Tyrwhitt can hold to this stricter sense of meter because he holds that the line Morell is excusing is actually corrupt (p. 82).

Passing from a warm commendation of Chaucer's achievements in his octosyllabic poetry ("if he had given no other proofs of his poetical faculty, these alone must have secured to him the preeminence, above all his predecessors and contemporaries, in point of Versification," p. 83), Tyrwhitt's "Essay" moves to a description of Chaucer's achievements "in that kind of Metre which we now call the Heroic." This Tyrwhitt defines: "The Heroic Metre with us, as with the Italians, is of the Iambic form, and consists of ten, eleven, or twelve syllables; the tenth, however, being in all cases the last accented syllable" (p. 83n.). On the empirical evidence of his own reading Tyrwhitt credits Chaucer with introducing the heroic meter into English ("as I have not been able to discover any instance of this metre being used by any English poet before him, I am much inclined to suppose that he was the first introducer of it into our language"; p. 84). Recalling Chaucer's debt in *The Knight's Tale* to Boccaccio's *Teseida* and revealing his own discovery of the source of *Troilus* in *Filostrato*,[2] Tyrwhitt comments that as both Chaucer's source-texts were "written in the common Italian hendecasyllable verse, it cannot but appear extremely probable that his metre also was copied from the same original" (pp. 85–86), though the origin of his rhyme-royal stanza ("This Stanza of seven verses, being introduced, I apprehend, by Chaucer"; p. 87n.) seemed to Tyrwhitt French rather than Italian.

In assessing Chaucer's meter, Tyrwhitt works from the assumption that "the correctness and harmony of an English verse depends entirely upon its being composed of a certain number of syllables, and its having the accents of those syllables properly placed" (p. 88). Accordingly, "it is necessary that we should know the syllabical value (if I may use the expression) of his words, and the accentual value of his syllables, as they were commonly pronounced in his time" (p. 88). From this Tyrwhitt proceeds to present an analogy of how an Augustan Roman critic would approach from first principles the task of editing the text of Ennius, assuming that "the old Bard" was aiming to write metrical lines and attempting to remove scribal corruption from them.[3] The Ennius example prepares the way for Tyrwhitt's similarly reasoning approach as an editor to the meter of Chaucer, as observed on first principles from the evidence of the manuscripts. For Tyrwhitt, "The great number of verses, sounding complete even to our ears, which is to be found in all the least corrected copies of his works, authorizes us to conclude, that he was not ignorant of the laws of metre." And working from this, Tyrwhitt continues; "Upon this conclusion it is impossible not to ground a strong presumption, that he intended to observe the same laws in the many other verses which seem to us irregular" (p. 91). In this context Tyrwhitt sets himself to account for irregularity from observation of manuscripts. Little time is taken over "any Superfluities" in syllabic content of lines, for these "may be reduced to just measure by the usual practices of even modern Poets" (p. 92).

It is lines that "labour under an apparent Deficiency of a syllable, or two" which Tyrwhitt admits as the greater problem. In earlier sections of his "Essay," Tyrwhitt had given an account of Middle English grammar—less than completely accurate by later standards but very adequately learned for Tyrwhitt's own period—and drawing on this, Tyrwhitt indicates how the regularity of Chaucer's meter is assisted by the pronunciation of -es in the genitive singular and the plural form of nouns, together with -ed in past tenses and participles of verbs. But any attempt to indicate such pronunciation through an editorially imposed uniformity of orthography or by typographical means is scorned by Tyrwhitt.[4]

Beyond this, however, "nothing will be found of such extensive use for supplying the deficiencies of Chaucer's metre as the pronunciation of the e feminine" (p. 96), and Tyrwhitt gives an account of its pronunciation in words first of Romance origin, then of Old English. After suggesting how the en termination of verbs developed into a pronounced e termination (and noting how the pronounced final -e in such adjectives as swete or trewe would also be pronounced in their adverbial forms swetely, trewely, etc.), Tyrwhitt concludes: "What is generally considered as an e mute in our language . . . was antiently pronounced, but obscurely, like the e feminine of the French" (pp. 100–102). Proceeding from this account of syllabic irregularity to accentual irregularity, Tyrwhitt comments: "I am persuaded that in his French words [Chaucer] most commonly laid his accent according to the French custom" (p. 103), yet although he has been successful "without rule or example to guide him" (p. 106), "we are not to expect from Chaucer that regularity in the disposition of his accents, which the practice of our greatest Poets in the last and present century has taught us to consider as essential to harmonious versification" (pp. 104–105). It is thus appropriate that the first eighteen lines of The General Prologue, marked as Tyrwhitt feels they should be read, conclude the "Essay," which is written very much as an expression of Tyrwhitt's understanding of his practical role as an editor of the medieval manuscripts of a medieval poem, for his assessment of their evidence for Chaucer's meter is part of the general respect that he shows for his "best Mss."

Sources

The sources for Tyrwhitt's edition are acknowledged by the editor, for Tyrwhitt gives a full list of the manuscripts he used ("A List of the Mss. collated, or consulted, upon this occasion is subjoined"; 1. 1) and indicates also those manuscripts he most highly regarded ("Of these Mss. the most credit is due to the five following . . ."; p. xxiii).

Below are listed the manuscripts cited by Tyrwhitt in his list, with his sigils for them:

1. *British Library*

A.	Harley 7335	F.	Harley 1758
B.	Royal 18 C ii	G.	Sloane 1685
C.	Harley 7334	H.	Sloane 1686
D.	Royal 17 D xv	I.	Harley 1239
E.	Harley 7333		

2. *Bodleian Library*

B.α.	Bodley 686	B.δ	Selden Arch B 14
B.β.	Laud 739	B.ε.	Hatton Donat. 1
B.γ.	Laud 600	B.ζ.	Barlow 20

[*Also at Oxford*: NC (New College D.314).]

3. *At Cambridge*

C.1.	University Library Dd.4.24
C.2.	University Library Ii.3.26
T.	Trinity College, R.3.3
Tt.	Trinity College, R.3.15

4. *Then in private hands*

Ask.1.2. "Two Mss. lent to me by the late Dr. Askew." [Now British Library Egerton 2864 and Add. 5140.]

HA. "A Ms. lent to me by Edward Haistwell, Esq." [Now British Library Egerton 2726.]

W. "A Ms. in the possession of the late Mr. P. C. Webb." [Now British Library Lansdowne 851.]

Ch.N. [Two other manuscripts Tyrwhitt knew from collations by Thomas for Urry's edition: Cholmondeley (the Delamere manuscript) and Norton (Egerton 2863).]

Important additional insights into Tyrwhitt's editing process are also provided by the survival of his collation papers (now Harvard University, Houghton Library, fMS Eng. 1219)[5] and the "printer's copy" prepared by Tyrwhitt for his printer (now University of Virginia, Alderman Library).[6] The collation papers reveal that Tyrwhitt worked by "cannibalizing" a copy of the edition of 1687 of Speght, taking out its pages and using them as the "base" against which his manuscripts were collated. Blank pages were interleaved with the pages of the Speght text and grouped in a series of booklets for ease of working. Tyrwhitt then recorded variant readings from his manuscripts on the blank pages and made changes on the printed text itself. Changes of spelling and punctuation are indicated on the printed text by written-in corrections, crossings-out, and marginal notes. For his printer's copy Tyrwhitt made use of a copy of the Speght edition of 1602, and he has again incorporated a mass of fine corrections in the text, consisting both of his emendations from the manuscripts and also of his emendations to a more uniform system of orthography.[7]

From the collation papers it soon becomes clear that when Tyrwhitt refers to "a List of the Mss. collated, or consulted" he indicates a real distinction in his own practice. After his list of manuscripts he specifies as "A, C. 1, Ask. 1&2, HA," as those to which "the most credit is certainly due." His collations make most use of A, C. 1, C, T, W. Most other manuscripts are evidently collated more sporadically, and the Oxford manuscripts relatively infrequently (although their readings are considered at some cruces and are sometimes cited in Tyrwhitt's notes). The manuscript to which Tyrwhitt's collation practice reveals that he gave most authority was A, though it unfortunately lacked part of the whole, as the Preface notes. In the absence of A, Tyrwhitt makes most use of C. 1, and failing both of these he tends to use C.[8] Tyrwhitt's preference of A to C has been confirmed by subsequent editorial opinion, but he is careful to collate C generally. His attention to the Askew manuscripts would not be followed by modern scholarship, but his regard for HA characteristically shows his textual discernment, as does his regard for A and C. 1—these were the best manuscripts available to him.

There are then a number of sources for the study of Tyrwhitt's editing: direct comparison of his text with his manuscripts, his own comments on textual matters in his notes, and the collation papers and printer's copy. The overall impression given by Tyrwhitt's method of working on the Chaucer text is one of detailed attention to manuscript evidence, but Tyrwhitt's respect for the manuscripts is a critical and reasoning one.

Some of Tyrwhitt's editorial principles are implicit in his procedure in the collations. The Speght text is evidently used for the convenience of collating against a printed base, which is not apparently accorded any authority in itself, though some features of the Speght text may slip through despite Tyrwhitt's painstaking marking of the printer's copy, as he perhaps acknowledges when correcting in one note the reading printed in the text ("I have here inadvertently followed the printed copies"; 3.288). Against the Speght lines Tyrwhitt compares principally the manuscripts he has discovered to be most reliable, and in cases of difficulty he enquires more widely. In a note to his "Essay on Language and Versification," Tyrwhitt reveals his belief that the text of *The Canterbury Tales* is not in any case radically corrupt. Doubting that syllabic deficiencies in some lines are likely to be remedied from any manuscript, Tyrwhitt adds: "I would not be thought to undervalue the Mss. which I have not seen, or to discourage those who may have inclination and opportunity to consult them. I only mean to say, that, where the text is supported (as it generally is in this Edition) by the concurrence of two or three good Mss. and the sense is clear and complete, we may safely consider it as tolerably correct" (4.93n.). It is consequently not surprising that Tyrwhitt's holds with his "best Mss." where they seem self-evidently best, as he acknowledges in a note on the text: "Ver. 10977, 8. are also transposed; but upon the authority of Mss. A. C. 1. and, I believe, some others; though, being satisfied of the certainty of the emendation, I have omitted to take a note of their concurrence" (4.294).[9]

Tyrwhitt's collation papers are accordingly not as thickly annotated as they would be by a more modern editor who was consulting the number of manuscripts that Tyrwhitt lists. They are personal papers toward the practical end of achieving the most satisfactory reading. They are not intended to record a complete corpus of variants for its own sake, but nonetheless they do record how carefully Tyrwhitt consulted his manuscripts in cases of doubt. Indeed, Tyrwhitt's own published annotations show his openness to manuscript evidence and his candor in acknowledging doubts, as appears in his note on *SqT* F 349:

> Ver. 10663. That mochel drinke and labour] So Mss. C. 1. HA. In Ms. A. it is, *That mirthe and labour*. In Ask. 1.2. *That after moche labour*. In several other Mss. and Editt. Ca. 1.2. *That moche mete and labour*. We must search further, I apprehend, for the true reading. [4.292]

The same self-deprecating tone marks his note on *KnT* A 2683: "I have patched up this verse, as well as I coud, out of the different copies" (4.231).

Tyrwhitt's editing method may thus be characterized by his disposition in the first place toward the readings of a number of manuscripts discerned to be the best in terms of general accuracy within the body of manuscripts available to him. But where those manuscripts cannot offer a satisfactory reading, Tyrwhitt is very willing to consider the readings of the whole body of manuscripts. As an editor working without a recensionist approach, Tyrwhitt has no concern to group manuscripts off against each other as wholes. Indeed, beyond his general approval of certain manuscripts, he shows himself very willing in practice to seek the best reading in each line and context, though this may mean departing from his main manuscript source at that point. In this Tyrwhitt is winningly flexible and undogmatic, and he is by no means producing an edition based simply on a single corrected manuscript. Is Tyrwhitt's method then to be termed "eclectic"? It is certainly eclectic if that means that Tyrwhitt has used his knowledge and intelligence to find the best readings he could, while alerting the reader to what he has done. For Tyrwhitt—as for his age—there is no attempt to conceal that the editor has inevitably made subjective decisions of his own, for there is no sense that the editor should not apply his experience and judgment to his task.

Emendation: Editorial Practices

> This was a work which Pope seems to have thought unworthy of his abilities, being not able to suppress his contempt of "the dull duty of an editor," . . . but an emendatory critick would ill discharge his duty, without qualities very different from dulness. . . . Out of many readings possible, he must be able to select that which best suits with the state, opinions, and modes of language

prevailing in every age, and with his authour's particular cast of thought, and turn of expression. Such must be his knowledge, and such his taste. Conjectural criticism demands more than humanity possesses, and he that exercises it with most praise has very frequent need of indulgence. Let us now be told no more of the dull duty of an editor.

Johnson, *Preface to Shakespeare*[10]

Tyrwhitt's main "large-scale" editorial achievement is in his work of establishing the order of the tales and their links much as in later editions, with a few minor points of difference. Tyrwhitt disentangles the very confused and corrupted tale order in Speght, for while he assumes that *The Canterbury Tales* is unfinished precisely in matters like the disposition of its parts, Tyrwhitt perceives that the manuscripts support better arrangements than those that had previously been printed.[11]

Tyrwhitt's opinions on tale order are discussed in the "Discourse" and complemented in the notes to the tales. As the "Discourse" works through the tales in their order in his edition, the first major textual topic is the absence of *The Cook's Tale*. As in most other textual matters, Tyrwhitt is influenced by his manuscript A, which omits the tale, and (always alert to Chaucer's own inconsistencies) Tyrwhitt recalls that *The Manciple's Prologue* later assumes that the Cook has not told a tale, "however, as it is sufficiently certain, that the *Cokes* Prologue and the beginning of his Tale are genuine compositions, they have their usual place in this Edition" (4.144). The claims of *Gamelyn* are naturally discounted in the only terms that count: "it is not to be found in any of the Mss. of the first authority" (p. 145).

A more radical correction occurs after *The Man of Law's Tale*, which Tyrwhitt follows with the Wife-Friar-Summoner fragment rather than the Squire and Merchant as in Speght. As Tyrwhitt comments, the latter order makes the Merchant refer to the *Wife's Prologue* before it has been uttered: "Such an impropriety I was glad to remove upon the authority of the best Mss. though it had been acquiesced in by all former Editors" (p. 152). In his notes to the *Wife's Prologue*, however, Tyrwhitt notes that in some manuscripts it is preceded by a link of some lines connecting it with *The Merchant's Tale* ("I print them here, in order to justify myself for not inserting them in the text"; p. 261).

In Tyrwhitt's edition *The Merchant's Tale* is accordingly made to follow *The Clerk's Tale*, and the jumbled order of stanzas in the Clerk's Envoy in Speght is emended, so that the new tale's opening echoes the Envoy's last line ("This arrangement, which recommends itself at first sight, is also supported by so many Mss. of the best authority, that, without great negligence or dullness, I coud not have either overlooked or rejected it"; pp. 158–59). But it is typical of Tyrwhitt's scholarly candor that after giving his authorities in his notes he adds: "But I must not conceal a circumstance, which seems to contradict the supposition that the *Marchant's* Prologue followed immediately" (p. 281). Tyrwhitt here prints the text he finds in the same manuscripts of the stanza of "murye words of the Hoost" (Robinson, 4.1212a–g). Robinson suggests that this is the original ending, and, similarly, Tyrwhitt concludes that Chaucer "may be supposed . . . to have left this Stanza for the present uncancelled in his Ms." (p. 282).

Very comparable principles guide Tyrwhitt in his printing of what he calls the "Squire's Prologue" (in Robinson the Epilogue to *The Merchant's Tale* and Introduction to *The Squire's Tale*. He remarks that this link "appears now for the first time in print. Why it has been omitted by all former Editors I cannot guess, except, perhaps, because it did not suit with the place, which (for reasons best known to themselves) they were determined to assign to [*The Squire's Tale*], that is, after [*The Man of Law's Tale*] and before [*The Merchant's Tale*]. I have chosen rather to follow the Mss. of the best authority in placing [*SqT*] after [*MerT*], and in connecting them together by this Prologue, agreeably, as I am persuaded, to Chaucer's intention" (pp. 161–62).[12]

Both Speght's and Tyrwhitt's editions have by this point reached *The Franklin's Tale*, though Tyrwhitt points out that former editions had run together the link passage of exchanges between Franklin and Squire and Host (Robinson, 5.673ff.) with *The Merchant's Prologue* and placed both before *The Merchant's Tale*. Pointing out the incompatibility of a prologue that talks of a marriage two months old and another about the speaker's grown-up son, Tyrwhitt restores the link to before *The Franklin's Tale* with the support of both common sense and the manuscripts ("This therefore, upon the authority of the best Mss. I have restored to *the Frankelein*"; p. 163).[13]

In making *The Physician's Tale* follow on to *The Franklin's Tale* in his edition, Tyrwhitt again differed from previous editorial tradition, which had placed *The Second Nun's Tale* and *The Canon's Yeoman's Tale* before *The Physician's Tale*. But as Tyrwhitt remarks: "The best Mss. agree in removing those Tales to the end of [*The Nun's Priest's Tale*], and I have not scrupled to adopt this arrangement" (p. 170). Moreover, as Tyrwhitt points out, since the Monk begins his tale near Rochester and the Canon's Yeoman overtakes the pilgrims near Boughton-under-Blee, then fragment VIII cannot logically precede the *Monk's Tale–Nun's Priest's Tale* sequence.

It is in his provision of a prologue for *The Physician's Tale* that Tyrwhitt makes one of his few decisions about the order and linking of tales that has not been confirmed by subsequent editing. It is, however, a decision that Tyrwhitt is at pains to emphasize as provisional. His important achievement lies in placing *The Physician's Tale* after *The Franklin's Tale*, "but how they are to be connected together, and whether at all, is a matter of doubt" (p. 171). As Tyrwhitt explains, the six-line prologue he has printed is found "in one of the best Mss. but only in one: in the others it has no Prologue" (and in his notes to *The Physician's Tale*, Tyrwhitt identifies the manuscript as A, p. 304). Tyrwhitt is strongly persuaded of only the first line's authenticity: "I would therefore only wish these lines to be received for the present (according to the Law-phrase) *de bene esse*, till they shall either be more authentically established, or superseded by the discovery of the genuine Prologue" (p. 171).

Tyrwhitt's next significant decision in the disposition of the tales happens to be the other main instance in which his decision has not been absorbed into later editorial opinion. This is his printing as *The Shipman's Prologue* of that passage which in Robinson is printed in brackets as the *Epilogue* to *The Man of Law's Tale* (lines 1163–90). Tyrwhitt is candid with the reader of the "Discourse" about the conjectural nature of his emendation: *The Shipman's Tale* has no prologue in Tyrwhitt's "best Mss."; the prologue given in previous editions is "evidently spurious"; to remedy this, Tyrwhitt has moved to *The Shipman's Tale* a prologue "which has usually been prefixed to [*The Squire's Tale*]," though he admits he has done this "upon the authority of one Ms. (and, I confess, not one of the best)" (p. 172).[14] Like later editors Tyrwhitt feels the genuineness of the passage: "As this Prologue was undoubtedly composed by Chaucer, it must have had a place somewhere in this Edition, and if I cannot prove that it was really intended by him for this place, I think the Reader will allow that it fills the vacancy extremely well" (p. 173).

By contrast, Tyrwhitt rightly rejects a spurious link between the lines printed by Robinson as *Epilogue* to *The Nun's Priest's Tale* and *The Second Nun's Prologue* (this actually indicates within the text that *The Second's Nun's Tale* is to follow: Tyrwhitt gives these forged link lines in his notes to the passage, 3.295). And with his usual sense of manuscript support Tyrwhitt ejects *The Plowman's Tale* from its place in Speght between *The Manciple's Tale* and *The Parson's Tale*: "As I cannot understand that there is the least ground of evidence, either external or internal, for believing it to be a work of Chaucer's, I have not admitted it into this Edition" (pp. 185–86).

Tyrwhitt's establishment of one of the most widely accepted versions of the order of *The Canterbury Tales* (and his lucid presentation of his case throughout the "Discourse") is an achievement characteristically built on respect for the manuscripts and disregard for the nonsenses of early editions. A note in his account of his manuscripts in the "Appendix to the Preface" reveals the main influence on Tyrwhitt in his establishment of the tale order in his edition: "Of these Mss. the most credit is certainly due to the five following, viz. A. C. 1. Ask. 1. 2. and HA. The four last exhibit the Tales in exactly the same order in which they are printed in this edition; and so does A. except that it wants the *Cokes* Tale . . . and has the *Nonnes* Tale inserted between the *Sompnoures* and the *Clerkes*" (1.xxiii). In short, Tyrwhitt's "best Mss." are the most convincing example to him of the best tale order, though his meticulous notes to the tales show how careful Tyrwhitt is not to mislead the reader about the range of manuscript variation.

To turn now from tale order to examine Tyrwhitt's emendations within the texts of the individual tales, a comparable respect for that manuscript evidence which the editor is to interpret is discernible in his approach to a range of textual problems, from missing, transposed, or interpolated lines to the smaller-scale but equal difficulties within the phrasing of individual lines.

Tyrwhitt's regard for manuscript testimony to authenticity is well brought out where he accepts the authority of the manuscripts that certain lines are authentic, even where they may not be to his taste. Variant ribald lines interpolated into the pear-tree incident in *The Merchant's Tale* in some early editions are scornfully dismissed ("the lowest and most superfluous ribaldry that can well be conceived"; 4.288), not simply for themselves, however, but because the manuscripts indicate they are forged: "It would be a mere loss of time to argue from the lines themselves, that they were not written by Chaucer, as we have this short and decisive reason for rejecting them, that they are not found in any one Ms. of authority" (pp. 288–89). By contrast, certain lines in *The Wife of Bath's Prologue* were missing from some of Tyrwhitt's "best Mss.": 3.609–12, 619–26 ("I took no kep, so that he liked me"). Tyrwhitt's textual acumen is such, however, that he sees that the lines are authentic, despite the disruption of normal manuscript support and his own view of their content: "These four lines are wanting in Mss. A. Ask. 1. 2. and several others. And so are the eight lines from ver. 6201. to ver. 6208. incl. They certainly might very well be spared" (4.264). Here Tyrwhitt has instead accepted the superiority of his manuscript C.1.

This care and discernment with which Tyrwhitt has collated his manuscripts does lead him to some impressively astute comments on problems of authenticity in several passages of the *Tales*. In the instance of the six lines early in *The Wife of Bath's Prologue*, which Robinson gives in a footnote (3.44a–f), Tyrwhitt prints the lines in his notes, specifying the supporting manuscripts ("C.1. HA. C.2. and in Edit. Ca. 2.") and commenting: "If these lines are not Chaucer's, they are certainly more in his manner than the generality of the imitations of him. Perhaps he wrote them, and afterwards blotted them out" (IV. 4.262). In this, Tyrwhitt's judgment anticipates Robinson's. A comparable astuteness marks Tyrwhitt's note on the "modern instances" of tragedy in *The Monk's Tale*, which occur in the manuscripts either between Zenobia and Nero or at the end. For Tyrwhitt's analysis of the advantages of either position anticipates Robinson's own analysis of the problems (his notes, pp. 746–47), and although Tyrwhitt places the modern instances at the end ("I have followed the order observed in the best Mss." 3.285), he has alerted his reader to the merits of the alternatives.

Tyrwhitt's characteristic assumptions in his editing are also revealed by his approach to problems raised by various omissions and interpolations in manuscripts of *The Franklin's Tale*. In some instances (lines 1289–90, 1423–24, 1434–36) Tyrwhitt would find in collating against the printed copy that Speght had omitted authentic lines, and there, following his trusted manuscripts, Tyrwhitt correctly restored the text. On the authority of manuscript A, Tyrwhitt moves the exchange between Aurelius and Dorigen (Robinson, lines 999–1000) to follow a consequently longer speech by Dorigen (i.e., after line 1006). The flat last lines of Dorigen's soliloquy (lines 1455–56) were omitted from manuscript A and some others, and so Tyrwhitt "was not unwilling to leave them out" (4.303). Similarly, the six lines (1493–98, available to Tyrwhitt only in Caxton's second edition) are omitted: "These lines are more in the style and manner of Chaucer than interpolations generally are; but as I do not remember to have found them in any Ms. I coud not receive them into the text. I think too, that, if they were written by him, he would probably, upon more mature consideration, have suppressed them, as unnecessarily anticipating the catastrophe of the tale" (4.303–304). Robinson includes lines 1455–56 and also lines 1493–98 (noting "Only in [Ellesmere and Add. 35286] . . . but apparently genuine," p. 894). Since Tyrwhitt did not see these manuscripts, he was in his own terms justified in excluding the lines, and he also revealed his interest in detecting signs of unfinishedness in Chaucer's autograph, preserved by the errors of scribes.[15]

Space allows only a representative selection of the instances in which Tyrwhitt, collating his manuscripts against Speght, has preferred the manuscript reading, and thus restores some Middle English word or idiom or undoes the garbling of sense in Speght. Tyrwhitt's grasp of Middle English guides him, as in *KnT* A 2114, where Speght reads "They would all full faine willen," but Tyrwhitt reads "They wold hir thankes willen" (Tyrwhitt's line 2116), drawing on his manuscripts A, C.1., C, and Ask. 1 and 2, and noting in the glossary: "The phrases, *his thankes, hir thankes* . . . answer to the French, *son gré, leur gré* " (5.211). Several other idiomatic lines are corrected through Tyrwhitt's collations. In *MilT* A 3709, Speght reads: "As helpe me God and sweet saint Jame," but Tyrwhitt corrects to "As helpe me God, it wol not be, compame" (Tyrwhitt's line 3709). His collations show that he noted readings in A, Ask. 1 and 2, C.1, and C, though in his note he glosses *compame* as "friend" rather than as "come kiss me" (4.245). In *RvT* A 4101, where Speght has "With kepe, kepe, iossa, iossa, warth there," Tyrwhitt shows a sense of idiom and prints "With kepe, kepe; stand, stand; jossa, warderere" (Tyrwhitt's line 4099). Here he seems indebted to manuscript C.1, and his glossary shrewdly surmises the meaning of *warderere* as "perhaps a corruption of the Fr. *Garde arriere*" (5.232).

Tyrwhitt's following of his manuscripts produces a text marked in this way by more authentic diction than that of some earlier texts. In *KnT* A 2883, Speght reads "With glitering beard & ruddie shining heres," but Tyrwhitt corrects from manuscripts A, C.1, and Ask. 1 and 2 to read "With flotery berd, and ruggy asshy heres" (Tyrwhitt's line 2885) and in his notes compares *Teseida* and comments: "*Flotery* seems literally to mean *floting*; as hair dischevelled (*rabbuffata*) may be said to flote upon the air. *Ruggy* is *rough*" (4.234). In *RvT* A 3864, where Speght has the corrupt reading "Soothly (qd. he)," Tyrwhitt has seen from his manuscripts the dialect line lying behind the corruption and prints "So the ik, quod he" (Tyrwhitt's line 3862), explaining in his notes: "so may I *the*, or *thrive*. This ancient phrase is terribly corrupted in most of the Mss. and Editt." (4.246–47). The Speght text is comparably corrupted in *RvT* A 3870 ("Which somtime yelow was, now white ben min heres"), but from his collations Tyrwhitt reads instead "Min herte is also mouled as min heres" (Tyrwhitt's line 3868), which his glossary duly explains as "grow mouldy" (5.135). Or again, in *KnT* A 2550, Speght reads "Foin if him list on foot, *the same he shall were*," but Tyrwhitt reads (from manuscripts A, C, T) " . . . himself to were" (Tyrwhitt's line 2552), and glosses *were* as "To defend" (5.236).

As he collated the Speght copy against the manuscripts, Tyrwhitt also corrected many garbled lines in the printed text. Thus, Speght's version of *SNT* G 536 ("With shetes home full faire they her hent") does not survive Tyrwhitt's collations against the manuscript: he emends to "With shetes han the blood ful faire yhent" (Tyrwhitt's line 16,004; cf. manuscripts A, C.1, C, HA). Such garbled lines as *KnT* A 1968, in Speght ("The purgatory that was thereabout over all") becomes "The purtreiture, that was upon the wall" (Tyrwhitt's line 1970; cf. manuscripts A. C. 1). But the use Tyrwhitt makes of his manuscripts is careful: in *SqT* F 516, Speght's line "With his dissimuling and fair assemblaunce" is emended to "And kepeth in semblaunt alle his observance" (Tyrwhitt's line 10,830), and here Tyrwhitt follows C.1 rather than A ("And kepith semblable . . . "), his usually preferred manuscript. Tyrwhitt's attention to the manuscripts ensures many correct emendations to a harder reading: thus *MerP* E 1236, Speght's "Hath wedded be, though men him rife" becomes Tyrwhitt's "Wifles hath ben, though that men wolde him rife" (Tyrwhitt's line 9112), or Speght's account of Venus with her brand (cf. *MerT* E 1778), "So fresh she was, and thereto so licand" becomes Tyrwhitt's "As that she bare it dancing in hire hond" (Tyrwhitt's line 9652). And similarly, some of Speght's more plausible lines (as in *MerT* E 2072: "His death therefore desireth he utterly") are emended through Tyrwhitt's appraisal of the manuscript evidence; thus, following manuscripts A, C.1, C, and Ca. 2, he emends Speght's line into "He wepeth and he waileth pitously" (Tyrwhitt's line 9946).[16]

Tyrwhitt's experience in using manuscript sources enables him to detect some of the processes of scribal corruption, and as an editor who prefaces his edition with an essay on Chaucer's language and versification, he indicates in his notes his concern with how the poet's meter has often been inseparable from his editing work. Two notes by Tyrwhitt on *The General Prologue* and *The Knight's Tale* can help distinguish his ideas. In his note on the Pardoner's song "Come hider, love, to me!" (*GP* A 674), Tyrwhitt comments that "*Love*, is here a dissyllable" (4.214), and scans some other nearby lines: "In lóvedáys, ther cóud he móchel helpe" (Tyrwhitt's line 260; *GP* A 258), or again: 'Ful sóth is sáyde, that lóve ne lórdship' (Tyrwhitt's line 1627; *KnT* A 1625). From the rhyme of the couplet containing the Pardoner's song Tyrwhitt now proceeds to make that deduction often made since about final -*e*: "The double rime of *to me*, answering to *Rome*, proves evidently that Rome in this place is to be pronounced as a Dissyllable. We need therefore have no scruple, I think, of pronouncing it in the same manner wherever the metre requires two syllables. . . . A like use may be made of other similar rimes in Chaucer for establishing the pronunciation of the *e* feminine" (4.214), and Tyrwhitt gives examples. The nature of Tyrwhitt's metrical understanding is suggested by his note scanning his line 2469 of *The Knight's Tale* ("Min ben alsó the máladíes cólde"), which differs textually from Robinson's line ("And myne be the maladyes colde," line 2467). Tyrwhitt's point is to alert his reader that "I apprehend that *maladies* in this verse is to be pronounced as of four syllables" (4.229), and to consolidate his point Tyrwhitt gives two further examples of scansion. While one example broadly agrees with modern versions (Tyrwhitt's line 2495: "Ther wás in th'hóstelríes áll abóute"; cf. *KnT* A 2493), the other instance is less accurate (Tyrwhitt's line 2591: "Ther n'ére swiche cómpagníes néver twéy'; cf. Robinson, line 2589: "Ther nere swiche compaignyes tweye"). This brings out the way that Tyrwhitt's practice may be faulty, despite the general soundness of much of his metrical principle. Yet it is difficult not to admire Tyrwhitt's devotion to his purpose: he concludes his note on his line 2469: "However, if any one should prefer a hobbling line with another syllable in it, he may read with the best Mss. *And* min ben also &c." (4.229). Here Tyrwhitt's two devotions, to the idea of Chaucer's metrical regularity and to the "best Mss.," are evidently in conflict. But Tyrwhitt's approach even to good manuscripts is never merely passive, and here he is more concerned to avoid that Chaucer should ever write "a hobbling line."

Accordingly, a number of Tyrwhitt's notes recording his metrical emendations admit that he has introduced a conjectural reading to regularize the meter. In the note on his line 2872 ("And after this, this Theseus hath sent"), Tyrwhitt comments: "The second *this* is from conjecture only. Some Mss. read—And after this Theseus hath *Ysent*—which perhaps is right" (4.233), and indeed this is the reading adopted by Robinson (*KnT* A 2870).[17] But Tyrwhitt's notes on his conjectures reveal that the right metrical idea often occurred to him, even if he preferred his conjecture. Thus, on his line 2559 ("No longer shal the tourneying ylast") Tyrwhitt comments: "The prepositive *y* is an addition of my own, for the sake of the metre; but perhaps we might read, "No longer shal the tourneyinge last" (4.230), and in fact this corresponds to the form in Robinson.[18]

In brief, Tyrwhitt's notion of how closely Chaucer's text supported the metrical principles that he had established led the eighteenth-century editor into more conjectural emendation on metrical matters than he allowed himself in other aspects of his editing activity. It is here that his feeling for the manuscripts is weakest (while in interpreting their sense in any line he is so assured), and Tyrwhitt's mistakenness in metrical practice stems not only from some intermittent failings in grammar but also from attempts to apply his metrical principles without always enough allowance for permissible variations. Thus Tyrwhitt's notes recurrently list his conjectural emendations of "headless" and other "deficient" or irregular lines.[19] On Tyrwhitt's line 2866 ("Of funeral he might all accomplise") his note admits that *"Of* is a conjectural supplement." The line stands without it in Robinson (*KnT* A 2864). On his line 393 ("All in a goune of falding to the knee") he notes, "I have added *All*, for the sake of the verse" (4.208).

The form of Tyrwhitt's notes to his edition suggests that his approach to the editing of the poetic text itself is not, in his eyes, distinct from his work of explication in the edition as a whole, for the determination of the correct reading will necessarily often overlap with the larger task of the commentary on the poem. Thus in his line 2014 (*The Knight's Tale*, line 2012) Tyrwhitt correctly prints *outhees*, explaining its meaning as "outcry" and noting that it had usually been corruptly printed as *on theft* (4.223). Again Tyrwhitt learnedly corrects previous editions on the reading *thyn ore* (in his line 3724; *MilT* A 3726), with references to Robert of Gloucester and the manuscript of *Li beaus disconus*. In *RvT* A 4320 (Tyrwhitt's line 4318, "Him thar not . . ."), Tyrwhitt declares, "I have restored this old word, upon the authority of the best Mss. in this and other places" (4.254). In such contexts Tyrwhitt's concern for the authentic language of Chaucer's text naturally involves the work of commentary too, as in Tyrwhitt's note on his line 11,807 (*FranT* F 1503): "As she was *boun*] *Ready*. This old word is restored from Mss. A. Ask. 1.2." Indeed, Tyrwhitt's editorial interests in the *lectio difficilior* in his manuscripts—the underlying principle in his approach to textual cruces—sometimes constitute his keenest notes on the poem's language, as in the Pardoner's "saffroning" of his preaching: "To saffron] So Ms. A. and Ed. Ca. 2. I have preferred it to the common reading *savor*, as more expressive, and less likely to have been a gloss" (4.307). Similarly, Tyrwhitt notes on the phrase *crowned malice* in his line 10,840 (*SqT* F 526): "The reader of taste will not be displeased, I trust, at my having received this reading upon the authority of Ms. A. only. The common reading is *cruel*" (4.293).

Tyrwhitt is not the first editor to find that some hard readings are so hard as to be almost inexplicable. As he comments on his line 3768 (*MilT* A 3770): "the viretote]   This is the reading of the best Mss. The explanation of the word I leave to the reader's sagacity" (4.246). On the phrase *out of relees* (Tyrwhitt's line 15,514; *SNT* G 46) Tyrwhitt notes, "All the best

Mss. concur in this reading, and therefore I have followed them, though I confess that I do not clearly understand the phrase" (3.295). In some instances by shrewd detective work in the sources of a passage Tyrwhitt can retrieve the correct reading from beyond the corrupt English line. Thus Tyrwhitt notes on his line 2686 (*KnT* A 2684): "a fury]   Most of the copies have *a fire*. Ms. A. reads *a fuyr*. from which I have made the present reading, as in the Theseida it is *Herinis*, i.e. *Erinnys*, one of the Furies" (4.231). Similarly, Tyrwhitt gives this note (4.217):

> Ver. 886. And of the temple]   The Editions, and all the Mss. except two, read *tempest*. But the *Theseida* says nothing of any *tempest*. On the contrary it says, that the passage
>
> > Tosto fornito fu et senza pene.
>
> I have therefore preferred the reading of Mss. C.1 and HA. as Theseus is described making his offerings, &c. upon his return, in a temple of Pallas. Thes. 1.ii.

In such instances textual and annotatory activity are at one,[20] but in other instances the problem remains unsolved, as Tyrwhitt's notes admit. Thus he notes on his line 14,123 (*MkT* B² 2117): "saith Trophee]   As all the best Mss. agree in this reading, I have retained it, though I cannot tell what author is alluded to. The margin of C.1. has this note. *Ille vates Chaldæorum Tropheus*. The Editt. read—*for trophee*." (3.282). More revealing again is Tyrwhitt's comment on his line 8258 (*ClT* E 382): "ful of *nouches*]   The common reading is *ouches*; but I have retained the reading of the best Mss. as it may possibly assist somebody to discover the meaning of the word" (4.279). For all the scholarly uncertainty, Tyrwhitt's characteristic faith in the manuscripts and the Middle English text is striking here—as throughout his editing—and the learned seriousness and respect with which Chaucer's poem is taken is typical of Tyrwhitt's work both as editor and annotator of *The Canterbury Tales*.

Commentary

> You have shewn to all, who shall hereafter attempt the study of our ancient authours, the way to success; by directing them to the perusal of the books which those authours had read.
>
> Dr Johnson to Thomas Warton[21]

In the "Introductory Discourse and Notes" to his edition, Tyrwhitt assembled the first effective modern commentary on Chaucer, not only through the range of his reading (exceptional especially in the wide and sympathetic familiarity with medieval writings in manuscripts) but also by the skill and grace with which the great mass of knowledge is brought to bear at important points. Very many now-accepted explanations and annotations of Chaucer's text are first put forward in Tyrwhitt's notes.

Tyrwhitt's Preface declares his intention "to distinguish the parts where the author appears as an inventor, from those where he is merely a translator, or imitator; and throughout the whole to trace his allusions to a variety of forgotten books and obsolete customs" (p. ii), and Tyrwhitt presents a cogent account of very many of the important general questions about the work that have since concerned subsequent editors. Before looking at Tyrwhitt's more detailed notes, it will accordingly be best to consider the main contributions of his "Discourse."

Opening on the background to works like *The Canterbury Tales*, Tyrwhitt compares the format of the *Decameron*, of which he comments: "There would be no great harm, if the Critics would permit us to consider the Decameron, and other compositions of that kind, in the light of Comedies not intended for the stage" (4.116). Yet Tyrwhitt shrewdly notes the real distinctions between Chaucer's and Boccaccio's works, contrasting the open-ended form of *Decameron* and its lack of differentiated narrators with the pilgrimage setting and the variety of character in Chaucer's company of tellers. The tale-telling competition in turn raises the question of how many tales were really to be told and thus how far completed the *Tales* are. On this, assuming that the return journey to London was to have been included, Tyrwhitt notes that of the projected whole "more than one half is wanting" (4.120). And working from allusions in the *Prologue* to *The Legend of Good Women*, Tyrwhitt concludes that Chaucer could scarcely have begun *The Canterbury Tales* in earnest before 1389, the more remarkable when it was assumed in the eighteenth century that Chaucer was born in 1328.

Throughout his annotation Tyrwhitt makes strenuous attempts to explain Chaucer's references to time, especially all astrological allusions.[22] By later ideas he is sometimes mistaken in these matters, yet his endeavors are always distinguished by a respectful attitude to his original, an implicit trust in the sense and accuracy of Chaucer, despite the apparent corruptions of his meaning in transmission. This also distinguishes his discussion of the number of pilgrims really present at the Tabard—that problem depending on whether the Prioress is really accompanied by three priests. Tyrwhitt scrutinizes the text with his characteristic combination of an editor's eye for scribal corruption and a background knowledge of the period (he includes a note on what female religious could and could not do). Eventually he is forced to conclude that the line is corrupt, just as—when he considers whether each pilgrim was to tell one or two tales—Tyrwhitt is forced to conclude that this is an aspect of the unfinished nature of *The Canterbury Tales*. In both these sensible conclusions he has been followed by later critics. Tyrwhitt is distinctive in the way that he does bring to Chaucer's text such a searching eye for inconsistency and loose ends. Meaninglessness must be explained, and if meaning cannot be found, then it is Tyrwhitt's idea of his duty to inform the reader as much as he can or, failing all else, to signal clearly editorial defeat.

The greater part of the "Discourse" is taken up with brief general discussions of each of the *Tales*. Great erudition and critical sense are at work here. For *The Knight's Tale*, after speculating on its earlier form before the *Tales* were written, Tyrwhitt gives an excellent summary of its source, *Teseida*, with some shrewd footnotes that point out some significant differences that Chaucer made in his version, forming a succinct and impartial presentation of "the parts where the author appears as an inventor" (Preface).[23] Throughout his annotation Tyrwhitt is astute in his feeling about sources and unafraid to differ from received opinion: he records the supposed derivation of *The Reeve's Tale* from the *Decameron* but points out that he believes it more likely to be modeled on a French fabliau (p. 144; cf. his similar observation on *The Shipman's Tale*, p. 173). A comparable sense of the interrelatedness of medieval texts marks his comments on *The Man of Law's Tale*, for although Tyrwhitt misses the source in Trivet and mistakenly believes that Chaucer took the tale from Gower, he is nevertheless learned enough in medieval romance to comment, "I find among the *Cotton* Mss. . . . an old English Rime, entitled '*Emare*,' in which the heroine under that name goes through a series of adventures for the most part exactly similar to those of Constance" (p. 150); but further, Tyrwhitt notes that this romance itself acknowledges a French source. With *The Wife of Bath's Tale*, Tyrwhitt also suggests Gower as a possible source, though speculating on some other traditional version of the Florent story, and he gives a succinct account of the sources behind her *Prologue*.

In his discussion of *The Clerk's Tale*, Tyrwhitt provides a coolly learned note on the possibility that Chaucer ever really met Petrarch. His review of the actual historical records reflects his own scholarly distaste for surmise, while his note on the origin of the pear-tree episode in *The Merchant's Tale* reflects as throughout his scholarly concern for manuscript authority. Quoting a rare Latin analogue of the bawdy incident in an early edition, Tyrwhitt comments, "I dare say the Reader will not be very anxious to see any more" (p. 160), but then learnedly notes that he has been unable to find a manuscript of this text. As ever, Tyrwhitt preferred to consult manuscripts of early literature and distrusted all editions. Indeed, the discussion of medieval lays (with a sympathetic account of Marie de France) that accompanies Tyrwhitt's introduction to *The Franklin's Tale* reveals his extensive familiarity with manuscripts of medieval literature in the British Museum. He quotes Marie and other texts, including "An old English *Ballad of Sir Gowther*," from manuscripts, though reaching the conclusion that any immediate source of the tale in a lay is not now available ("The Lay itself is either lost, or buried [perhaps for ever] in one of those sepulchres of Mss. which, by courtesy, are called Libraries"; p. 166–7).

In this way the "Discourse" maintains a remarkable concentration of learning in placing Chaucer's works in the context of classical and medieval literature. *The Prioress's Tale* is related to the traditions of child martyrs, and

Tyrwhitt's comments on *Sir Thopas* accurately convey how its comedy exists in relation to its times (". . . clearly intended to ridicule the 'palpable-gross' fictions of the common Rimers of that age, and still more, perhaps, the meanness of their language and versification"; p. 175). Of *Melibee*, Tyrwhitt notes (accurately enough for his times) that it is "a mere translation," but he gives some references to manuscripts of its French source and offers a characteristic defence of the work: "It is in truth . . . *'a moral tale vertuous,'* and was probably much esteemed in its time, but, in this age of levity, I doubt some Readers will be apt to regret, that he did not rather give us the remainder of *Sire Thopas*" (p. 176).

After suggesting some of the sources of *The Monk's Tale*, Tyrwhitt then attributes the fable behind *The Nun's Priest's Tale* to a fable of Marie de France, printing the text from manuscript for the first time "and the more willingly, because it furnishes a convincing proof, how able Chaucer was to work up an excellent Tale out of very small materials" (p. 177–9). In the instance of *The Second Nun's Tale*, Tyrwhitt indicates it is "almost literally translated" from the *Legenda aurea*, while also noting those details in the *Prologue* which suggest that it has been hurriedly prepared for its present position ("Such little inaccuracies are strong proofs of an unfinished work"; p. 181n.). A learned note on alchemy accompanies Tyrwhitt's brief introduction to *The Canon's Yeoman's Tale*, which (with rather uncharacteristic speculativeness) suggests that Chaucer was motivated by some personal grudge against alchemists. On *The Manciple's Tale*, Tyrwhitt comments upon Chaucer's use of the traditional materials: "His skill in new dressing an old story was never, perhaps, more successfully exerted" (p. 184). When the spurious *Plowman's Tale* has been dismissed, Tyrwhitt continues with a discussion of the problematic references to time in *The Parson's Prologue* (p. 186), and after speculating on the probable source of *The Parson's Tale* in some treatise on penance (in which, of course, he has been proved right), Tyrwhitt moves on to a brief discussion of Chaucer's *Retraction*. His "Introductory Discourse" ends with the surmise that the missing tales "might, and probably would, have served to link together those which at present are unconnected; and for that reason it is much to be regretted, that they either have been lost, or (as I rather believe) were never finished by the Author" (p. 188).

Tyrwhitt's "Discourse," which is presented in such a way as to produce a general description built up out of a very minute and careful observation, is balanced by the meticulously detailed scholarship of his notes, which will now be considered in terms of their great general range of erudition, their particular knowledge of English and French medieval literature (especially from manuscript sources), and their use of other sources in chronicles and official documents.

Of Tyrwhitt's ranging erudition as it is applied in many cases throughout his notes to the *Tales* it is implicitly difficult to give a summary account.

His learning enables him to fill in the background to the Knight's campaigns, as well as annotating *The Knight's Tale* with reference to *Teseida*, especially in difficult passages (pp. 233–34). Tyrwhitt is effortlessly at home with his sources and slips into his notes his observations (Tyrwhitt's line 1920; *KnT* A 1918) that the temple of Venus from *Teseida* has already been used in *The Parliament of Fowls*, and (Tyrwhitt's line 2813; *KnT* A 2811) that the flight of Arcita's soul to the spheres has been used instead in *Troilus and Criseyde*. His familiarity with learned sources is effectively brought to bear: Bernardus Silvestris is cited as the source of a passage in *The Man of Law's Tale*, and quoted from a Bodleian manuscript (4:258); Geoffrey of Vinsauf is cited in *The Nun's Priest's Tale* (3:294); Gervase of Tilbury is cited apropos of the spell in *The Miller's Tale* (4:243); Vincent of Beauvais is cited in connection with *The Wife of Bath's Tale* (4:271); an allusion to the *Secreta secretorum* is fully explained (3:300). Names and allusions are corrected by Tyrwhitt in emendation of earlier confusion: concerning "Lynyan," mentioned in *The Clerk's Prologue*, Tyrwhitt comments drily, "His name of late has been so little known, that I believe nobody has been angry with the [Editions] for calling him *Livian*" (4.277), and goes on to give an account of the figure. Again he restores the reading *Chichevache* (*ClT* E 1198) "upon the authority of the best Mss." and explains the joke by reference to "an old Ballad, which is still preserved in Ms. *Harl.* 2251" (p. 280). It would be a simple matter to go on accumulating the instances in which Tyrwhitt throws light on the text by his learning, providing notes on the significance of Pamphilus (4.298), Lepe (p. 308), Stilbon (p. 309), and so on. He gives a sympathetic account of the achievements of Wace (p. 267); he argues succinctly for Benoit de St. Maure as a source for Guido delle Colonne (p. 289); he pays tribute to the materials of the *Gesta Romanorum* (4.288; 3.319).[24]

Yet his learning is to do with not only—in the words of his own Preface—"forgotten books" but also with "obsolete customs," and Tyrwhitt provides long studies on such varied subjects as the status of yeomen (4.195), the real nature of a *dais* (p. 205), the meaning of *tregetoures* (p. 299) and *gestours* (p. 319), not to mention an essay upon fairies (p. 268). For help with the terms of medieval medicine and cookery Tyrwhitt has frequently resorted to information in medieval manuscripts and other very early accounts.

Many of Tyrwhitt's annotations of Chaucer bear witness to his special range of sympathy with other medieval English writing, much of it quoted by Tyrwhitt from unedited manuscripts in the British Museum. Tyrwhitt's notes to *Sir Thopas* particularly reveal this keen knowledge of Middle English literature, for, as he comments in the "Discourse," "It is full of phrases taken from *Isumbras, Li beaus desconus*, and other Romances in the same style, which are still extant" (p. 175); and by setting *Thopas* in its contemporary literary context through his notes Tyrwhitt locates the nature of its humor. Thus, citing British Museum manuscripts, he quotes from William of Nassyngton on *gestours* (4.319), and from *Ywain and Gawain* on *royal romances* (p. 320). He explains *lere* (Tyrwhitt's line 13,786; *Th* B^2 857) by reference to a manuscript copy of *Isumbras* and compares the arming of the hero in *Li beaus desconus* (p. 321). Succeeding notes on *Sir Thopas* refer to the *Tournament of Tottenham, Perceval le Galois, Emaré,* and *Gamelyn.*

The romance of *Isumbras* is also alluded to in Tyrwhitt's note on "the Grete See" (p. 193), and the chronicle of Robert of Gloucester is mentioned a number of times in notes (pp. 204, 210), as is Peter of Langtoft (p. 252). An Oxford manuscript of Robert Mannyng of Brunne's *Handlyng Synne* is consulted for help with the difficult word *squaymous* (Tyrwhitt's line 3337; *MilT* A 3337). An English legendary in the Bodleian is quoted for the note on Saint Julian the hospitable (p. 203), while "that curious old Ballad, *The turnament of Tottenham*" (p. 232) is used to illustrate *the gree* (Tyrwhitt's line 2735; *KnT* A 2733). On the harrowing of hell, after citing the Gospel of Nicodemus, Tyrwhitt gives references to an English poem in a Bodleian manuscript and to the Chester Plays in a British Museum manuscript (p. 243). Again, in *The Nun's Priest's Tale* he notes that "Burnell" is used as a nickname for the ass in the Chester Plays (3.293). For the term *prime* Tyrwhitt also gives a number of references to English manuscripts (4.247–48), as he also does in annotating the term *cokenay* (p. 253) or *payndemayn* ("I find it twice in a Northern tale called 'The freiris of Berwick' "; p. 315).

Several Middle English works are particularly cited in Tyrwhitt's notes, including *Piers Plowman* and a text of *Mandeville's Travels*. Thus Mandeville is cited in connection with the location of the "Grete See" (4.193); the cult of the Holy Nails (p. 309); Saint Helena's discovery of the True Cross (p. 311); references to *clowe-gylofre* (p. 316), and "Sire Oliphaunt" (p. 318). Tyrwhitt's references to *Piers Plowman* draw on the poem for a range of annotation, to explain both words and also customs and concepts. Once again, Tyrwhitt goes directly to a manuscript, not caring to trust the old editions, as he reveals when citing *Piers Plowman* in his note on the *rekkeles* Monk: "In P. P. according to Ms. *Cotton.* Vesp. B. xvi. (for the passage is omitted in the printed editions) a similar saying is quoted from Gregory" (4.198). In his notes to the *Prologue* description of the Friar, Tyrwhitt draws on *Piers* in his explanation of *love-dayes* (p. 201) as of *courtepy* (p. 201). Similarly, Tyrwhitt draws on *Piers* for his glosses to *howe* (p. 248), *Malkins maidenhede* (p. 255), and a *sommergame* (p. 265).

Tyrwhitt's familiarity with apposite medieval literary parallels in French literature similarly produces a stream of references in his notes. Although some of these would not now appear in modern annotation, they do show Tyrwhitt's concern to set Chaucer in the context of medieval literature, as when—in his notes to *The Franklin's Tale*—he cites a selection of passages from Marie de France (taken from the manuscript) to illustrate her approach to the Breton lays. A number of references of this kind occur, as when

Tyrwhitt, in annotating "*In principio,*" quotes "an old French Romance" (p. 200), or in annotating *sausefleme* cites "an old Fr. book of Physick" (p. 212). Indeed, Tyrwhitt's note on "Termagaunt" in *Sir Thopas* shows he had looked at the Oxford manuscript of *La Chanson de Roland,* for he cites instances of "this Saracen deity, in an old Romance . . . The author's name was Turold, as appears from the last line" (pp. 318–19).

But the most frequently cited French medieval text is the *Roman de la Rose,* which produces a number of telling notes: the Prioress's table manners are compared with the account in the *Roman* (4.196); use of the *Roman* in *The Wife of Bath's Prologue* is pointed out (p. 264), as also in *The Physician's Tale* ("I find that our author has drawn more from thence, than from either Gower or Livy"; p. 305), and links are also noted with the Monk's tragedy of Nero (3.283). Apart from such larger uses, the *Roman* is frequently cited by Tyrwhitt in his interpretation of difficult single words and phrases (4. 258, 263).

The other French text recurrently cited in Tyrwhitt's notes is that of Froissart's *Chronicles.* Thus, on the description of Arcite's body on a bier "bare the visage," Tyrwhitt very appositely notes, "Froissart says, that the corpse of our Edward III was carried '*tout au long de la cité de Londres,* à viaire decouvert, *jusques à Westmonstier*' " (4.233). Froissart naturally is consulted on such historical matters as *Belmarye* or the *lord of Palatye* in the description of the Knight (4.192, 194), or on the identity of King Pedro's murderer (3.285–86). Even greater use of Froissart's writing is made to explain difficult idioms or words in the Chaucer text: thus, in glossing *to dien in the peyne,* Tyrwhitt vividly echoes from Froissart the very words of Edward III (4.219), and other phrases that are glossed with the help of parallels in Froissart include *exiled on his hed* (p. 220), *the maister strete* (p. 234), *his vassalage* (p. 235), *more tawe on his distaf* (p. 246), *riding fro river* (p. 270), *to hevy or to hote* (p. 272–73), *cuirbouly* (p. 322), and *thurgh jupartie* (3.299). Many references to chronicles, various medieval documentary evidence, and parliamentary records also throw light on every manner of "obsolete custom" (Preface): Walsingham is cited on the siege of Alexandria or on *Lettow* (4.191, 192), and some directions in French to the nuns of *Sopewell* are cited in connection with the Prioress's use of French (p. 196).

In brief, Tyrwhitt's commentary is characterized not only by its richness of information but also by the critical understanding of Chaucer that it often reflects. Thus, on Theseus's speech at the end of *The Knight's Tale,* Tyrwhitt notes: "Ver. 2993. that fayre chaine of love] Our author's philosophy is borrowed, as it is usually, from Boethius" (4.235). And on a passage in *The Nun's Priest's Tale,* Tyrwhitt comments: "One might be led to suspect that [Cicero] was here quoted at second hand, if it were not usual with Chaucer, to throw in a number of natural circumstances, not to be found in his original authors" (3.289).

Achievements

Ver. 307. in forme and reverence] *with propriety and modesty*. In the next line *"ful of high sentence"* means only, I apprehend, *"full of high*, or *excellent sense."*—Mr. Warton will excuse me for suggesting these explanations of this passage in lieu of those which he has given in his *Hist. of Eng. Po.* p. 451. The credit of good letters is concerned, that Chaucer should not be supposed to have made "a pedantic formality," and "a precise sententious style on all subjects," the characteristics of a scholar.

—Tyrwhitt, on *The General Prologue* portrait of the Clerk (3.315)

It is time to attempt some assessment of Tyrwhitt's achievements when compared with the preconceptions of his own period, and also of his influence on the editing of Chaucer. Inevitably modified by subsequent philological scholarship, Tyrwhitt's perception of Chaucer's metrical regularity still underlies later editing, while the centrality and rightness of so many of Tyrwhitt's explanatory notes has ensured that later commentaries have been founded upon them. But several other features of Tyrwhitt's edition have constituted comparable watersheds in the development of Chaucer editing—particularly the Glossary and the determination of the canon of Chaucer's works presented in the fifth (Glossary) volume of 1778.

In the Preface to the first four volumes (1775), Tyrwhitt commented that a glossary based on only part of Chaucer's works, even *The Canterbury Tales*, "must necessarily be a very imperfect work, the utility of which would by no means be proportionable to the labour employed in compiling it" (1.iii). Accordingly, in his later, fifth volume Tyrwhitt published a Glossary based on Chaucer's complete works. In the "Advertisement," Tyrwhitt acknowledges consulting Timothy Thomas's glossary to Urry's edition. This acknowledged debt apart, however, Tyrwhitt has gone much further and more rigorously than had previous studies of Chaucer's language. In each word entry Tyrwhitt aims to define "the part of speech to which each word belongs, and to distribute all homonymous words into separate articles [here Tyrwhitt comments sharply on Hearne's practice].[25] . . . The numbers, cases, modes, times, and other inflexions of the declinable parts of speech are also marked" (p. iii). Etymologies are not generally given, though Tyrwhitt briefly indicates the original language of a word. Taken together with the many glosses within his notes, the Glossary volume consolidates a study of Chaucer's language exceptional in its time and not soon superseded.

But to produce this Glossary based on Chaucer's whole oeuvre, Tyrwhitt needed to give an account of "what I conceive to be *the genuine* works of Chaucer, and of those which have been either falsely ascribed to him, or improperly intermixed with his, in the Editions" (5.i), and his work toward determining the Chaucer canon is among his most important. Tyrwhitt lists the following as Chaucer's works apart from the *Tales*: *The Romaunt of the Rose; Troilus and Criseyde* (with an estimate of how many lines are indebted to *Filostrato*); *The Court of Love* (included from "internal evidence"); *The Complaint Unto Pity; Anelida and Arcite; The Assemblee of Foules* (i.e., *Parliament*); *The Complaint of the Black Knight; An ABC; The Book of the Duchess; The House of Fame*; "Chaucer's Dreme" (i.e., *The Isle of Ladies*: "There is no ground for doubting the anthenticity of the poem itself "); *The Floure and the Lefe* ("I do not think its authenticity so clear as that of the preceding poem"); *The Legend of Good Women; The Complaint of Mars; The Cuckoo and the Nightingale*; the shorter poems, *The Envoy to Bukton, Lak of Stedfastnesse, Truth, Fortune, The Envoy to Scogan, The Complaint of Chaucer to His Purse, Gentillesse, To Adam*, and *Proverbs; Boece; A Treatise on the Astrolabe;* and *The Testament of Love*. Of all these Tyrwhitt declares: "The foregoing I consider as the genuine works of Chaucer" (5.xvii), commenting, "It would be a waste of time to sift accurately the heap of rubbish which was added, by John Stowe, to the Edit. of 1561" (5.xxii).[26] It is characteristic of Tyrwhitt not to repeat the earlier "Lives" of Chaucer that deduced and inferred from the spurious works, instead confining himself to printing a list of the known documentary references to Chaucer.[27]

This scholarly discipline over what relation the extant works may bear to the poet's life is typical of Tyrwhitt, who can comment drily on *Lak of Stedfastnesse*: "This balade is said to have been made by Chaucer *'upon his death-bed, lying in his anguish'*; but of such a circumstance some further proof should be required" (5.xv). Similarly, Tyrwhitt can differ over the authenticity of the *Retractions* with Hearne (who would reject them as a monkish adaptation) in a way that brings out both Tyrwhitt's discernment of what is Chaucerian and also his hesitation over "biographical" evidence: he accepts the *Retractions* as the authentic conclusion of *The Parson's Tale* but believes that it has been corrupted into a personal statement by "Chaucer" through the interpolation of the listing of his works, which Tyrwhitt prints in brackets. Yet it is Tyrwhitt who can recognize the authentic role of the tale in itself, as he comments in his "Introductory Discourse": "I cannot recommend it as a very entertaining or edifying performance at this day; but the Reader will be pleased to remember, in excuse both of Chaucer and his Editor, that, considering the Canterbury Tales as a great picture of life and manners, the piece would not have been complete, if it had not included the Religion of the time" (4.187). This range of sympathy and of reading in medieval literature means that Tyrwhitt is less likely to be misled by what he is able to see and can be explained through knowledge of medieval literary tradition. Thus Speght's identification of the daisy in *The Legend of Good Women Prologue* with Margaret, countess of Pembroke, can be dismissed by Tyrwhitt in the light of his own knowledge of the Marguerite poems of Machaut and Froissart (1.xxxiv–xxxv).

It is this exceptional respect for evidence within medieval tradition— seen throughout his editing of *The Canterbury Tales*—that distinguishes Tyrwhitt even from those in his own age who loved and honored the Middle

Ages, as is shown by two of Tyrwhitt's references to Bishop Percy and Bishop Hurd. On Percy's suggestion of a source for *The Wife of Bath's Tale*, Tyrwhitt remarks: "The old Ballad entitled "The Marriage of Sir Gawaine" [*Ancient Poetry* . . .], which the learned Editor thinks may have furnished Chaucer with this tale, I should rather conjecture (with deference to so good a judge in these matters) to have been composed by one who had read both Gower and Chaucer" (4.154). And in a note on *Thopas*, Tyrwhitt comments: "The very learned and ingenious author of *Letters on Chivalry*, &c. supposes, 'that the *Boke of The Giant Olyphant and Chylde Thopas* was not a fiction of Chaucer's own, but a story of antique fame, and very celebrated in the days of chivalry.' I can only say, that I have not been so fortunate as to meet with any traces of such a story of an earlier date than the Canterbury tales" (4.318). Not only in these comments on Percy and Hurd but also in his whole achievement in the edition of *The Canterbury Tales*—the tale order, the canon, the commentary, the Glossary, and the essay on meter— Tyrwhitt demonstrates what the *Gentleman's Magazine* praised in him (2 [1786]:718):

> His mode of criticism is allowed to have been at once rigorous and candid. As he never availed himself of petty stratagems in support of doubtful positions, he was vigilant to strip his antagonists of all such specious advantages. Yet controversy produced no unbecoming change in the habitual gentleness and elegance of his manners. His spirit of enquiry was exempt from captiousness, and his censures were as void of rudeness, as his erudition was free from pedantry.[28]

7. Thomas Wright
(1810–1877)

THOMAS W. ROSS

T HOMAS WRIGHT'S edition of *The Canterbury Tales* (vols. 1 and 2, 1847; vol. 3, 1851) appeared between the monumental editions of Tyrwhitt and Skeat. Although Wright's work is not comparable to that of either his predecessor or his successor, it is of lasting significance for two reasons. First, Wright chose, or perhaps happened upon, the best-text editorial method, which all subsequent editors of Chaucer have followed to a greater or lesser degree. Second, his explanatory notes, while not extensive, were the result of a lifetime devoted to medieval literature. They were incorporated by Skeat into his own massive annotations, which have, in turn, been used by all later editors. I shall return to these matters in due course.

In the *British Library Catalogue*, Thomas Wright has 129 entries, testimony to his remarkable industry, which filled a life that did not quite reach three score and ten. He died in 1877, at the age of sixty-seven.

Viewed from today's perspective, Wright's many publications would perhaps be considered antiquarianism rather than rigorous scholarship. Sir Sidney Lee called him an "enthusiastic pedestrian,"[1] which, while it is intended to describe Wright's delight in walking (and in writing about his walks), might be applied, if one were so unkindly inclined, to his antiquarian investigations. Indeed, Wright styles himself, not surprisingly, as an antiquary in the title of one of his works, *Wanderings of an Antiquary* (1854).

Pedestrian though some of his works might seem to us today, his publications indeed evince a contagious enthusiasm. Most of us will recall the delights that he made available to us in potpourri collections such as the *Reliquiae antiquae*, still the only available source for many curious and quaint medieval writings.

His broad interests were surely fostered by his education and are given testimony to by his early publications. He took his B.A. at Trinity College, Cambridge, in 1834; his M.A., in 1837. As an undergraduate he published his first piece of antiquarianism, the *History and Topography of Essex* (1831–36). Of it Lee writes, "He had many correspondents in the county, but he seems rarely to have visited it,"[2] perhaps an indication of Wright's attitude toward some of his publications that dealt with the past.

At Cambridge he also made the acquaintance of James Orchard Halliwell (later Halliwell-Phillipps), who remained a lifelong friend and collaborator. Both show a similar breadth of interest, though neither approached the scholarly attainments of a Tyrwhitt or a Skeat.

Upon leaving the university, Wright continued his career as an editor of medieval English and Latin works. He made his living by his pen—then, as now, a precarious livelihood. He held no academic positions and received no preferments until late in life. He was granted a stipend from the civil-list of £65 (1865), increased to £100 in 1872. This recognition of a lifetime's work may have come too late, for "after 1872 his mind failed, and he sank into imbecility before his death."[3]

Like most other eighteenth- and nineteenth-century editors of Chaucer, Wright seems to have trained himself in paleographic skills. Before the publication of his Chaucer edition, a quarter century's work had produced editions of both English and Latin pieces that demonstrate his thorough acquaintance with late medieval scribal habits. Further, he had amassed an impressive store of medieval lore which he could call upon in his introductions and annotations.

Like most other scholarly and antiquarian publication, Wright's work was not profitable. Much of it was printed at the expense of wealthy patrons—e.g., his volume of *Vocabularies* (1857), financed and privately printed by Joseph Mayer. Many of his works were supported by the various antiquarian societies that in nineteenth-century Britain were major publishers of scholarship.

Lack of money did not deter an enthusiast like Wright. By the time he turned to Chaucer, he had published a remarkable number of works. These include:

Early English Poetry (an anthology in black-letter, 1836)[4]
Alliterative Poem on the Deposition of Richard II (Camden Society, 1838)
Early English Literature (sketch, 1839)
Political Songs of England (Camden Society, 1839)
Reliquiae antiquae (with Halliwell, 1839–43)
Latin Poems Commonly Attributed to Walter Mapes (Camden Society, 1841)
Vision and Creed of Piers Ploughman (1842)
The Chester Plays (Shakespeare Society, 1843–47)

These selected titles show a pattern: Wright moved toward more substantial and important literature as his career progressed. He had also done work for the Percy Society, for which he eventually published fifteen volumes. Included among these was his edition of *The Canterbury Tales*.

His career did not, of course, end with the Chaucer, to which I shall return in a moment. He went on to compile the volume of *Vocabularies* (Latin-English glosses similar to the *Promptorium parvulorum*), to edit John of Garland's *De triumphis ecclesiae*, to edit *The Book of the Knight of the Tour-Landry* (for the EETS), and to provide two volumes for the Rolls Series. He also directed the excavation of a Roman city at Wroxeter, publishing his findings in 1859 (a fuller account in 1872).

Wright's work with *Piers Plowman* is indicative of his later practices as well. He printed the B version as it occurs in Trinity College, Cambridge (his old college), B.15.17, a good manuscript though, according to Skeat, inferior to Laud Misc. 581 (Bodleian Library), which the later editor used for his own B-text version.[5]

This editorial experience with a major work of fourteenth-century English literature was to be repeated when Wright eventually edited *The Canterbury Tales*: he chose as base text a good manuscript but one inferior to others (or another) that later scholarship has judged to be better.

After having edited *Piers*, the Chester Plays, and a great number of both important and nugatory *disjecta membra* of medieval literature, Wright turned to Chaucer. He professed to see the shortcomings of Tyrwhitt's edition (1775–78), of which he said in his Preface: "Tyrwhitt's entire ignorance of the grammar of the language of Chaucer is exhibited in almost every line, few of which could possibly have been written by the poet as he printed them."[6] Such an evaluation of Tyrwhitt is uncharitable and, as B. A. Windeatt's chapter on Tyrwhitt in this volume indicates, it is also inaccurate. Elsewhere, in his notes, Wright showed cordial regard for his great predecessor. Perhaps his real motive for attacking Tyrwhitt was not that he was sure that he could produce a better text than that printed in 1775 but that by denigrating Tyrwhitt's learning his own edition might expect some sales.

It must be confessed, however, that there is little in Wright's edition of *The Canterbury Tales* which was designed to correct whatever errors Tyrwhitt might have made in describing Chaucer's grammar or in transcribing his poetry. Wright was shrewd enough, on the other hand, to perceive that there were pitfalls in his great predecessor's editorial method. Wright's broad editorial experience, especially with *Piers*, gave him the confidence to point out that Tyrwhitt had formed his Chaucer text "from a number of different manuscripts, written at different times and at different places," a method that he called "the most absurd plan which it is possible to conceive."[7]

Although he considered the plan absurd, he nonetheless made extensive use of the great edition. But in an important sense, Wright was correct in

his censure of Tyrwhitt. The latter claimed to have used twenty-six manuscripts in preparing his edition. He did his work with disarming modesty,
and he usually made clear the provisional nature of his conjectures. His
respect for the manuscripts with which he worked entitles him to be called
the first critical editor of Chaucer.

Tyrwhitt's actual working procedure was to use Speght's second edition
of 1602, emending, in its margins, as his good editorial sense prompted
him. This was his printer-ready copy. He did not use his great wealth of
primary materials, the manuscripts, in a consistent fashion, and this
eclecticism was the basis for Wright's censure. Tyrwhitt knew enough
about Middle English verse to perceive that the poet's lines could be made
to scan if one took into account the final -e's. When Tyrwhitt did not find
what he wanted in Speght, he emended from whatever manuscript provided
him with an acceptable reading,[8] or he went back to Urry's edition, or he
simply made up the best reading to fit his ideas of Chaucer's regular iambic
pentameter. The result is a smooth Augustan version of Chaucer.

On the other hand, Wright could not have failed to be impressed and
influenced by Tyrwhitt's annotations and explanations of "hard words" in
The Canterbury Tales. He profited from his predecessor's erudition, as has
every subsequent editor, though his own edition has fewer notes than did
Tyrwhitt's, as we shall see.

By 1840 or so, the best-text method seems to have been established by
the classicists as a viable way—perhaps the only dependable way—of
editing a poet's works. Benedict Gotthelf Teubner, of Leipzig, had begun
his great series of classical editions, the Bibliotheca scriptorum Graecorum et
Romanorum Teubneriana. The first volume did not appear until 1849, but it
is possible that Wright knew of it earlier, and in any event the European
scholarly community must have been aware of this "new" editorial approach
to literature. Because it employed the best-text method, the Teubner Series
"attained high renown as containing the best available texts of the
classics."[9]

Among the twenty-six manuscripts consulted by Tyrwhitt was Harley
7334 (Ha[4]), though it is not one of the five to which he gave "most credit."
It is a handsome volume that contains a text of deceptive smoothness and
fluency. Actually it is extensively editorialized and inauthoritative. It is
independent of other major manuscript groups, but it shows contamination
from the Ellesmere (El) and the Hengwrt (Hg).[10]

Wright described his editorial method thus:

> . . . to form a satisfactory text of Chaucer, we must give up the printed
> editions, and fall back on the manuscripts; and . . . instead of bundling them
> together [as, in his view, Tyrwhitt had done] we must pick out one best
> manuscript which at the same time is one of those nearest to Chaucer's time.
> . . . At the same time, it cannot but be acknowledged, that the earliest
> manuscript might possibly be very incorrect and incomplete, from the

ignorance or negligence of the scribe who copied it. This, however, is fortunately not the case with regard to Chaucer's *Canterbury Tales*. The Harleian manuscript, No. 7334, is by far the best manuscript of Chaucer's *Canterbury Tales* that I have yet examined, in regard both to antiquity and correctness.

From the scribe's hand, Wright dated Ha^4 "a few years after 1400," which later scholarship has proved to be correct. Wright continued: "Its language has very little, if any, appearance of local dialect; and the text is extremely good, the variations from Tyrwhitt being usually for the better." He claimed to have collated *The Canterbury Tales* throughout with manuscript Lansdowne 851 (La), "which appears to be, of those in the British Museum, next in antiquity and value to the MS. Harl." He also claimed to have collated, as far as *The Wife of Bath's Tale*, Cambridge Mm.2.5 and Ii.3.26 but concluded: "In general, I have reaped little advantage from collating a number of manuscripts."[11] Manuscript La has some interest for present-day editors of Chaucer (it along with Ha^4 is included among the base group used for the Variorum Edition), but neither of the Cambridge manuscripts consulted by Wright has any authority.

Wright's statement is revealing: his antiquarian knowledge and his paleographical experience made it possible for him to date Ha^4 accurately. On the other hand, the remark about the absence of dialectical forms strikes the modern Chaucerian as peculiar since it is not a very useful basis for the judgment of the quality of a source. The reference to Tyrwhitt shows Wright's respect for his predecessor's work, even though he had roundly criticized it; furthermore, it indicates that Wright compared his transcription, with some consistency, with Tyrwhitt's edition. Finally, he coolly dismissed the value of methodical collation, thus betraying his impatience with this part of scholarly procedure.

Later in the century Chaucerians somewhat younger than Wright were to become interested in Ha^4, and it is possible that in his conversations with fellow antiquarians he heard its qualities praised.[12] But other than Wright's statement that Ha^4 was "by far the best manuscript of Chaucer's *Canterbury Tales* that I have yet examined," we have no explanation for the choice. It is not a dependable basis for an edition. Wright's younger contemporaries eventually lost their original enthusiasm for Ha^4 and ultimately rejected it as inauthoritative, though its importance as an early version of the *Tales* continues to be recognized. As the nineteenth century drew to its close, El emerged as editors' choice of best text, and it is the basis for Skeat's *Canterbury Tales* that appeared as part of his great edition of the *Works* in 1894. Oddly enough, the appearance of Wright's edition and its reviews may have been responsible for the ultimate recognition of the superiority of El, which had been ignored by Tyrwhitt and by Wright himself.[13]

Because of his new editorial method and his experience, Wright felt on sure editorial ground. He also had a good printed text, by a truly learned editor, which he could use as a guide—Tyrwhitt's. It should be observed in passing that Chaucer's editors have the disconcerting habit of making (sometimes extensive) use of their predecessors' work, which they criticize and claim to supersede. Tyrwhitt did this with Urry. Wright did it with Tyrwhitt. Skeat did it with Wright (see below). In a sense, Manly-Rickert did it with Skeat, since his *Student's Chaucer* was the printed edition that they used in their preparation for the recension that they hoped would produce O′, and some modern editors do the same, professing to have evolved authoritative texts from fresh sources while actually following others' printed texts more faithfully than they would like to admit.

Wright's choice of Ha^4 was unfortunate, as was his selection of base text for his edition of *Piers*, mentioned above. If he had copied the manuscript faithfully, he could have provided us with a diplomatic transcript of an important version of *The Canterbury Tales*. Furnivall eventually published such an edition.[14]

Nonetheless, Wright's methods, however faulty, broke new ground and lighted the way for all subsequent editors of Chaucer. The complete title of his work reads *The Canterbury Tales by Geoffrey Chaucer: A New Text with Illustrative Notes*. As do all the other good manuscripts, Ha^4 presents the *Tales* in a plausible order, though of course it does not correct the inconsistencies that have plagued so many commentators. Wright did not deal with the problem of order—merely following that of his manuscript—and thus avoided the question that was confronted, if not solved, by both his predecessor and his successor, Tyrwhitt and Skeat.

As his title page promised, there are notes, and many of them were incorporated into later, more prestigious editions. In view of Wright's erudition—and his use of Tyrwhitt as a model—the notes are oddly scanty. Perhaps the publisher, who may have hoped for some commercial success with this edition of Chaucer, enjoined the editor to keep his explanations at a minimum. For the 745 lines of *The Miller's Tale*, which I shall use to illustrate his methods, he provided only 35 notes. By comparison, Tyrwhitt has 48, many of which were cited by Wright, and Skeat has 118, several of them extensive excursuses. Some of Wright's notes consist of a single line; almost none is supported by authority; and later scholarship has shown some to be downright wrong.

Here is a typical Wrightian note:

> 3216. *Angelus ad virginem*. One of the hymns of the church service. It is more difficult to say what was the *kynges note* in the next line.

In fairness it should be admitted that we are still not sure what the "kynges note" was, though there have been several conjectures in our century. Wright confessed his ignorance with beseeming modesty (as before him Tyrwhitt had done) but it would not have taken much labor to have ascertained that the *Angelus ad virginem* is an Annunciation hymn. Later commentators have of course made much of the ironic relevance of such a song issuing from the mouth of the adulterous Nicholas.

It will be remembered that in his preface Wright expressed open contempt for Tyrwhitt's knowledge of Middle English. Nonetheless, he respectfully cited his predecessor in matters of metrical judgment. Obviously he had Tyrwhitt's edition open before him as he made his line-by-line transcription of Ha^4, though he did not "cannibalize" the earlier work. He quoted with approval Tyrwhitt's idea that "Now, deere lady, if thi wille be" (line 3361) contains internal rhyme—a notion at which Skeat (5.104) sneered in a note which begins "Tyrwhitt absurdly says." Skeat went on to point out that Chaucer could never have rhymed "lady" with "be," though Wright agreed with Tyrwhitt that such a rhyme was possible.

In his note to line 3358, Wright surmised that a "shot-wyndowe" was one from which inhabitants shot at those trying to break in. He dismissed all previous conjectures but provided no basis for his own, which has been accepted by no subsequent editor.

He correctly identified "him that harwed helle" (line 3512) as "Our Saviour" but did not point out the apocryphal basis for the legend. Instead he provided the information that the Harrowing was presented in the mystery plays (in which play or plays he did not say, though he had edited the Chester cycle), "from which representations the lower orders obtained their notions of scripture history and theology." He can be forgiven the reference to the "lower orders," which strikes us today as supercilious, but in view of his own experience and knowledge the explanation is curiously sketchy.

On the other hand, his notes provided original and useful information, as that for line 3767 (3769 in Robinson and other modern editions), where he correctly glossed "gay gerl" as "a young woman of light manners." To substantiate this reading, he adduced a parallel use of the phrase from the time of Henry VIII. Neither Skeat nor Robinson offers an explanation of "gay gerl" in his notes, though a search of their glossaries will give the reader the appropriate sense.

He did not even offer a conjecture for the meanings of "hard words" like "gnof" (line 3188), "derne" (line 3200), or "i-dight" (line 3205), but, then, neither had Tyrwhitt. There are, of course, still plenty of unsolved puzzles in *The Miller's Tale* (and elsewhere in Chaucer's works). Unfortunately, Thomas Wright did not have the time—or perhaps space—to bring his erudition to bear upon them. The reader of his text would understand the events of *The Miller's Tale* but would be left with countless questions about details.

In transcribing the manuscript, Wright chose to normalize spelling and to introduce modern punctuation, both of which are an editor's privilege, especially if he intends the text for the general reader. Actually *The Miller's Tale* comes out better in this regard than it had in Tyrwhitt's edition, where

one is confronted by superfluous punctuation such as "n'as" for Wright's
"nas."

The edition itself was, however, unsatisfactory. An editor who follows
the best-text method will emend on the basis of authority when he finds it
necessary, as I said above. When Wright decided to alter an Ha⁴ reading, he
sometimes appended a note but seldom did he provide authority for the
change:

> 3203   A chambir had he in that hostillerye
> Wright's note: *that*. The MS. Harl. reads *in his hostillerye* [Wright followed
> Tyrwhitt's *that* but with no acknowledgment]. It may be observed that it was
> usual in the university for two or more students to have one room.

> 3255   For brighter was the schynyng of hir hewe
> Wright's note: *schynyng*. The MS. Harl. reads *smylyng*, contrary to the other
> MSS. that I have examined [Tyrwhitt has *shining*. Wright perhaps got the *sch-*
> from La. It is probably just as likely to have been a deliberate archaism, a
> "quaint" spelling].

Sometimes Wright chose not to emend but cited Tyrwhitt in a note:

> 3322   Schapen with goores in the newe get
> Wright's note: Instead of this line, Tyrwhitt reads,—*Ful faire and thicke ben
> the pointes set* [which is the reading in all the best MSS—except Ha⁴].

> 3367   That chaunteth thus under oure boure smal
> Wright's note: Tyrwhitt, with some MSS., reads *boures wal* [as again do all the
> best MSS].

Similarly in his notes to lines 3377 and 3485 Wright gave obeisance to
Tyrwhitt while retaining the Ha⁴ reading.

Sometimes Wright kept the Ha⁴ reading in preference to that in Tyrwhitt but did not justify his choice. For the following he provided no note at
all—an example that could be multiplied many times:

> 3110   In all the route nas ther yong ne old
> Tyrwhitt: In al the compagnie n'as ther yong ne old

Occasionally he mustered the courage to reject Tyrwhitt's reading in favor
of that in his base text:

> 3378   And sent hire pyment, meth, and spiced ale
> Wright's note: *pyment*. Piment was a kind of spiced wine. Tyrwhitt's reading,
> *pinnes*, is certainly much inferior to the one in the text.

Most reprehensible was his habit of emending silently:

> 3420   That Nicholas stille in his chambre lay
> Ha⁴ reads: Tha Nicholas in his chambre lay

> 3586   That non of us ne speke not a word
> Ha⁴ reads: That not of us ne speke not a word

3605 What al this queinte cast was for to seye
Ha⁴ reads: What al this wente cast was for to seye

3618 He weepeth, wayleth, maketh sory cheere
Ha⁴ reads: He weepeth wayleth he maketh sory cheere

Tyrwhitt was clearly the source for all four of these emendations, but Wright cited neither him nor any manuscript.

Understandably the reception of Wright's text was not favorable. When the first volume appeared in 1847, there was published an unsigned article (by Richard Garnett)[15] that lumped together Wright's earlier publications with the edition of *The Canterbury Tales*. Evidently Garnett had seen the first volume of the edition, but there is no evidence that he had examined it with care. He had certainly read the Preface (see his remarks below concerning the attack on Tyrwhitt). The review is astonishingly bitter and personal. It is couched in terms that would be considered libelous today. There is no mention of Wright's choice of Ha⁴ as copy text or of his editorial methods or notes, though Garnett sometimes attacked explicit deficiencies in Wright's earlier publications.

The following are typical excerpts: "We have our own reasons for distrusting everything done under [Wright's] superintendence, if the task demand the smallest possible amount of critical skill or acumen. . . . Blunders of this sort are simply the fruits of ignorance and carelessness." Wright is compared with earlier scholars, including Percy, Warton, Ellis, and Price, who were "something more than mere mechanical translators of ancient poetry."

Garnett continued with heavy irony, lauding Wright for the "singular grace and propriety [with which] he vituperates his predecessor Tyrwhitt for *philological deficiencies!*" [italics Garnett's]. Wright is one of the swarm of "half-learned smatterers [who are the] very plague and pestilence of our literature."

The hapless editor was ridiculed for glossing "brok" in *Piers Plowman* as "an animal of the badger kind." And finally, while acknowledging Wright's industriousness, Garnett concluded that "his activity is so counter-balanced by want of scholarship and acumen, that he can never be more than a third or fourth rate personage."

One is reminded of the infamous (and mortal?) attacks upon Keats that appeared in *Blackwood's* and the same *Quarterly* that published Garnett's article. Surely there must have been personal animosity between the reviewer and the unfortunate "third or fourth rate personage," Thomas Wright. Perhaps it was the familiar self-made-man's suspicion of the university graduate. Garnett was not a college man but had taught himself all the major European languages, including Celtic, in which he was an expert. Wright was B.A., M.A., Cantab. One is inevitably reminded, too, of Chaucer's own carpenter and miller (in the tales told by the Miller and the

Reeve) who express open contempt for university clerks and their "learning."

No review of Wright's complete three-volume edition ever appeared in the *Quarterly*, perhaps because their reviewer Garnett died in 1850. But in 1851 the *Athenaeum* published a gentler, but still censorious, review upon the appearance of the third volume.[16] The writer praised Wright for his method: the editor had adhered to the "sound principle" of a single manuscript as the basis for his text—in contrast to Tyrwhitt's eclectic employment of several manuscripts. The reviewer took Wright to task, however, for emending without reference to source, for using Tyrwhitt without acknowledging the debt, and for intruding words of his own to mend the meter.

At the same time the *Athenaeum* writer expressed surprise that Wright (and all other editors of Chaucer) had ignored a splendid manuscript. It is the Ellesmere, though it was not then known by that name:

> . . . the venerable volume in the library of the Marquis of Stafford . . . with elaborate illuminations. . . . If we are not mistaken, it will be found to afford a purer, if not an older, text than any similar authority by which editors have assisted themselves; and we are not a little surprised that anybody should have thought of publishing a new impression of the "Canterbury Tales" without first having recourse to it.

The reviewer was right about El, except for his judgment of its age. It was composed about the same time as Ha^4. The world had to wait for Skeat's edition of 1894, however, before that manuscript was used in an intelligent way by an editor. Perhaps Skeat had read the *Athenaeum* and had tracked down this most beautiful of all of the manuscripts of *The Canterbury Tales*.

Oddly enough—and sadly enough, too—despite the bad reviews Wright's text was reprinted in the popular series of English authors published in 1854–56 by Robert Bell and again in 1890 by Blackwood, apparently from old stereotype plates. In America, Thomas Y. Crowell brought out his own *Poetical Works of Geoffrey Chaucer*, again with Wright's introduction and his text of *The Canterbury Tales*. More curious is that in 1878 Skeat, who was later both to praise Wright's work and to revile it in terms almost as strong as those of Garnett, published a Chaucer edition as it had been printed by Bell. The revision of this four-volume work consisted in Skeat's identification of the spurious poems, which he placed in a separate volume. Wright's text of the *Tales* remained unchanged.[17]

Thus during the last half of the nineteenth century, on both sides of the Atlantic, Wright's text was standard for *The Canterbury Tales*. As early as 1862 his work was given a stamp of approval by no less an authority than F. J. Child, of Harvard. Child used it as the basis for his study entitled *Observations on the Language of Chaucer*. He described Wright's edition thus: "Though the editor informs us that he has corrected many obvious errors, we may regard the text as essentially a reprint of Harleian MS. 7334. As such it is of great value, but it is, nevertheless, by no means a satisfactory, or even a comfortably readable text." Child admitted that there were errors both manifest and probable, but maintained that "there are long passages which appear to be but very slightly corrupted from the original, the metre being regular, and certain plain grammatical laws uniformly observed."[18]

Child thus exhibited the same familiar equivocal view of Wright's text as did Skeat, who, as we have seen, gave his own imprimatur to his predecessor's work by reprinting the text of *The Canterbury Tales* unchanged. Skeat also had fulsome praise for Child, the American professor from Harvard, and for his definitive work on Chaucer's language, even though it was based on Wright's "reprint" of Ha[4].[19]

After he had completed his own monumental edition of Chaucer's *Works*, Skeat ceased to equivocate. He gave Wright's edition its coup de grace in 1900, beginning with the old antiquarian's preface, which he reprinted with a running commentary (here enclosed in brackets):

> Tyrwhitt's entire ignorance of the grammar of the language of Chaucer is exhibited in almost every line, few of which could possibly have been written by the poet as he printed them. [Skeat: A gross exaggeration; very many lines are correct.] It need only be stated, as an instance of this, that in the preterites of what the modern Teutonic philologists term the strong verbs . . . Tyrwhitt has inevitably placed a verb in the plural with a noun in the singular. [Skeat: Not invariably; Tyrwhitt has *slep*, Prol. 98; *carf*, Prol. 100.] Examples of this (in the verbs *to bear*, of which the correct forms were, s. *bar*, pl. *bare* [Skeat: The more "correct" form is *beren*; both *baren* and *beren* occur in Chaucer, though not (perhaps) in the C.T. Wright was thinking of Prol. 105, 108, where Tyrwhitt has *he bare*.]; *to come*, s. *cam*, pl. *come*; *to swear*, s. *swor*, pl. *swore*; *to give*, s. *gaf*, pl. *gave* [Skeat: We should expect sing. *yaf*, pl. *yeve*; he refers to Prol. 177, where Tyrwhitt has *He yafe*, Wright *He gaf*, and the Harl. MS. *ȝaf* (= *yaf*).]; *to speak*, s. *spak*, pl. *spake*; *to rise*, s. *ros, roos*, pl. *rose* [Skeat: This is truly astonishing; the pl. form is *rise(n)*, but it does not occur So also the pl. of *rood* (he rode) is *riden*, as printed by Tyrwhitt (and by Wright!) in Prol. 825 (or 827)] . . . occur in almost every sentence. [Skeat: Yet the strong verbs in the pt. t. are rare.] In the verb *to sit*, of which the pret. s. and pl. was *sette* [Skeat: Not so; the pt. t. was *sat*, pl. *sēte*. And both Tyrwhitt and Wright (!) have *sat*, Prol. 469 (or 471).].

Skeat continued in the same vein with "but *crepen* had . . . and Wright himself prints. . . . How so? . . . Yet . . . Wright himself has. . . . It will be seen that the case is overdrawn, and that Wright knew but little better than his predecessor."

Thus Skeat exposed both Wright's and Tyrwhitt's ignorance of Middle English. His treatment of Wright's editorial methods was no less scathing. As I have done above, he pointed out instances of silent emendation and emendation-without-authority (except sometimes for Tyrwhitt) to mend the meter. He concluded thus:

Truly the fates were strongly against the early production of a good text of the Tales. All the black-letter editions were very unsatisfactory, owing to their unphonetic spelling [but surely much more significantly because of their use of inferior manuscripts and because of their dependence upon their predecessors' printed editions]. Urry's edition was much worse, and is quite the worst on record. Tyrwhitt trusted too much in the old editions, and too little to the MSS. Wright took as the basis of his text the faulty and treacherous Harleian MS. [see above, footnote 12, for evidence that Skeat himself sometimes respected and used Ha^4]; and Bell followed Wright blindly, exclaiming all the while that he did so with open eyes. . . . Nevertheless, Mr. Wright's edition was long accepted as being almost the best possible.[20]

Poor Thomas Wright: the "half-learned smatterer" had actually chosen an editorial practice that might have produced truly the "best possible" text of *The Canterbury Tales*—if only he had selected a more authoritative manuscript as his copy text and had emended sparingly, and with authoritative basis—not to smooth the meter, but to try to reproduce, as accurately as possible, what Chaucer wrote. Yet his edition represented Chaucer's most famous work for almost a half century. His learned annotations, though regrettably sparse, were incorporated in later editors' notes.

Most significantly, Wright's editorial method paved the way for all later Chaucerians who undertake the editing of *The Canterbury Tales*.[21]

8. Frederick James Furnivall (1825–1910)

DONALD C. BAKER

I T IS DIFFICULT to discuss F. J. Furnivall's contribution as an editor to the history of Chaucerian textual studies without divagations upon his remarkable character and life, but no extensive discussion is required at the outset, for inevitably any treatment of his work must at least by indirection touch upon his personal qualities, his enthusiasm, his zest for work, his admiration for learning wherever he found it, and, above all, his love for Chaucer, whom he names his favorite poet after Tennyson.[1] As he tells us in his *A Temporary Preface to the Six-Text Edition of Chaucer's Canterbury Tales, Part I*,[2] he was moved to make accessible the principal manuscripts of the great poet, as far as he, with much help from others, could determine them, by the pleas of the great American scholar F. J. Child, in the aftermath of the American Civil War. Furnivall was stirred by the fact that the most important work in the language of Chaucer had been done by a foreigner, and by one who had spent an important part of his life engaged otherwise in a noble cause, that of fighting slavery (a legacy of the English, as the liberal Furnivall bitterly remarked),[3] and felt that the least an Englishman of kindred spirit could do was to provide the important texts of one of England's greatest poets (and greatest spirits) for the study and enjoyment of all who shared the language of England. Because the efforts and resources of Furnivall's other society founded for similar purposes, the Early English Text Society, were fully employed in providing the grist for the great *New English Dictionary*, it was for this purpose of serving the international fellowship of good men who admired good work that the Chaucer Society was formed with Furnivall's characteristic directness, suddenness, and enthusiasm. The society was, in a sense, dedicated to Child (the Six-Text edition is specifically dedicated to him), and to foreigners, such as the great European scholars (the *Parallel Print of the Minor Poems* is dedicated to ten Brink), who had brought so much light to a cultural heritage shrouded in darkness, except for the labors of Tyrwhitt. Furnivall's contempt for his own countrymen who were content to remain ignorant of the real text of Chaucer, or in the case of the noble lord who refused to part with his manuscript for the purpose of letting it be copied, was unbounded.[4]

Furnivall's contribution to the history of Chaucer's text *as an editor* may not be easily assessed. The Six-Text edition and the subsequent editions of Harleian 7334 (H^4) and Cambridge Dd.4.24, as well as the texts of *Troilus and Criseyde* and of the minor poems, are perhaps not editions as we would use the term normally. Furnivall's chief contributions must be said to have lain in the selection of the texts, seeing to it that they were well copied, printed (Furnivall raising the money), and well proofread (most of which work Furnivall did himself). Furnivall was clearly not a textual scholar, in the sense that Henry Bradshaw was, but he was fully aware of this, and at every step he generously gave credit to his chief advisers, Bradshaw, Morris, Ellis, and others. But, however regretfully one must assess the genuinely editorial capacities of Furnivall, one must not, as we will see, be led into the assumption that Furnivall was merely an ignorant enthusiast. On the contrary, he was an extremely learned man in certain ways, and part of the reason for our dismissal of his more narrowly textual abilities can be found in the readiness with which he admitted his own mistakes; surely no editor has ever been so willing to admit his own error and seize upon a correction by another instead of stubbornly clinging to error and only grudgingly and silently admitting mistakes by quiet emendation in subsequent printings. Furnivall fell upon accurate scholarship with enthusiasm and gratitude, as will be evident in the following pages. It is owing to Furnivall's own blunt honesty that we are as aware of his imperfections as we are. His works are sprinkled with footnotes almost gleefully announcing that his conclusions or facts have been challenged and corrected by another scholar.

Imperfections there must have been, if we survey his work in the Chaucer Society alone, forgetting completely that he was at the same time fully engaged in the Early English Text Society, the Philological Society, and many others, and engaged always also in the steady compiling of slips and of cajoling, arguing, and maneuvering to achieve the lifetime's dream that he knew well he himself did not have the final qualities necessary to bring about, the great *New English Dictionary*.[5] The texts of Chaucer were printed over a period of thirty-four years (1868–1902), with the great majority being copied, printed, and proofed in an amazingly short period of eight years (1868–76). For this great project Furnivall not only selected the manuscripts after considerable deliberation and assistance from others but oversaw the copying, devised the scheme of presentation, hit upon the method of representing the manuscript's written forms on the printed page, read the proofs—after having arranged by a variety of means to pay for the printing and the distribution of the fascicles (for the subscriptions were never in themselves enough to support the project). It is not exaggeration at all to say that the selection and printing of this series of texts was the most important contribution by one man to the tradition of Chaucerian textual study, quite different in kind from the work of Tyrwhitt and Furnivall's colleague Skeat, and far different indeed from that of Manly and Rickert and the Chaucer Laboratory at Chicago. This is not to say that the later work would not have been ultimately possible, but certainly it would have taken very much longer. Someone would, for example, have *printed* Chaucer in the late fifteenth or early sixteenth century if Caxton had not done it, but Skeat's edition would have been impossible within the lifetime of that scholar, and the Manly and Rickert *Text*, which used Skeat as a copy text, and must have had its origins in the evidence of the Six-Text print, would have been difficult in the extreme (difficult as it *was*) without so much of the ground having been broken by Furnivall's labors.[6] Finally, however, in justice one must say that Furnivall never edited Chaucer and that the edition of which Child had dreamed and toward which Furnivall worked so mightily, was to be the work of Skeat, culminating the labors of the Chaucer Society, though it did not, of course, appear under their imprint.

In an attempt to present a fair summation of Furnivall's contribution to Chaucer's text, I shall discuss Furnivall's procedures in selecting his texts, the nature of his collaboration, if it can be called that, with Henry Bradshaw, and then, in connection with the description of Furnivall's text, the very important question of his accuracy in representing them.

Furnivall's major contribution to the study of the text of *The Canterbury Tales* must, of course, be the Six-Text parallel edition together with the subsequent separate publication of the Harley 7334 (H^4) and the Cambridge Dd.4.24. In his *A Temporary Preface to the Six-Text Edition* (the word "temporary" fits like a glove Furnivall's own always modest assessment of his own work) he provides a grab bag of material on the text and other matters, the most important of which is his section on the "Specialties" of the principal manuscripts, the first reasonably detailed comments on the strengths and weaknesses of the various manuscripts, however superficial the discussions may seem today. One is struck by the fact that Furnivall goes right to the best manuscripts, Hengwrt and Ellesmere. Although Hengwrt receives little discussion, Furnivall recognizes it, in spite of its poor condition, as a manuscript of the first importance, the "second best" to Ellesmere. While Furnivall is still impressed by Harleian 7334, that manuscript's weaknesses are exposed by the detailed comparisons provided by Morris (pp. 70–87), and Furnivall did not include it in the Six-Text edition. Most of the material for the discussion of Cambridge Gg.4.27 was provided by Bradshaw, who had labored to bring that important manuscript to public attention. Furnivall's acceptance of its importance, in spite of its many peculiarities, which had at first put him off, is a good indication of Furnivall's instinct, which is an extremely important factor in assessing the value of his work. Furnivall preferred Cambridge Dd.4.24 and had intended it for the Six-Text but discarded it (to be printed later) because of its incompleteness and because of Bradshaw's cogent arguments. Likewise, Murray's analysis of the linguistic peculiarities of Lansdowne 851 (La) played an important role in Furnivall's deciding to print that manuscript (though it must be admitted that perhaps its beauty played a part, too).

Throughout Furnivall's discussion in his Preface of the reasons for choosing this manuscript and excluding that one, there runs this mixture of the textual and the personal. This method of assembling the texts combines those features which every scholar would approve with elements at which one can only stand aghast. Although the results were excellent, one can only muse at the principle which he describes (pp. 5–7): that of the plan of getting the three best texts from public institutions and the three best in private hands. This would seem to be a strange method indeed by which to select texts, but one must take into account Furnivall's political motivations (which in a sense underlie all of his work). He was by conviction opposed to national literary treasures belonging to individuals, and it was very important to him, on the basis of that principle, to print the best manuscripts so excluded from the public domain that he could procure, and so to publish them, in the broadest sense. Having acquired Ellesmere, Hengwrt, and Petworth from the "private sector," he determined then "to turn to public Libraries; and with the desire of choosing, if possible, one from each of our great stores of MSS, London, Cambridge, and Oxford" (p. 6). To think of impartially representing both Oxford and Cambridge in such a matter (Furnivall being a Cambridge man) and bringing in London to act as a proper balance! But it made for a kind of crazy sense as well as neat symmetry. On this basis he describes (pp. 6–7) the agony of choosing between Gg.4.27 and Dd.4.24 at Cambridge. In spite of the "offensive" language of the former it was finally selected, as we have observed, as being the more nearly complete (and because of Bradshaw's persuasion). The importance of Dd.4.24 did not escape Furnivall, however, and he caused it to be copied against its later publication (1902). The Corpus Christi presented fewer problems at Oxford, though Furnivall was sorely tempted by Arch. Seld. B.14, the only manuscript which had the Man of Law preceding the Shipman, which was the order roughly bearing out the Bradshaw Shift in the order of the *Tales* which Furnivall had enthusiastically embraced. The obvious inferiority of the Selden, however, caused Furnivall to select the Corpus Christi, though he continued to play with the idea of printing all or part of the Selden at a later date. Furnivall was guided throughout by the advice of others, as he makes clear, notably Morris, Bradshaw and Earle, but the selections were finally his own. The three primary considerations for Furnivall throughout, then, were (1) the desire to bring together manuscripts from private and public libraries, (2) the desire to print, whenever possible, *complete* manuscripts, and (3) the desire to print the best manuscripts that could be found. I do not mean to suggest that these three motivations were always in that order, but that is the order in which Furnivall actually discusses them, and we know from his correspondence that his priorities were in fact roughly in that order.

The problem of the order of the tales forced itself upon Furnivall because, if he was to arrange the manuscripts in a parallel-text edition, obviously there had to be congruity in order, or else the order had to be changed for printing (as was to be the case anyway, particularly with the Hengwrt). He followed basically the order suggested to him and worked out by Bradshaw,[7] whom he lavishly acknowledges. Furnivall's own contribution to the order was the shift of fragment C (*The Physician's Tale* and *The Pardoner's Tale*) to place no. 4 largely on the strength of the Pardoner's indication that he was hungry. Although the Chaucer Society order and numbering has had much influence in the tradition of the text of *The Canterbury Tales*, this particular shift of fragment C has been largely ignored since it was enshrined in Skeat's edition. Furnivall's speculations on the number of days that the pilgrimage required, and so forth, are of no particular importance for the history of the text of *The Canterbury Tales*, but his adoption of "the Bradshaw shift," that is, moving fragment VII (*The Shipman's Tale* through *The Nun's Priest's Tale*) up to the position following *The Man of Law's Tale*, a position that in the lettering of the fragments caused it to become B[2] (*The Physician's Tale* and *The Pardoner's Tale* being C and *The Wife of Bath's Tale, The Friar's Tale,* and *The Summoner's Tale* being D) has been quite important and continues to be debated,[8] though it was later abandoned by Skeat himself, as we shall see.

It might be worthwhile at this point, in which the collaboration of Furnivall and Bradshaw is germane, to illustrate their relationship so that a just balance can be struck in assessing their proper roles in the creation of the Six-Text edition. Two letters may be submitted as fair evidence of the sort of collaboration, if one may use that term, that occurred between the two, letters which attest to almost everything of importance: the respect of Furnivall for Bradshaw (a respect not fully returned), the former's willingness to put himself to school to Bradshaw, Furnivall's artless admission of his own inadequacies (above all, the stunning admission that he had not even read Tyrwhitt before beginning his textual preparations), but finally Furnivall's unswerving idealism which had Chaucer as its center, and his determination to cling to his great idea, however much Bradshaw might bully or ridicule him.

The first is Bradshaw's, to Furnivall, dated from the University Library, Cambridge, August 6, 1868:[9]

Dear Furnivall,

Thanks for your letter and its enclosures—The skeleton is admirably done if you had but gone a little further. Not having any definite point of view as a reason for your subdividing I suppose it doesn't matter to you; but if your object were, as mine is, to see how they [the *Tales* and links] were actually written, with a view of seeing how the work may be partially reconstructed, you would see that the three most important subdivisions are ignored in your scheme.

When I wrote my notices of the Fragments which you read and discussed last September, I only refrained from *printing* the notices with the list of contents because it seemed absured to print so much in such an utterly unreadable form, and I hoped to get the collection done before it could be really wanted.

When you determined to start a Chaucer Society, you remember we discussed the way of printing. You were for doing what you still insist upon doing, printing the copies parallel. I urged what I consider the only rational way, printing a manuscript as it stands, only with all the divisions and subdivisions marked.

Once break up the work into its 47 pieces, and give a skeleton in which every one of these parts has been numbered, & you have only to go through a MS. and take down the order in which the pieces come & you are master of the subject.

Had you adopted my plan, it was necessary to have carefully laid down *before you start*, exactly what division & subdivision you would recognize. But with your plan, there could be no call for this until you reached The Reves Tale at earliest. Otherwise I should have printed my notices months ago. I did not see the object of printing merely to be penny-a-lined about—& at that time there was no prospect of anything else. When I learnt from M\u02b3 Hall that you were at work on the skeleton I thought I might as well print that it might possibly be of use to you—accordingly I sent my papers to the press just as you saw them last year, & I shall merely put a postscript adding what had occurred to me on the subject since.

[Goes on to say that he cannot work as fast as Furnivall.]

My only comfort in the turn-up is that you are at last beginning to appreciate Tyrwhitt. I never could understand how a professed lover of Chaucer could despise Tyrwhitt. It is this alone which has given me that extreme prejudice against your Morris's and Skeat's Chaucer work. I am quite willing that you should think as you now believe that I have been palming off as my own what I merely stole from Tyrwhitt. As long as you will be grateful to him and read him, I shall be content . . . .

                                                                    H Bradshaw

To Bradshaw, from 3 Saint George's Square, August 6, 1868:

My Dear B

So long as you print, I am satisfied. But I must say, in answer to your notes
(1) I wished to follow your scheme; not to have the bore of making one out for myself. I wrote to you & asked for yours, telling you I had lost my copy. You wouldn't, or at least didn't, send me another copy, which wouldn't have taken you 2 min. to write. So I had to make out my own, & found that for my 1st purpose the mere tabulation of Tyrwhitt would do. I am going on to the

47 pieces or whatever no. they prove to be: but as yet the groups are not done. Till I've got a report of every MS. I can't say whether there are 47 or 57 bits. Of the Tales one can be sure: of the chats, not; at least, I can't.

2) You wouldn't let me have one of your proofs, tho' you knew it would have saved me time & trouble & money to.

3) I offered in every way but giving up the parallel plan to work out your notions, & printed the statement in the prospectives that a separate of each MS. would be given as well as the parallel one. [And, of course, it was eventually done.] It was you who refused to work with me, or let me work under you.

4) Till about 2 months ago I never owned a Tyrwhitt, nor had I ever read him. My impression of him was formed from what Wright & others had said of his text. You were the first that ran counter to this. About a fortnight ago, or whenever it was that I made up my mind you were ungenerously keeping back your plan of the Tales from me, I for the first time read a good bit of Tyrwhitt, & found that he did know his business—except the grammar, say—& found some at least if not much of what you had told me (assuming no doubt that I knew Tyrwhitt) was in him. You would not in talking say "That's T's, etc., That's mine" always, & my tendency is to put down to men whom I like more than they'd themselves claim. I have never been able to acknowledge the value of your work, & don't think I shall be.

Your holding it back, I don't like.

Talk of penny-a-lining as you choose, it enables one to interest a large circle of men not only in Chaucer but in other good men & good work. Had you just been willing to carry on a public with you in your work, it would have increased your usefulness & your power, & saved me & others a lot of trouble—There, that's over. Of course, I shall like to see your pamphlet or essay, & shall work on my own way now till I get to your results, or some others.

My second table went to the printers this morning; & soon I hope to have in type the varying prologues & chats from every MS. Then with the facts before me, I shall try what conclusions I can draw. At present the best result of what I have done is the drawing out of your essay.

Yours always

FJ Furnivall

Earlier, Bradshaw's criticism of Furnivall's mass-produced Early English Text Society volumes was even more trenchant and in many cases, of course, was accurate. Bradshaw wrote Furnivall in 1867 a blistering attack upon Panton's edition of Lydgate's *Troy Book*, pointing out that Panton's manuscript had been missing three whole pages which Panton had neglected to note, and ridicules Furnivall's attempt at what might be called a type facsimile with abbreviations and so on, carefully italicized or typographically represented: "At this point your notelet comes in. You now perhaps see what I mean by the remarkable absence of literary editorial power w[h] the Society's work displays. A great deal of care about marginal notes, italic abbreviations, etc., etc., etc., etc., but not a feather's weight of care for the substance of the matter."[10] Bradshaw later in the same letter continued the attack: "And what I insist on is that until some of you begin to *edit* books there is no chance for any of us learning anything."

As anyone who has studied the earlier productions of the EETS overall will recognize, Bradshaw had certainly got a point. Many of the early editions were slipshod, for which Furnivall frequently did not himself even read proof. The appearance of careful typesetting is particularly annoying when the material itself is shoddily represented, and some of the introductions are not only frivolous but downright wrong.

We are here concerned, however, with the Chaucer Society, in which Furnivall took a much more personal role, and with the great texts with which Furnivall was deeply concerned and which he, and his long-suffering copyists, printers, and fellow proofreaders produced. The texts themselves are much alike, in appearance like those of the EETS. Furnivall, as he tells us, aimed to reproduce the manuscript itself as closely as possible, expanding obvious abbreviations (with italics), but generally wherever there was a doubt about practice reproducing the brevigraphs used by the scribes with a variety of printed symbols. The appearance on the page, as Bradshaw noted of the volumes of the EETS, certainly gives an impression of scholarly impeccability. How accurate are these texts? I have certainly not checked them all against the manuscripts, but in preparation for some work in the Variorum Chaucer, I tried my own eye on the Ellesmere (both in film and in the Manchester facsimile) against Furnivall's printed text. Errors, of course, abound, but largely of a minor nature. The remarkable thing which I concluded was that, considering the amount of material, the errors are quite surprisingly few, and, more importantly, consist largely of inconsistencies in representing letters (*i-j*, *u-v*, etc.) and in expansions, all of which Furnivall freely admits in his *Temporary Prefaces*. Since I was interested in minutiae, I was annoyed by the number of times that human frailty slipped in, but in my overall assessment I was enormously impressed, and even more so later when I had the opportunity to read some of Furnivall's correspondence and got a clearer idea of the fury with which the man worked. I later did collations for the Variorum of a number of tales, which involved comparing manuscripts of the Six-Text edition, the Harleian 7334, and Cambridge Dd.4.24 with microfilms of the manuscripts, and frequently with some of the manuscripts themselves (the Cambridge manuscripts, the Corpus Christi, and the Lansdowne and Harleian), and continued impressed by the accuracy of Furnivall (particularly as my own errors began to pile up alarmingly). In one specific instance, when working on *The Manciple's Prologue* and *Tale* for the Variorum, I was particularly careful to check the Variorum's base manuscript, Hengwrt, and the Ellesmere and found in Furnivall's text two errors of spelling only, one in Hengwrt and one in Ellesmere. Two German late contemporaries of Furnivall, Koch and Flügel, did detailed studies[11] and concluded that, although, of course, there were errors, varying in number according to what one wished to consider an *error*, the faults were few. Koch (p. 9) calls into doubt the accuracy of the transcripts in a number of places by inference only because, as he says, he did not check the manuscripts directly. He draws our attention to the work of Flügel, who examined the Ellesmere thoroughly and found few mistakes, though his number of "variations" is large. Flügel was concerned with everything—consistency of representation of abbreviation, questions of word and letter separation (a question of millimeters), *i-j*, *u-v*, etc., as well as actual misreadings. It is best to quote Flügel himself (pp. 401–402):

Dear Dr. Furnivall,

I think few men have "poured" over your Chaucer texts—even if it was not "in cloistre"—during the last four or five years more assiduously than I. This means that few have a greater respect for the wonderful amount and quality of work which you have accomplished, few feel more grateful to you, and few love your editions more than I do.

But, of course, during my daily scrutiny of these texts doubts have not been lacking as to an "u" or a "v", an "i" or a "y" and for the last two years I have made it a part of my duties to look up, or have others look up for me, doubtful passages in the Mss. Naturally my inquisitiveness did not stop short at the Ellesmere Ms., a Ms. the value of which you first of all have impressed upon us. I became gradually determined to get the Ellesmere text in orthography and readings as absolutely perfect as I could . . . .

[Flügel then arranges the mistakes into categories; he is quite aware of the slimness of his garnerings.]

The list of real mistakes in readings is very short and very slight; there are not more than about fifty places where the whole text of 238 folios needs verification. My gleanings, as you see, are very few indeed; just as I expected it

ffor wel I wot that folk [viz. *Dr. F.*] han here beforn
Of makynge ropen & lad awey the corn.
    And I come aftyr glenynge here and ther
And am ful glad [No!] if I may fynd an er
Of ony goodly word that they han laft.

I have quoted this long passage to offset the strictures of Bradshaw upon quite different work.

In working since with Furnivall's prints of *Troilus and Criseyde*, I have again concluded that, in spite of annoying inconsistencies and some genuine errors, the texts are remarkably clean and, to put it bluntly, compare favorably with similar modern work. It just does not do to be contemptuous of work about which Furnivall cared so deeply. It is true that some EETS volumes were tossed off with little or no supervision or care by Furnivall. But one can only conclude that in the eight texts of *The Canterbury Tales*, and the important texts of the *Troilus* and the *Minor Poems*, Furnivall performed Herculean labors which cleared the way for better editors—

nearer Housman's sense of the word—but that his own achievement was breathtaking. I do not suggest that all the texts are equally consistent—the texts of the Minor Poems, I fear, are not as accurate as those of *The Canterbury Tales* (C. S. Wright, currently editing *The Legend of Good Women* tells me that, although there is overall accuracy, there are some major blunders). But one can understand Furnivall's impatience which finally broke through his ever-genial nature at Bradshaw's nitpicking. One can admire Bradshaw's scholarship, but without Furnivall there would have been nothing.

We must also be grateful for Furnivall's stubborn clinging to the parallel-text concept. With all the reordering of the tales that resulted, and in spite of the nonsense of the Bradshaw Shift, and in spite of Furnivall's "filling in" of lacunae with the texts of other manuscripts, the parallel text was and remains a brilliant idea. Being able to compare quickly the texts of principal manuscripts without having to chase through the orders of individual ones, has made the task of subsequent editors enormously easier, especially that of Skeat. This idea, as far as I can gather, was Furnivall's alone. He was, clearly, doubtful of his own ability as an editor to "strike" the "right" text, but his modesty should be praised in view of the editions which had preceded him and which had called forth Child's plea for help. The multitext "edition" of works which had so variously and incompetently been treated by others seemed a logical response to the problem. Furnivall, like the great German scholars, always had future students, scholars, and editors in mind. Along with assessing Furnivall's modest estimate of his own abilities, one must also concur that the solution he reached was, considering the state of Chaucer's text and the number of manuscripts, the best that could have been reached at the time. Even the printing of a number of bad manuscripts would have been a distinct advance over the textual state of Furnivall's day. But to have printed Hengwrt and Ellesmere was itself a triumph of judgment. All the manuscripts that he printed were important; of the manuscripts of *The Canterbury Tales* one could have wished only that BL Additional 35286 (Ad^3) and Christ Church 157 (and perhaps all of Egerton 2726–En^1) could have been added in separate prints: further parallel texts in the same print would have been physically impossible. Furnivall was certainly aware of the importance of these other manuscripts and made an effort to represent them, at least, in his *Specimens*, but there was clearly a limit to time and energy and money, and, after all, he had so many other important texts to print. He was, of course, aided by the advice of others, but, as I have said, Furnivall ran, finally, a one-man show, and the ultimate choice was his alone, for he paid the piper and saw to it that the work was done.

It will not do to leave the impression of Furnivall as merely an inspired textual amateur. True, he was not in the class of Bradshaw, or in the class which Skeat later joined (but those numbers were very few indeed); nevertheless, he was a keen student of the manuscripts. The Norlin Library of the University of Colorado possesses the fifth part of the Six-Text print that contains fragment E, which Furnivall owned. Its pages are covered with interlinear notations remarking similarities with other manuscripts (most not published by Furnivall) and tentative associations, in this fragment, in families of manuscripts. The learning and judgment displayed here, which is material for an interesting essay in itself, is impressive. Furnivall clearly saw the relation of Cambridge Dd.4.24 and Egerton 2726 (filling in the lacunae of the former with the latter), for example, and had worked out many of the details of what Manly was later to describe as the *a* group of *Canterbury Tales* manuscripts. Clearly, for all his disarming manner Furnivall was no babe in the woods.

From Skeat's rather brief discussion of the manuscripts of *The Canterbury Tales* and of his own methods in the introduction to volume 4 of his great edition, it is clear that he relied very heavily indeed upon the Six-Text print of Furnivall, together with the Chaucer Society's later publication of Harley 7334. It is doubtful that Skeat systematically consulted the manuscripts themselves, and indeed it would have been difficult for him to have done so, considering that three were still in private hands, and the owners had already rendered their service to scholarship by allowing them to be copied for just such a purpose as Skeat's. He did consult Dd.4.24, which he could do easily, being at Cambridge; this manuscript was the last to be published by the Chaucer Society, not appearing until after Skeat's edition was published. The latter manuscript then completed what Skeat was to assess later as *The Eight-Text Edition of the Canterbury Tales*.[12] Although Skeat rightly claimed there, as earlier, to have consulted a large number of other manuscripts, he makes perfectly clear that he considered nothing very important which was not to be found in the Six-Text print supplemented by Harley 7334 and Dd.4.24.

The principal disagreement between Furnivall and Skeat developed slowly; Skeat had adopted the "Bradshaw shift," which Furnivall had enthusiastically seized upon and which governed the numbering of lines and fragments. As he says, "In making my own edition, I had practically no choice in the matter. The matter had been already decided, and a new method of numbering the lines had already been established."[13] It is clear, however, that Skeat rejected the Bradshaw arrangement and Furnivall's own contribution of the arrangement of fragment C; he argued lengthily in *The Evolution of the Canterbury Tales*[14] and in his *The Eight-Text Edition* that there was no "correct" or "final" order but only a "last" order, that we could not go on rearranging tales by what seemed more logical references, place-names, and so on; he himself argued for the Harleian 7334 order as being not the final but the last order with which Chaucer was working, an order which would undoubtedly have continued to change, and it is upon this argument that he claims the chief importance for Harleian 7334, not because of its text, which is distinctly inferior to Hengwrt, the manuscript, he says, "to which I now always look *first*."[15]

In his selection of texts for the Minor Poems, Furnivall was equally useful. Seizing upon Fairfax 16, Cambridge Gg.4.27, and Tanner 346 as his "bases," he also recognized the extraordinary importance of the first Thynne edition, not only, of course, for those poems for which Thynne offered the only text but also for those texts from which Thynne printed which were no longer extant. And Furnivall's overriding purpose is well caught in the title page of the *One-Text Print of Chaucer's Minor Poems: Being the Best Text of Each Poem in the Parallel-Text Edition, for Handy Use by Editors and Readers*.

In his approach to the texts of *Troilus*, Furnivall was at least as accurate in his judgment (however well advised) as he was with those of *The Canterbury Tales*. In *A Parallel-Text Print of Chaucer's Troilus and Criseyde* (appropriately dedicated to "Henry Bradshaw . . . to help whom my Chaucer work was first begun") Furnivall selected the Campsall, Harley 2280 (H^1, according to Root's sigils), and Gg.4.27, all manuscripts of the first importance. He also published in *A Parallel-Text of Three More MSS. of Chaucer's Troilus* Corpus Christi, Harley 1239 (Root's H^3), and St. John's. Corpus Christi and St. John's again are of the very first importance, though H^3 is dismissed by Root as extremely corrupt. Harleian 3943 (H^2) was printed in the Chaucer Society's publication of Rossetti's *Chaucer's Troylus and Cryseyde compared with Boccaccio's Filostrato*. Root, in the preface to his edition, says (pp. v–vi):

> I have been reminded anew of the debt which all Chaucerians owe to the pioneer industry of Dr. Furnivall and his collaborators in the work of the Chaucer Society. It has materially lightened my labors to have in print *literatim* copies of seven of the manuscripts of *Troilus*, among them the two important manuscripts Cp and J, which have served as primary authorities for my text. I have also had in my possession a complete and careful transcript of H^4 made for Dr. Furnivall but never printed.

Root indicates that he has "verified anew" the readings of these prints, and he is much less dependent upon them than was Skeat, but his respect for the care with which Furnivall prepared or had prepared these precious documents is everywhere apparent.

Furnivall's work for Chaucer was so various that no account can cover all aspects of it with any adequacy. His publication in various places of the odd stanzas, his interest in the originals and parallels of Chaucer's stories, his own work on the *Life-Records*, the minutiae of his own speculations upon the actual organization of Chaucer's pilgrimage (with Bradshaw he *had* to see it, in his romantic way, as a realistic event which must be treated as if Chaucer's record were a factual one), his encouragement of Rossetti's study of *Troilus* and Boccaccio—the list goes on and on. These were the starting places of modern studies. As an *editor*, as I have remarked, his work cannot really be evaluated, for he never, in a sense, *edited* anything. He printed, but how fully, how gloriously, he printed! He made all modern editions possible. In every aspect of Chaucerian study his work is found. His role is, finally, the one that he would have wanted. He admired "good work," "good men," "good poets." He did enormous "good work" himself, he found and encouraged "good men" (he published, or made arrangements for publication before his death, work of Koch, Kittredge, Tatlock, Root, McCormick, Skeat, and so many others). Whether we condescend in our own day of supersophisticated (perhaps too sophisticated) concepts of editing even to admit Furnivall into our ranks, he is the giant upon whose shoulders we all stand—enthusiastic, genial, enormously hard-working, quick to judgment and quick to admit error, encouraging all who followed and criticized and bettered his own work. He would be pleased, even flattered, with the role that history may well assign him: the most important of all Chaucerians—not the best scholar, etc., but the most important—highly personal and yet curiously anonymous, who was able to devote only a small portion of his total working time to Chaucer but who shames us all who, in our serried ranks, minutely ponder the works of that highly personal and yet curiously anonymous poet.

9. Walter Skeat
(1835–1912)

A.S.G. EDWARDS

THE NATURE of Skeat's achievement in the Clarendon Chaucer[1] can be grasped to some degree by an appreciation of the state of Chaucer's text that existed before it. The editions of Bell (1782), Anderson (1793), and Chalmers (1810) were conflations or adaptations of the work of Tyrwhitt and/or Urry. Although regularly reprinted, they had no claims to authority, completeness, or reliability. None included Chaucer's prose works, possessed satisfactory notes or glossary, or afforded a reliable representation of the canon.[2] Thomas Wright's 1847–51 edition of *The Canterbury Tales* was notable as the first since Tyrwhitt to return to the manuscripts, albeit in a slapdash way. It is only with Richard Morris's 1866 revision of the 1845 Aldine Chaucer that there is the first serious attempt to use manuscript evidence as a basis for establishing texts, and this edition, which was the best available until the appearance of Skeat's, contains a number of important limitations, some of which it shared with its predecessors.[3]

Thus when Skeat undertook the preparation, for the first time in the history of Chaucer's text, of a complete works, he began a task of daunting complexity, a task for which the past afforded little practical help and much accumulated error. His achievement was to provide a series of authoritative texts and supporting apparatus that have become the foundations for most of the subsequent editorial work on Chaucer. Many of his conclusions may now be challenged; much of his work may be superseded. But Skeat's edition marks the beginning of a new epoch in Chaucer scholarship, signaling the beginning of its Modern Age.

171

I

The movement of Skeat's career toward its culminating achievement can be seen, in retrospect, to have an evolutionary inexorability about it. Born in 1835, Skeat was educated at King's College School in London, where, as he put it, "it was my singular fate to have as my class-master the Rev. Oswald Cockayne."[4] Cockayne (1807–73) was himself a philologist and editor of distinction, best known as the editor of *Anglo-Saxon Leechdoms* and of Ælfric's *Lives of the Saints*.

Cockayne's influence was not immediately apparent. Skeat went up to Cambridge to read mathematics. He took orders in 1860 and became a curate in Godalming, Surrey, until

> an alarming attack, of a diptheritic character, totally unfitted me for clerical work and rendered a long rest absolutely necessary; and thus I found myself, in the end of 1863, at the age of twenty eight, in the desolate condition of finding my chosen career brought to a sudden end, without any idea as to my future course.[5]

In October, 1864, he returned to his former college, Christ's, as lecturer in mathematics. By his own account this employment left him "a good deal of leisure time."[6]

The year 1864 was a particularly portentous one in which to be a young, underemployed scholar with an interest in medieval English language and literature. For in that year the indefatigable Frederick James Furnivall launched the Early English Text Society, dedicated to the editing of (particularly) Middle English texts, to provide material for his great dream, the *New English Dictionary*. As Skeat reports it, "My name was mentioned to him as one who was fond of Early English and had some leisure."[7] The account does less than justice to Furnivall's positive genius for talent spotting. Certainly the die was swiftly cast. On October 29, 1864, Skeat wrote to Furnivall agreeing to reedit *Lancelot of the Laik*.[8] "My objection, that I was unable to read a MS., was over-ruled on the grounds, first, that the sole MS. was always at hand in the Cambridge University Library; and secondly, that I could learn."[9] This undertaking was but the first of an outpouring of editions, books and articles, publications which by his death in 1912 could be numbered in the thousands.[10]

But from the outset it was inevitable that Skeat should be drawn to the editing of Chaucer. His letter of October 29, 1864, contains one particularly portentous passage. He writes, "It would be a great kindness if you would introduce my name to Mr Bradshaw's notice, that he might know who I was, should I call on him." Furnivall passed the letter on with the laconic annotation: "My dear Bradshaw, Please help W. Skeat if he should come & ask you any questions."[11] Thus was forged the next and possibly most crucial link in the chain of circumstances that was to lead to the Clarendon Chaucer.

By 1864 Henry Bradshaw was fellow and dean of King's College, Cambridge, and assistant with responsibility for rare and early printed books in the Cambridge University Library. Born in 1831, Bradshaw had graduated B.A. in 1854 and had taught for two years in Ireland before returning to Cambridge to pursue his growing interest in early books and manuscripts. Chaucer had been an enthusiasm since childhood, and Cambridge gave him the opportunity to focus it on the text of his works in manuscript.[12] His researches were notable for the extraordinary reputation they gained him, made even more notable by his almost total inability to bring most of them to a final, publishable form.[13] But by January, 1864, his reputation as a Chaucerian scholar was sufficiently established for Macmillan to approach him to undertake a new edition of Chaucer in collaboration with John Earle and Aldis Wright. "Bradshaw had it in his mind, in one form or another, for fifteen years, and made large preparations, but time and opportunity seemed always wanting."[14] Nonetheless, Bradshaw agreed, in 1866, to collaborate with Earle and Wright on a standard edition of Chaucer for the Clarendon Press.[15] A little later he had reverted to the idea of undertaking an edition for Macmillan, when progress on the Clarendon edition was foundering.[16]

And no discernible progress had been made on the Clarendon Chaucer when, in 1870, Earle resigned from it. Aldis Wright was first approached to take it over but declined. It is an indication of Skeat's rapidly growing stature as an editor of medieval texts that the delegates then turned to him. He referred them elsewhere: "I have little doubt," he wrote "that the man who knows the subject most thoroughly is Mr Bradshaw, and I should not be justified in putting myself before him."[17] Bradshaw agreed, having first secured the promise of Aldis Wright and Skeat to act as his assistants. Among his papers is the draft of a letter to Bartholomew Price, one of the Clarendon delegates, outlining his sense of the scope of the undertaking and including a tentative list of contents.[18]

Thus, for the first time, Skeat found himself drawn toward the editing of Chaucer. It may be surmised that he did not find the initial experience a rewarding one, for left to his own devices he was never one to delay overlong in bringing a project to completion. But there is no indication that Bradshaw, having accepted the delegates' commission, ever undertook its execution. Furnivall, in an unwontedly tactful letter of March 15, 1871, to Bradshaw remarks: "I'm glad to hear that the Oxford plan is only suspended. (That's clearly the right plan.) M[ark] Pattison said 'abandoned', but of course Price and you know better."[19] It would seem that Bradshaw's interest swung yet again to producing an edition for Macmillan.[20] But no progress seems to have been made on either front. All activity seems to have languished for an indeterminable period.

I have been unable to establish when the proposal for a complete works was revived and Skeat proposed as its editor.[21] But the passage of time,

Bradshaw's death in 1886, and Aldis Wright's defection to editing Shake-speare would have made Skeat an inevitable choice even if he had not already established himself as the chief editor of Chaucer for the Clarendon Press. He edited, for the Clarendon Press series, various selections from *The Canterbury Tales*: *The Prioress's Tale*, *The Tale of Sir Thopas*, *The Monk's Tale*, *The Clerk's Tale*, and *The Squire's Tale* in 1874 and *The Man of Law's Tale*, *The Pardoner's Tale*, *The Second Nun's Tale*, and *The Canon's Yeoman's Tale* in 1877 and reedited Richard Morris's edition of *The General Prologue*, *The Knight's Tale*, and *The Nun's Priest's Tale* in 1889. In addition, he had edited the *Minor Poems* in 1888 and *The Legend of Good Women* in 1889, for the same series. This was not the extent of his preliminary editorial activity. He had also edited Chaucer's *A Treatise on the Astrolabe* in 1872 for the Early English Text Society and undertaken a revision of Bell's edition of Chaucer in 1878. He thus had amassed experience unmatched by any of his contemporaries in the editing of Chaucer, credentials which made him the editor most fully equipped to prepare a standard edition.

The edition, as it initially appeared, was in six volumes, as Bradshaw had felt it should be in his original draft of the table of contents.[22] A seventh volume, titled *Chaucerian and Other Pieces* (but *The Complete Works of Geoffrey Chaucer* on the half title) appeared in 1897 in a uniform binding. But it was never conceived as part of the original edition and will not be discussed here.[23] The initial six volumes were published at roughly two-month intervals, between February, 1894, and January, 1895, at 12s 6d. a volume or three guineas the set.[24] Publication was assisted by a subscription to which a total of 1,013 persons, institutions, and booksellers subscribed for a total of 1,191 copies. There were some notable omissions from the list of subscribers: F. J. Furnivall, James Murray, A. S. Napier, George Lyman Kittredge, and Henry Sweet, among others. On the other hand, W. P. Ker put down for two copies (and wrote a lengthy review article for the *Quarterly Review*). A. C. Bradley did not subscribe, but his brother F. H., the philosopher, did. It bespeaks the polymathic interests of the later Victorians that others among the individual subscribers included J. G. Frazer, already at work on *The Golden Bough*, and N. Story-Maskelyne, the noted mineralogist.

The edition seems to have been a financial success for the press. As early as March, 1894, C. E. Doble, the assistant secretary, wrote to Skeat that "demand for the great Chaucer . . . seems very satisfactory."[25,26] The Clarendon Chaucer went into a second edition in 1900 and remains in print.

The critics were generally as satisfied as Doble. The *Athenaeum* declared roundly that "this edition marks an epoch in Chaucerian study,"[27] after the publication of only the first volume. W. P. Ker observed that "its value as the first critical text of Chaucer will scarcely be much impaired by the future edition of a hundred years hence, which will stand in the same relation to this edition as this to Tyrwhitt's."[28] Flügel acclaimed it as "the best edition [of Chaucer] extant, and the best edition ever published,"[29] while Kittredge spoke of "our deep sense of the obligation under which Prof. Skeat has laid all who care for learning or for literature."[30] Such comments are representative of the general acclaim of Skeat's achievement.

II

Such a widely acclaimed achievement did not spring into being *ex nihilo*. It is true that there was little in the existing editorial tradition to afford Skeat much to lean on with any expectation of firm support, apart from Tyrwhitt's edition, which Skeat characterized as "the first in which some critical care was exercised" (5.x).[31] But if the past afforded virtually no guidance to Skeat's undertaking, his own contemporaries provided compensating assistance. As a preliminary to assessing Skeat's edition, it is necessary to weigh his debts to three men: Richard Morris, F. J. Furnivall, and Henry Bradshaw.

Morris (1833–94) is best known as the first—and one of the best— editors for the Early English Text Society, for which he edited a number of texts between 1864 and 1878. He edited as well *The Prick of Conscience* (1863), which according to Skeat "laid the foundation of a more accurate study of Middle English";[32] an edition of Chaucer's *Boece* (1868); and the revision of the Aldine Chaucer (1866), already mentioned. He also produced in 1867 a selection from *The Canterbury Tales* for the Clarendon Press series. This edition of *The General Prologue, The Knight's Tale*, and *The Nun's Priest's Tale* went through a number of editions, and in several of its later forms it was revised by Skeat.

But Skeat was not linked to Morris simply, or even primarily, by a shared editorial interest in Chaucer. Even more important to Skeat than Morris' editorial labors was his *Specimens of Early English*, first published in 1867. The importance of this work lay, in Skeat's words, in the fact that

> he clearly made out the chief characteristics of the three main dialects, Northern, Midland and Southern. The results of his work are now [i.e., in 1896] common property, and almost every beginner of the study of Middle English is perfectly familiar with facts which, in 1866, were quite unknown. Every such student ought to know, further, what a debt of gratitude he owes, for this and many other lessons, to Richard Morris.[33]

Skeat's awareness of his own debt took immediate and practical forms: "His *Specimens of Early English* was, in my eyes, of such great value, that I could not rest till I had provided it with a new Glossarial Index and furnished the author with such notes and small emendations as it was in my power to offer."[34] In subsequent editions Skeat became Morris's collaborator.

It seems that it was to the stimulus of Morris that Skeat owed some important impetus to his own activities as glosser and annotator. In the

Clarendon Chaucer he observes with proper pride that "I think Dr. Morris and myself may claim to have done much for Middle-English by way of compiling glossaries." But, as he goes on, "Dr. Morris led the way by the very full glossaries to his Early English Alliterative Poems, Sir Gawayne and the Grene Knight, and Genesis and Exodus" (6.xxii). The recognition of the priority and importance of Morris for his own work in this respect indicates Skeat's appreciation of his debt to Morris's example. Ultimately he was to surpass his mentor's achievement, building on his foundation.

Morris was of some importance to Skeat's work as an annotator as well. As I have mentioned, Skeat also collaborated with Morris on later editions of his selection from *The Canterbury Tales*. He makes clear this aspect of his indebtedness in the Clarendon Chaucer (5.xxvi):

> Many of [the notes] on the Prologue and Knightes Tales were really written by Dr. Morris; but owing to the great kindness he shewed me in allowing me to work in conjunction with him on terms of equality, I should often be hard put to it to say which they are.

A comparison of the relevant sections of Skeat's notes in the Clarendon Chaucer with Morris's edition shows that many of his notes do come from Morris, generally without acknowledgment (this is true of *The Nun's Priest's Tale* as well, which Skeat—oddly—does not mention). Brief notes tend to appear verbatim; in the case of longer annotation Skeat has almost invariably enlarged upon Morris's initial comments.

In such respects Morris's importance is clear: he gave Skeat sound scholarly models for the supporting apparatus for his text, its notes, and its glossary, examples which he was to digest and improve upon but which were doubtless of crucial importance in helping him formulate his views on these aspects of editorial procedure in general and their applicability to Chaucer in particular.

Furnivall's role in Skeat's edition was very different, and much more important. It is hard now, after the unsympathetic account of him by Elisabeth Murray,[35] to appreciate the crucial importance of Furnivall to the growth of medieval studies in nineteenth-century England. I have already mentioned his gifts as a talent spotter. He was also an indefatigable founder of societies, assuring by the most important of these, the Early English Text Society and the Chaucer Society, that there was produced a steady flow of newly edited or transcribed medieval texts to provide both raw material for the *New English Dictionary* and important materials for the understanding of Chaucer's texts.

The role of Furnivall's Chaucer Society, founded in 1868, was to be of crucial significance to Skeat's Clarendon edition. It, in effect, provided him with the very bases for a number of his editions in the Clarendon Chaucer. Skeat makes this extensive debt quite explicit in his General Introduction (6.xviii):

As regards the texts, my chief debt is to the Chaucer Society, which means, practically, Dr. Furnivall, through whose zeal and energy so many splendid and accurate prints of the MSS. have been produced, thus rendering the actual readings and spellings of the scribes accessible to students in all countries.

Elsewhere he confirms and clarifies his debt to Furnivall's labors in respect of particular texts. In discussing his text of *The Canterbury Tales*, he observes (4.vii) that

it owes everything to the labours of Dr. Furnivall for the Chaucer Society, but for which no satisfactory results could have been obtained, except at the cost of more time and toil than I could well devote to the subject. In other words, my work is entirely founded upon the splendid "Six-text" Edition published by that Society, supplemented by the very valuable reprint in the celebrated "Harleian" manuscript [i.e. Harley 7334] in the same series.

The importance of Furnivall's Six-Text edition of *The Canterbury Tales* is fully discussed elsewhere in this volume by Donald C. Baker. As Baker rightly stresses, the important characteristic of Furnivall's editions was his almost intuitive perception of which were the important manuscripts of the *Tales*: Ellesmere, Hengwrt, Cambridge University Library Gg.4.27, Lansdowne 851, Corpus Christi, Oxford 198, Petworth, and Harley 7334. These were the manuscripts that Skeat was to employ in his edition—in effect, some of his most fundamental decisions in this respect were taken for him by Furnivall. It is fortunate that Furnivall's judgment seems in general to have been matched by his accuracy,[36] given the extent to which Skeat was to rely on them.

This indebtedness to Furnivall was not limited to his transcripts of the *Canterbury Tales* manuscripts. Skeat used the Chaucer Society transcript of the Campsall manuscript as the basis for his edition of *Troilus and Criseyde*.[37] *The Legend of Good Women* is also drawn from Furnivall's transcripts,[38] as are most of the *Minor Poems*[39] and the edition of *Boece*.[40]

Furnivall's willingness to allow such extensive use of his work was entirely characteristic of his modest and clear-sighted sense of his role. He once wrote to Bradshaw: "As to *editing*, I've no right to call my work that in your sense: that I leave to you: but put forth texts for others to edit, I do."[41] Or again (also to Bradshaw): "Don't be absurd. You're the man to *edit* Chaucer if only you will. I'm the man to print the text, if only you'll add your notes of MSS to mine, or tell me which book to look in to find the MSS."[42] It was through his promulgating of editorial raw materials, particularly in the form of parallel texts,[43] that Furnivall made Skeat's whole undertaking possible.

But it was Bradshaw who was without question the most important and at the same time the least easy to define influence on Skeat's edition. Skeat's sense of Bradshaw's importance to him is indicated publicly in his dedication of his final volume: "In grateful memory of Henry Bradshaw." He has left a private, fuller acknowledgment of his debt in a remarkable letter written to Bradshaw on April 8, 1878, after he had been elected Bosworth Professor of Anglo-Saxon at Cambridge—and nearly fourteen years after his letter to Furnivall seeking an introduction. It is worth lengthy quotation:

> And *now* let me say what I wanted to say before, but could not so well as now. You shall put your own interpretation on your work—and I will allow you to know best. But, at the same time, it is for *me* to know what you have been for me, & what you have done for me. In my beginning to study, I was with the best of intentions, all abroad. I could not read a MS., I did not know what a MS. was. I wanted to read books, but did not know what books. I wanted to understand Chaucer's rhymes (or rimes) & his grammar, & his ways in general & I had none but vague ideas. And in hundreds of ways I wanted to know (& still want to know) all sorts of things more or less connected with MSS. & literature. Well, it is the merest truth that it is, practically, to you that I owe all my best ideas. You have set me thinking where I was before thoughtless, you have helped me to read MSS., you have told me of this or that book or edition, over and over again & thrown out hints (so thankfully received) & told me of points, and in fact helped me, in & out, in hundreds of ways & thousands of times. Your remarks have always been *treasured*: some have seemed wrong to me at first, but they generally *came* right. And I can only say that I never remember a remark of yours that was not received with profound thankfulness, & with a determination to follow it out. It is merely and perfectly hopeless to say how much more I owe to you than to anyone else.[44]

This indicates Skeat's sense of the degree of indebtedness to Bradshaw but only hints at the diverse forms that such indebtedness takes. The desire "to understand Chaucer's rhymes" is presumably a reference to Bradshaw's attempts to develop rhyme tests as a criterion of canonicity, a technique that became particularly important in Skeat's slowly evolving views about the authenticity of *The Romaunt de la Rose*.[45] Bradshaw's, and hence Skeat's, thinking on this underwent considerable revision, moving from wholesale rejection to the final acceptance of fragment A as Chaucer's own. Skeat acknowledges in the Clarendon edition that the chief arguments for his final position "are not original, but borrowed from Mr. Henry Bradshaw, whose profound knowledge of all matters relating to Chaucer has been acknowledged by all students" (i. 1).

There are a few other explicit acknowledgments to Bradshaw. He is credited with positioning what in Skeat's edition becomes *The Shipman's Prologue* in *The Canterbury Tales* (B 1163–90, more generally known now as the *Man of Law Endlink*).[46] And he is acknowledged, a touch grudgingly, as the first to have identified the variant forms of *The Legend of Good Women Prologue*.[47] But Bradshaw's most striking contribution to Chaucer scholarship, one which Skeat employed in his edition, is passed over in silence.

The "Bradshaw shift" has been the subject of scholarly controversy ever since Bradshaw, with characteristic reluctance, permitted Furnivall to disseminate his arguments on the ordering of *The Canterbury Tales*. As is now common knowledge, he sought to reconcile the chronologically anomalous geographical allusions in the work by repositioning fragment B^2 so that it immediately followed fragment B^1. This was the order employed by Furnivall in his Six-Text edition for the Chaucer Society, which formed, as we have seen, the basis for Skeat's own. It is presumably for this reason that Skeat felt it unnecessary to indicate what is, in many respects, the most remarkable single editorial decision in his whole edition. I will return to this point in the next section. For the present it may be sufficient to indicate this specific instance as demonstrating the problem of pinning down with any precision how much Skeat really owed to Bradshaw. The two were in close, often daily contact for over twenty years. They had little occasion to write to one another. And the constant stimulus of Bradshaw's bibliographical, codicological, and palaeographical skills gave Skeat the tools and the impetus to do what Bradshaw was never capable of doing—bringing his researches to printed form. If Skeat failed to acknowledge at times his debt to Bradshaw as clearly as he might have been expected to, it was probably because after such close collaboration he often found it difficult to tell where Bradshaw left off and Skeat began.

It is, however, possible to discern a number of strands of influence of varying significance underlying Skeat's edition. To the cumulative impetus of Skeat's own editorial labors can be added the stimulus and example of these three contemporaries. With such perspectives it is now appropriate to turn to a consideration of some aspects of the edition itself.

III

Ker acclaimed Skeat's edition as "the first *critical* [my italics] text of Chaucer." One might assume that by this he meant what was specified by another reviewer in praise of Skeat's work:" . . . he has taken unlimited pains to furnish a satisfactory text, and what is more, to provide his readers with the means of appraising the value of the lections he adopts."[48] Obviously Skeat's work warrants initial inquiry at this fundamental level: his use of manuscript evidence and the nature and quality of the texts he established.

Any inquiry must begin with *The Canterbury Tales*. A crucial issue is the implications of Skeat's use of the Chaucer Society transcripts in the Six-Text edition and the separate transcript of Harley 7334. The decision may be defended without undue difficulty in many respects, though it must be appreciated that to do so is to commend Furnivall's judgment and accuracy as much if not more than Skeat's perception of these qualities in Furnivall's work. But if Furnivall gave him the basis for an edition, he also left Skeat in something of a quandary. For he seems to have felt that by committing himself to use Furnivall's transcripts he committed himself to Furnivall's ordering for *The Canterbury Tales*. And yet he found this ordering in at least one important respect to be unacceptable. He found the positioning of fragment C (*The Physician's Tale* and *The Pardoner's Tale*) immediately after the (emended) placing of B^2 to be unacceptable. He observes (3.434):

> In the best MSS., [*The Physician's Tale*] follows the Frankeleins Tale; and such is, in my belief, its proper position. This arrangement was arbitrarily altered by Dr. Furnivall, in order, I suppose, to emphasize the fact that the relative order of the Groups may be altered at pleasure; but this might have been understood without forcible dislocation; and I think that no good has been effected by it. I have been obliged to follow suit, but I wish to make a note that the right order of the Groups is A, B $[B^1, B^2]$, D, E, F, C, G, H, I.

It is not at all clear *why* Skeat felt constrained by Furnivall's ordering. And he himself seems to have felt the need for some greater justification of the acceptance of an order he found unacceptable. For in a footnote to volume 6 he comments on the problems of the numbering of *The Canterbury Tales*, which were "especially troublesome. I give three distinct systems of numbering the lines." The footnote to this comment reads: "This is the real reason why it is necessary to retain the unauthorised order of the Groups introduced by Dr. Furnivall. To initiate yet another mode of reference would have caused much inconvenience" (6.xi.fn.1).

It is possible to be unconvinced by this argument. One might feel that the function of the editor is, after all, to edit, and especially in a situation where various orders and lineations exist to have no compunction about imposing what he feels to be the proper one. The more so since there is no real problem of lineation, since the issue is really one of the positioning of a distinct fragment.[49] One must assume that for Skeat convenience took precedence over conviction here and that the ease of preparing copy using Furnivall's text outweighed presenting the text in an "incorrect" order.

A somewhat different pragmatism informs Skeat's decision to follow Furnivall in the use of the Bradshaw Shift. Clearly he felt there was no issue here that warranted discussion or justification. His only mention of this matter comes obliquely near the end of his discussion of the grouping of the *Tales*, where he discusses internal allusions to place and time: "The references to places on the road can cause no trouble; on the contrary, these allusions afford much help, for we cannot rest satisfied with the arrangement in Tyrwhitt's edition, which makes the pilgrims come to Sittingbourne before arriving at Rochester" (3.376).

For Skeat the issue devolves into questions of versimilitude and reason. The pilgrim is intended to be a realistic representation, hence logically the order must be adjusted to accord with what would appear to be the rational sequence of narrative. It has been pointed out that neither Chaucer's scribes nor his previous editors had been as worried about this as Bradshaw, Skeat, and Furnivall were. Indeed, it can be seen as part of a much larger texture of inconsistency and error in the verisimilitude of *The Canterbury Tales*.[50] Skeat's decision seems once again dictated by the Six-Text Chaucer rather than by convincing editorial practice. It is noteworthy that he subsequently became more hesitant about this aspect of his edition and seems to have verged on repudiating it.[51]

But what of Skeat's actual editorial method, the procedures and criteria adopted in the construction of his critical texts? Once again it may be appropriate to begin with *The Canterbury Tales*. The most substantial objections to Skeat's procedures here have been formulated by Eleanor Hammond:

> . . . an edition of the *Canterbury Tales* based on the seven MSS (out of more than fifty) which the [Chaucer] Society had issued when Skeat prepared his text cannot be considered as final, . . . although the text may upon this mode of procedure be satisfactory to the ear, we cannot follow the editor's reasoning in its establishment. For when after asserting that a certain group of MSS is "better" than another group—and here again we wish a reason—Skeat suddenly incorporates in his text readings from the "inferior" MSS, we look for an explanation which is not given. It is evident to any close student of the *Canterbury Tales* that Skeat has not devoted to the MSS such examination as Morell or Tyrwhitt made, and his editorial procedure, a century or more after Tyrwhitt, is guided by the erroneous supposition that the true Chaucerian readings may be picked out intuitively, instead of by the laborious and impartial comparison of all the authorities.[52]

These observations do raise some important questions about the nature and degree of Skeat's method. As we have seen, the actual choice of manuscripts collated is—thanks to Furnivall—very sound. One would hardly wish to criticize Skeat for failing to provide a collation of all the fifty-seven manuscripts of *The Canterbury Tales* that he records. The logistical problems would have been insuperable and the extension of his labors inordinate, and the results could hardly have been incorporated into his edition.

This much must be stressed in defense of Skeat's procedures—about which he is, in any case, quite candid. But other aspects are more obscure. He never provides, for example, any real demonstration of the textual reasons for his choice of Ellesmere for his base manuscript, simply asserting that "of all the MSS., E is the best in nearly every respect. It not only gives good lines and good sense, but is also (usually) gramatically accurate and thoroughly well spelt" (4.xvii). In some respects, as we will see, this assertion is at odds with Skeat's practice. But for the present one may simply note the degree to which he requires his audience to have confidence in his own confidence in his judgment without providing any analysis or comparison to support it.

Equally valid is Hammond's criticism of Skeat's seemingly arbitrary and random use of further manuscripts beyond the seven on which he principally relies. He observes (4.xviii):

> In very difficult cases, other MSS (beside the seven) have been collated, but I have seldom gained much by it. The chief additional MSS. thus used are

[Cambridge University Dd.4.24; Sloane 1685; Royal 18.C.2; Harley 1758, and the Lichfield MS] and others that are sufficiently indicated.

This account is both unclear and misleading. Of the manuscripts he mentions, he uses only the Lichfield manuscript to any degree, and that only in *The Canon's Yeoman's Tale*. Harley 1758 is employed not for the text of *The Canterbury Tales* but as an authority for *Gamelyn*. Royal 18.C.2 seems to be used only for one brief passage along with Sloane 1685.[53] Cambridge University Dd.4.24 is used intermittently at a very few points.[54] No reasons are given for the use of these manuscripts in particular.

As puzzling is Skeat's failure to provide clear indication of the further manuscripts he used or (again) the reasons why they were used. The most striking instance occurs in his use of Arch. Selden B.14 as an authority for *The Parson's Tale*.[55] In addition, Royal 17.D.15 is employed at some points,[56] as are British Library Add. 5140[57] and the Christ Church manuscript.[58] Since all these are relatively late manuscripts, one would wish to know what belief Skeat had in their authority rather than that of other manuscripts and why that belief was so intermittent.

Other aspects of his editorial procedure are more enigmatic. In particular, the recording of variants for *The Canterbury Tales* poses great difficulties. Skeat's statement of his procedures is clear and unequivocal (4.xx):

> The footnotes do not record various readings where E[llesmere] is correct as it stands; they have purposely been made as concise as possible. It would have been easy to multiply them fourfold without giving much information of value; this is not unfrequently done but the gain is slight. With so good a MS. as the basis of the text, it did not seem desirable.

This is not unreasonable as a procedure—assuming, that is, that criteria for "correctness" are satisfactorily defined. But examination of the printed variants suggests that it is not one that is adhered to with any consistency. It is untrue, for example to claim that the variants "do not record various readings where E[llesmere] is correct as it stands." At various points Skeat uses readings from other manuscripts apparently to justify the *retention* of Ellesmere readings.[59] At other points he rejects readings from Ellesmere but provides no indication of the readings of other manuscripts, even when they support his emendation.[60] At still others he includes, apparently randomly, variants that provide no basis for emendation.[61] The recording of variants seems to be wholly devoid of consistency and method.

Similar difficulties obtain in the treatment of emendations. Skeat's statement about this is once again categorical and misleading. He announces that "as a rule I have refrained from all emendation" [in *The Canterbury Tales*]" (4.xx). He gives only one instance (B^2 1189) where he has emended the text. One must assume that he means emendations for sense rather than for orthography or meter since there is considerable adjustment in these respects to his base manuscripts, as we will see. But even if Skeat's assertion can be understood as limited solely to substantive emendation, he crucially misrepresents his activity in this respect, which is far more extensive than he indicates.

I have not attempted a full count of Skeat's departures from Ellesmere in his text of *The Canterbury Tales*. One of the difficulties in attempting such a count is that the form in which Skeat presents his emendations is not conventional, clear, or consistent. Thus the one emendation to which Skeat draws attention in his statement of editorial principles is printed in italics.[62] So far as I can determine, this is the only point where Skeat employs italics to denote an emendation (elsewhere italics are reserved for words or phrases in Latin or French). Elsewhere square brackets are used infrequently to indicate some conjectural emendations.[63] But at other points readings lacking any manuscript support are not placed in square brackets or otherwise indicated as conjecture.[64] And Skeat does not seem to employ square brackets within his text to indicate points where he departs from Ellesmere and has the authority of other manuscripts. Skeat's attitude towards emendations and their representation with his text seems unsupported by any controlling principles.

However, Skeat does seem to have been relatively cautious in making conjectural emendations, but he was much more willing than he indicates to tinker with his text when there was manuscript support—*any* manuscript support. An examination of Skeat's emendations to *The Canterbury Tales* gives some support to Hammond's criticism of Skeat's apparent belief that it was possible to pick out Chaucerian readings "intuitively instead of by the laborious and impartial comparison of all the authorities."

As we have seen, his use of manuscript evidence in itself tends to imply this cavalier attitude. Some particular examples of Skeat's practice may also suggest something of the variable nature of his editorial judgment. Obviously it is possible here to give instances only very selectively, with the attendant dangers of misrepresentation and distortion. But it is nonetheless possible to indicate certain general tendencies that limit Skeat's editorial judgment.

There is in many of Skeat's emendations a general inclination to render Chaucer more explicit and accessible, in effect more prosaic, than either sense or meter warrants. It is an inclination of a piece with Skeat's concerns about the ordering of *The Canterbury Tales* and his preoccupation with verisimilitude and logic and his concern to make the text smooth, neat, and tidy. At times this expresses itself in an attempt to clarify Chaucer's sense.[65] At other points he is willing to go against Ellesmere on simply quantitative grounds.[66] Elsewhere, in spite of his stated principles Ellesmere is rejected quite arbitrarily, no authority being given for the emendation.[67] And yet elsewhere he refuses to emend even though he believes the text to be incorrect.[68]

These limitations impose some qualification on Skeat's skill and judg-

ment as an emender, one of the most important aspects of his achievement.
It is that very skill which makes it hard to look objectively at this particular
editorial function. Looking at later editions of *The Canterbury Tales*, one gets
the impression that subsequent editors have let themselves be led by the
nose somewhat by Skeat and in certain cases (it would be discourteous to
offer names) to endorse his conjectures as if they were the received text.
Hence Skeat's dexterity as emender has served to interpose a layer of
editorial conjecture between manuscript and printed text that is not easy to
penetrate, given the vagaries of Skeat's printed variants.

One can say, however, that the layer seems thicker than it need be. Such
an opinion is hard to substantiate adequately except by a full reediting of
The Canterbury Tales. Failing that, the evidence of a sample examination of a
single tale may help make my point a little more clearly. I have compared
Skeat's edition of *The Nun's Priest's Tale* (B^2 4011–4636) with the separate
edition of the tale undertaken by Kenneth Sisam and published in 1927.
This is still a most useful edition, produced by a scholar of the highest
editorial judgment. Both used Ellesmere as their base. A comparison of
their emendations is instructive. So far as I can determine, Skeat acknowledged sixty-three substantive emendations in his edition,[69] and Sisam
endorses thirty-two of these.[70] Sisam in addition makes another thirteen
emendations.[71] Of these, two seem to be errors.[72] In the remaining eleven
cases he either adopted different emendations or emended different points
in the text.

This illustration, rough and ready though it is, may be suggestive. An
editor, with expertise comparable to Skeat's own, found himself much more
inclined (about a third more) to adhere to the readings of his base manuscript than was Skeat. It suggests the possibility that Skeat may have
exercised a degree of emendatorial impetuosity that may in some respects
obscure his very gifted attempts to reconstruct Chaucer's text.

The problems with Skeat's overconfidence and suppression of evidence
occur elsewhere in the Clarendon Chaucer. On the unwarranted eclecticism
of his treatment of *Troilus and Criseyde*, Root may speak with some authority:

> Though Skeat examined all the extant manuscripts, he collated carefully only
> those which had been then printed by the Chaucer Society. . . . With such
> authorities to guide him, it was inevitable that Skeat should have printed a
> γ text of the poem. His authorities, outside of the γ group, are both so
> corrupt that it is not strange that he failed to discriminate between scribal
> corruptions and authentic variants.[73]

While Root's own views on the text may leave him vulnerable to criticism
in other respects, there can be little doubt that Skeat's failure to collate such
manuscripts as the St. John's[74] or Arch Selden B.24 or his perfunctory
discussion of the early printed editions[75] renders him particularly vulnerable. This is not untypical of Skeat's way of proceeding. For example, in the

case of *Truth* (1.390–91) he collates only six of the seventeen manuscripts of which he was aware.[76] For *Gentilesse* (1.82–84) he elects to reject all of the six manuscript authorities and base his text on Caxton's print. With respect to certain works, most notably *The Parliament of Fowls* (1.66–75) and *Anelida and Arcite* (1.76–78), Skeat fails to provide any textual justification for his choice of base manuscripts at all. Skeat's gifts as an editor did not include the patient sifting of manuscript evidence. He possessed a clear conviction of his capacity to get to the heart of the matter without any sense of the necessity of communicating to his reader the bases on which decisions had been arrived at.

This lack of total editorial candor extends into another aspect of Skeat's treatment of his text. I am thinking of his quest for orthographic "regularity," a quest that led to extensive adjustments of his various base manuscripts. It is fair to say that phonetic considerations weighed heavily with Skeat in his treatment of manuscript spelling. Of his text of *The Canterbury Tales* he observes, "I suppose this is the first complete edition in which the spelling has been tested by phonetic considerations" (4.xviii–ix). Elsewhere he praises the Ellesmere manuscript for "the highly phonetic quality of the spelling. The future editor will probably some day desire to normalize the spelling of Chaucer throughout his works. If so, he must study the spelling of the Ellesmere and Hengwrt MSS." (5.xx). Or again, "the spelling of the Ellesmere MS. is phonetic in a very high degree. Pronounce the words *as they are spelt* [Skeat's italics], but with the italics vowel sounds and the German final *e*, and you come very near the truth" (5.xxv).

The obvious conclusion to be drawn from these reiterated assertions is clear: they suggest a high degree of regard for the orthography of Ellesmere that leads one to suppose that he is generally faithful to it. He does offer a full statement of principles for his deviations from Ellesmere spellings (4.xviii–xx). He concludes his statement (4.xix–xx):

> These minute variations are, I trust, legitimate, and I have not recorded them. They cause trouble to the editor, but afford ease to the reader. But the scrupulous critic need not fear that the MS. has been departed from in any case where it could make any phonetic difference without due notice.

There are some basic difficulties with the claims made here. In the first place, given the previous stress on the soundness of Ellesmere, one might suppose the "variations" to be "minute" in number as well as in kind. But this is not the case. My impression, from spot collations against the Six-Text edition, is that Skeat's silent changes, orthographic or substantive, probably average at a minimum about one every line when one takes into account his treatment of manuscript capitalization, flourishes that Furnivall expands as final -*e*'s, and the silent suppression of manuscript thorn and yogh.

This is not, in particular cases, all that crucial. A number of Skeat's consistent changes are very minor, such as the printing of consonantal *u* as *v*.

But in their overall effect they do serve to alter the texture of Ellesmere's accidentals significantly, making it appear far more regular than is the actual case. And, beside that, one can ponder Skeat's pursuit of a chimerical consistency at all. A point in *The Second Nun's Tale* is revealing here. Skeat emends Ellesmere's *swete* at G 251 to *sote*. His reasoning is set out in a footnote (4.517):

> The MSS have *swete* here; but in 1. 247 we find only *sote, soote, swote, suote*, except *swete* in [Petworth]; in 1. 229 [Ellesmere, Harley 7334 read] *soote*; [Hengwrt] *swote*; [CUL Gg.4.27] *sote*; [Corpus, Petworth, Lansdowne] *swete*.

Actually Ellesmere reads *soote* at both line 229 and line 247. But the form *sote* never occurs in Ellesmere. Confronted with evidence of orthographic inconsistency, Skeat invents a new form. Even though the manuscripts offer clear evidence of a range of forms within and among themselves, Skeat feels it possible and appropriate to pursue a chimerical notion of consistency in spelling.

But the question of spelling obviously appealed to Skeat's sense that the problems of Chaucer were susceptible to resolution by the application of reason by a superior intellect. In this conviction he was further sustained by the comforting knowledge that if fifteenth-century scribes did not know how to spell Chaucer's works, he did. He is quite frank about this (6.ixn.):

> There can be no harm in stating the simple fact, that a long and intimate acquaintance, extending over many years, with the habits and methods of the scribes of the fourteenth [*sic*] century, has made me almost as familiar with the usual spelling of the period as I am with that of modern English.
>
> It is little more trouble for me to write a passage of Chaucer from dictation than one from Tennyson. It takes me just a little longer, and that is all.

It is, of course, unsurprising, given this conviction, that Skeat felt it necessary to demonstrate that he knew better than the scribes—or Chaucer.

An equally unsurprising corollary of his orthographic changes is the appearance of a Chaucer who generally wrote verses of great regularity. Skeat's "Germanic -*e*'s" rarely are heard, and in many cases are not even visible. In *The Canterbury Tales*, for example, he seems to have suppressed many of the final -*e*'s that Furnivall printed.[77] He also silently changed readings he felt to be metrically inappropriate, irrespective of their "phonetic difference."[78] Once again, the treatment of versification is neither consistent nor clear.[79]

IV

Skeat's texts for the Clarendon Chaucer were generally constructed in ways which subsequent scholarship has found unsatisfactory: the erratic presentation of manuscript evidence, arbitrary emendation and excessive interference with the accidentals of his texts tend to misrepresent the nature of

Chaucer's received texts in ways that make his editing ultimately unsatisfactory, though immeasurably superior in most respects to that which
preceded it.

It remains to consider Skeat's most enduring achievements. His greatest
gifts seem to lie in his skill as a glosser and annotator of Chaucer's text and as
a purger of his canon.

Skeat's Glossary to Chaucer's works is among the most considerable of his
achievements. It runs to 310 double-column pages, with an additional
Glossary for fragments B and C of *The Romaunt of the Rose*. A comparison
with the Glossary which Skeat's mentor Richard Morris appended to his
Aldine edition of *The Poetical Works of Geoffrey Chaucer* (1866) may indicate
the extent to which Skeat advanced Chaucerian lexicography. The comparison is an appropriate one, for, as we have seen, Skeat acknowledged a
general debt to Morris. But both qualitatively and quantitatively Skeat's
Glossary represents an extraordinary advance in method. For example, the
letter *C* in Morris's edition contains 317 entries. In Skeat's there are 810.
One might not wish to place too much weight on the increased number of
entries, since Skeat included the *Romaunt* as well as the prose works, *The
Tale of Melibee, The Parson's Tale, A Treatise on the Astrolabe*, and *Boece*. The
difference may be both confirmed and clarified by a single illustration under
the letter *C*. For *cas* Morris has only "sb. chance" and a single reference.
Skeat's entry contains 26 separate references and 14 separate glosses (exclusive of plural forms) and a cross reference to a variant spelling with
additional entries. And all the references are to poetic texts. The example
suggests the new standards for the glossing of Chaucer which Skeat set,
standards which no subsequent edition has equaled.

Skeat's commentaries on particular works have inevitably suffered more
from the passage of time and the acquisition of new information. Such a
difficulty was aggravated by the way in which Skeat prepared the various
commentaries for his texts. For as we have seen, before undertaking the
Clarendon Chaucer, he had engaged in intermittent and piecemeal editorial
activities on Chaucer, mainly for the Clarendon Press series for which he had
edited *The General Prologue* and eleven of the *Tales* and most of the other
works except for *Boece, Troilus and Criseyde*, and the fragment of the
Romaunt. As he explains, "It will now be readily understood that nearly all
the notes and illustrations that have appeared in these various books are here
collected and reproduced (with corrections where necessary) and that many
others have been added of a like kind" (6.xvii).

In fact, the process of revision of earlier work was more intermittent than
Skeat indicates here. For example, the *Astrolabe*, Skeat's earliest editorial
engagement with Chaucer, was published in 1872. But the notes are
reprinted verbatim in the Clarendon Chaucer with no additional material of
any kind.

In most of the other texts that he had previously edited a similar process occurs, though, since they were undertaken closer in time to the Clarendon edition, the situation is less serious. The editions of the *Minor Poems* (vol. 1 of the Clarendon Chaucer) are taken over with only occasional deletions and small additions from Skeat's 1888 edition. Similarly, his Clarendon edition of *The Legend of Good Women* relies almost wholly on his 1889 edition, apart (mainly) from a few isolated references to Lounsbury's subsequent *Studies*.[80] The situation with the annotations to *The Canterbury Tales* is similar. Many of the texts that Skeat had previously edited had, however, been reprinted on more than one occasion before the Clarendon edition. Skeat does seem to have attempted to revise the notes on such occasions. But he does not seem to have undertaken any but the most perfunctory revisions between the latest reprinting and the appearance of the Clarendon edition, an omission which at times leads to errors and omissions. Of the works for which he first produced a commentary in the Clarendon Chaucer his observations on *Troilus and Criseyde* received their share of unfavorable comment.[81]

But local disagreements should not be permitted to detract from the overall excellence of Skeat's Commentary. Flügel's observation on the Commentary on *The Canterbury Tales* can be extended to the rest of Skeat's annotation:

> This is the most complete commentary on the Tales; and even if Dr. Skeat had never written anything but this commentary, it would have been sufficient to ensure the honorable association of his name with that of his author and to win for him the lasting gratitude of Chaucer students.[82]

The most tangible and most significant manifestation of this gratitude has been the number of subsequent editors who have felt it proper to appropriate Skeat's notes silently.[83]

Skeat's final enduring achievement is a negative one. It consists in what he did *not* include in the Clarendon Chaucer. With Skeat's edition we approach very close to the final stabilization of the Chaucer canon, to the achievement of a complete works purged of the accretions of insubstantial attributions of earlier editors. Chaucer is finally and authoritatively liberated from the authorship of such works as *The Plowman's Tale, Jack Upland, The Assembly of Ladies, The Craft of Lovers*, and Usk's *Testament of Love*, as well as large portions of *The Romaunt of the Rose*. Particularly by the use of rhyme tests, pioneered by Bradshaw,[84] Skeat was able to provide plausible criteria and hence new standards for canonicity.

He was somewhat less successful in adding to the canon. He did find the lyrics *To Rosemounde* (1.389)[85] and *Womanly Noblesse* (4.xxv–xxvi). But the three lyrics he printed as possibly Chaucer's (vol. 1, nos. 21–23) have not won a more secure place in the canon. And the two poems he belatedly added in volume 4 (apart from *Womanly Noblesse*)[86] have not gained even qualified support from later editors. He was perhaps disposed to place too heavy a weight on internal evidence and the conjunction of a few poems with others of certain authorship in particular manuscripts. He was triumphantly vindicated in the case of *A Complaint to His Lady* (1.360–64) which he had placed in the canon before Furnivall found the Chaucer ascription in Phillipps 9503.[87] But in other cases his judgments seem marked by a curious insistence on the need to examine manuscripts—curious, since it does not clearly bear on the issue and does not seem to warrant the warmth with which he was prepared to attack unnamed detractors.[88] Such intemperate defences of tenuous and relatively minor positions is an odd feature of some of Skeat's more implausible attributions.

This overassertiveness in defending the canonicity of a few lyrics contrasts markedly with his attitude towards Chaucer's authorship of "The Romaunt of the Rose. Rarely did he arrive at his final position so painfully and after such changes of heart. Originally, he seems to have shared Bradshaw's view that none of the work was Chaucer's.[89] Then he was, for a time, prepared to admit only fragment C. Finally he came to espouse the view reflected in his edition—that fragment A alone was Chaucer's. I have no wish to chronicle these changes of heart more fully.[90] It is a testimony to Skeat's flexibility of mind that he was willing to wrestle for such a length of time with the problem and to abandon (and acknowledge that he had abandoned) positions he no longer believed in. Subsequent scholarship has tended to endorse his final position.

V

Skeat has profoundly affected the way we read Chaucer. He was the first to attempt a comprehensive edition of the works, he provided for the first time an apparatus to illumine them that was reliable and compendious, and he set standards in critical editing which, if they have been subsequently raised, have been raised as a consequence of his work. Whatever failures of method and accuracy I have noted must be offset by an appreciation of these fundamental achievements, achievements which laid a firm foundation for modern Chaucer scholarship.[91]

10. Robert K. Root
(1877–1950)

RALPH HANNA III

OBERT KILBURN ROOT belonged to the last Victorian generation—
those young people who came to maturity in the 1890s—a generation which also included John M. Manly. Root's editing of Chaucer's *Troilus*, only a small portion of his total service to scholarship and
academia, was and is a landmark in medieval studies. Heralded even a
quarter century after its appearance as the best edition ever made of a
medieval text, Root's *Book of Troilus* still merits admiration, for it represents the first modern critical edition of any Middle English poem.[1] It is
thus the book from which we all have, in some sense, learned our trade. But
its achievement, however commanding, needs to be carefully measured. For
Root's *Troilus* remains a product of a late Victorian approach to texts, and
although it is a fine and monumental example of the approach, it is also,
lamentably, compromised by its Victorian rationalist methodology.

Root's Victorian legacy takes two forms. One is creative and extraordinarily helpful. Root was the beneficiary of a traditional literary
education, a product of late-Victorian humanism. The imperative that the
past must be comprehended in its fullness and otherness inspires, I think, a
great deal of Root's best work. He was a massively learned man and
possessed that rare ability to draw together, almost effortlessly, it seems, all
his diverse erudition. Moreover, he was imaginative, tireless, and tasteful:
able to recognize potential literary problems, quick to recall and find
information which would resolve them, and willing to eschew pedantry.
These impressive qualities, nurtured at that font of American humanistic
studies, A. S. Cook, produced Root's most lasting contribution—his
exhaustive annotation of Chaucer's text.

Unfortunately, there was another side to Root's Victorian legacy which
compromised his best efforts. As an editor, Root indulged too often a view

that the past is fully comprehensible through rational exercise alone. This insistence upon the universality of logical processes (often carried to the point of speciousness and basic logical error) tainted Root's endeavors to establish the text of the *Troilus*.

Two separate sorts of logical exercise proved particularly debilitating for Root. On the one hand, he believed unswervingly, I think, in the possibility of a scientifically verifiable text, one uncontaminated by any touch of merely human judgment. This great hope, always associated with Lachmann's edition of Lucretius of 1850, takes the form of a belief that the relations of witnesses to a text can be resolved by purely logical processes. It is perhaps Root's tragedy to have been laden with a text not susceptible to such procedures, for Root's failure as editor is predicated upon a series of logical operations inspired by the inability of a genetic Lachmannian system to produce results. In the absence of the accepted "scientific" method to produce a text, Root had to create a new method and fell back upon a faith in logic, not observed fact, as a guide.

Even this effort became compromised because of failures peculiar to Root's logical system. For Root's logical views were fundamentally Darwinist and developmental: all human action, including that of both scribes and poets, reflected the same general laws. Broadly speaking, action had to move from simplicity to complexity, from mediocrity to greatness, for that was the nature of things. Both sorts of logical exercise—textual theory and developmentalism—had a place in Root's faulted effort to establish the text of *Troilus*.

Root's effort to determine what Chaucer wrote was perforce a complicated affair. The relationships among the witnesses remain unresolved today, and this untidiness of manuscript affiliations had been established long before Root became involved in editing *Troilus*. Sir William Symington McCormick, whose materials Root inherited, had found himself incapable of describing any coherent manuscript relations. After extensive collation and comparison of variants, McCormick could find no coherent genetic groups which would enable him to edit the text through the Lachmannian principle of recension. As McCormick saw, the manuscripts agree erroneously in such an incoherent variety of patterns that no single stemmatic diagram can reveal their relationships. Thus an editor lacks the evidence to create a pattern which may reveal the readings of the archetype of all surviving manuscripts.[2]

Although McCormick had found that manuscript relations showed a confusion impossible to deal with genetically, he had made a second, and rather different, discovery of vital importance for Root's view of the editorial problem. McCormick was convinced that not all the variants differentiating the manuscript versions were the result of scribal copyings. Although incapable of grouping the texts on a genetic basis, McCormick believed that he could subdivide the witnesses on other grounds. He thought that the manuscripts of *Troilus* split into the two groups, α and β; these, he thought, reflected two different stages of publication, rather than the residue of scribal activity. He identified α as an unrevised state of the text, extant in Ph H_2 (first scribe, the same copyist as Ph), for much of the poem in Gg H_5, and for later portions in J. In contrast β represented a fully revised state, appearing in R Cx, for most of the poem in J, and in several other texts showing shifting affiliations. And, at a later stage, McCormick identified a third textual state γ, typified by Cp C1 H_1; this he thought the last version, but he was simultaneously troubled by many scribal errors associated with this recension. Ultimately McCormick excluded γ from consideration in his provisional edition, published in The Globe Chaucer.[3]

McCormick had thus strikingly redirected the focus of textual studies. Rather than the removal of scribal *corruptela*, the editor of the *Troilus* would henceforth be engaged in a more exciting task. Because textual variants could be identified as signs of revision, the editor would find himself in the position of literary critic, investigating those changes made by Chaucer himself in the production of his masterwork.

One should note in passing that McCormick's findings are not mutually exclusive. If, as McCormick (and later Root) believed, the manuscripts reflect revision states, this fact alone will not edit the text. Discovery of revisions allows elimination of some texts from serious consideration (a text of "the early recension of Chaucer's *Troilus*" cannot logically rely on the corrected β γ evidence, for example), but it does not direct the editor in his handling of those texts he does use. That is, within separate revision states variation occurs, and the elimination of nonauthorial variants remains a requirement for the production of a critical text. This necessity becomes an especially acute problem when one recognizes that the β copies, the center of McCormick's final version, turn out on inspection to be those man-uscripts least susceptible to consistent genetic analysis. And without such grouping their nonauthorial readings cannot be removed by stemmatic analysis. McCormick's view of the text requires two different sorts of procedures: the identification of revision states and the identification, within these states, of clear genetic relations.

These conclusions Root knew and reverified, and they posed for him a dilemma of no mean sort. For the failure of the manuscripts to group genetically left Root with no "scientific" method for arriving at the text. At the very best in this situation, he might construct a version of *Troilus* unacceptably eclectic. He might prepare a text based upon a single "best" manuscript corrected from the rest where manifestly deficient. Or he could produce a "Chaucerian text" by choosing on the basis of taste alone preferred readings from the total variant corpus and intercalating them. No such alternative seems to have been particularly inviting for Root: to accept such a text would surrender the editor's hope that the text of Chaucer was rationally recoverable.

Moreover, Root must have seen that McCormick's conclusions compromised one another to an unsettling degree. The lack of clear genetic relationships, if pursued, could call into question whatever had been gained by the discovery that the manuscripts reflected revision states. On a strict genetic basis there could be only one way to account for the situation McCormick had uncovered. Manuscripts of a work which will not group genetically represent one of two situations to which Victorian editors refer by the general term "conflation." They may reflect scribal conflation in the strict sense, deliberate efforts to produce a text which fuses the readings of two or more exemplars.[4] Or they show convergence, scribal errors produced independently by individual copyists and accidentally coinciding with similar independent errors.[5] Conflation proper produces texts which join readings from more than one discrete genetic tradition. Convergence produces texts which appear to shift genetic affiliation constantly.

In spite of the logical necessity of "conflation" to explain the situation McCormick had found, Root strenuously denied this conclusion. Although seldom dealing with the *Troilus* manuscripts on a genetic basis, Root insisted that the textual tradition of the *Troilus* was unconflated.[6] Indeed, upon this obiter dictum, an assertion or assumption held quite in defiance of the facts, Root built his theory of the text.

Such an assumption (or denial of McCormick's logical conclusion) was an utter necessity. Root must have seen clearly that to accept a conflated scribal tradition might thoroughly undermine the usefulness of McCormick's theory of revision states. Admitting the presence of conflation could potentially distort not only scribal relationships but also the precise delineation of the revisions. One could no longer be certain that readings peculiar to one recension of the poem had not traveled into another or that some texts on a local basis had not fused different recensions. There would then be no basis for a text short of already rejected eclecticism. But a rigorous and scientifically derived text was to be had by some means; Root's unswerving belief in the recovery of authorial readings by rigorous rational exercise had to be served. What resulted, the elegant, rationalistic construction of a complete chimera, explained everything about the text of *Troilus and Criseyde* except the most palpable and obvious facts.

At the center of Root's reconstruction stood McCormick's discovery of revision states. However, to judge from McCormick's surviving statements, Root did not inherit but had to create an editorial tool out of a general theory of how Chaucer composed. Here Root must have been concerned with two problems. First, the evidence for revision in the poem is not exceptionally clearcut. The only palpable evidence which might conduce an editor to believe that *Troilus* may exist in revised and unrevised versions comes from five isolated passages and an at least partly mistaken scribal note in J.[7] And even if all these passages are taken as proof positive of revision (which they cannot be),[8] no information exists to deal with the thousands of other manuscript variants which an editor must ultimately accept into or exclude from the text. Simply identifying what are only by assumption examples of revision gives no tool for identifying possible revisions elsewhere.

Second, to invert McCormick's original view, Root had to be aware that not all differences between the manuscripts can be ascribed to the effects of revision. A priori one might reasonably expect that a substantial portion of manuscript variation reflects scribal, rather than authorial, behavior. One must, then, be able to separate possible Chaucerian readings from non-authorial errors. Something more than a theory of revision is needed to have a scientific editorial tool.

These difficulties Root resolved by a stroke of brilliance, but a brilliance fraught with foolish self-deception, for all difficulties in McCormick's theory of the text finally depended upon a single conception—scribal error. Error in the manuscripts occurred in such confusing combinations that no consistent disposition of the variants emerged; error potentially called into question any information about revision. Root apparently saw an extra-ordinary way around this impasse: to banish error from the discussion.

Although to say that Root banished error of course overstates, his editorial activity removed manuscript relations from the center of the discussion and made a rational critical edition of the sort he desired possible. Root reduced to far below any acceptable minimum editorial interest in the scribal transmission of the text and thus in genetic relations per se. That the manuscripts would not group genetically could be ignored. Root accomplished this act by declaration; he simply decreed that scribal error was recognizable and simple-minded: ". . . some [readings] present but a slight variation, such as a simple transposition in word-order or a trifling substitution, which could be explained as a scribal corruption. Others, however, involve so considerable a difference in phrasing that the variation can be explained only as due to deliberate revision."[9] This statement may be a logical extension of factual observation—scribes do, on a demonstrable basis, often make trivial changes in the texts they copy. But the fact that scribes sometimes make trivial errors neither supports nor approximates the two propositions Root conceived as the equivalent of that fact: (1) all trivial errors are scribal; (2) no scribe ever makes a substantial error (or a substantial deliberate change). Both these propositions, central to Root's view of the text, are only counterfactual inferences. Some trivial errors represent authorial *lapsus calami* (as, in other contexts, Root was well aware); some scribes (the very clever copyist of Ph, for example) can change the texts they inherit in quite radical ways.[10]

Having by logical extension rendered scribal error only the easily recognizable trivial corruption, Root further minimized the usefulness of error in constructing the text. In the tradition of the *Troilus*, Root saw the major problem requiring resolution as a substantial variety of large-scale disagreements among manuscripts. Shared palpable errors also occurred, but these usually distinguished only pairs of texts (though there was, as we shall see, one large family) and were, for Root, mainly useful in restraining editorial enthusiasm for isolated readings. He thus chose to exert his energies on large multitext variants and in this process relegated interest in scribal error (as he conceived it) and genetic relations to a secondary position. [11]

Moreover, Root's purely logical definition of scribal activity allowed the elevation of McCormick's revision theory to a central position. For by Root's definition the major disagreements among the manuscripts could not have been scribally produced. If scribal behavior was trivial and recognizable, all other disagreements had, logically, to be nonscribal. By fiat Root had denatured all these disagreements: they had lost the moral stigma of being mere scribal errors and were effectively neutralized as variant forms of the text. And because they had become, by a priori definition, nonscribal, such variants could have been produced by only a single mechanism: all such readings probably came from the pen of Chaucer. By minimizing errors, Root increased exponentially the evidence that the text of Chaucer's *Troilus* exists in two or more states of revision.

This process, Root's journey toward a position from which a critical edition could be produced, represents a perverse inversion of the editor's task—all in the service of escaping fact through easy logical inference. Rather than identifying wrong readings, errors inadmissible to the text, Root placed himself in the position of being the advocate for a great number of competing variants. Such readings, because by theory "nonscribal," were probably Chaucer's: Root's editorial activity became the demonstration that nearly all such readings could be conceived as indeed authorial. In adopting this stance, Root not only relied upon circular reasoning but abandoned that discrimination central to textual criticism since Bentley. And he replaced discrimination with a tolerance and susceptibility which could accept even the flimsiest scribal creations as lines from the pen of Chaucer himself.

But this same foolish brilliance made an edition possible. For by daring to be catholic, to accept every possibly defensible reading as Chaucerian, Root was able to generate vastly more revisions than hitherto suspected, to analyze them, and to explain their genesis. And having assumed that scribes do not perform sweeping changes in their exemplars, Root had a nearly automatic (though wrongheaded) system for constructing a text. All that remained was the assignment of certain manuscript variants to particular stages of revision. And *The Textual Tradition of Chaucer's Troilus* meticulously performs this task to provide the underpinnings for the subsequent critical text.

But this triumph was a pyrrhic one. First, the proliferation of proven revisions reached such proportions that the original excitement and attractiveness of the theory was lost. Were the *Troilus* to exist in revision states, one should hope to learn from these something of Chaucer's methods of composition and something of his intent in writing *Troilus*. But as the number of discovered and proven revisions snowballed, a sense of any end Chaucer had in revising became blurred. Finally Root had to throw up his hands; revision, rather than clarifying authorial method, made no sense at all. Rather than revealing the plans of a master poet, it created mysteries.[12]

Second, and more regrettable, Root's urge for an utterly scientific and automatic system for creating a text led him to jettison his most valuable tool, his own literary judgment. For as we have seen and will see again, Root's pursuit of an impeccable text was based upon a hope that logical rigor could solve all textual problems. But, in the event, this rigor (tempered by constant logical error) produced a text which included a substantial number of readings which good taste should have rejected. Having thrown away the conception of scribal practice as an editorial tool, Root had no mechanism to distinguish among the plausible readings his revision states provided. Consequently, he took for revision (and frequently for the final authorial version) a number of lines most modern critics schooled in the study of scribal practice would see as nonauthorial productions.[13] What resulted, *The Book of Troilus*, is an extraordinary scholarly paradox, a careful scholarly edition of great acumen, the text of which has been rejected (and properly so) by every subsequent major editor.

The Textual Tradition is a selective account, though it examines more evidence for the text of a Middle English poem than any other study until the Manly-Rickert *Canterbury Tales*:

> The investigation of the MS. relations has been based on a minute examination of about 2500 lines chosen from all parts of the poem, after a more cursory comparison of the authorities in their entirety. The lines chosen for careful study include: (1) the stanzas printed in the Chaucer Society's volume of Specimen Extracts; (2) the whole of the soliloquy on free choice in Book IV; (3) all lines in which there is a significant variation found in two or more MSS.; (4) all lines in which there is a variation, however slight, affecting the two main types of text α and β, or the important group designated as γ.[14]

In this volume Root analyzed about one-third of the poem's lines, but his principles of selectivity prejudged the issues. His decision to analyze selectively was not necessarily an evil one and, given the amount of variation to deal with, very likely appeared a necessity. Root could not, for example, utilize the method later suggested by Dom Henri Quentin—extensive analysis of a limited but consecutive chunk of the poem[15]—for the witnesses shift affiliations with frequency. But the choice of where to analyze reveals a bias toward seeing only certain types of variation as potentially significant. Categories (3) and (4) above suggest that Root especially sought readings involving splits within the manuscript tradition, places where largish variant groupings occurred. And Root apparently chose such readings for analysis in the hope that they would provide the clearest and most incontrovertible evidence about revision states. But the nature and extent of revision was what Root should have been investigating; the careful, but apparently unconscious, preselection of material for analysis meant that Root presumed that revision had occurred and was to be found in variants such as these. Thus, while avoiding the scribal detritus with which McCormick could not deal, Root persistently begged the question he sought to pose.

This illogical simplification of the issues left Root with a small and soluble group of problems. Once he arrived at his conception of the textual issues, he had to perform four steps to create a text. First, manuscripts had to be grouped on the basis of sharing certain variants (not errors): this step established the different states of the text. From these groups any readings palpably erroneous had to be removed: at this stage the different states might be presumed to represent groups of purely authorial revisions. The different revisions then had to be time-ordered from earliest to most recent: this procedure would allow identification of a last state, presumably Chaucer's final and considered intention and thus the basic text for an edition. Finally, Root had to explain the genesis of the individual states of the text; the necessity for such an analysis would have become apparent in sorting the data, for the evidence, even after Root's preselection, did not clearly support a first text α changed to produce a final text β.

Root's account was also colored by the form in which he chose to analyze his evidence. He considered each of these four problems simultaneously and on a book-by-book basis. This form of analysis seems, given the shifting manuscript affiliations, a natural one, but it gave to book 1 a perhaps undeserved prominence. Analyzed first, book 1 came to typify Root's conception of the textual relations, for that portion of the poem allowed a straightforward analysis of the generation of manuscript versions. What in later books was obscure and often baffling was in book 1 clear, and this introductory analysis came to govern the entire argument. Root could (and did) assume that this simple situation in fact reflected the underlying structure of the entire textual tradition and that this structure elsewhere was merely obscured by a patina of local difficulties.

In book 1 Root could distinguish with relative ease the three stages of the text McCormick had earlier discovered.[16] The α manuscripts formed a group by virtue of their inclusion of a stanza lacking in other copies, one of the major readings always taken as revision evidence. In addition, Root showed a number of other loci where α manuscripts agreed against other texts in variation; a great many of these readings Root found too extensive to be scribal productions and elevated to authorial status as the remains of Chaucer's first recension.

Within book 1 Root also discovered what he took as evidence for time ordering α against the other texts. On a number of occasions Root believed he could show α readings to be more direct representations of Chaucer's Italian source, Boccaccio's *Filostrato*, than were the readings of other versions. With impeccable Victorian evolutionary logic Root argued that these agreements of α and the Italian proved that α was the first recension. Second drafts should, in this theory, show a poetic freedom and individuality not to be expected in a first effort; there the poet tries to convey only the sense of his source. Such an assertion again begs the question: poets may work this way, but it remains to be demonstrated that Chaucer worked so. And in asserting α's unique similarity to the Italian, Root was aided by the partitioning of his argument on a book-by-book basis, for at many later points by his own account β or γ resembles the Italian more nearly than does α. [17]

Root's discussion of the β version of book 1 was relatively unproblematic. Just as α, the β texts grouped in a number of agreements in variation. Root identified these readings as a fully revised second authorial version, and he expended a good deal of energy in defending these readings as plausibly authorial, rather than scribal. Largely through the criterion of extensiveness of variation, Root removed any tincture of scribal activity from the β readings. As a result of this question begging, β was never distinguished by a single error common to all manuscripts and became a purely authorial text.

This argument, the effort to render even palpable β scribalisms authorial, was a necessary corollary to Root's revolutionary view of the γ texts. Whereas Skeat believed γ the only basis on which to construct the text and McCormick thought it a scribally deformed final version, Root set about to debunk its readings. He properly noted that all γ manuscripts agree in a large number of lections which are palpable (and usually trivial) errors. But Root could not live with the apparent paradox that a copying might be inattentive and careless, thus producing predictable minor errors, while simultaneously offering readings which might be of substantive value. In yet another sweeping logical extension he excluded γ from textual consideration. Because γ manuscripts agreed in unique scribal errors, all unique γ errors became, for Root, scribal errors. For all the appearance of logic here, Root failed to note that "some *A* are *B*," and "all *A* are *B*" are not equivalent propositions. The elevation of β to authorial status was balanced by denigrating γ to a purely scribal version.

Here one has to be surprised that Root did not recognize the disparity between his logical constructions and the palpable facts. For although γ texts do include a number of clearly scribal boners, they also quite often manage to support β manuscripts in readings Root thought authorial. Indeed, for about five hundred lines of book 2, γ manuscripts are the only source for Root's revised version and only in 3.400–4.170 did Root believe they differed markedly from β. [18] The ability of γ texts to preserve readings Root thought in other contexts correct should have led him to reconsider his logical animus against all γ readings.

Beyond his rejection of these γ readings, Root's explanation of how γ had
been produced was revolutionary. On the basis of the disposition of readings, especially in book 3, Root argued that γ, rather than a final version of
the text, as McCormick believed, was a middle version. For much of the
poem it shares readings with β and thus must have been produced after
Chaucer's revisions. But in book 3, wherever γ differs from β, it lacks
Chaucer's final revisions. It thus must have been produced after α but before
β and, given its frequent errors, was produced by scribal, rather than
authorial, means.

But Root could never acknowledge the problems inherent in such a view.
For if γ manuscripts represent a "mediate version" of the text, they do so
only metaphorically and not in fact. In book 3, where γ is, in Root's view,
unrevised, it simply represents an expansion of the α-manuscript group.
And in other contexts, where γ has revised readings, it is merely an
expansion of the β revision group. All that Root means by a "middle
version" is a text that shifts apparent affiliations, at times agreeing with an
early version α and at times with a later version β. But that view is not
logically the same view as Root's claim that because γ forms a "middle
version" it was produced second, before β. Nothing prevents γ from being,
as McCormick thought, the last version produced. Moreover, because Root
refused to accept unique γ readings as evidence for Chaucer's text, he could
ignore entirely certain situations (notably book 5) where in his account no
revision went on. In such situations α and β usually agree, sometimes
against γ. Many less wedded to their own a priori logical constructions than
Root might be tempted to see in this situation a sign that γ was indeed a
revised version.

Such objections Root tried to forestall but lacked the evidence to do so. In
only a few and very isolated instances do α, β, and γ actually coexist as
separate versions of the text. And of this small number of cases, in only a
handful, perhaps no more than four or five instances, could Root convince
himself that all three variants were authorial. When this situation
occurred,[19] Root tried to argue that γ was a "middle version" in a second
and very different way. In these few readings Root tried to analyze the γ
variants as merely combinations of α and β versions and thus typical of only
a partly revised state of the text. But since Root still viewed γ as a scribal
version, he could provide no clear evidence that this version was not an
eclectic combination of two preexisting ones. Nor could this sparse evidence for the simultaneous existence of three separate versions carry conviction: a handful of variants in an eight-thousand-line poem proves very little.
Indeed on a purely factual basis Root had almost no evidence for his three
states of the poem.

The three time-ordered states discovered in book 1 could not, however,
explain even Root's selected evidence. No amount of work could render β,
the basis for Root of Chaucer's final text, a fully consistent group of

manuscripts and readings through the entire poem. Indeed through much of books 2 and 3 β does not exist at all as a coherent group; rather, some witnesses follow the α version (Root's Chaucerian first draft), some follow γ (Root's mediate scribal version), and a very few (J R H_4) show unique readings. With his typical search for revision rather than error Root ignored the palpable evidence that β simply does not here exist and identified J R H_4 as the β tradition.

But this decision did not lay all problems to rest. The β texts show frequent and unpredictable agreements in variation.[20] Many manuscripts at odd points desert the identifiable β tradition altogether and agree with α or γ texts in scattered readings. And the faithful J R H_4, although the only source of a revised authorial text in book 3, provide such bad readings in book 2 that even Root could find no way to defend them as authorial. If β was, as it seemed to Root from "clear" portions of the text it must be, the revised text prepared by Chaucer, considerable explanation of the vagaries of the manuscripts had to be undertaken.

Here Root, in his effort to preserve β's integrity and explain its waverings, had to rely upon a fantasy. He interwove expert literary history, his own valuable knowledge of publication in the age of the manuscript book, with a surprising scholarly credulity. Root recognized, correctly, that if two versions of the *Troilus* had achieved manuscript circulation, they had probably been published—as that process was understood in the fourteenth century. That is, Chaucer, when ready to publish an early α version, would have had a scribal fair copy made from his drafts. After an authorial check this text would provide copy for the actual publication, the production of a series of purely scribal manuscripts.[21] And, Root reasoned, Chaucer would probably have prepared a second recension on this fair copy: β would in effect be only a corrected text of α itself.

But into this reasonable theory of textual production Root imported a literary fiction.[22] He took the lyric *Adam Scriveyn*, with its references to Chaucer's correction of *Boece* and *Troilus*, as if a literal historical document standing as fully valid external evidence. Root introduced into his argument as a historical figure a doltish Adam whose fair copy included a batch of miswritings and mismetrings. By this construction Root was able to place the source of a great many variations which distinguish the surviving manuscripts in Chaucer's own fair copy. After Adam's careless transcription Chaucer proofread the newly prepared manuscript. Some errors Chaucer noticed and corrected, with much of the rubbing and scraping mentioned in *Adam*, but other mistakes eluded his scrutiny. And his revision to produce β turned the halting fair copy, already overlaid with corrections, into an even messier document, one filled with new authorial readings.

Adam's unsightly and doubly corrected fair copy—a text we have no assurance ever existed—became Root's method for handling all the loose ends left by his prior theorizing. This document, in Root's construction, included a variety of readings: the original text of α (in some cases with Adam's uncorrected errors), corrections of Adam's errors, and a number of revisions which comprised the β version. Root never stopped to consider that, if production of fair copy was a prerequisite for medieval publication (a view invoked in discussing α), Chaucer should have had a second fair copy produced in order to publish the β version. Instead he assumed—because it could produce that chaos he found typical of the manuscript relations—that all extant γ and β manuscripts had been produced by consultation of this draft manuscript—part scribal fair copy, part authorial corrections.

This putative manuscript in some sense accounted for all the extant versions of the text. The α manuscripts derived from a copy of the original scribal draft (in some cases uncorrected). After this scribal draft had been partly corrected and revised by the poet, the archetype of the γ manuscripts was copied from the manuscript. But the γ scribe, in addition to introducing a number of errors through carelessness, frequently copied not the revised β text but the canceled, yet still legible, α readings.[23] Finally, after a further revision of book 3, the β manuscripts were copied. The surviving β copies reflect at least five further independent transcriptions of the fair-copy draft. In each of these copyings the scribes independently replicated the activity of the γ scribe; that is, in a substantial but various group of readings, the five β scribes chose to reproduce not the revised β text but the canceled γ readings.[24] And before three of these copyings, those which eventually produced J R H_4, the draft text had lost leaves from book 2 which contained extensive Chaucerian revisions; these pages had been replaced from another, but unrevised, manuscript and accounted for the peculiar behavior of these manuscripts.[25]

On this basis Root could solve to his satisfaction the conundrum posed by shifting affiliations of the β texts. Wherever, Root argued, manuscripts representing any three of the original β copyings agreed in a reading, that reading provided the text of β. The other β manuscripts, which would usually agree with unrevised α or γ in these places, simply represented cases where individual copyists had chosen canceled, rather than final, readings. This analysis allowed Root to construct an archetypal β text, the form (in his theory) of Chaucer's final revision, while at the same time remaining consistent with his original supposition that much manuscript variation reflected authorial readings, rather than scribal errors.

After this lengthy aprioristic procedure, the actual construction of a text of Chaucer's *Troilus* becomes relatively mechanical. Root had simply to reproduce the revised β version (save in book 2, where γ is the revised text). Having "proved" that most important variation stemmed from a recoverable Chaucerian fair copy, Root had created the situation he had sought, one in which a text could be automatically generated. And because that text reflected a copy overseen by Chaucer, Root was absolved of any worries over the authority of the version produced. Having sought situations where judgment could have no play, Root had created an ideal text. Because all its readings had been authorially supervised, there was no necessity for any emendation whatever, and the editor could adopt the ultraconservative and ostensibly "scientific" role of mere textual annotator.

Root's actual practice in *The Book of Troilus* wavers little; the text, given the principles on which it is constructed, is a monument to sober conservatism. Although Root was forced to adopt a somewhat artificial normalized spelling for his presentation,[26] his adherence even to his artificial spelling rules is finicky almost to a fault. Thus he refuses to change to a spelling not attested by the manuscripts to present a Chaucerian Essex-Kentish rhyme. He refuses to add or delete final -*e* without manuscript support and prefers to defend metrical gibberish or to posit implausible disyllabic Chaucerian forms rather than to emend.[27] Root's handling of substantial readings shows much the same sobriety. He preserves a number of obvious minor *corruptela* because they occur in all, or very nearly all, the texts: these in his theory represent Adam's uncorrected errors in Chaucer's fair copy. In a minute number of cases where he could persuade himself that most manuscripts showed independent scribal errors, Root emended against his principles. But for the most part even minority readings which had attracted him in *The Textual Tradition* were rejected as good scribal guesses and consigned to the variant apparatus without regret.[28]

This apparatus shows a similar conservatism and adherence to principle. The presentation of textual evidence follows closely the logic for an edition developed in *The Textual Tradition*.[29] Since α represents, in Root's argument, a fully authorial version, even if superseded, all clear α readings are recorded. All possible, but not certain β readings, because evidence about Chaucer's final intention, are also recorded; these typically reflect loci where two of the five separate β groups share a common reading. And all common γ readings also appear: these have no value for determining the text but do reflect the forms of the largest genetic manuscript family and Root's rejection of his base text Cp. The apparatus does not present those readings Root had long since excluded—the greater mass of variation he believed totally scribal.

In its adherence to principle the *corpus lectionum* is the most irritating and irresponsible portion of Root's work. By his selective presentation Root forced all readers of *Troilus* to adopt his view of the text and denied them any evidence which would allow an independent assessment. Unlike *The Canterbury Tales*, where the evidence for the text is totally available, thanks to the efforts of Manly and Rickert, the evidence for the text of *Troilus* remains inaccessible and unknown. One can only make a guess about how much a new and open-minded attempt at the text would seek to change; on the basis of such collation as Root printed and the readings analyzed in *The Textual Tradition*, Root's printed text probably differs from Chaucer's actual intent in at least 10 percent of the lines.

As an example of the kinds of adjustments to Root's text which editors should make, we can survey a ten-stanza block for which full evidence is available in Chaucer Society prints. This passage, Pandarus's speech at 3.253–322,[30] occurs in a portion of the poem Root found uninteresting because he believed it unrevised. But an assessment of the facts—in this case the complete scribal evidence—shows that in every major problematic reading where Root followed his logical principles he reproduced a text not Chaucer's. Only when he deserted principle, when (in effect) taste overcame theory, did he manage sometimes to give the authorial reading.

In these seventy lines Root generally printed what he took to be the Chaucerian unrevised text provided by α and β manuscripts. As a result of this decision the reader is given at least twelve lines containing non-Chaucerian scribal readings. In two of the cases these readings reflect Root's doubts; he inserted readings shared by α and two (rather than his preferred three) β subgroups. But abandoning principle gave at least proportionately better results than following it. On two further occasions when Root forsook theory, which would have generated additional scribalisms as authorial, he printed the correct readings provided by γ manuscripts.[31]

Root's longing for an automatically generated text, one which would involve no editorial judgment, is finally an illusory hope. Editors do nothing except make judgments. In the long range, Skeat's claim of utter eclecticism, that he possessed the ability to recognize Chaucerian lines when he saw them, has much more to recommend it than Root's laissez-faire attitude that any bit of Middle English could be conceived as "Chaucerian." Root's efforts with the *Troilus* are a salutary lesson that the act of discrimination can be avoided only with peril.

But if Root reduced overmuch his activity as textual critic, this choice freed him to perform other editorial tasks superlatively. For as an annotator of the text, a provider of basic literary documentation, Root proved tasteful and learned. The ways in which he set about explaining the text for his readers established a standard and model which all subsequent texts, consciously or not, emulate. Indeed, until J. A. W. Bennett's Gower and Langland texts in the 1970s probably no editor has offered so extensive and so apposite a commentary as Root.

Root's mode of explanation was revolutionary and, to a certain extent, daring. He put behind him that philological approach which characterizes most earlier editions of Middle English texts. Having dealt extensively with the manuscript readings elsewhere, he saw little need to fill his notes with cogitations on difficult readings (though a number of these occur). Further, he let ten Brink's study and Tatlock and Kennedy's *Concordance* define the norms of Chaucerian usage. Thus *The Book of Troilus* has no glossary; discussions of "hard words" and of some niceties of Chaucerian forms and syntax are handled through notes and cross references.

In subordinating philology, Root emphasized in annotation problems of literary history. This interest is first signaled in the proportions of the Introduction. Although nearly half of the frontmatter of the volume is given over to the text (much of it a sketchy summary of work published elsewhere), most of the remainder treats literary issues: "Sources," "The Range of Chaucer's Reading," and "Moral Import."[32] And this attractive bias toward literary annotation similarly dominates the textual notes.

Root offers especially thorough and helpful annotation (the Introduction giving a general overview and the notes precise information appropriate for specific textual loci) on two themes. Taken as a whole, the volume provides exhaustive information on the tradition of Troy narratives, especially Boccaccio's *Filostrato* and Chaucer's handling of it. And Root was utterly indefatigable in finding other sources and analogues used by Chaucer in the poem. Particularly impressive is his attention to subliterary sources: he noted Chaucer's interest in proverbial wisdom and assembled evidence to show the prevalence of about sixty of these saws.

At general literary annotation Root was also extremely thorough. His explanatory notes are crammed with brief essays which elucidate a variety of Chaucer's references. Root is particularly helpful on astrological references, but his learning is not limited to this area. He also shows an adept's knowledge of such diverse topics as geomancy, medical theory, scholastic thought, the iconography of the virtues, and the rules of "hazard" (the medieval forerunner of crap shooting). And a number of notes join Chaucer's scattered uses of the same word or idea or connect Chaucer's uses with those of authors as diverse as Rabelais and Marlowe.[33] All in all, Root provides almost a textbook model for how to annotate a text.

Root's great strength remains his power as an explainer of the text. Regrettably, the text he undertook to annotate was a far from satisfactory representation of what Chaucer wrote. But the same Victorian milieu in which Root's illogical rationalism was fostered also bred his sense of fitting textual explanation. The industrious ferreting which produces such elaborate and helpful exemplification of Chaucer's words reflects the same high Victorian rationalism as Root's disastrous theories of textual transmission. Both share the same faith in the comprehensibility of the past, and Root's mixed achievement as editor combines both the powers and weaknesses of his historically localizable methodology.

11. John M. Manly (1865–1940) and Edith Rickert (1871–1938)

GEORGE KANE

ECAUSE John M. Manly and Edith Rickert's edition of Chaucer came out in 1940, not long before America's entry into World War II, it received less notice than its size and pretensions merited. There seem to have been few reviews, and those generally muted from consideration of Manly's recent death.[1] The work was evidently important. No Chaucer edition before it had been supported by such an elaborate apparatus: six volumes to accompany less than two of text. The appearance of authority from this was bound to be immense.

That appearance, the difficulty of the subject, and, it must be said, the opacity of the presentation, have protected the authority from challenge for more than a generation. Its import has been, principally, to question the originality, even respectability, of the texts of other editions of the *Tales*, to devalue the previously esteemed Ellesmere manuscript (El) and to give currency to the proposition that the main difficulty with the textual criticism of the poem is the result of the combined effects of authorial revision and what these editors call "editing."

To question the originality of existing texts is healthy, and not just as an antidote to complacency or sloth. It is part of a gradual process by which the damage done to literary works of art in the course of manual transmission is repaired. It took about five centuries of the process to attain such consensus as now exists about the texts of Greek and Roman antiquity.[2] In that perspective we in Middle English have only just begun to edit,[3] and the Manly-Rickert results accordingly represent an early rather than a late or final stage in the establishment of the text of *The Canterbury Tales*. That reduction of its authority can be held to apply particularly to the discrediting of the text of the Ellesmere manuscript, for the proposition that Ellesmere's occasional superior readings should be excluded from the text of

the tales because "it is very clear that an intelligent person, who was
certainly not Chaucer, worked over the text" when the manuscript was
copied[4] is a crucial one.

The postulate of authorial revision involves the most problematic factor
in textual criticism. One way of knowing that authorial revision occurred is
from external information, but none is available here. It can be fairly
presumed to have occurred in certain classes of situation, such as will be
allowed to exist in parts of *The Canterbury Tales*. But where there is no
external information, and where such situations do not obtain, the only
means by which authorial revision might be identified is editorial judgment. And once the likelihood of its occurrence in a textual tradition is
admitted, it must figure in every comparison of variant readings. It is
hardly possible to exaggerate the importance of assessing the likelihood of
its occurrence correctly.

From those considerations, which bear ultimately on every detail of the
text of *The Canterbury Tales*, the importance of a correct evaluation of the
edition must be apparent. For instance, the text, without any punctuation,
has a most authentic appearance; one would think it based on the ideal copy
text; only by the way, and under other headings, does one discover that its
form of language is synthetic (1.x, 151). The editors tell us that their basis
of collation was "Skeat's 'Student's Edition' " (2.5), but not whether they
took into account the extent to which that is an edited text. There is
frequent reference to variants "of classificatory value" for establishing
genetic relation, but no information about how the editors assessed that
value. There is mention of Maas's *Textkritik* (2.20), but no account of
whether or how Maas's general prescriptions were translated into a practical
system for editing. We are not clearly informed what sorts of variants are
excluded from the apparatus,[5] or for that matter, how the variants at the
foot of the text in Volumes 3 and 4 were selected; I have not yet found out.
From the theoretical information supplied it is impossible to establish what
the editorial procedures were, and thus also how effectively they were
applied.

The first determinant of the quality of any edition must be the method
adopted by its editors and their understanding of that method. Here the
method is recension (1.xii), a process originally devised to exclude subjective judgment from editing. In theory it applies information about the
genetic relation of the manuscripts of a text to eliminate their scribal
readings and by that means to recover the archetype, or exclusive common
ancestor, of the manuscripts. The effectiveness of recension as a control of
editorial judgment and a means of recovering the archetype is necessarily in
absolute and direct relation to both the completeness and the correctness of
the "family tree," or stemma, of the manuscripts. Without a complete
stemma, recension, in any meaningful sense of the term, is logically
impossible.

The governing principle of the classification of manuscripts is that there is no other evidence for genetic relation than agreement in unoriginal, that is, scribal or "wrong," readings. From this arises an immediate difficulty of distinguishing between agreements in original and agreements in unoriginal readings. To collate manuscripts a base is needed, a norm from which to record their divergences of reading. Obviously not all the groups formed by agreements in variation from such a base are necessarily genetic. Where the base has unoriginal readings the group-forming agreements may be in original, in right, readings and thus have no genetic significance. To distinguish the genetic groups it is necessary to identify originality in the base. That can be done only by prior editorial judgment, by establishing a hypothesis of direction of variation in as many as possible of the instances where variational groups founded on rival readings have taken shape. The edition does not refer to this operation.[6]

There is a second difficulty to compound the first, namely, that not all agreements in unoriginal readings are products of vertical transmission: some must have come about by lateral transmission, that is, contamination, whether deliberate and visual, or unconscious and memorial, and some by coincident variation. Thus, further, not all agreements in unoriginal readings are necessarily evidence of genetic relation. The editor is again thrown back upon his judgment: to classify the manuscripts he must somehow distinguish between genetic and random variational groups, identify the evidentially valid agreements.

Manly and Rickert were aware that agreement in original readings is "non-classificatory" (2.24), but the edition does not show that they were troubled by the indeterminate originality of their base for collation, "Skeat's 'Student's Edition' " (2.5).[7] What seems to have preoccupied them was the second difficulty of classification, that created by convergent variation (2.20–27). To counter this they made an independent venture into the rationale of textual criticism with the postulate that "The law of probability is so steady in its working that only groupings of classificatory value have the requisite persistence and consistency to be taken as genetic groups" (2.22). That postulate is a fallacy, for it assumes that manual transmission is uniformly erratic (all texts are equally corrupt), that there will always be relatively abundant agreement in error between genetically related manuscripts. Scribes copying Middle English manuscripts were not generating "mass phenomena" in respect of which "the regularity of the operations of chance" (2.23) can be invoked, but operating as highly specialized individuals in sets of highly individuated situations. Of course the editors knew that the assumption was baseless; they appear not to have seen how it affected their postulate.

The data to which, according to the account in Volume 2, such editorial thinking was applied were full of bewildering contradictory indications inherent in the textual situation: from the work being unfinished, the possibility of authorial revision, of arrangement by a literary executor or by stationers; from the divisibility of the work, from its status and evident popularity, the possibility of unauthorized copying; from "correction" and sophistication. The editors show no awareness that in such a situation the genetic relation of the manuscripts might be irrecoverable. Indeed, they imply that they were successful by publishing their text as one "established by the process of recension" (2.40), the text of the exclusive common ancestor of the surviving manuscripts, one determined by "a scientific process" in which the role of individual judgment had been reduced to the minimum.

In fact it is the product of an immensely complex system of contingent hypotheses which seldom account for all the data and are sustainable only by the constant exercise of that editorial judgment which the editors set out to exclude. In the classification of the manuscripts editorial judgment is constantly applied to dismiss contradictory evidence. The classifications exist only by virtue, first, of the unremittingly expeditious, indeed opportunistic, agility of editorial distinctions between vertical and lateral transmission, and then by identifications of "borrowing," "editing," and authorial revision which by their frequency come in time to acquire an appearance of *petitio principii*.

The demonstration of the inadequacy of the classifications as instruments of recension is the complexity of the explanations in *Survey of the Classification* (2.41–44), and the struggles with discrepant evidence in the successive parts of that volume: twenty pages on the manuscript relations in *The General Prologue*, forty-one for *The Knight's Tale*, twenty-seven for *The Wife of Bath's Prologue* and *Tale*, almost never a clearly defined situation. In *The Merchant's Tale* the classification invokes two changes of exemplar implying revision (3.375); it proposes seven lines of descent for *The Physician's Tale* (4.65) and eight for *The Shipman's Tale* (4.108), and twelve for *The Franklin's Tale* (4.34). Occasionally what is presented as a classification looks like an admission of defeat (3.39). The classification repeatedly begs the question of its completeness by use of the expression "independent groups and MSS" (cf., for example, 4.83): within a stemma, by definition, no groups or manuscripts are in any significant sense "independent." And the expression evidently means "unclassified and probably unclassifiable here." Whenever one examines the evidence for a group, it is unimpressive in its variants being indistinguishable in kind from those dismissed as "non-classificatory." How the editors differentiated between the two sorts is obscure.[8]

It is hard to believe that they were unaware of the limitations of their results, here and throughout. For every classification that involved "un-placed groups" or "independent manuscripts and small groups" or "variable groups, loosely related" amounted to an admission of failure to classify, and every new explanation of such discrepancy would increase the scale of the *petitio principii.* That fallacy stands out very clearly at one point in the Introduction (2.39, 40).[9] We read how, notwithstanding "the fact that in many of the tales the text is derived not from a single archetype but from texts which sometimes represent different stages of composition," the editors "proceeded as if all MSS were from the same archetype, being on the watch, however, for indications of separate origin and separate lines of descent," in the confident certainty that "the ordinary processes of classification would call attention to readings and MSS not derived from [a single archetype] and would enable the textual critic to distinguish such varied sources as had not become entirely unrecognizable by the spread of vulgate readings." By that fine language the editors were effectively if not consciously announcing that in carrying out "the ordinary processes of classification" they would prejudge their results. There is a warrant for critical interpretation of the results of collation—which is what Manly was writing about here. But where the textual situation is extraordinary, the "ordinary processes of classification" are inoperative.

It comes to this: that we do not have a complete, or even a reliable partial, stemma of the manuscripts of *The Canterbury Tales.* Even the one discernible family, $\langle a[b(cd/d^*)]\rangle$, is, as Root (*SP*, pp. 6, 7) pointed out, imperfectly defined and unstable because of—other qualifications apart—the paucity of clear evidence for *d.* The editors must have understood that in the best circumstances, where the manuscript reading of this family could be confidently identified, its evidential weight was that of precisely one manuscript. But there is no sign in the edition that they faced the implication of this: that one single substitution at the group-ancestor stage would differentiate all members of that family from the "unplaced, independent copies and small groups." What is presented as an archetypal text is at best the text of the exclusive common ancestor $\langle a[b(cd/d^*)]\rangle$. Its dignification by the symbol 0^1, which is bound to suggest a text at one remove from the author's copy, has no warrant.

Such, however, is the opacity of the presentation that the classification has in effect gone untested. Manly expressed concern that the "impression of complication and variability" made by it would raise the question of its correctness (2.41), and Root (*SP*, p. 7) discussed this. *Pace* Root, who thought it might take "at least a year" to test that correctness, the manner of presentation makes it virtually impossible to test it from the information given in the edition.[10] Much of the work will have to be done again,[11] and if it is to produce results worth the name, the analysis of variant groups will have to be conducted by a better rationale than any discernible in the Manly-Rickert edition.[12]

The object of classifying the manuscripts was to enable recovery of the text of the *Tales* by recension, that is, in simplified terms, the elimination of scribal error through identification of the point in the manuscript tradition where it was introduced; the editors also call it the "genealogical method"

(1.xii; 2.12, 40, etc.). That both its logic as a rationale and its practical feasibility are open to question they nowhere recognized. Its operation is far from simple,[13] but one searches Volume 2 in vain for any account of how Manly and Rickert understood and carried out recension. Root suggested that "the failure of the editors to explain the procedure adopted in constituting the text must . . . mean that they found it impossible to follow any uniform procedure" (*SP*, p. 10). Dempster, in a loyal attempt to interpret the edition, admitted that "there is no short road to the understanding of Manly's choice of readings,"[14] and the way her attempts to find some principle tail off into lame discussions of particular instances suggests that there is no long road either. Sometimes the apparatus does not even list the manuscripts in support of the reading adopted.[15] The notes where one was led to expect discussion (2.40) are sometimes perfunctory or even noncommital. But if there was no uniform procedure, what did the editors substitute for one?

They were not subject to the first fantasy of textual criticism, that all texts are sound.[16] As for the second, the fantasy of a "safe" method, one affording reassurance, which would eliminate the need for "unscientific" critical thinking, indeed for any critical thinking at the crucial final stage of *examinatio*,[17] there are unmistakable signs of this in Volume 2. But that volume as a whole and with it the critical notes to the text reveal that, far from fulfilling any hope of a "scientific process" (2.20), the editors' "system" grew into a monster both tyrannous and inefficient, which gradually forced them into the position of having to rationalize its discrepant or speculative results, to exercise "judgment" constantly, in the determination of "classificatory value," of whether readings were "errors," that is, accidental, or "editing," that is, sophistication, of what was an inferior reading or an authorial variant. In short, the edition shows them carrying out editorial processes not in the determination of originality but in defence of a dubious stemma from which initially they had expected support and direction.

The arguments of their apologists must in justice here be set down. The edition was published under pressure. The editors did not receive the expected financial support. The edition does not fairly represent their intellectual quality or their command of textual criticism. Their failure to describe their procedures adequately should not be taken to imply that they had no rationale. The exposition in Volume 2 is "so cryptic and confusing at times" because much was lost in the final revision: "Lack of space forced [Manly], as nearly the last act of a sick man, to cut that account to the bone." A main element in the original conception of the undertaking had been "to test recension." The published text of the *Tales* represents an earlier stage in editorial thinking than that of Volume 2.

Some of those considerations cannot fail to elicit sympathy from anyone with experience of large projects, and doubtless in sum they account for certain features of the edition. But the eight volumes loom massively in Chaucer scholarship, exercising effect and influence without qualification by the editors' biographies. Therefore, in the end, the edition must be assessed per se, to establish whether the influence it has exerted and might continue to exert was warranted.

The authority of any edition involving textual criticism, whatever its theoretical basis, necessarily relates largely to the quality of the editorial judgment applied to the individual textual situations. Such judgment develops with experience of scribes and their ways. The accumulated generalizations about scribal proclivities[18] become real through sustained observation of the behavior of particular scribes during the long labor of collation. It is forced upon the editor that because scribes did not copy by the word, but took into their memory blocks of text such as stanzas or paragraphs, many variations with an intrinsic appearance of deliberateness are likely to have been subconsciously induced, especially if the scribe had previously copied the same text. The editor gets a sense of probable direction of variation, of scribal as well as authorial *usus scribendi*. He learns to distinguish the effects of carelessness and to predict variation. By observation of visible variation of individual manuscripts from a putative group reading, he acquires insight into the possibilities and likelihoods of variation at the level of subgroup and group. He develops the flair of the textual critic, Maas's *Fingerspitzengefühl*. The editorial judgment exhibited in this edition is not distinguished for that quality.

There are, for a start, occasions when the editors show no sign of awareness that there is an editorial problem. At 3.146: A 3592 *go god thee spede* there is variation *go/so*, and a strong likelihood that *so*] *go* variation occurred coincidentally through inducement of following *god* or of *Go*, line 3596, or of both, but there is no critical note or any sign of awareness that this is a minor crux. For 3.399: E 1909 *He is as wys discret and secree* with variants *and as secree/and eek secree* there is a critical note, "Some such word as 'eek' or 'as' was omitted by 0^1" (3.476), but at 2.280 agreement of El and Cambridge University Gg.4.27 (Gg) in reading *as secree* is classified as "patently by *acco*," that is, by coincident variation. This is a weird logic which, having correctly identified direction of variation, i.e., that there was an omission, and recognized the likelihood of coincident variation in the alignment of agreements, stops short of the obvious interpretation of the evidence: that from there being two inducements (*a-nd a-s* and *a-s s-ecree*) to omission of *as*, it was likely present in the original. Then El and Gg agree not by coincident variation but in preservation of the original. If there was coincident variation, it was in omission of *as*, and possibly also in supply of *eek*. For 3.163, A 4020 *Iohn knew the wey hym neded no gyde* with *hym/hem* variation, the note (3.443) reads, "The original reading seems to have been 'hym.' The alteration by (sc. to) 'hem' by El and others is unnecessary." How the editors formed their judgment of originality here is not clear. In the sense that the context accepts either number of the pronoun, the "alteration" they assume would be unnecessary. But experience would have indicated that the likelier variation was *hem]hym* through inducement of singular *Iohn* and *he* 4021, and protected them against the question-begging term "alteration." So too in 4.273: B 4438 *Though god forwoot it er that it was wroght* with a variant *I was wroght*: here it is allowed that "The attractive reading 'I' may be original," but laid down that "the variation between 'I' and 'it' is intentional" (4.515). Here is a situation where unconscious variation either way would be easy: through inducement of the philosophical cliché, or of preceding *it* (4437, 4438). And, of course, with the strong inducement to substitution goes a corresponding likelihood of coincident substitution.

The editors misread various classes of typical evidence. For instance, at 3.251: D 368 *Ben ther noone othere resemblaunces* there are variants *other(e) manere, other(e) of thees, other(e) of thy, other(e) of youre*, described as "four different attempts to emend" (3.458). But this is a clear case of loss of original *manere* by homoeoteleuton. A slightly more complex instance is 4.139: B 1883 *Til that oure hoost iapen to bigan* with variants *to iapen po, to iapen, iapen tho, to iapen he, iapen he*. For the editors the original was "obviously" *iapen tho* (4.499). But that original is unlikely to have generated the pattern of variation. The original likeliest to have produced that pattern is *to iapen tho* or *to iapen po*, where simply the consideration whether to spell the last word *tho* or *po* would be distraction enough to cause random variation. Of this a first stage might be *to iapen to*. From that, *to iapen he* is explicable as a sophistication, *iapen to* as a confused correction (the scribe having meant to omit the first *to*). At the next stage *iapen he* and *iapen tho* are sophistications of *iapen to*. This kind of pattern is not uncommon and becomes familiar with experience. So do accidental omissions like that of A 637, 638 (3.28) from Hg Bodley 686 (Bo^2) occasioned by homoeo- and homoarchy: *And . . . drynke . . . wyn* line 635; *And . . . dronken . . . wyn* 637, *Thanne wolde he speke* 636, 638. The editor who can recognize them is in less danger of suggesting that the lines are "a happy afterthought" of the poet (3.425); he will also appreciate the possibility that omission might occur coincidentally.

It is not clear that in their judgments the editors took account of the tendencies discernible in scribal variation, subconscious, indeterminate or conscious; they miss very obvious instances. At 3.313: D 1983 *And chiden heere this sely innocent* the critical note (3.467) is preoccupied with a variation of little difficulty, *sely] holy*, induced by the common collocation "holy innocents," and impossible in the context. They miss or ignore the good possibility that the original read *hir the, heere* having been caught up from line 1981, and *this* being a more explicit substitution. At 3.272: D 929 *Somme seyde that oure herte is moost esed* there is a variant *hertes be* which the critical note (3.460) describes as an "intelligent emendation." In fact it is a variation to an easier reading from the more difficult distributive singular, called a "bad reading" by the editors.

At 3.44: A 974 *ther is namoore to telle* the predictable variation *is/nis* occurs, as also at, e.g., A 901, 1274, 2722, 2847. I find it hard to believe that the editors did not know how freely these expressions would replace each other, or to see the inducement here to *is] nis* by *n-amoore* or by the tendency to increase emphasis, or that to *nis] is* by the common collocation *ther is*. But they apparently did not: the critical note (3.427) solemnly treats this as a crux, even raising the question of "archaizing." At 3.304: D 1696 *And thurgh out helle swarmeden al aboute* a number of copies lack *al*, which is, however, taken to be the archetypal reading. There is no note to this line and no sign of awareness that *aboute] al aboute* is in this context a predictable variation to a more emphatic reading by an enthusiastically participating scribe. At 3.351: E 583 *And bad this sergeant that he pryuely / Sholde this child softe wynde and wrappe* there is variation *wel/ful softe*. The note (3.472) explains these variants as "emendations by early scribes" because the line "seems to have lacked a syllable." Whether or not the line seemed so to the "early scribes," the adverbs are more likely to be variations, very possibly unconscious at that, to more emphatic readings. The same is true of 3.162: A 3977 *The person of the toun for she was feir / In purpos was to maken hir his heir* with variation *feir] so feir*, that is to a reading more emphatic and explicit both. Had the editors been more famililiar with the *usus scribendi* of scribes, they would not have observed, after excluding *so* on manuscript evidence, that is, presumably by recension, that "stylistically 'so fair' seems necessary" (3.443).

Familiarity with the ways of scribes should have enabled the editors to interpret slightly more complex situations like 3.383: E 1436 *And streight to the deuel whan I dye*, with variants *so streight, so go streight, go streight*. Here they found the evidence "on the whole . . . to be in favor of a headless line lacking both 'go' and 'so' " (3.474). Actually it favors *so streight*. The variation *so] go* will have been by unconscious misreading, probably of 8-shaped *s* for *g*, or by inducement of the concept of motion in the line; *so] so go* will be a separate variation to a more explicit reading; and *so streight] streight* omission by homoarchy. At 3.47: A 1031, where the adopted text reads *Dwellen this Palamon and eek Arcite*, there is a variant *This Palamon and his felaw Arcite*. The critical note (3.427) seems to mean that *Dwellen* was first accidentally omitted, and in a copy of the manuscript so affected, *his felawe* later substituted for *eek* to fill out the line ("it is obvious that this reading is an editorial emendation"). Actually the following considerations obtain. First, the line and its immediate context do not seem to have any obvious features that would have induced accidental omission of original *Dwellen*. Second, if it had nevertheless been omitted, the likeliest sophistication would have been supply of a verb, of *Lyueth* on the suggestion of line 1028, or even, by felicitous restoration, of *Dwelleth*, of which the sense "continue to be" stands out in the context. Third, the line without a verb is vastly *durior lectio*. Either a verb must be understood, or else Palamon and Arcite are by ironic syllepsis additional subjects of *lyueth* in line 1028. Fourth, as between *eek* and *his felaw*, the former is the likelier padding to the experienced eye. It is from this sort of misinterpretation that the "intelligent editor" of Ellesmere[19] derived his existence.

There are situations where the editors react to the text like scribes. An instance is 3.47: A 1038, 1039 *For with the rose colour stroof hir hewe / I noot which was the fairer of hem two* with *fairer/finer* variation. Of the alternatives the scribal one is almost certainly *fairer*, either a thoughtless, more explicit substitution, or because scribes misread line 1039 to be comparing the rose and Emelye, not the color of the rose and her complexion, for which *finer* is the appropriate term (*MED* s.v. *fin* adj. 5). Our editors identify *fairer* as original, presumably by recension, and explain *finer* as "an emendation by the El group" (3.428). The possibility is not raised that *fairer* might have been substituted coincidentally.

There are some indications of superficial reading of the text. At 3.300; D 1647 *After the text of Crist Poul and Iohn* with variants *text crist of Poul, text of Poul*, and *text Crist Poul* the editors presume loss of *and* between *Crist* and *Poul*, and find it strange that "none of the scribes supplied the obvious lack" (3.465). But *and* is not obviously lacking: the three names are not a set of equivalents. Just conceivably the line as the editors print it is original, meant to be read with a portentous pause after *Crist*, a kind of colon of silence to introduce the Scripture references. More likely it read *of Crist in Poul and Iohn*; the preposition written as *i* with a suspension would easily be lost without trace, or even obscured by a cæsural punctuation. At 3.314: D 1993 *Be war from hire that in thy bosom slepeth* with *hire/ire* variation the editors rightly connect substitution of *hire* with the second half of the line, but their note (3.467) seems to suggest that *ire] hire* might be by deliberate substitution and indicates no awareness that the words were as good as identical phonetically, that Chaucer had made a pun and probably intended it.[20] Those considerations would have prevented them from taking manuscript alignment seriously, printing *hire* as the archetypal reading, and speculating why Chaucer failed to correct it. At 3.169: A 4171 *Lo swilk a couplyng is ymel hem alle* there is variation *complyn/complyng/copil/compen/ company*. For the editors *complyn* is "probably an emendation by a few scribes who independently sought for a better meaning than was suggested by the ancestral reading 'coupling' " (3.445). That is to stand the concept of coincident variation on its head. They are proposing repeated independent scribal substitution of a reading which happens to be conveniently introduced by *melodye* 4168 and *sang* 4170 and ironically anticipates *the feend is on me falle* of 4288,[21] in fact a much harder reading. Had they borne in mind that the speaker is a clerk, they might have taken note of how the word is woven into the texture of the narrative. As for the actual coincidence, that will have been in variation from *complyn*, possibly spelled *complyng* (see *MED* s.v.); written with a suspended *m*, and given the expectation of the genre, this would inevitably be corrupted to *couplyng*, and coincidentally. There is little likelihood that *couplyng* was the archetypal reading.

Whether or not this is a fair representation, some editorial judgments suggest insufficient familiarity with Middle English. Everett noticed "either carelessness or uncertainty in the handling of linguistic material."[22] There is amateurishness in their treatment of problems involving language, as, for instance, in two successive critical notes, where one reads that "modern idiom, no doubt, prefers 'out swarmen from,' but Chaucer seems to have been influenced by 'out of,' " and that "the uses of prepositions are so different in early and modern English that one is often surprised."[23] Had the editors turned to the articles on the prepositions *from* and *of* in *OED*, they would have not have written the nonsense about Chaucer being "influenced by" *out of*.

The dictionary is an editor's primary instrument, but it is not often cited in the critical notes, where there are some unmistakable indications that they underestimated the difficulties of Middle English lexicography, to the detriment of their interpretation of the evidence.

At 3.103: A 2527 *Honoured weren into the paleys fet* there is *paleys/place* variation. The critical note (3.433, 434) observes that "by making the place of assembly the courtyard of the 'paleys' Chaucer got a more definite picture." This seems to mean that *paleys* is an authorial revision of *place*; the suggestion implies that the editors did not know that *paleys* and *place* have an area of synonymity (*OED* s.v. *Place* sb. 5b). Actually *place* is *durior lectio* both from its polysemy and because it must be given dissyllabic value for the metre. Either reason could induce random substitution of *paleys*. At 3.18: A 383 *He koude rooste and sethe and broille and frye* the variation *broille/boille* is troublesome because it does not correspond to genetic pre-conceptions: this generates an elaborate note (3.424). They evidently did not consult *OED*, where both words are shown to have only recently come into use in Chaucer's time to denote cooking processes. With considerations of relative difficulty out of the way, they might have noticed the contextual features likely to induce unconscious, therefore possibly coincident *broille*] *boille*: that is, the presence of *boille* in line 380 and of *sethe* later, in line 383. For 3.334: E 137 *That thurgh youre deeth youre lyne sholde slake*, with *lyne / lynage* variation, the note reads: "The change from 'lynage' to 'lyne' was possibly made by Chaucer himself, for greater accuracy, but it is confined almost entirely to the independent MSS of Group IV, and may be a purposeless scribal substitution" (3.469). In fact, *lyne*, as highly polysemous, is much the harder, and *lynage* the more explicit and easier reading, therefore likely to have been substituted independently. There is no basis at all for talk of revision. At 3.252: D 387 *I koude pleyne and I was in the gilt* the variation *and*] *and ʒet, whan, thogh* is called "scribal efforts to

subject Chaucer's colloquial construction to formal grammar" (3.458).
This is hard to credit, but the editors evidently did not know the senses "If,
supposing that, and "Even if," of *and* (*OED* s.v. *And* Conj. C 1, 2) and were
reading this construction as paratactic. At 4.259: B 4045 *By nature he knew
ech ascensioun* the significant variation is *knew/krew*. Again the editors had
genetic problems: a factor in their choice of *knew* as archetypal was that *krew*
"seemed the more likely emendation" (3.514). Leaving aside the consideration that the one manuscript reading *krew* is Hg, distinguished by "entire
freedom from editorial variants" (1.276), the quasi-transitive use of *krew*,
"announced by crowing," as in *There is no cock to crowe day* (*OED* s.v. *Crow* v.
lc), is a much harder reading and probably original here; the obvious and
easily coincidental substitution is *knew*.

   In all those instances consultation of the dictionary would have safe-
guarded the editors. It is ironic that when once (apparently) they did
consult it, for 3.135: A 3265 *A broche she bar vpon hir loue coler*, it dis-
appointed them by not giving *lou* as a variant spelling of the adjective *low*:
"No one seems to know the term 'loue coler.' " They missed the help it
afforded (" 'Lowe coler' is equally unknown" (3.440)) in offering them the
sense "Situated not far above the ground or some other downward limit"
(*OED* s.v. *Low* a. and sb. 2), for which the context would have made the
"downward limit" clear. Although *loue* here may not be a "true form," it
unmistakably stands for the weak form of the adjective; one is surprised that
they did not recognize it as such.

   Where aids were less readily available, the editors' inexperience of the
language shows even more. Of 3.348: E 508 *Ne I desire no thyng for to haue /
Ne drede for to lese saue oonly ye* with variation *yel pe* they comment, "Chaucer
undoubtedly wrote 'ye' for the sake of the rhyme" (3.471). The confident
"undoubtedly" will have been evoked by the circumstance that Hg, El, and
Gg read *pe*. But there is doubt. Chaucer's practice elsewhere, as in *Troilus
and Criseyde* I 5, where he rhymes *Troye: joie:fro ye*, at least raises the question
whether he would have used the reduced form of the objective case of the
plural pronoun in a stressed position to rhyme with the [e:] of *me* and *be*.
Moreover, Griseldis's use of the familiar singular pronoun here cannot be
ruled out: the usage of singular and plural in address was far from systematic
in Chaucer's time. Even in this tale where social distance is emphasized it
fluctuates. At lines 127–40 the spokesman for his people, addressing the
Marquis, uses a plural imperative in line 127 and singulars in lines 134 and
135; and for his part the Marquis occasionally uses the formal plural to
Griseldis (e.g., at lines 350ff., and —interspersed with singulars—in lines
477–97). Indeed, the circumstance that elsewhere she always addresses him
with the deferential plural makes the singular *durior lectio* here and so liable
to be corrupted. Above all the resemblance of *p* and *y* in many fifteenth-
century hands would promote misreading, especially with inducement
from the sense of social difference between Griseldis and Walter. Any one of

those considerations should have given rise to editorial doubt. Moreover, a very plausible dramatic reason can be found for Griseldis lapsing into the singular at this moment of acute stress. At 3.281: D 1189 *But he that noght hath ne coueiteth to haue* a number of manuscripts do not read the infinitive sign. Their genetically embarrassing agreement is explained as "a bit of editing done independently at least three times" (2.215). It is, however, more likely that *to* was supplied independently in variation to a historically easier reading. At 4.263: B 4174 *Oon of the gretteste auctor that men rede* the note (4.514) shows no awareness that the line in this form was produced by unconscious overlay of two constructions by a scribe or scribes uncertain which to write down. At 4.265: B 4226 *A dong carte wente as it were to donge lond*, where several manuscripts do not have *wente*, the explanation offered for the line in the text is that *wente* "was a marginal correction for 'were' and was misunderstood by the scribe of 0^1" (4.515); in other words, he added it instead of substituting it for *were*. But *wente* is not a "correction"; it is a variation to a more explicit reading, and the probably original *as it were to donge lond* is respectable Middle English for "as if for the purpose of manuring land."[24] At 3.185: B 47–49 *I kan . . . no thrifty tale seyn That Chaucer . . . Hath seyd hem* the grammar embarrasses the editors: "Chaucer is sometimes confused in sentences involving a negation in a subordinate clause. We shall doubtless come nearest to his intention if we read 'that' in this line (47) and 'nath' in 49" (3.447). It is not impossible that Chaucer did write *Nath* and that this was corrupted to *Hath* through misreading of the initial capital. But if he wrote *Hath*, which seems likelier, the confusion is not with him, for *That* in line 47 has the good Middle English meaning "Because."[25] Of 3.135: A 3285 *Wy lat be quod ich lat be Nicholas* with *ich/she* variation, the critical note (3.440) classes *she* as "an easy scribal error caused by the resemblance of 'ich' and 'sche' (with long *s*)," the whole of line 3285 being "the exclamation of Alison." But *quod ich* is simply not Middle English for "I said" in "Stop it, I said! stop it!" It is an unemphatic formula signifying report of direct speech. Middle English equivalents of "I said!" here would have subject-verb order and be in the present tense.[26] The original was almost certainly *she*, with substitution induced by *I, my* in line 3284 and *I* in line 3286. *N-ich-olas* following could have induced the spelling.

There is a strong suggestion in these instances, which are typical, that the editors did not sufficiently respect the difficulties of Middle English and were overconfident about their knowledge of the language. That circumstance, along with their inexperience of and misconceptions about the scribal mentality, accounts for the inability to read manuscript evidence which their edition exhibits time and again. It accounts, also, to some extent at least, for their having formed and insistently postulated the notion of the scribal "editor" and his activities in the manuscript tradition of *The Canterbury Tales*.

It has not been the general practice to use the terms "editing" and "emendation" to denote scribal substitution. For scribal variation presumed deliberate the usual term is "sophistication." Knowledgeable editors use it cautiously, aware of the degree and variety of change that the scribal subconscious can effect in a text between its being taken through the scribe's eye into his memory and being set down, laboriously letter by letter, on the page. They know that between, at the one extreme, the wholly accidental error produced by a simple failure of signals between eye and hand, and at the other the calculated, purposeful alteration, there is a huge area of uncertainty. Here even the limited degree of scribal participation implied in the effort to comprehend could set up distractions. Distraction could originate in anything the scribe had ever copied before, including the text at hand, and produce memorial contamination, or in his own experience, or in his sense of grammar, in all the patterned forms of language he habitually used or avoided, in his response to what he had just copied or preoccupation with development to come. Almost every element of interest or response he was capable of was a potential source of distraction and of consequent variation without his being fully or even at all aware of what was happening.

Of course, sophistication did occur, and must be allowed as a factor in the restoration of texts. It can be identified in the visible effort of the scribe of the single manuscript or subgroup ancestor to improve a group reading corrupt in his exemplar, in additions that expand to the detriment of the formal or generic integrity of the text, in changes that have an appearance of being systematic, or changes of a scale or manifest intention beyond the conceivably subconscious, like the adaptations of the links in Hengwrt. Manly had at hand the opportunity of studying sophistication in the manuscript Harley 7334 (Ha⁴) which is extensively so affected.[27] He does not seem to have taken it.

The absence of any systematic thought about the nature of scribal variation, indeed, a general poverty of editorial insight, shows itself particularly in the treatment of the Ellesmere manuscript. This is of such a character as to suggest that it was emotionally based, as if the editors were under some compulsion to discredit the manuscript which clouded their judgment. Was it a need to produce a conclusion different from the current one? Robinson, it will be recalled, had in 1933 described Ellesmere as "the best copy."[28] Or did Ellesmere have to be put down because they could not classify it, because its existence outside their already dubious stemma was a potential dismissal of the whole hypothesis? For there will have come a stage of commitment when retreat, the admission of failure, became impossible and counterattack the only course. In whatever event, the Ellesmere variants are the subjects of a long succession of rationalizations and opportunistic explanations as discrepancies that do no credit to Manly and Rickert's editorial expertise. This will appear from scrutiny of a sample of the variations designated as "emendations" in Volume 2 and the Critical Notes.

At 2.91 there is a list of seven instances of Ellesmere editing in the *Prologue*. Two are more likely to be scribal substitutions of more emphatic readings: 188 *his*] *his owne* and 824 *in*] *alle in*. At 234 *faire*] *yong* will be unconscious substitution on inducement of *y-euen* before it and *yonge* 213. At 421 *engendred*] *they engendred* is a more explicit variation. In 612 as between *coote* and *gowne* (also, incidentally, the reading of group *a*) one variant will be a substitution of a more habitual collocation: the question is, which? The scribe had read *coote and hood* in line 103 preceding, and the words were apparently connected in a proverb.[29] To anyone uncommitted to recension, *gowne* can thus seem the likelier original. Either way substitution will have been unconscious. So also at line 858, where *in this manere* (*a* reads it too) is "editing"; in fact, it may easily have been the original, with *as ye may here* induced by *herkneth what I seye* 855 and *seyde* 858. That leaves 240 *euery/alle the*: originality here is indeterminable, since we do not know what was the friar's territory. But, then, neither did the scribes, and between the two readings *euery* is unmistakably the more emphatic, not to mention a practical impossibility.

In *The Knight's Tale* the editors identify thirteen "unique readings in El showing a possible editorial intention" (2.127). Three of these are accidental: 1260 *thyng that*] om (by homoeoteleuton, *wh-at, th-at*); 1337 *somer*] *sonne* (by confusion over minims or an *er* suspension); 2828 *and folk*] *and eek* (by inducement of the common collocation). One variant is more explicit: 871 *yonge*] *faire*. One is an easier reading: 1560 *lynage*] *kynrede* (compare the same substitution by Gg at 1110). One is more emphatic: 2219 *and with*] *with ful*. In four instances the Ellesmere reading can have, to an unprejudiced judgment, the appearance of originality. At line 876 the original certainly contained *yow*, whatever its position. At 931 *waille/crie* the likelier substitution is *waille*, on inducement of the common collocation *wepe and waille*. In line 1156, Ellesmere's past tense, required for the meaning "You did not know until just now," is incidentally attested in other manuscripts. In line 2874 loss of original *hadde* will have been by homoarchy. In one instance, line 1933, the Ellesmere reading is to be classed with the other attempts to come to terms with an original necessarily difficult on the showing of the variation. Was this because of syllepsis in an original reading *Of loue that I rekned haue and shal*? The two readings that remain resist explanation. But at line 2220 variation between the formulas *as ye shal heere* and *in this manere* recalls that at line 858 preceding (see above). And at 2952 *fyr*] *place* is unmistakably variation to an inferior reading with a scribal quality about it.

In *The Miller's Tale* the editors identify three classes of Ellesmere variation relevant to this examination. In the first class there are eleven "certain errors"; in the second, six which "may have been deliberate changes" (2.149). All but one of these, however, are explicable as unconscious variations: 3575 *shaltow*] *shal I* induced by following *I*; 3599 *teche*] *preche* induced by *sermonyng* 3597; 3608 *dede*] *lost* induced by the common collocation; 3540 *gete*] *brynge* variation to an easier reading (*geten* in this sense was just coming into use in the fourteenth century). One Ellesmere reading, 3810 *amydde*, looks original; it would have been replaced on the inducement of the common collocation *smiten in*.

Then there is a group of variants where, we are advised, a change has been made "for the purpose of correcting and regularizing the line" (2.149). The description does not stand up to scrutiny. At 3228 *men/man* is simply morphological: these are two forms of the indefinite pronoun. Two variations are mechanical: at 3624 *he* was omitted through attraction between *hand* and *made*; at 3735 *were*] *was* was induced by following *wa-r*. Four are substitutions of more explicit readings: 3541 *had*] *had be*, 3621 *after*] *after that*, 3626 *Vnto*] *Into* and 3778 *I*] *And I*. In 3576 the probable original was not *his* but *the*, and Ellesmere's *hir* is simply another variation to a more explicit reading.

Next there are four "errors in which editing is clear" (2.150). One of these, if not a substitution of an easier reading, is a misreading of a difficult because unanticipated original: 3697 *cougheth*] *knocketh* (compare *tougheth* Harley 7335 [Ha⁵], where the scribe's eye simply refused the difficult original sense). In the other three instances it can be argued that Ellesmere preserves a reading both archetypal and original. At 3251, between *silk* and *grene*, it is possible to account for *grene*] *silk* variation by the recurrent suggestion of *silk* 3235, 3240, 3243. But no scribe is likely to have had the leisure to hit on the appropriately obscene suggestion of a leather purse with a "green" tassle. At 3362, as between *rewe* and *thinke*, *rewe* is too easy to have been corrupted, whereas polysemous *thinke*, apt only in the sense "remember, bear in mind" (*OED* s.v. *Think* v.² 5) is likely to have been ousted by the easier word. For 3810 *in/amydde*, which reappears here, see above.

The instances of "editing" I have examined are typical of the editors' evidence for the occurrence of that process, which they represent as a deliberate and systematic undertaking to improve the text: "it is very clear that an intelligent person, who was certainly not Chaucer, worked over the text when El was copied" (1.150). It is in fact anything but clear. Ellesmere's status has still to be assessed, but it is certainly not to be measured in terms of the editors' evidence for "editing."

Their evidence for authorial revision is no better. This can be illustrated from *The Miller's Tale*, where they find nineteen lines in Ellesmere with variants which are "as readings just as acceptable as those supported by the stronger authority," a part of the evidence which for them "points perhaps to ultimate derivation of El from a working copy containing about 20 alternative readings which may have originated with Chaucer" (2.150, 151). These will now be examined.

For a start, three of these variations are classical instances of indeterminacy: 3620 *And/He*, 3654 *in/of* and 3819 *sette/sit*. These are scribal variables with nothing to choose between them where the substitution can as easily have gone either way. In four others Ellesmere probably reads an unconscious variation; in 3289 *hym*] *hire* can have been induced by *hir* 3291, 3293; in 3505 omission of *it* can have been caused by attraction between *telle* and *man*: in 3637 *seten*] *sitten* can have been induced by *st-i-lle* following; in 3761 *clepen*] *cleped* can have been caused by following *d-aun*. Four Ellesmere variants are more explicit: 3333 *a*] *his*, 3443 *And*] *Til*, 3660 *With*] *With a*, and 3828 *lay*] *he lay*. Those at 3443 and 3660, notwithstanding their possible status, are excluded from the apparatus at the foot of the text. One Ellesmere variant, 3482 *on* (2)] *of*, is an easier reading. Two, at 3477 *loke*] *what loke* and 3828 *That*] *That yet*, are more emphatic. That leaves six which, because they could readily have generated the readings preferred in the text by very common processes of corruption, have the appearance of being original. In three the reading of the text looks like unconscious substitution: 3466 *heuest of*] *heuest vp* and 3470 *haf of*] *haf vp* by inducement of the common collocation *heuen vp*, and 3593 *folk*] *men* by inducement of surrounding *wh-en . . . be(e)n*. In 3519 *than an*] *than in an* will be variation to a more explicit reading; 3418 *thyng*] *nothyng* and 3510 *am*] *nam* variations to more emphatic readings.

These are typical instances of Ellesmere variants represented by the editors as products or possible products of authorial revision. Along with the others like them so classed at various points in Volume 2 and in the Critical Notes, they form part of the question-begging system, involving also "editing" or "emendation" and "borrowing," by which the discrepancies in their classification are excused. To examine them all will be a major study in itself. But there are two lists of presumed authorial revisions, at 2.38, 39 and 2.495–518. Manly offered the second list in part tentatively, as "possible slight retouching of some of the tales" and in part apologetically as unfinished work by Rickert (2.501), but the first apparently had his backing and may fairly be here examined.

For a start there are the prologues and endlinks. Here simply the likelihood that Chaucer had not decided on any final order of tales when he stopped writing[30] carries with it a corresponding one of revision. Moreover, the passages in question are long enough to enable the unavoidable critical judgment, whether they are Chaucerian, to be attempted with some degree of confidence. Even so only some of the editors' instances are clear cases.

One is B 1163-90, the *Man of Law Endlink*; this, from the existence of D 1665–1708, which dispose of the Summoner otherwise, can be presumed to have no longer any function, though "superseded" would be a better description than "cancelled," since the passage has survived. Here there is every warrant for inferring authorial change of intention or enlargement of conception. So also the longer form of *The Nun's Priest's Prologue*, B[2] 3961–80, very likely registers a heightening of Chaucer's dramatic conception by insight into the possibilities of contrasting responses by the Knight and the Host. But in the instance of the *Physician-Pardoner Link* at C 287–300 the situation is not as clear because of the undismissed possibility of split variation.

The Host's mockery of the Nun's Priest, B^2 4637–52, is correctly describable as "undeveloped" rather than as "cancelled." On indication of line 4652, Chaucer intended it to lead to another tale. The likelihood is that he never decided who was to tell this: nothing could be more characteristic of an unfinished work. The explanation of the absence of the passage from many manuscripts may be simply that there were arrangers of the tales who disliked its inconclusiveness more than they relished the Host's mockery.

A more problematic instance is E 1212a–g, spoken by the Host at the end of *The Clerk's Tale* and classified by the editors as "Remnant of a cancelled link." There is no actual evidence of the act of cancellation, only a disturbance of the editorial hypothesis of classification. When that consideration is set aside, *The Merchant's Prologue* follows on well enough from E 1212g across the change to couplets that was bound to come in any event. And actually E 1212a–g as a final stanza of rhyme royal appropriately fastens the Clerk's ironic lyric[31] to his tale and, far from breaking the continuity,[32] sets up another pair of contrasting responses like that to *The Monk's Tale* noted above.

A different situation exists at B^2 3568 in the *tragedie* of Pedro of Castile. The editors explain the two forms of this line, *Thy bastard brother made the to flee* and *Out of thy land thy brother made thee flee* as revision occasioned by the topicality of the subject: the reference to bastardy became impolitic when the claimants to the throne were reconciled. There is unquestionably that possibility. But there is another, that the line with *thy bastard brother* resulted from scribal variation to a more emphatic reading. Indeed the line without the sense "into exile," *out of thy land*, is not notably apt. There is enough doubt here to make the line poor evidence for inference about early and late forms, or about cancellation of the "modern instances."

Within the actual tales likelihood of revision is not so easily presumed, and does not show as clearly. The issue arises in the tales mainly from the presence or absence of material. There decision about revision will relate to how both presence and absence can be accounted for.

Critical opinion about the literary quality of the material confuses the issue in the case of Dorigen's list of instances of heroically chaste women, F 1426–56. It was evidently the editors' violently unfavorable opinion which directed their judgment that the archetype was at this point "an unpolished working draft" (2.314, 315). The oracular voice of the classification seems, however, to have been ambiguous, for earlier in the same volume (2.39) the passage was labeled "Possibly not in early version." They seem not to have allowed that a fourteenth-century response to the list might have differed from theirs, or even that the length of the list might be a Chaucerian

correlative of Dorigen's hysterical state. Scribes had great difficulty with
the spelling of the proper names here, and the absence of the passage from
some copies may relate to this.

By contrast there should have been no problem for the editors with the
five passages (D 44a–f, 575–84, 609–12, 619–26, 717–20) in *The Wife of
Bath's Prologue* but not found in a good many copies. None of these passages
could bring any discredit on Chaucer. All can be read as meaningful
additions. And no reasons suggest themselves for the cancellation or
accidental omission of any one. From those features they compel a hypothesis of authorial revision, but for the editors they constituted a predicament
from the need to account for their presence or absence in terms of the
classification. The extreme complexity of the resulting explanations is a
further criticism of that hypothesis.

How plausible we find the classification will determine whether we
accept the description of F 1493–98 as a "late addition" (2.39). There is
certainly an element of doubt. Why should the lines not come from an early
version for reading aloud and be generally absent because the poet suppressed them when he took the tale into the Canterbury scheme? More
seriously, because the passage breaks the narrative flow just before a climax,
it was particularly liable to omission by oversight. And there are features, in
effect homoeoarchy of this and the following paragraph, that could occasion
accidental omission: *Parauenture* 1493, *Of aventure* 1501; *heep* 1493, *happed*
1501; *yow* 1493, *hir* 1501.

The recurrence of propositions about authorial revision that arise from
genetic considerations is notable. There is the instance of A 3721, 3722, a
"late couplet, copied only by El and borrowed thence by other MSS" (2.38,
150–51).[33] This is the only Ellesmere variant in *The Miller's Tale* to be taken
seriously as a possible revision. But the lines could have been accidentally
omitted. They interrupt the action just before a climax and would be liable
to omission simply from that feature; or they could have been lost by
homoeoarchy: *Thanne . . . thee* 3720, *Now . . . thou* 3722. Accidental loss
would explain the situation in Selden, where the couplet is at the foot of the
page in the main hand with a direction to its right location (3.442); that is
how scribes who caught themselves out in omission commonly put the
matter right. Coincident omission is an easier explanation of this situation
than revision and borrowing from Ellesmere. Other considerations apart,
its pristine condition argues against Ellesmere having been available for
general consultation; and as for that manuscript "very close to it" (1.536),
where are its progeny? All the while the absence of these lines from some
manuscripts questions the classification.

At A 3155, 3156 similarly, the genetic hypothesis dictates: "Obviously
these lines were not in 0[1]." They were, variously, "procured by the ancestor
of El from some other Chaucerian copy" or "may well have been composed
by the intelligent editor of El" (3.439, 440), or they were, "if by Chaucer,

cancelled later" (2.38). It should by now have appeared that creating the delicious irony whereby the drunken Miller rebuking the Reeve echoes the God of Love rebuking the Dreamer is not in that intelligent editor's style. The lines were most likely omitted through eye skip: *goode . . . oon* 3154, 3155; *knowes-tow . . . thow* 3156, *ar-tow . . . now* 3157. Whether the omission was coincidental would be determinable only if an effective classification was available.

A similar bias of editorial judgment appears in the treatment of D2159–2294, the last episode of *The Summoner's Tale*, not found in the manuscripts of one group, $d*^1$. From that absence the editors infer that the lines were "possibly not in the earliest draft" (2.38), that the group text "represents an earlier and unfinished form" of the tale (2.229). But lack of the passage is the main evidence for the existence of the group here, which "is held together primarily by [its] absence" (2.228). The editors know an easier explanation: loss of a folio with the very usual content of thirty-four lines per side. But they reject this in favor of a speculative preconception.

So also in the treatment of two adjacent instances, at E 1170–1212, where 1170–76 are taken to have been "absent from the pre-CT version," and 2101–2112 to have preceded 1195 in the "first draft for CT" (2.38). To judge by manuscript evidence, some manuscripts lack 1170–76 because of a physically defective exemplar. As for the presumption of transposition, the "first draft" order, from the poor sequence of discourse it affords—*hem* 1201 lacks a gramatically plausible antecedent—is very likely scribal, and can have come to be by several of the processes in which text is disordered. In this category belong F 1001–1006, described as "not in the early draft and misplaced by the scribe of 0^1" (2.39). There was probably displacement here, but the likelihood is that the disordered lines were 999–1000, omitted from an original position as in the adopted text through attraction between 998 and 1001 and copied in at the next convenient point.[34] The extreme instance of prejudicial interpretation is D 829-56, "Possibly not in the earliest draft of WBP" (2.38). The lines are absent from one single manuscript. To be sure, the proposal is only tentative (cf. 2.194, 195), but it should not have been made. We have here the loss of the content of a last leaf of a gathering.

In the instances so far examined, there was nothing about the quality of the alternatives to exclude the possibility of authorial revision. That is not the case with the rest of the proposed revisions. The instance of 3.81: A 1906, "Left unrevised" (2.38) is simply an irrelevancy. It is clear from the apparatus that there was random variation here, and we have no assurance that the archetype read like the text. The speculation in the critical note (3.430, 431) does not merit taking seriously.

The remaining instances have to do with scribal variation. Thus 3.28: A 637, 638 are absent from two manuscripts by homoarchy (*And* 635, 637, *Thanne wolde he speke* 636, 638); the speculation about a happy authorial afterthought inserted in the margin of the text (3.425) is gratuitous. If Hg had not been one of the manuscripts concerned, the omission might well have passed unremarked. 3.12: A 252a, b, "Preserved by Hg and borrowed thence by five other MSS" (2.38), were most probably lost for the very reason our editors think Chaucer might have canceled them, "as interrupting the flow of the narrative" (3.424). Intervening syntactical units are particularly liable to omission. An added source of distraction might have been the contextual difficulty of *vertuous* 251. The lines are actually necessary to the sense, to make 256 intelligible. Another couplet so lost is 3.109: A 2681, 2682, "If by Chaucer, cancelled later" (2.38). Here a contributory circumstance might have been *And* 2680, 2683, which could conduce to eye skip. At 4.238: B² 3616 *he spak right noght*] *he saugh it noght*, "Rewritten" (2.39), substitution for the undoubtedly original *spak* (*Inferno* 33, *sanza far motto*) occurred because preceding *herde* suggested the common collocation *herde and saugh*. At 3.45: A 992 *freendes*] *housbondes, lordys* is variation to more explicit readings. This instance occurs among the proposed authorial revisions, but in the critical note (3.427) both variants are called "emendations." At 3.44: A 980 *wan*] *slough* is a scribal substitution of an easier reading: *wan* with the object *penoun* and the special sense "earned the right to display"[35] is difficult without close attention, and substitution of *slough* on the inducement of *Mynotaur which that he* preceding would be predictable. There is no critical note. At 4.53: F 1321 *Repenteth*] *Bithynke* is another scribal substitution of an easier reading: the sense "Think better of it" (*OED* s.v. *Repent* v.3) is not an obvious one. This instance does not figure in the apparatus at the foot of the page. Finally, at 3.108: A 2655-56 there is a confusion symptomatic of the editorial predicament. As between "He cryde hoo namoore for it is doon / Ne non shal lenger to his felawe gon" and "Vnto the folk that foghten thus echon / He cryde hoo namoore for it is doon," the second couplet, from its flabbiness and lesser advancement of the sense (whom, after all, could Theseus be shouting to?) is the scribal one. It may have seemed the necessary archetypal reading because it is in the manuscripts of standing, Hg, El, Gg—how can they be wrong together, agreeing in error as if genetically related? So at 2.38 this difference is by authorial revision, "Couplet rewritten." But in the master apparatus one alternative is presented as accidental omission made good by supply of a spurious line (5.258), and in the critical note there is wavering between that explanation and "Chaucer having written a new couplet"; the expeditiously available O² turns up here (3.434). What we actually have is either subconscious recasting of a difficult line in the scribal memory or sophistication. The reason for the variation will have been the contextually difficult use of *felawe*, "one of a pair of opponents" (*MED* s.v. *felau*(e n. 10).

All this is regrettable. There is, after all, a rationale for identifying authorial revision. It is not foolproof, but it can protect thoughtful editors. Identification of revision is necessarily subjective, for it assumes the critic's or editor's capacity to identify a superior quality in the author's writing, to distinguish between the *usus scribendi* of author and scribe. The subjectivity is, however, directed and controlled by experience of the extent to which scribes can deface a text and the characteristics of such defacement. Part of the act of judgment will be discernment of authorial intention, on a presumption that when the author made a change he had an object in view and that it has been attained. Scale is a factor: if the area of the text affected is large, there will be more information available for the critical act; in small instances the determinant will be more likely whether a direction of variation by characteristic scribal substitution suggests itself.

A further generalization arises from the unfinished state of *The Canterbury Tales*, but it must be correctly understood. Thus, because the parts are generally complete in themselves but the assemblage (*after the newe gise*, the compilation) was not completed, the likelihood of both revised and un-revised forms surviving is not uniform: it is obviously greater in passages with structural function. Where the text survives in both earlier and revised forms, there are, also obviously, at the points of revision two manuscript traditions. But in good logic these cannot be postulated until revision has been otherwise established; they cannot be argued from alignments of variational groups, since these become genetically significant only when the variants in which they agree are identified as unoriginal readings.

The time has come to look at the structure of arguments that sustains this edition.

First, the editorial proposition that a classification of the manuscripts has been accomplished from which by recension an archetypal text of the poem can be recovered has no foundation. There is no such serviceable classification. At almost every stage, and making generous allowance for the possibility that different tales may have different manuscript traditions, the scheme of relationships leaves a greater or lesser residue of manuscripts unaccounted for. Thus, even supposing any proposed stemma to be locally accurate, what has been accomplished is only a partial classification, the identification of a family, or complex of groups, not the relation of all the manuscripts. That information can at best reach back only to the group ancestor: this must be understood to be the limit of its serviceability. The editors' 0^1 is no more than that—supposing their classifications to be correct.

Second, the proposition that explains the failure of the classification to account for all the manuscripts by postulating differentiation of archetypes has not been demonstrated. The evidence for the "intelligent editor," for "borrowing," and for widespread authorial revision does not bear examination. The Ellesmere variants proposed as evidence for editorial activity turn out to be the very commonplaces of scribal substitution—unless they appear as original and the probable sources of the other variants. The "borrowing" depends on a *petitio principii* of genetic relation and on dis-regard of the frequency of coincident variation, and it further postulates a fifteenth-century clearing house for *Canterbury Tales* readings that is hard to believe in. As for authorial revision, with some striking exceptions the editorial proposals are not firmly based.

Third, the quality of judgment exhibited in all the editorial processes, the theorizing, the interpretation of detail, and the general conclusions, has an amateurish look. This can be masked by the very obfuscating codifica-tion of the data in many parts of the edition, but it shows, naked and unhappy, in the earlier part of Volume 2, and especially in those ultimate moments of editorial self-exposure, the Critical Notes. One can trace the growth of an increasingly severe predicament. The editors committed themselves to recension, in itself a logically questionable method. Then they discovered that their subject resisted it. They disregarded the basic principle of manuscript classification in favor of a romantic confidence in the uniform operation of the laws of probability in a situation composed of factors calculated to disturb such operation. What they call recension turns out to be a succession of adventitious accommodations to conflicting evidence. From the number of mistaken identifications of direction of variation in simple instances, let alone misinterpretations of more complex variation, they seem to have been grievously handicapped by inexperience of the processes of scribal variation.

Whatever other limitations their edition may be judged to have, Manly and Rickert's troubles began with the procedures for classification that they adopted, apparently without adequate consideration or real understanding of the implications. There is an a priori unlikelihood of their results being sound. Either to dispose of their consequent propositions or to reinstate them, the classification will have to be attempted again: their results are untestable from the information given in the edition because of the virtually impenetrable system of symbols they employed in presenting their evi-dence. There is no telling what the result may be if the attempt is expertly carried out.[36]

Meanwhile, it will be judicious to abstain from using the propositions of this edition as bases for further argument, especially about the prehistory of the manuscript tradition of *The Canterbury Tales* or about the superiority of this or that manuscript.

F. N. Robinson's "Tentative Rule." Reprinted by permission of Charles W. Dunn, Harvard University, Robinson's literary executor. Photo provided by the Archives of Harvard University.

12. F. N. Robinson
(1872–1967)

GEORGE F. REINECKE

Genesis

IN 1904, only a few years after Skeat had completed his massive edition of Chaucer, Bliss Perry, a well-known figure in publishing and belles lettres, had been holding conversations with another resident of Cambridge, Fred Norris Robinson, then in his tenth year on the Harvard English faculty. Perry was best known as editor of the *Atlantic Monthly*, but doubled as chief editor for trade books at Houghton Mifflin. A former teacher of English at Williams and at Princeton, Perry was in charge of Houghton Mifflin's well-established Cambridge Poets series. In a letter of December 1, still in the publisher's files, he formally proposed that Robinson edit Chaucer for the Poets.[1] Obviously, the matter had been talked about previously. In a handwritten letter Robinson replied, accepting the terms of Bliss's letter and undertaking "to begin supplying copy in January 1908 & to complete the editorial work within a reasonable time thereafter."[2] This elastic clause Robinson was to stretch beyond the ordinary; the edition would not appear until 1933.

The earlier volumes of the Cambridge Poets, with their characteristic maroon bindings and gold stamping, are familiar to all haunters of bookstores. Horace Scudder's *Browning* (1895) may serve as an indication of what the publishers expected from Robinson nine years later, for Scudder worked for Houghton Mifflin and had preceded Bliss as general editor of the series. His *Complete Poetical Works of Browning* contained a thousand pages of Browning and about thirty of apparatus, into which Scudder squeezed a biographical sketch, "Notes and Illustrations," a list of the poet's writings, and indices of first lines and titles, but very little (sometimes nothing at all) on the text. Scudder's was what the trade calls a "library edition," suitable for the nonspecialist's bookshelf. Chaucer, of course, presented problems of text and language much greater than did the Victorian poet, but it seems clear that Bliss and his principals were thinking of a volume comparable to Lounsbury's unpretentious effort for Crowell or perhaps Macmillan's very reputable Globe edition of 1897, with its seventy pages of introduction. Of course what Houghton Mifflin finally published in 1933 was infinitely more elaborate and scholarly than Lounsbury's small effort and much better received, in the long run, than the meritorious but less ambitious Globe. Small as was the type chosen for the introduction, notes, and glossary of Robinson's edition, concentrated and pruned as these perforce became, they eventually contended in bulk with the text itself. The good but ordinary library edition *in posse* had become what in time was recognized as the standard work from which the learned might quote and the best-known Chaucer textbook of the twentieth century.

Twenty-nine years is an extraordinarily long time to intervene between the signing of a book contract and the eventual publication. The high standards Robinson set himself must in some measure explain the delay. Ought we, however, to attribute this pace, slower than empires, only to the editor's ever-growing wish to add scope to his apparatus? I think not. Robinson spread himself thin. When we recollect his decades of national eminence in the field, his presidency of the Modern Language Association, his years in a prominent teaching position, we must be surprised by the small bibliography the scholar left when he died in April, 1967, at the age of ninety-five.[3] But he was born in a more leisurely time and grew up in a world where American college teachers were either drudges or else gentlemen, and publication did not necessarily suggest the alternative of perishing. Besides, he was much involved in departmental administration. Further, he was quite as concerned with Celtic studies as with Middle English; after taking his doctorate at Harvard in 1894 (his dissertation was on Chaucer's grammar), he had gone to Freiburg to study the new field of Celtic philology with Rudolph Thurneysen. When he returned, he initiated Celtic studies at Harvard, and even such seniors as Kittredge sat at his feet to acquire some knowledge of the "new" subject.

A third component in the explanation of the delay is Robinson's personality, combined with his financial security. He was not a stern heroic taskmaster like his first Chaucer teacher, George Lyman Kittredge. One university can accommodate only so many Kittredges. He modeled himself less on Wotan and more on Geoffrey Chaucer. "Robbie," or "Uncle Fritz," as he was called, was gregarious, decorously jolly, and avuncular. Short and solid of build, he enjoyed the atmosphere of Boston clubs and of resort hotels in summer, scholarly conversations with the learned and *thé-dansants* at the Copley with his nieces and their friends. Late in life he took a fine delight in name dropping, *épatant la jeunesse* with such phrases as "I remember hearing Matthew Arnold say . . . ." Long after his wife's death he maintained a comfortable house (and rather impressive address) in "Long-fellow Park" near the poet's Craigie House and just a few streets from Harvard Yard.[4] There were no children.

I worked for him for two years, and he was ever charming, courteous, and kind far beyond the ordinary. In the mid-1950s he gave the impression of thriving on a chaos of papers. His study in Widener Library was rather sparsely furnished, but the desk and other flat surfaces were covered with mountains of dusty letters, notes, and offprints. The reality must somehow have belied the appearance, or nothing at all would have been accomplished, yet the disorder must have slowed down his work. But this was long after his retirement and not long before the second edition of *Chaucer* appeared. One cannot be sure when this disorder began. In a generously detailed letter to me, B. J. Whiting, now Gurney Professor Emeritus but secretary to Robinson during the last stages of the first edition, recalls some of the conditions of work at that time. He seems to emphasize Robinson's order and Yankee thrift:

> By chance I seem to have preserved a page of R's manuscript of the *Troilus* notes, which I am happy to give to you. As a matter of fact the page tells rather more about his practices than I have. It is a bluebook paper. R. through the years had systematically torn unused pages from examination books before returning or destroying them. Second, you see how neatly he wrote things off—although there is a chance that he was copying the page before us from an earlier draft. . . . He didn't really trust typewriters.[5]

What emerges is that Robinson was more in the tradition of Dr. Johnson than cast in the mold of the twentieth-century organization man; Jere Whiting characterizes his own share of the work as "base and mechanical," and I can testify that my own work twenty-five years later was void of decision making and required only as much scholarship as permitted intelligent verification of notes and informed proofreading. All along Robinson was determined to do all the significant work himself; he had found, as he told Jere Whiting, that the first of his assistants (later a well-known Chaucerian himself) was too willing to take on the task of coeditor; thenceforward he "made it quite clear that [the assistant's] function was to verify references."[6]

Thus the Celtic studies, the administrative duties, the prosperity, and the gregarious disposition, as well as his determination to "go it alone," were all factors which, along with his determination to produce much more than the ordinary trade edition, explain the elephantine gestation of *The Complete Works of Geoffrey Chaucer*. The decades passed, and the growing number of American Chaucerians, many of whom were Robinson's pupils and even his academic "grandchildren," impatiently awaited the slow delivery.

Reception

Much as his contemporaries and juniors may have teased him about his slowness in the years before 1933—Robinson did not mind a degree of discreet fun—the other members of the "Chaucer Trust" were loud in their praise when it appeared that spring. Many of their congratulatory letters survive, most at Harvard, a few in the hands of Mrs. Robinson's family.[7] A characteristic response was that of Walter Clyde Curry, at Vanderbilt: "Now that it has come, it surpasses anything I could have anticipated. Your text, as far as I am able to judge, is more to be relied upon than any heretofore printed; it supersedes all other editions.[8]

Henry Noble MacCracken, president of Vassar, was even more complimentary. Himself the editor of a Chaucer textbook, MacCracken (in a letter of May 1, 1933) called the newborn edition "a great achievement, and an honor to our scholarship." In his presidential address at the Vassar commencement of 1933, MacCracken was heard to "call your Chaucer 'a monument to American philological scholarship.' "[9] Later that year he wrote a short notice for Canby's *Saturday Review of Literature* and called it "by far the best text of a first-grade English poet." There is one phrase in this review which gets to the heart of the matter: "good sense always is his guide."[10]

Other extant congratulations, some mingling small criticisms with the praise, are from G. H. Gerould, Emile Legouis, Tarquinio Vallese, G. G. Coulton, Carleton Brown (" . . . realizes what seemed to me impossible"),[11] Roger Sherman Loomis, Howard Patch, Edgar Shannon, Theodore Spencer, Hyder Rollins, Karl Young ("I find delight and satisfaction in every detail I examine: textual firmness, preemptive exposition, gracious expression and unparalleled completeness."),[12] Henry Hinckley, Stith Thompson, J. Burke Severs, and E. P. Kuhl.[13]

Of course, the printed reviews were later in coming out. On the whole they were not nearly as flattering or encouraging to Robinson as had been the personal communications; indeed, the Chaucer student who has grown up in a world where Robinson is something of a fixture may well be surprised at the inconclusive nature of these evaluations, the rather small number of which is also surprising. J. S. P. Tatlock and M. B. Ruud did the only extensive American reviews (Albert Marckwardt did another for *English Journal*).[14] Dorothy Everett's in *Year's Work in English Studies* was the only major English account except for the nonspecialist review in the *Times Literary Supplement*.[15] In Germany, Hermann Heuer wrote for *Anglia Beiblatt* a longish review, largely descriptive, but concerned about the fact that Robinson was admittedly not of the "severest textual school."[16] Old Alois Brandl, editor of *Herrigs Archiv*, may have taken his cue from the new masters of Germany when he wrote his own patronizing review: "Who is this F. N. Robinson?" asks Brandl. "One seeks his name in vain in all the bibliographies of English." He then praises the editor for his introductions and explanatory notes, only to attack him severely for not having been possessed by the spirit of Lachmann and pretending to a "critical edition" while his true basis of textual judgment was his common sense.[17] Of course, Brandl was not too wrong about what Robinson did; the difference lies in the German's unhesitant adherence to Lachmann's apparatus for establishing a critical text.

Everett views the new edition from a rather superior height: "The book is in many ways well suited to the needs of those who are beginning the serious study of Chaucer." She too brings up the textual issue and raises objections to Robinson's claim that he had produced a critical or nearly critical edition. Like Brandl she questions the "dangerous" practice of adopting readings "because of their greater metrical regularity, even making use . . . of the suspect Harleian 7334."[18] Part of her position is doubtless traditional British coolness to things American, but she is obviously troubled by the challenge to nineteenth-century German textual orthodoxy, especially in the name of a revived, purified eclecticism.

At the hands of the Americans, Robinson fared a little better. M. B. Ruud, reviewing the *Works* in *Modern Language Notes* two years after publication, ran counter to Brandl and Everett. Although by no means willing to suggest that Robinson might rival the forthcoming Manly and Rickert study of *The Canterbury Tales*, he finds that, for what it is, it is good. His appraisal of the quality of the text suggests that he was impressed in spite of his preconceptions: "His introductions, explanatory notes and glossary are models of what such things ought to be."[19] But the "Textual Notes" leave Ruud unhappy, especially because not all departures from the Ellesmere have been recorded. He is doubtless right in sensing that Robinson's thin selection of text notes requires us to take more on faith than would be ideal beyond the undergraduate level. In this connection, however, one ought to review Robinson's own explanation of why he abandoned his original intention of publishing a full apparatus criticus (Preface, p. vii). Beyond the mere question of bulk, there was the fairly recent appearance of Root's *Troilus* and the expectation of Manly and Rickert's *Tales*. This last must have been the chief factor; every time Robinson explained his reasonings on the basis of the eight published Chaucer Society texts, the Cardigan manuscript and the Morgan, he was leaving himself open to embarrassment when the Chicago monument superseded all previous textual opinions.

Returning to the text itself, Ruud continued his praise, specifically lauding Robinson for not "perpetuating the ignorance, the vagaries, and the carelessness of the fifteenth century copyists," i.e., for *not* preparing a critical edition in the approved Lachmann form.

J. S. P. Tatlock, Robinson's brilliant former colleague and friendly enemy, did the review for *Speculum*.[20] This six-page study is a mixture of insight and niggling complaints. Unlike Dorothy Everett and the Germans, he likes the text because, though far more conservative than Skeat, it

avoids the mechanical fidelity to the best manuscripts found in contemporary editions of some of Chaucer's works (this perhaps aimed at Koch and
Root, but more particularly, I believe, at Manly's school text). More than
any other reviewer, Tatlock saw to the heart of Robinson's textual problem:

> Since the scribes paid little careful heed to the orthography of their
> predecessors, an editor is confronted with what is almost an *impasse*. We not
> only have none of Chaucer's original manuscripts; we have none . . . directly
> derived from them, only manuscripts at an unknown number of removes. It is
> from such that we get all our knowledge of Chaucer's own grammar and
> metrical usage. But these last are the only basis, *except our idea of literary fitness*
> [italics mine] on which we can judge among alternative readings. . . . The
> editor's policy of adjusting the conflicting claims of the manuscripts and of *a
> priori* theory by means of both the knowledge of the scholar and the wisdom of
> the literary man seems to the reviewer that likely to lead nearest to what
> Chaucer wrote.[21]

Tatlock next turns to the subject of the introductory essays and commentary (i.e., "Explanatory Notes"), concerning both of which he joins in
the general critical praise. We will further advert to this aspect of Tatlock's
review later. He left the nit-picking for last; there follow four pages of
indications of glossarial omission, challenges of minor historical and biographical data, and finally, detailed attacks on the dating of *Troilus* and
Robinson's perpetuating the fragmentation of the later marriage group and
the Manciple-Parson sequence.

All in all, the reviews did not suggest that Robinson's *Works* was
gradually to become the standard edition of Chaucer, though this outcome
would have been clearer if the reviewers had spent more time comparing the
new edition with its alternatives. It is pretty hard to decide what distinguishes a "standard edition" in makeup, but it is easy to know one from the
use to which it is put: it is the edition from which other scholars take their
citations. Before 1933, most Chaucer scholars tended to quote from Skeat,
though others seem to have turned to the Six-Text edition and used the
Ellesmere transcript there or determined their own text on the basis of all
the transcripts provided by the Chaucer Society or the Ellesmere facsimile.
Modern Language Notes was then the typical place to publish a short Chaucer
piece in America; in 1933 (the last year before Robinson's impact might
reasonably be expected), there were twelve Chaucer articles in that publication. Five had no quotations, two acknowledged using Skeat, and the
remainder quoted their Chaucer without text acknowledgment. In *Publications of the Modern Language Association* of the same year there were four
Chaucer articles, one quoting Skeat's text, one specifically quoting manuscripts, and one quoting Chaucer without acknowledgment. In *Modern
Language Notes* for 1936 there were thirteen Chaucer articles; only one used
Robinson's text, but three others refer to Robinson in notes, and four
acknowledge no source for their quotations. In 1940, *Notes* had eleven

Chaucer papers; six use Robinson, three of them for Chaucer quotations, while only two use Skeat, Chaucer Society, or Kaluza (for *The Romaunt of the Rose*). By World War II, Robinson's prestige was gradually gaining.

To see how positively it grew between that time and the postwar era, one can consult the anthologies of Chaucer criticism, Owen's, Wagenknecht's, and Shoeck and Taylor's. These have the advantage of representing the more important or esteemed scholars at their presumed best.

If one omits matter published before Robinson's first edition and articles with no quotations from the poet (or passages so brief as to make text source unclear), and if, further, one does not count doubly those selections which appear in more than one anthology, the articles come to forty-three. Thirty-three (77 percent) use Robinson's first or second edition. The remaining ten use no special rival: John Spiers and E. M. W. Tillyard (1934) closely approximate Skeat's text. Clawson uses Manly's *Canterbury Tales* of 1928. Arnold Williams acknowledges use of Manly and Rickert; Sams and Mizener, writing about *Troilus*, quote from Root. Tatlock and Kemp Malone seem to be using their own never-printed texts, presumably made for the occasion. It is not possible to decide whose text W. Owen utilized. Thus we see that the minority who did not use Robinson fall into four classes: first, Robinson's contemporaries (Malone, Tatlock), who had not yet accepted the Robinson as a standard edition; second, Englishmen who remained loyal to Skeat (Tillyard, Speirs); third, a loyal Manly contingent (Clawson, Arnold Williams); and, fourth, students of *Troilus* who preferred, doubtless with good reason, to use Root. J. A. Burrows's critical anthology of 1969, *Geoffrey Chaucer*, could not be used, because he normalized almost all quotations, even the earliest, to conform to Robinson's second edition, as he acknowledges in his Preface.[22] Added together, these facts (especially taken with Bateson's recognition of Robinson as the standard edition of Chaucer)[23] are a powerful indication that after a slow start Robinson's work gained general acceptance among Chaucerians on both sides of the Atlantic in the three decades or so after its appearance. A brief scan of eleven periodicals appearing in 1981 in America, England, and on the Continent suggests that the use of Robinson continues. All the articles in *Chaucer Review*, perhaps because of policy, use Robinson's second edition; so do all the others which quote from Chaucer at all (articles in *Studies in Philology, Speculum, English Studies, English Language Notes*), except for Norman Blake, who cites his own York edition of *The Canterbury Tales*.

The Text (Theory)

The materials for discussion of Robinson's text theory are the brief remarks in his Preface, the section on text in the Introduction, and the headnotes to the textual notes for each individual work. To these can be added several manuscript papers relating to text which have survived among Robinson's papers at Harvard. The only way to date these is to see how much they resemble the final print. By this norm the most primitive is the single sheet with many examples reproduced in this volume, the "Tentative Rule." A second item, a booklet, largely blank, is divided into the several sections, much as they appear in the present Table of Contents. The fifth sheet is marked marginally "The Text," and is quoted later in this chapter. A third manuscript piece relates specifically to the text of *The Canterbury Tales*.

The statement entitled "The Text" in the Introduction to the first edition (henceforward called RB^1), pp. xxxii–xl, ought to be reread in full. It remains almost intact in the second edition, pp. xxxvi–xliv, except for the added first paragraph. The second paragraph (third in RB^2) must be carefully examined:

> The entire text has been made afresh by the editor. It is based on his examination of all the published manuscript materials and photographs or collations of some of the more important published sources. Account has been taken of the numerous studies that have been made of the character and relations of the manuscripts, and it has been the editor's intention to pay due regard to critical principles. In fact the text may be called a critical edition, with one reservation. In the case of the more important works, including the Canterbury Tales, the manuscript materials accessible to the editor have not been exhaustive. But the best copies . . . and enough others have been compared to make possible, in the editor's belief, the establishment of trustworthy texts.

This is a little disconcerting, because of the ambiguities and subtle guardedness of "due regard to critical principles," "best copies," and "enough others." It is just this paragraph that the reviewers tended to fall upon. Surely Robinson knew that when he spoke of archetypes and critical editions nearly all would take him to mean what the German textual-criticism tradition had meant for a century. He knew and used the work of Continental scholars on the classification of Chaucer manuscripts. He attempted no new classifications himself but followed Zupitza, Koch, to some extent Brusendorff, and, for *Troilus*, McCormick and Root. When he speaks of *Canterbury Tales* manuscripts of type A, like Zupitza he means the subcategories α (Ellesmere, Hengwrt, etc.), β (Cambridge Dd, Egerton 2726, etc.), and γ (Cambridge Gg etc.). When he says type B, he refers to the many generally inferior manuscripts (see ε and ζ as listed on p. 1003, RB^1). Usually he also includes under type B the δ manuscripts, one of which is the controversial but now generally rejected Harleian 7334, in which Robinson retained a certain lingering faith (strengthened somewhat by Brusendorff) even after Tatlock had demonstrated that it had no authoritative claims.[24] He very rarely adopted unique readings of Ellesmere, though he believed it the best surviving manuscript. He generally preferred A over B readings and usually tells us in the textual notes when he chooses B. Yet there is a telling phrase in the second rough statement on text among the Harvard papers, which otherwise resembles the wording of the published paragraph pretty closely:

> Not called a crit. text for two reasons: Edited with due regard for critical principles. Not called a crit. text because accessible materials far from complete and because the editor has *not always adopted the readings which the strict critical process would yield. Some eclecticism inevitable; editor has not hesitated to abandon critical reading* rather than put unreasonable or unmetrical lines into text. [Italics mine]

Was Robinson aware of Joseph Bédier's devastating critique of the strict *Stammbaum* method in the Introduction to his *Lai de l'ombre* (1913)?[25] This French scholar's analysis of the German method led him to adopt a procedure very similar to that which Robinson actually used for his *Chaucer*: choose a "best" manuscript and edit it in the light of the others, using common sense and scholarly knowledge and experience.

Bédier was of course already very well known, but this decision on his part was a volte-face. Although French medievalists generally accepted his new conclusions, the Paris-trained André Morize, Robinson's younger colleague at Harvard, still inculcated (in his well-known *Problems and Methods of Literary History*, 1922) a strict Lachmann-derived method and exemplified it by quoting Bédier's early application of the German method to a text of Pascal.[26] It is therefore quite possible that Robinson did not know Bédier's revisionist essay; if not, there is nothing too surprising in the similarity of procedure, since Bédier's conclusions are essentially reactionary; they follow logically from his demonstration that the *Stammbaum* method, rigidly applied, contains many assumptions which cannot be proved (e.g., absence of contamination) and that when there is a two-against-one choice among hypothetical ancestors absurd readings often emerge as "archetypal," whereas when the *Stammbaum* (perhaps unconsciously so manipulated) leads to a one-against-one choice (by far the more common event), then the textual critic makes his choice at each lemma just as he would if Lachmann had never existed.

Deciding after collation that his A is the best manuscript, Bédier then finds thirty-four places where he thinks he must depart from it. He divides his readings thus:

> 1. There are eleven cases where "A" yields nonsense or countersense which the editor would correct immediately even if only one manuscript survived.
> 2. Ten copying errors exist which an editor would probably have sought to mend by conjecture, if only "A" survived.
> 3. Eight cases of error detectable only with the other MSS in hand, where the others furnish better readings, or where "A" omits verses.
> 4. Five instances, not too different from those of "3" where "A" readings, even those supported by another good MS, seem somewhat less good than those of other MSS.[27]

Evidently decisions like those indicated by Bédier can be reached only with a full knowledge of the lexicon and grammar of the author and his contemporaries, a knowledge of the mores and social history of his time and place, and a grasp of his principles of versification.

Compare with the above Robinson's remarks on the page immediately following the debated claim that he had made "a critical text" (RB[1], p. xxxiii):

> . . . the present editor does not belong to the severest critical school. When the readings of the "critical text" or of a superior archetype appeared unsatisfactory or manifestly inferior, he has accepted help from other authorities more often than the strict constructionists might approve. . . . in making his decisions he has endeavored to give constant attention to the relation of the manuscripts and *to all relevant consideration of language, meter and usage.* [Italics added]

Though there is no reason to doubt this statement, Robinson's emphasis on "the relation of the manuscripts" often in application seems secondary. Even though Tatlock's *The Harleian Manuscript 7334 and Revision of the Canterbury Tales*[28] appeared as early as 1907, and Robinson accepted its demonstration that Harleian's variants are mostly scribal, and not Chaucer's revisions, he tended to cling to this manuscript even though it was outside the charmed A circle, and finally accepted some of its unique readings, a few of which we must approve. For instance, Harley 7334 (Ha[4]) reads *sterres* at *KnT* A 2037, and so does Robinson, whereas Manly and Rickert (MR)[29] read *sertres* without gloss and admit in a note (3.432): "Editors who read 'sterres' are undoubtedly giving what Chaucer wrote." In other instances, however, the unique readings of Ha[4] indicate only that an unknown fifteenth-century scribe-editor had the same metrical and conservative grammatical tendencies as had Robinson five hundred years later. He wanted, like Robinson, to restore his text intelligently where the scribally transmitted text failed him. But if Robinson was a latter-day confrère of the Harleian scribe, he was also of Bédier's party, even if, as is possible, he did not know it existed. Robinson's stemmata come from the Continental scholars named earlier. As Bédier could have guessed, not only *The Canterbury Tales* but also *The Book of the Duchess, The House of Fame, The Parliament of Fowls, Anelida and Arcite, Boece,* and *The Legend of Good Women,* as well as many of the short poems, are divided by the stemma makers into two hypothetical lines of descent. But a few of the short poems do survive in three classes and so allow for a clear application of the majority principle. The briefest examination of the textual notes for two of these, *Truth* and *Lak of Stedfastnesse,* bears out the fact that Robinson abandoned the Lachmannist procedure. In *Truth* the large number of manuscripts and the variants which cross classification lines show either that much contamination exists or that the classification which Robinson adopted in its entirety (Koch, Brusendorff) is itself unreliable. From Bédier's point of view, the probable contamination is grounds enough for rejecting traditional critical method. Robinson states that he will print from (*British Library*) Additional 1034, one of the two members of α, but, with the probable intention of improving the meter, he rejects the α reading at line 11 for one which occurs in some γ manuscripts only. In the notes to *Lak of Stedfastnesse*, Robinson tells us, "of 'α' and 'β' neither is consistently superior, but in most cases 'β' readings are given the preference" (RB[1], p. 1038). Such a procedure is surely a departure from the "two-against-one" principle, but then Robinson had already concluded that γ represents an inferior text, so that, a priori, if α agrees with γ, that is a point against it, not for it.

It is therefore best to define Robinson's text as conservative, highly informed, and eclectic, though arrived at after much of the procedure for establishing a critical text had been performed. He was careful about his choice of copy text; he rarely accepted unique readings. When he did depart from his copy, it was usually for a reading connected either with grammar or with metrics. In the editing of *The Canterbury Tales*, the utilization of only ten manuscripts (the eight published by the Chaucer Society, the Cardigan—no previous editor had used this unpublished manuscript, now at Austin, Texas—and the Ashburnham, now the Morgan, also not published) along with Skeat's reproduction of the print of 1532[30] was a sensible decision; this number included all the manuscripts commonly termed "good," and going further would mean competing with Manly and Rickert, though it promised ever-diminishing textual returns.

The Text (Practice)

I have already referred to Robinson's "Tentative Rule," which he established fairly early in the course of his work, and which is reproduced herewith. Stripped of the examples, these five practical rules are as follows:

> 1. Modernizations, *f* for *ff*, *th* for *þ* and crossed *d*, *v* for *u*, *j* for *I*; apostrophe in *t' n'*, etc.
> 2. Necessary changes for meter or sense. (Use Harl. to support older forms linguistically?)
> 3. Correct ungrammatical spellings. (Normalize rimes. Keep cases of MS apocope and elision when correct.)
> 4. Accept other MSS when clearly preferable and authority good.
> 5. Accept other MSS when evidence is very strong and reading good.

No date can be put on this document, and it may well antedate Bédier's *Lai de l'ombre*, but one is struck by how germane it is to Bédier's categories previously quoted. From the facsimile one can read the many examples Robinson found to clarify and illustrate each rule.

The best way to see what Robinson did with his texts is to examine closely several passages of medium length. The beginning of *The Pardoner's Tale* lines, C 463–504, lends itself well to an examination of tentative rule 1, because it is free of substantive lexical textual problems, save at line 475, where Robinson, Skeat, and Manly-Rickert agree, except for the error by omission of *noght* in MR. This allows us to see the modernizations without distraction (Robinson's spelling is first, then Ellesmere's):

f for *ff*: line 463, *fflaundres*; line 478, *ffetys, ffrutesteres*
th for *þ*: lines 475, 485, *þt*.
v for *u*: line 465, *Tauernes*; 468, *ouer*; 469, *deuel*; 470, *deueles*; *perseuereth*, 497.
j for *I*: lines 475, *Iewes*; 482 *Iohn* (Robinson capitalizes).

Expanded abbreviations are at lines 475, 485, *þt*, and line 479, *wᵗ*; the backward *er* superior flourish at line 466, *Gyternes*, is expanded, as it is in *perseuereth*, line 497, where the first *er* is expanded from the descender crossbar of *þ*.

Line 465, *Tauernes*; line 465, *Riot*; line 466, *Gyternes*; line 477, *Tombesteres*; line 479, *Baudes*, all represent dropped capitals, whereas *lordes*, line 474, is an instance of modern capitalization.

Robinson has made one word of El *With inne*, line 470; *vn to*, line 482; and *who so*, line 488.

The forty virgules of the passage in Ellesmere are wholly omitted.

Also suppressed are the Latin marginal glosses "Nolite inebriari vino in quo est luxuria" at line 485 and "Seneca" at line 492.

Robinson's punctuation is wholly modern, and his own. Substantial as these modifications may seem collectively, they are much what one will find in most nondiplomatic Middle English texts.

The second rule calls for changes to improve meter and meaning; the third, for the correction of "ungrammatical" endings and the normalization of rimes. The parenthesis of rule 3 may seem almost as elastic as Robinson's original contract; "when correct" must mean either "when there is a great deal of evidence that Chaucer did thus elsewhere" or "when the editor's informed taste directs it." Yet, as different as these two might sound, most of the time they would produce much the same textual result at the hands of a major scholar. Robinson, however, had marked preconceptions about Chaucer's meter and did not view the poet's grammatical usage either as tolerant or as marked by flux.

To illustrate the degree to which rules 2 and 3 were actually imposed on the text, I have collated about four hundred lines of the Ellesmere, consisting of well-known passages from *The General Prologue*, *The Knight's Tale*, *The Wife of Bath's Prologue*, and *The Franklin's Tale* with the Robinson text. It would seem that there are some variants in meter, a small number relating to sense, and very few indeed relating to ungrammatical spellings. Of course, Ellesmere tends to conform to the orthodox opinion of Chaucer's grammar, so that there is a chance of circuitous reasoning here. The passages examined are *GP* A 748–856 (end of *The General Prologue*), *KnT* A 3005–3108 (Theseus's discourse), D *WBP* 503–604 (Jankin), and F 729–838 (the Franklin's *raisonneur* speech on love and marriage). In none of these is the spelling or metrical deviation very marked. Significant differences from Ellesmere are shown in the following table:

Line	El	RB[1]
GP A 752	*to been*	*to han been* [From Ha[4], justified grammatically in RB[1], p.xxxiv, but decided, I believe, on meter.]
A 756	*lakked*	*lakkede* [Grammatical restoration of Chaucer's usual weak preterite ending, yielding a decasyllable.]
A 783	*hond*	*hondes* [Counterindicated metrically but necessary for sense and supported by other MS.)
A 803	*my self*	*myselven** [RB[1] adopts a B reading for meter; the three-syllable form exists elsewhere in Chaucer and Gower.]
A 812	*would*	*wolde* [the E reading in the Six-Text edition is probably in error; cf. the Hg *Facsimile* for El *wolde*. If *would* is the right El reading, the normalization to Chaucerian *wolde* is either monosyllabic or contrametrical]
A 822	*gan for to*	*bigan to* [A decision on basis of taste? both seem equally grammatical and metrical. A "critical" decision.]
A 829	*it yow recorde*	*I it yow record** [RB[1]'s form demands elision to make hendecasyllable; the sense in RB[1] somewhat clearer. *I* is a B reading; El might have *ye* as subject; the Six-Text's unwarranted bracketed insertion of *I* may have influenced RB[1].]
KnT A 3018	*sprynge*	*to sprynge* [A Cardigan (Cn) reading, noncritical; it makes the line hypermetrical unless *begynneth* is contracted to two syllables. Reading without *to* would conform to Chaucer's grammar. A puzzling choice.]
A 3036	*that*	*the which** [The Ha[4] reading to circumvent the difficult meter.]
A 3059	*flour*	*the flour** [A majority, mostly B reading, running against the meter unless the *e* of *chivalrie* is silent.]

Line	El	RB[1]
A 3071	*we make*	*that we make* [So Ha[4] and Cn. Not critical, but on solid metrical grounds.]
A 3079	*syn that*	*syn* [The E reading, also in some B manuscripts, in hypermetrical.]
A 3100	*that it*	*that hath it* [RB[1] takes the decasyllabic reading of the other Six-Text MSS.]
WBP D 511	*bet'*	*bete* [The flourish after *t* in El and Hg probably = final *-e*, which the grammar seems to call for.]
D 588	*weepe*	*weep* [A grammatical choice of no metrical significance supported by Hg and Gg.]
D 604	*seint*	*seinte** [An emendation; all MSS like El. A grammatical decision; a weak declension adjective as in category c of RB[1]'s p. xxix.]
FranT F 772	*auantate*	*avantage* [A corrected scribal lapse.]
F 814	*stynten*	[El's extra syllable kept by RB[1] in spite of evidence from other A MSS.]
F 815	*Dorigene*	*Dorigen* [An orthographic change for consistency with later spellings. No change in meter.]

* Robinson adds a textual note

Few of these are grammatical, even if we include conformity to Chaucer's precise putative dialect. Even with this broad inclusion, only lines A 756, D 511, 588, 604, and possibly A 812 can be so classed. Tentative rule 3 seems to apply at lines A 783, 822, and 3059 (perhaps), 3079, 3100, D 604, and F 772. On the other hand, rules 4 and 5, essentially nonamenable to science, were doubtless used to justify such decisions as A 752, 829, 3018, 3036, 3071 and, in a slightly different way, the keeping of the Ellesmere reading at F 814. Of the nineteen instances in about four hundred lines, only five are mentioned in Robinson's textual notes. One must agree with Ruud's review that the edition would have been improved by inclusion of notes on the remainder.

Classics scholars tell us that *Oedipus* fits perfectly Aristotle's definition of tragedy in the *Poetics* because Aristotle was describing *Oedipus* rather than the whole genus. Since Ellesmere was the chief basis for Robinson's ideas of orthography and grammar, we must also examine a text in which Robinson has opted for a manuscript with scribal atypicalities. For this purpose we turn to two hundred lines of *The Parliament of Fowls* based by Robinson on Cambridge Gg.4.27. This manuscript had previously been judged best by

Koch and by Heath in the Globe edition.[31] In the Introduction Robinson says (RB[1], p. xxv):

> Professor Koch . . . has defended the opinion that Gg goes back in some fashion to an original above the archtype of the other manuscripts and that its variant may therefore be accepted freely. . . . It is not easy to decide this question. The present editor finds about twenty readings, either peculiar to Gg or having slight support in other manuscripts, which are clearly right, or . . . strongly preferable to the critical text. . . . Some thirty-five more appear to deserve consideration, and a few of them have been hesitatingly adopted. . . . But the evidence of [Gg's independence] is insufficient, and it has seemed safest to give the preference in general to a critical text, resorting to Gg only where there is special need or justification.

A comparison of the first 203 lines of Robinson's *Parliament* with D. W. Brewer's recent edition (a conservative Gg text with substantial textual notes)[32] and Koch's *Chaucer's Kleinere Dichtungen*, also based on the Gg manuscript (as found among the diplomatic texts in the Chaucer Society's *Parallel Text Edition of Chaucer's Minor Poems*, ser. 1, no. 21, pp. 50ff.) will demonstrate what Robinson actually did with a somewhat aberrant scribal text. First, it shows Robinson's orthographic normalizations and his necessary emendations of gross scribal errors. The passage also illustrates some of his "critical text" changes of Gg and a few of his retained unique (or nearly unique) Gg readings. Robinson makes a dozen or so departures for several reasons, including the metrical, from Gg's final -*e*. Further textual decisions are for metrical regularity, though these usually have manuscript support. Thus the "Tentative Rule" is generally brought into play, but, additionally, the orthography is normalized to approximate Ellesmere.

All the editors using Gg agree with Robinson in such changes as *Scipioun* for *sothion*, *Galaxye* for *galylye*, and *blosmy* for *blospemy*. In addition to the modernizations typical of the treatment of Ellesmere (thorn, yogh, *ff*, etc.) we find the following normalizations *to* Ellesmere English:

1. -*ed* for -*yd*; -*en* for -*in*; -*eth* for -*yth*.
2. *sh* for *sch* (*schewede*, *fisch*, etc.).
3. Omitted final -*n* in pronouns (*thyn*, *myn*, *thynself*).
4. *i* for *e* (*ferbrond*, *swemyn*, *iwrete*).

A few of the critical-text readings running counter to Gg are noted by Robinson at p. 1020: the inversion of *hard* and *sharp* at line 2; *And ful of torment and of harde grace* (so in most manuscripts) for Gg's hypermetric *And was sumdel disseyvable and ful of harde grace* (here Robinson's tentative emendation in the note for line 65 was accepted later by Brewer); *al hir wikked dede* (a reading found in all manuscript categories) for Gg's *is his weked dede*.

The minority or unique Gg readings preferred above the critical text include the following:

Line	Reading
PF 14	*swich* [So Koch and Brewer; other MSS, *such* etc.]
35	*seyn* [So Koch and Brewer; other MSS, *tel, sey.*]
46	*other* [So Koch and Brewer; the rest of the MSS, *eyther, or.*]
84	*comyn* [RB[1] *comen*; other MSS, *come, com.*]
166	*wher* [So Koch and Brewer; other MSS, *wether.*]
197	*acord* [So Koch and Brewer; other MSS, *ac(c)orde.*]

Robinson's treatment of Gg's final *-e* in *Parliament* can be judged from the following:

Line	Gg Reading	RB[1]
PF 11	*hise*	*his* [Scribal final *-e*; impossible metrically.]
12	*wele*	*wol* [Also grammatical change, normalizing; the final *-e* is hypermetrical.]
72	*weye*	*wey* [Optional save for the meter.]
117	*seye*	*sey* [Final *-e* metrically silent.]
118	*sweuene*	*sweven* [Final *-e* nonhistorical, nonmetrical.
193	*litele*	*litel* [scribal final *-e*; the change improves the meter.]

Robinson adds a desired final *-e* as follows:

Line	Gg Reading	RB[1]
PF		
33	*thereon*	*therinne* [A critical change normalizes the meter.]
72	*bliss*	*blisse* (Grammatical, but also critical.]
123	*iwrowht*	*ywroughte* [Also normalized spelling.]
176, 178	*assh, lasch*	*asshe, lashe* [*Asshe* is historical; *lashe*, a normalized rime.]
201	*myght*	*myghte* [Grammatical, but silent.]

In the two categories above (except in line 193) Koch anticipates RB[1]. Brewer follows in most of the first category, but in only half of the second.

Other instances of textual decisions found in the same passage were presumably influenced by metrical considerations, notably line 40, *betwix* for *betwixsyn*; line 83, *come* for *comyn*; line 91, *nadde* for *ne hadde*; line 124, *iwriten* for *I-wrete*; line 155, *stondeth* for *stant*; and line 165, *at the wrastlyng* for *at wrastelyng* (the *e* of Gg is probably silent, but RB[1]'s B reading forces us to give *liketh* only one syllable; this choice is surprising). Last, one can cite Robinson's emendation at line 39, where *telleth it* is adopted for sense against all manuscripts.

In his general remarks on the text in the Introduction, Robinson makes it fairly clear that he is uncomfortable with McCormick's and Root's belief in the three stages of *Troilus and Criseyde*, especially with Root's insistence that β represents a revision of γ and is therefore more authoritative, in spite of the superior quality of the best γ manuscripts. Robinson lauds Root for his recognition of the high quality of Corpus Christi 61 (a γ manuscript which Robinson had chosen as his base text long before Root appeared, but disagrees with him in denying the desirability of the peculiar readings of the β version. He therefore undertakes to offer a γ text: "The authority of the 'gamma' group, even when it stands alone, seems better to the present editor than it does to Mr. Root" (RB^1, p. xxxvi). He also speaks of the β category as "reconstructed" and "doubtful." "It should be added, however-er," closes Robinson, "that the differences between the 'gamma' text and Mr. Root's 'beta' version are few and unimportant" (RB^1, p. xxxvi).

It is not known just why Robinson altered in *Troilus* his *Canterbury Tales* practice of restoring grammatical but silent final -*e*, but he states at p. 1024 they are omitted more often from Corpus Christi 61 than from Ellesmere. To show variations in editing between Robinson and Root in matters other than a preference for β readings in Root, I have compared two hundred lines of book 2. Examples follow:

Line	Root	RB^1
TC 64	*sorwful*	*sorowful*
66	*evere* (silent)	*ever*
69	*Tereux*	*Tereus* [Robinson's note points to -*s* spelling in *LGW*.]
74	*plite* (silent)	*plit*
75	*wey*	*weye* [Silent]
109	*tel*	*telle* [Silent before a consonant.]
115	*sore*	*soore* [Inconsequential.]
117	*satte*	*sate*
121	*yit*	*yet* [In keeping with *PF* normalization.]
142	*eyen*	*eyghen* [Both spellings are found in good MSS.]
146	*nat*	*nought* [Both, with *not*, are found in MSS.]
152	*met*	*mette* [Silent before a vowel.]
193, 194	*ben, flen*	*been, fleen* [The disyllable is Chaucer's usual form.]
197	*her*	*here* [Silent before a consonant.]
201	*hire* (silent)	*hir* [Before a consonant.]
214	*or*	*er* [Robinson glosses both forms of the preposition.]
222	*widwes*	*widewes* [The meter calls for two syllables.]
230	*yit*	*yet* [Robinson's preferred spelling, also in Campsall.]
236	*witynge*	*wyttynge*

Of course, in the same passage there are eleven instances in which Robinson follows γ readings and Root, β. These may be readily consulted in Root: see 2.51, 86, 110, 124, 135,139, 176, 192, 217, 221, 224. What may be said of this passage is that, whereas the β theory of Root produces some substantial differences in reading, they can hardly be called major; as for the differences not related to the β preference, they are few, trivial, and mostly orthographic. Noteworthy as regards Robinson's position on the γ text is that E. Talbot Donaldson and Albert Baugh in their subsequent editions have also used Cp 61 as their base manuscript, John Hurt Fisher has followed Campsall (Morgan), a closely similar γ manuscript; thus Root's hard-to-follow argument has not had many takers.

The Headnotes and Critical Notes

To say anything against the notes would be to come out against God, home, and mother. Ever since 1933 an enthusiasm like the reviewers' has remained in the mouths of most Chaucer scholars and teachers. It is very hard for me to separate Chaucer's poetry from this apparatus, which accompanied it when I first encountered Chaucer and which I have used in teaching Chaucer for decades. To a somewhat lesser extent, this sentiment must be shared by most students of Chaucer now functioning. The early reviewers praised the notes' compactness, their inclusiveness, their fairness, and their wisdom. All these the introductions still seem to possess. If the Explanatory Notes need revision fifty years after their publication and twenty-five after their reediting, it is because they belong largely to what DeQuincey called the "literature of knowledge"; they are by their nature ever to be renewed. When I first taught Chaucer, I found the introduction to *The Canterbury Tales* a little frightening because it seemed to leave me with so little of my own to say. Having overcome that hurdle, I still find it remarkable, and the *Troilus* essay even better.

The Glossary

The Glossary has been the source of the most commonly recurring complaints about the two editions of Robinson. Mabel Day concerned herself chiefly with RB[1]'s Glossary in her review in *Review of English Studies*.[33] Her first concern is that the spellings in the Glossary do not always match those in the text. My own observation is that the glossarial entries do sometimes match Skeat's. It is a fair guess that Skeat was utilized as a sort of secondary copy text during the early stages of work on RB[1] and that his spellings thus crept into the Glossary.[34] Much of the Glossary may have been done before Robinson decided finally about his normalizations. This is a real fault. For instance, Day finds the Glossary lagging behind the notes on words like *yve* and *vache*.

Robinson's glossarial count is considerably less than Skeat's, but in spite of the short list of omissions in Day, and another in Tatlock's review already discussed, when I set myself for this chapter the task of comparing letter *N* in the Glossary of RB[1] with Tatlock's *Concordance*[35] for the same letter, I was truly surprised that there were but few additional words which I would wish to include. Perhaps the greatest difficulty students have with Robinson's Glossary is that he took no notice of spellings in vocalic *y* except under *i*, though he did not normalize in the text. A few technical alterations of this sort would render the Glossary more useful; so, of course, would line-number references, even partial.

The Edition of 1957

The second edition was planned to bring the Explanatory Notes up to date and to acknowledge Manly and Rickert's text of 1940 (MR) by certain changes in the text of *The Canterbury Tales*, which changes were listed at the beginning of the Textual Notes, though the old notes were perpetuated more or less unchanged, an action Robinson justified at p. 883 (RB[2]). He also stated that he had not tried to incorporate all the new information from Manly. A quick comparison of *The Miller's Tale* in RB[2] shows five changes from RB[1], not all taken from MR, while thirty-three variants from MR remain as in RB[1]. I judge eleven of these to have been passed over because the differences were inconsequential and manuscripts divided. Others were probably shunned because to adopt them would have left the lines a syllable short (A *MilT* 3236, 3292, 3485, 3519, etc.). Of the remaining eleven, keeping *man* for *men* (line A 3228) reflects Robinson's disagreement with Manly about the poet's own usage. At line A 3625 he kept *lowe coler*, doubtless because he took MR's naïveté into account. Rejection of MR's *quod ich* at line A 3285 was already a puzzling decision in RB[1]; it is in Ellesmere and Hengwrt and is more colloquially vivid. Grammatical as well as metrical reasons may have dictated keeping *wolde* at line A 3292, and the rejection of *his* before *duck* in line A 3576. There is no real artistic excuse for rejecting *thy derelyng* for *my derelyng* at line A 3793 or for keeping *shapen him a wyle* against MR's *shapen hem*. In giving three *what*'s to line A 3477, Robinson retains an Ellesmere reading, against MR's conclusion that the archetypal line was defective. Where Manly and Rickert point out such archetypical defects, Robinson commonly supplies emendations.

Of course, all the above comments assume that Robinson indeed compared the whole MR text systematically with his own first edition. It is barely possible that he made skimming choices; his failing eyes and very advanced age might be responsible. I find it, however, hard to believe that the Robinson I knew would have capped a meticulous lifework with such a slipshod procedure.

What changes did Robinson actually accept from Manly and Rickert? The first quasitextual change in *The Miller's Tale* (RB[2] list) is *tour* at line A

3256; it does not follow MR. At line A 3350 he yields to MR's aesthetic argument that the absence of *ne* before *took* makes "the stress fall effectively on 'no' and 'noon.' " (MR, 3.437). This overrides Robinson's usual preference for the decasyllable. MR's preference for *breke* over *broke* is probably accepted because it significantly alters the sense of the passage: the ax is stored among the tubs so that when the flood starts it can be used to break out of the attic. The tense change alters the entire picture one has of the denouement and is the most important of all MR's differences from RB[1] in *The Miller's Tale*; surely if any MR reading was to be accepted for literary reasons, this must be the one. At line A 3672, Robinson accepts MR's *to wake* for *wake* in spite of its being hypermetric, probably because it is authorized by Ellesmere and Harley 7334, though he passed over many similar readings. A similar scrutiny of *The Manciple's Prologue* and *Tale* shows that there too RB[2]'s new MR readings (four) are greatly outnumbered by loci (twelve) where MR's variance from RB[1] was not accepted.[36]

Thus we may conclude that in 1957 Robinson was no more strongly moved by Manly and Rickert's new but still systematic if not mechanical way of establishing the text than he had been by their Germanic predecessors' methods a quarter century before, no matter what lip service he had given them then. It would seem that he treated their findings in an aesthetic way; his choices are those of a learned literary critic. His chief preoccupation was the printing of regularly scanned, craftsmanlike, artistically significant lines conforming to his already determined opinions about Chaucer's grammar and meter.

It is surprising, remembering Robinson's dedication to Ellesmere, to note that fully 53 percent of the listed changes at the head of RB[2]'s Textual Notes conform to the Hengwrt manuscript. An additional 15 percent revert to previously rejected Ellesmere readings supported by Hengwrt. Thus fully two-thirds of the new readings (excluding those not manuscript-related) follow Hengwrt.

Late in the preparation of the RB[2] copy, editors at Houghton Mifflin asked Robinson to revise and greatly expand his Glossary. The use of Tatlock's *Concordance* for that purpose was mentioned but quickly abandoned. Robinson was too kind to say that he would not want to entrust such a task to his secretary, an untried Ph.D. candidate. He was probably not up to undertaking it himself. Thus he resisted the publisher, with the result that the new Glossary differs very little from the first.[37] For instance, under the letter *C* the new edition adds only two new words, *closet* and *college*. Some of Day's list of twenty-three years before he did insert: *leigh* as part of *lyen*, *brede* for roast meat, *in steere* for *astern*. Tatlock's list fared worse: only one word, *ale-stake*, appeared in the revision. I believe that Robinson disliked glossaries because they suggested that his readers were not learned gentlemen but mere students. So too, I know, when the new quarto format was adopted for RB[2] he protested that it looked like a schoolbook.

Here and there one finds in the text of RB^2 significant punctuation changes which are nowhere referred to. Two of these deserve mention here. In the beginning of *The Wife of Bath's Tale*, Skeat and RB^1 leave one with the impression that women go about in bushes and under trees (line D 879). Robinson abandons Skeat for the reading of Pollard's *Globe*, replacing the semicolon with a comma, so that the incubi, not the women, lurk in the shrubbery. So too in *Troilus* 2. 198, *Troilus* now ends with a period, whereas it was previously the subject of *hurte* in the next line.

It is unfortunate that RB^2 was set in Linotype, a process that bred new errors in each line to be corrected. A good many errata newly made by the typesetters in correcting their errors in the page proofs found their way into the first printing, though most of these have since been caught in the second or subsequent printings of RB^2.

To sum up, the second edition is an extension of the first, save for the updating of the Explanatory Notes, chiefly in a bibliographical vein, the textual changes in *The Canterbury Tales*, and the enlarged format. Consequently, it must be judged along with the first, for it shares its failings and many virtues.

F. N. Robinson formed two generations of Middle English teachers while he worked at his first edition. In his fortieth year as a member of the Harvard faculty, the book appeared, and even then, foreseeing a second edition, he began taking notes. Sixty-three years after he began his teaching career, he was still working on his *Chaucer*. Today, fifty years after its first appearance, it is much used and honored. Few scholars and teachers can have had so long and influential a career. His text, though we may cavil at it, *is* Chaucer to millions in the twentieth century. His Introduction and notes have set the tone for college lectures and student thinking about Chaucer for half a century both in the United States and, to a great degree, in the rest of the English-reading world.

Notes

Chapter 1

1. The best and most recent study of Caxton's life and works is that of George Duncan Painter, *William Caxton: A Quincentenary Biography of England's First Printer* (London: Chatto and Windus, 1976). All dates given here are from this source.

2. Walter John Blythe Crotch, ed., *The Prologues and Epilogues of William Caxton*, EETS, o.s., no. 176 (London: Milford, 1928), pp. 90–91.

3. Norman Francis Blake, *Caxton and His World* (London: Deutsch, 1969), passim; see also Norman Francis Blake, *Caxton and Chaucer,"* LeedsSE*, n.s. (1967):19–36.

4. The evidence is examined by Painter, *William Caxton*, pp. 43–46.

5. Crotch, ed., *Prologues and Epilogues*, pp. 2–8.

6. *The Game and Play of the Chess Moralized*, from Jacobus de Cessolis, *De ludo Scachorum*, principally through the French version by Jean de Vignay; see Painter, *William Caxton*, pp. 62–64.

7. Painter, *William Caxton*, pp. 72–77.

8. Ibid., pp. 54–57.

9. For the most recent chronological list see ibid., pp. 211–15.

10. Ibid., p. 12.

11. J. W. Adamson, "The Extent of Literacy in England in the Fifteenth Century: Notes and Conjectures," *Library*, 4th ser. 10 (1929–30):163–93.

12. For a discussion of early humanism in England, see Roberto Weiss, *Humanism in England During the Fifteenth Century*, Medium Ævum Monographs, no. 4 (Oxford: Blackwell, 1941).

13. Eugène Vinaver, ed., *The Works of Sir Thomas Malory*, 2d ed. (3 vols.; Oxford: Clarendon Press, 1973), 1.xxxvi–xxxvii.

14. Ibid., 1.ix. Caxton's book 5, which Malory had adapted from the alliterative *Morte Arthure*, was shortened through modernization. For discussion and photographs of offsets, see Lotte Hellinga, "The Malory Manuscript and Caxton," in Toshiyuki Takamiya and Derek Brewer, eds., *Aspects of Malory* (Cambridge: Boydell and Brewer, 1981), pp. 127–41.

15. Edward Gordon Duff, ed., *Fifteenth Century English Books: A Bibliography of Books and Documents Printed in England and of Books for the English Market Printed Abroad*, Bibliographical Society, London, Illustrated Monograph no. 18 (Oxford: The University Press, 1917); Seymour de Ricci, *A Census of Caxtons*, Bibliographical Society, London, Illustrated Monograph no. 15 (Oxford: The University Press, 1909); Alfred William Pollard and Gilbert Richard Redgrave, ed., *A Short-Title Catalogue of Books Printed in England, Scotland, and Ireland and of English Books Printed Abroad, 1475–1640* (London: Bibliographical Society, 1926; reprinted, 1946); Frederick Richmond Goff, ed., *Incunabula in American Libraries: A Third Census* (New York: Bibliographical Society of America, 1964; reprint ed., 1974). See

also John Cloud Trewhart Oates, ed., *A Catalogue of Fifteenth Century Printed Books in the University Library, Cambridge* (Cambridge: The University Press, 1954).

16. For the history of paper see Dard Hunter, *Papermaking: The History and Technique of an Ancient Craft*, 2d ed., New York: Knopf, 1957).

17. Examples are given by William Blades, *The Life and Typography of William Caxton, England's First Printer* (2 vols.; London: Lilly, 1861, 1863; reprint ed., New York: Burt Franklin, 1971), vol. 2, plate IV.A. Blades's work was long the authoritative study of Caxton and his press.

18. For Caxton's types see Daniel Berkeley Updyke, *Printing Types*, 2d ed. (Cambridge, Mass.: Harvard University Press, 1937). Both Blades and De Ricci also give plates of Caxton's types, though more types have been recognized since Blades wrote.

19. See, for example, Francis Jenkinson, *The Story of Queen Anelida and the False Arcite* (Cambridge: The University Press, 1903); *Geoffrey Chaucer: The Canterbury Tales* [Caxton, 1483] (Cambridge: Cornmarket Reprints in Association with Magdalene College, Cambridge, 1972).

20. Norman Francis Blake, *Caxton: England's First Publisher* (London: Osprey, 1976), plate 38 and pp. 85–119.

21. For discussions of proofreading in Caxton's time see Douglas Crawford McMurtrie, *Proofreading in the Fifteenth Century: An Examination of the Evidence Relating to Correctors of the Press at Work in Paris Prior to 1500* (Greenwich, Conn.: Condé Nast, 1921); Curt Ferdinand Bühler, "Variants in English Incunabula," in Deoch Fulton, ed., *Bookmen's Holiday: Notes and Studies Written in Tribute to Harry Miller Lydenberg* (New York: New York Public Library, 1943), pp. 1–16; see also Blake, *Caxton: England's First Publisher*, pp. 101–105.

22. The standard edition of Chaucer's works is still Fred Norris Robinson, ed., *The Works of Geoffrey Chaucer*, 2d ed. (Boston: Houghton Mifflin, 1957). All quotations not otherwise designated are from this edition.

23. Blake, *Caxton: England's First Publisher*, pp. 83–119.

24. Painter, *William Caxton*, p. 84; see also Copeland's preface to *Apollonius of Tyre* (*King Appolyn of Tyre*, translated by Copeland and printed in 1510 by Wynkyn de Worde).

25. Charles Moïse Briquet, *Les Filigranes* (4 vols.; Amsterdam: Labarre Foundation, 1968), 1.*27. The possibility of an earlier date for the first edition of *The Canterbury Tales* based on its relationship to Type no. 1 is under study by Paul Needham and Lotte Hellinga.

26. Crotch, ed., *Prologues and Epilogues*, pp. 90–91.

27. For a full discussion of the order of *The Canterbury Tales*, see John Matthews Manly and Edith Rickert, eds., *The Text of the Canterbury Tales* (8 vols.; Chicago: University of Chicago Press, 1940), 2.475–94 and charts I–V; see also Robert Armstrong Pratt, "The Order of the Canterbury Tales," *PMLA* 66 (1951):1141–67.

28. For descriptions, see Manly and Rickert, eds., *The Text of the Canterbury Tales*, 1.256–65, 381–86, 527–31. Descriptions of other manuscripts of *The Canterbury Tales* can also be found in this volume.

29. Ibid., 2.57.

30. Virginia Everett Leland, "A Study of Scribal Editing in Twelve Manuscripts of the Canterbury Tales," (Ph.D. diss., University of Chicago, 1940), pp. 34–38.

31. Robert Kilburn Root, "Publication Before Printing," *PMLA* 28 (1913):420–21.

32. Manly and Rickert, eds., *The Text of the Canterbury Tales*, 1.530.

33. Ibid., 1.533–34.

34. Painter, *William Caxton*, p. 70.

35. Francis Thynne, *Animadversions uppon the Annotacions and Corrections of some imperfections of impressions of Chaucer's workes . . . reprinted in the yere of oure lorde 1598*, Chaucer Society, 2d ser., vol. 13 (London: Trübner, 1876), p. xii.

36. Thomas F. Dunn, *The Manuscript Source of Caxton's Second Edition of the Canterbury Tales* (Chicago: University of Chicago Libraries, private ed.; part of a dissertation, 1940).

37. Ibid., pp. 5–6.

38. Ibid., pp. 9, 14–15. The lines dropped are A 2681–82 (Out also in thirteen manuscripts) and E 2364–65 (Out also in three manuscripts, owing, Dunn thinks, to an eye-skip error).

39. Leland, "Scribal Editing," p. 26.

40. Dunn, *Manuscript Source*, p. 5.

41. Ibid., pp. 6–7.

42. Blake, *Caxton: England's First Publisher*, pp. 61–63.

43. Arthur Mayger Hind, *An Introduction to a History of Woodcut* (Boston: Houghton Mifflin, 1935).

44. Painter, *William Caxton*, p. 132.

45. For a discussion of Chaucer's sources, see Beverly Boyd, *Chaucer According to William Caxton:* Minor Poems *and* Boece, *1478* (Lawrence, Kans.: Allen Press., 1978), p. xvi.

46. Bernard L. Jefferson, *Chaucer and the* Consolation of Philosophy (Princeton, N.J.: Princeton University Press, 1917), pp. 16–25.

47. For work in progress, see Boyd, *Chaucer According to William Caxton*, p. xxvii.

48. For discussion see ibid., pp. xv–xvi.

49. For discussion see ibid., pp. xvii–xviii.

50. Weiss, *Humanism in England*, pp. 138–39; Painter, *William Caxton*, pp. 92–93.

51. Boyd, ed., *Chaucer According to William Caxton*, pp. 1–28 (*The Parliament of Fowls*), 29–39 (*Anelida and Arcite*).

52. Robinson, ed., *Works*, p. 796.

53. See ibid., textual notes, passim.

54. Painter, *William Caxton*, pp. 93–95.

55. Blake, *Caxton: England's First Publisher*, pp. 141–42.

56. Crotch., ed., *Prologues and Epilogues*, p. 69; he properly does not include the patch.

57. Robinson, ed., *Works*, p. 899; see also H. Frank Heath, in Alfred W. Pollard et al., eds., *The Works of Geoffrey Chaucer*, Globe edition (London: Macmillan, 1953), pp. xliii–xliv; Aage Brusendorff, *The Chaucer Tradition* (London: Oxford University Press, 1925), pp. 151–53.

58. Robinson, ed., *Works*, p. 899.

59. Blake, "Caxton and Chaucer," p. 25. Blake says that Caxton evidently took no steps to discover whether what his source had of the poem was all that was extant.

60. Painter, *William Caxton*, p. 135.

61. Robert K. Root, *The Textual Tradition of Chaucer's* Troilus, Chaucer Society, 1st ser., no. 99 (London: Kegan Paul et al., 1916 for the issue of 1912).

62. Robinson, ed., *Works*, p. xl.

63. Root, *Textual Tradition*, pp. 6–8.

64. Described by Painter, *William Caxton*, p. 135.

Chapter 2

1. William Thynne, ed., *The Workes of Geffray Chaucer newly printed, with dyuers workes whiche were neuer in print before . . .* (London: Thomas Godfray, 1532; *STC* 5068). There are two facsimiles of this edition: Walter W. Skeat, ed., *The Works of Geoffrey Chaucer and Others . . . from the Copy in the British Museum* (London: Alexander Moring and Oxford University Press, 1905); Derek S. Brewer, ed., *The Works, 1532, with Supplementary Material from the Editions of 1542, 1561, 1598 and 1602* by Geoffrey Chaucer (Menston, Yorkshire: Scolar Press, 1969). The Preface was actually written by Sir Brian Tuke, an officer in the king's household. Henry Bradshaw's account of his discovery of Tuke's own statement of authorship in the Clare College copy of Thynne's edition appears in Frederick J. Furnivall's edition of Francis Thynne, *Animadversions uppon the Annotacions and Corrections of some imperfections of impressiones of Chaucers workes (sett downe before tyme, and nowe) reprinted in the yere of oure lorde*

1598, Chaucer Society, 2d ser., no. 13 (London: Trübner, 1876), p. xxvi, and is reprinted in Skeat's facsimile edition of Th, pp. xxi–xxii. Tuke's handwritten note can be seen in Brewer's edition of Th, which is a facsimile of the Cambridge copy. However, because William Thynne presumably subscribed to everything that Tuke wrote in the Preface, I will maintain the fiction of the Preface and refer to it as Thynne's. All citations from the Preface come from pages A 2r through A 3r.

2. Robert A. Hall, Jr., *A Short History of Italian Literature* (Ithaca, N.Y.: Linguistica, 1951), p. 97.

3. Michele Barbi, *Life of Dante*, trans. and ed. Paul Ruggiers (Berkeley and Los Angeles: University of California Press, 1954), pp. 109–10.

4. Detlef Brüning, *Clément Marots Bearbeitung des Rosenromans (1526)* (Berlin: Erich Schmidt Verlag, 1972), pp. 41–43.

5. Thynne, *Animadversions*, p. xxi. Furnivall's assumption that the Thynne referred to as hunting with the king by Erasmus in a letter written in 1516 is not William Thynne is a conservative assumption, but not a certain one.

6. *Ibid.*, pp. xxi–xxii, xxvi–xxvii. On p. xxviii, Furnivall cites a document that he dates 1538 in which Thynne is called chief clerk of the kitchen; J. S. Brewer gives the date 1532 for the same document. See J. S. Brewer, James Gairdner, and R. H. Brodie, eds., *Letters and Papers, Foreign and Domestic, of the Reign of Henry VIII*, 23 vols. in 38 parts (London: Longmans, 1862–1932), vol. 5, item 1222.

7. Thynne, *Animadversions*, pp. xxviii, xxix.

8. *Ibid.*, p. xxix.

9. *Ibid.*, p. viii.

10. Geoffrey Elton, *The Tudor Revolution in Government* (Cambridge: Cambridge University Press, 1953), pp. 376–78.

11. Thynne, *Animadversions*, p. xxiii.

12. Brewer, Gairdner, and Brodie, eds., *Letters and Papers*, vol. 5, p. 332; vol. 5, item 1065, p. 311.

13. *Ibid.*, vol. 10, p. 674.

14. Elton, *The Tudor Revolution*, p. 42. For a specific example of the kinds of duties that might have been expected of Thynne, see ibid., pp. 58–59.

15. Marjorie Blatcher, ed., *Report on the Manuscripts of the Most Honourable the Marquess of Bath Preserved at Longleat* (London: Her Majesty's Stationery Office, 1968), 4.6.

16. Thynne, *Animadversions*, p. xxii; Brewer, Gairdner, and Brodie, eds., *Letters and Papers*, vol. 21, pt. 2, item 476, par. 37.

17. Thynne, *Animadversions*, pp. xxi, xxii.

18. *Ibid.*, pp. xxvi–xxvii, xxviii–xxix. The second item is the one mentioned in n. 11 as misdated. Brewer, Gairdner, and Brodie, eds., *Letters and Papers*, vol. 6, item 281.

19. Thynne, *Animadversions*, pp. xxvii–xxviii; Brewer, Gairdner, and Brodie, eds., *Letters and Papers*, vol. 6, item 561.

20. See n. 1 above.

21. Thynne, *Animadversions*, pp. 9, 10.

22. *Ibid.*, p. 9.

23. H. L. R. Edwards, *Skelton: The Life and Times of an Early Tudor Poet* (London: Jonathan Cape, 1949), pp. 209–10. On pages 208–10, Edwards gives a highly speculative, but perhaps likely, account of a friendship between Thynne and Skelton founded on their common devotion to Chaucer.

24. Thynne, *Animadversions*, pp. 9–10.

25. Various efforts have been made to reconcile the inconsistencies in Francis Thynne's account: see *Animadversions*, pp. 75–76, where Furnivall prints Henry Bradshaw's attempt; Thomas Raynesford Lounsbury, *Studies in Chaucer: His Life and Writings*, 3 vols. (New York: Harper & Brothers, 1892), 1.461–69; John M. Berdan, *Early Tudor Poetry* (New York: Macmillan, 1920), p. 118.

26. Caroline F. E. Spurgeon, *Five Hundred Years of Chaucer Criticism and Allusion, 1357–1900*, 3 vols. (Cambridge: Cambridge University Press, 1925), 1.lxxvi.

27. Veré Laurel Rubel, *Poetic Diction of the English Renaissance* (New York: Modern Language Association, 1941), chaps. 3–5, passim, in particular, pp. 14–30, 46; Raymond Southall, *The Courtly Maker: An Essay on the Poetry of Wyatt and His Contemporaries* (Oxford: Blackwell, 1964), pp. 11–14, 35–39.

28. John C. Bale, "The Place of Chaucer in Sixteenth Century English Literature" (Ph.D. dissertation, University of Illinois, 1953), pp. 230–43.

29. Thynne, *Animadversions*, p. 6.

30. *Ibid.* No record of this commission has survived. Having such a commission antedating the dissolution of the monasteries raises some questions, but John Leland received a similar commission in 1533; Lucy Toulmin Smith, ed., *The Itinerary of John Leland in or about the Years 1535–1543* (1906–10; reprint ed., London: Centaur Press, 1964), 1.xxxvii–xxxviii.

31. Not every text in Th has been examined closely for this chapter; evidence for Thynne's use of more manuscripts may come from work such as that in progress with the *Variorum Chaucer*.

32. Gl is described in Aage Brusendorff, *The Chaucer Tradition* (Oxford: Clarendon Press, 1925), p. 295. The fullest description of Lg is Eleanor P. Hammond, "MS. Longleat 258—A Chaucerian Codex," *MLN* 20 (1905): 77–79.

33. Caxton's edition of *Boece* is described in William Blades, *The Life and Typography of William Caxton* (1863; reprint ed., New York: Burt Franklin, n.d.), 2. 66–71.

34. All the following concern similarly marked manuscripts: Gavin Bone, "Extant Manuscripts Printed from W. de Worde with Notes on the Owner, Roger Thorney," *Library*, 4th ser., 12 (1931–32): 284–306; John Bromwich, "The First Book Printed in Anglo-Saxon Types," *TCBS* 3 (1962):265–92; R. W. Mitchner, "Wynkyn de Worde's Use of the Plimpton Manuscript of *De Proprietatibus Rerum*," *Library*, 5th ser. 6 (1951–52): 7–18; Margery Morgan, "Rylands English MS. 2—Lydgate's *Fall of Princes*," *BJRL* 33 (1950–51):194–96; Margery Morgan, "Pynson's Manuscript of *Dives and Pauper*," *Library*, 5th ser., 8 (1953): 217–28: H. C. Schulz, "Manuscript Printer's Copy for a Lost Early English Book," *Library*, 4th ser., 22 (1941–42): 138–44; H. S. Schulz, "A Middle English Manuscript Used as Printer's Copy," *HLQ* 29 (1966):325–36; Percy Simpson, *Proof-Reading in the Sixteenth, Seventeenth and Eighteenth Centuries* (London: Oxford University Press, 1935), chap. 2, "Early Proofs and Copy," passim.

35. A detailed proof for these statements can be found in my article "Some Printer's Copy for William Thynne's 1532 Edition of Chaucer," *Library*, 6th ser., 1 (1979):97–113.

36. An unsigned typescript of this transciption is inserted loose in Lg. Derek Pearsall refers to the inscription in what is the best summary of the external evidence associating Lg with Th; see Derek Pearsall, ed., *The Flower and the Leafe and The Assembly of Ladies* (London: Nelson, 1960), pp. 2–4, 7–8.

37. John M. Manly and Edith Rickert, eds., *The Text of the Canterbury Tales* (Chicago: University of Chicago Press, 1940), 1.342, 348. Manly and Rickert's discussion of the manuscripts' provenance, while citing no positive evidence for Thynne's ownership, does not preclude the possibility.

38. *Ibid.*, p. 294.

39. *Ibid.*, p. 293.

40. Brewer, Gairdner, and Brodie, eds., *Letters and Papers*, vol. 5, item 119, paragraph 52; see note 1 above for Tuke's authorship of the preface to Th.

41. Manly and Rickert, eds., *The Text of the Canterbury Tales*, 1.72–73, 133.

42. Eleanor P. Hammond, *Chaucer: A Bibliographical Manual* (1908; reprint ed., New York: Peter Smith, 1933), p. 338.

43. F. N. Robinson, ed., *The Works of Geoffrey Chaucer*, 2d ed. (Boston: Houghton Mifflin, 1957), pp. 912, 919.

44. E. Krausser, "The Complaint of the Black Knight," *Anglia* 19 (1897): 218–20; Charles Shepard Rutherford, *"The Boke of Cupide*: A New Edition" (Ph.D. dissertation, Indiana University, 1969), p. 151; V. J. Scattergood, *"The Boke of Cupide*—An Edition," *EPS* 9 (1965):51.

45. For a discussion of Th's unique, however corrupt, text of *The Testament of Love*, see Skeat's facsimile edition of Th, pp. xxxviii–xl. For Th's text of *The Testament of Cresseid*, see Denton Fox, ed., *The Poems of Robert Henryson* (Oxford: Clarendon Press, 1981), pp. xciv–xcv, c–cii.

46. Much fuller discussion of the textual relationships described here and below can be found in my "William Thynne and His 1532 Edition of Chaucer" (Ph.D. dissertation, Indiana University), *Dissertation Abstracts* 36 (1976):5311-A.

47. Skeat had already noticed Thynne's use of Pynson's text and his departure from it for the final six stanzas; see Skeat's facsimile edition of Th, p. xxxv.

48. Caxton's edition was printed at Westminster about 1477; see the facsimile edition, F. Jenkinson and P. Dujardin, eds., *The Story of Queen Anelida and the False Arcite* (Cambridge: Cambridge University Press, 1905).

49. For this stanza Skeat, who argues that Thynne emended Cx[1] with Lg, acknowledges that Thynne "had access to some other authority" (facsimile edition of Th, p. xxxvi). He does not grant another authority for the whole poem.

50. In the introduction to his facsimile edition of Th, Skeat maintains that Th's text of *The Complaint of Mars* was printed from Lg with emendations from Julian Notary's edition of *Mars* from about 1500 (ibid., p. xli). Given that, in comparison to the figures cited for F and T, there are 109 readings in Th not found in Lg and 194 not found in Notary's edition, it seems unlikely that Thynne established his text as Skeat suggests. The four readings that Th does share with Notary's edition against Lg, F, and T can be found in other manuscripts; Thynne may not have consulted Notary's edition at all.

51. [*The Parliament of Fowls*] (Westminster: William Caxton, [ca. 1477]; *STC* 5091); The explicit entitled *The Temple of Bras*, [*The House of Fame* and other poems] (London: Richard Pynson, [1526]; *STC* 5088); also includes *The Parliament of Fowls* and *La Belle Dame sans Merci*.

52. For manuscript groupings, see Robinson, ed., *The Works of Geoffrey Chaucer*, p. 902.

53. The shifts between compositors and copy do not coincide regularly within the signature with half signatures, whole sheets, or half sheets. Failing any such regular starting point for the second compositor, it is difficult to see how the arrangement saved much time at a time when the long galley had not yet supposedly come into use.

54. W. W. Greg, "The Early Printed Editions of the *Canterbury Tales*," *PMLA* 39 (1924):737–61.

55. Thomas Tyrwhitt, ed., *The Canterbury Tales of Chaucer*, 2d ed. (Oxford: Clarendon Press, 1798), 1.xl.

56. Robert Kilburn Root, ed., *The Book of Troilus and Criseyde, by Geoffrey Chaucer* (Princeton, N.J.: Princeton University Press, 1926), pp. lxiv–lxv.

57. John Strong Perry Tatlock and Arthur Garfield Kennedy, *A Concordance to the Complete Works of Geoffrey Chaucer and to the Romaunt of the Rose* (Washington, D.C.: Carnegie Institution, 1927).

58. In general the changes in Cx are very much like the ones in a Latin manuscript used as printer's copy, described by Bertram Colgrave and Irvine Masson in "The *Editio Princeps* of Bede's Prose Life of St. Cuthbert, and Its Printer's XIIth Century 'Copy,' " *Library*, 4th Ser., 19 (1938–39):289–303.

59. W. F. Bryan and Germaine Dempster, eds., *Sources and Analogues of Chaucer's Canterbury Tales* (1941; reprint ed., New York: Humanities Press, 1958), p. 402.

60. All quotations from the *Roman de la Rose* are from Ronald Sutherland, ed., *The Romaunt of the Rose and Le Roman de la Rose: A Parallel-Text Edition* (Oxford: Blackwell, 1968).

61. *Le Roman de la Rose*, 5 vols. (Paris: Librairie de Fermin and Didot et Cie., 1914–24).

62. For a description and explanation of the transposition, see W. W. Skeat, ed., *The Works of Geoffrey Chaucer*, 2d ed. (Oxford: Clarendon Press, 1899), 1.12–13.

63. In the footnotes to these lines in Max Kaluza, ed., *The Romaunt of the Rose from the Unique Glasgow MS*, Chaucer Society, 1st ser., vol. 83 (1891; reprint ed., New York: Johnson Reprint Corporation, 1967). Aage Brusendorff credits Thynne with the last four lines (p. 324); he is also willing to credit Thynne with line 6318, since it "corresponds so badly with the French text" (*The Chaucer Tradition*, p. 300). On the other hand, he takes issue with Kaluza's "entirely arbitrary view" that Thynne composed all the lines in Th that are omitted from Gl and asserts—rather arbitrarily, one could think—that lines 892, 1553, 3136, 4856, 6205 "do not look like having been made up by Thynne" (ibid., p. 297 and n.3).

64. This tale was supposedly printed first as a separate volume by Thomas Godfrey in the mid-1530s. See Skeat's facsimile edition of Th, p. xviii.

65. This entire sequence of editions, including the details about their contents, is described by Eleanor P. Hammond in *Chaucer*, pp. 116–28. Derek Brewer provides similar information in the unpaginated introduction to his facsimile edition of Th.

66. The material available about these printers' practices is too extensive to include here, but along with my own analysis includes items cited in note 34 above and the editorial commentary in several volumes from the EETS.

67. Quoted in H. S. Bennett, *English Books and Readers, 1475 to 1557* (Cambridge: Cambridge University Press, 1952), p. 199.

68. J. Schick, ed., *The Temple of Glas*, by John Lydgate, EETS, e.s., vol. 60 (London: Kegan Paul, Trench, Trübner & Co., 1891), p. xlvii.

69. Quoted in Bennett, *English Books and Readers*, p. 110.

70. E. Gordon Duff, *The Printers, Stationers and Bookbinders of Westminster and London from 1476 to 1535* (Cambridge: Cambridge University Press, 1906), p. 157.

71. Thynne, *Animadversions*, Furnivall citing Bradshaw, p. xxvi.

72. Thomas Berthelet, ed., *Confessio Amantis*, by John Gower (London: Thomas Berthelet, 1532), p. aa iii v a.

73. Henry Bergen, ed., *The Fall of Princes*, by John Lydgate, pt. 4, EETS, no. 124 (London: Humphrey Milford and Oxford University Press, 1927), pp. 119, 120.

74. Quoted in Bennett, *English Books and Readers*, p. 200.

75. Henry Bergen, ed., *Troy Book*, by John Lydgate, pt. 4, EETS, e.s., no. 126 (London: Humphrey Milford and Oxford University Press, 1920), pp. 62–65.

76. The English translation is from T. R. Lounsbury, *Studies in Chaucer*, 1.139; the original Latin text is reprinted in Hammond, *Chaucer*, p. 4.

77. The paragraph is reprinted in William L. Alderson and Arnold C. Henderson, *Chaucer and Augustan Scholarship*, English Studies (Berkeley: University of California Press, 1970), 5.211–12.

78. See n. 55 above.

79. Charles Muscatine, *The Book of Geoffrey Chaucer* (San Francisco: Book Club of California, 1963), p. 17.

Chapter 3

1. See, for instance, Walter W. Skeat, ed., *The Complete Works of Geoffrey Chaucer*, 7 vols. (Oxford: Oxford University Press, 1894–97), 1.41–43; W. W. Skeat, *The Chaucer Canon* (Oxford: Oxford University Press, 1900), pp. 117–26; Eleanor P. Hammond, *Chaucer: A Bibliographical Manual* (New York: Macmillan, 1908), pp. 121–22; Rossell H. Robbins, "The Chaucerian Apocrypha," in A. E. Hartung, ed., *A Manual of the Writings in*

Middle English 1050–1500 (Hamden, Conn.: Archon/Shoestring Press, 1973), 4.1070; a more measured assessment appears in George B. Pace and Alfred David, eds., *The Minor Poems, Part One*, vol. 5 in Paul G. Ruggiers and Donald C. Baker, gen. eds., *A Variorum Edition of the Works of Geoffrey Chaucer* (Norman: University of Oklahoma Press, 1982), p. 32.

2. Thomas Tyrwhitt, ed., *The Canterbury Tales of Chaucer* . . . (London, 1775–78), 5.xxii–xxiii.

3. For some consideration of this question see Francis P. Magoun, "The Chaucer of Spenser and Milton," *MP* 25 (1927):129–31; Alice S. Miskimin, *The Renaissance Chaucer* (New Haven and London: Yale University Press, 1975), esp. pp. 230–61.

4. Most helpful is C. L. Kingsford, ed., *John Stow: A Survey of London* (Oxford: Oxford University Press, 1908), 1.vii–xxviii; in the reprint of 1971 of this work is incorporated Kingsford's supplementary pamphlet of 1927, and this reprint has been used here. There are also some useful comments, but of Stow's method as a historian rather than on his life, in F. J. Levy, *Tudor Historical Thought* (San Marino, Calif., Huntington Library, 1967), pp. 167–69, 181–96, and M. McKisack, *Medieval History in the Tudor Age* (Oxford: Oxford University Press, 1971), pp. 82–85, 111–14, 131–33.

5. W. Ringler, "Lydgate's *Serpent of Division*, 1559, edited by John Stow," *SB* 14 (1961):201–203; the responsibility of Stow is accepted in the revised *STC* 17028.

6. Revised *STC* 17027.5, undated.

7. For this rivalry see Kingsford, ed., *John Stow*, 1.ix–xii; Levy, *Tudor Historical Thought*, pp. 178–81.

8. The revised *STC* distinguishes the works and editions confused in the original *STC*; see here *STC* 23319–25.2.

9. Revised *STC* 23325.4–23332.

10. Revised *STC* 23333–40.

11. See my "Robert of Gloucester and the Antiquaries, 1550–1800," *N&Q* 214 (1969):323–26; and A. S. G. Edwards and J. I. Miller, "Stow and Lydgate's 'St. Edmund'," *N&Q* 218 (1973):365–69.

12. Kingsford, ed., *John Stow*, 1.xxi–xxii; Levy, *Tudor Historical Thought*, p. 195.

13. Revised *STC* 23341–43; Kingsford's edition is of the last of these.

14. Revised *STC* 17652, 19209, 25004–25005; *Annales*, 1600, p. 1150, expanding the edition of 1592, p. 1161.

15. W. Ringler, "John Stow's Editions of Skelton's *Workes* and of *Certaine Worthye Manuscript Poems*," *SB* 8 (1956):215–17; the books are revised *STC* 22608 and 21499, where the responsibility of Stow is accepted (in the second instance with a query).

16. See Kingsford, ed., *John Stow*, 1.xix–xxv.

17. Ibid., pp. lxxxvi–xciii; and my "Robert of Gloucester," p. 325; to these others could be added.

18. See E. Arber, *A Transcript of the Registers of the Company of Stationers of London. 1554–1640 A.D.* 1 (London, 1875), fols. 181–181b; Kingsford, *John Stow*, 1.xvi–xviii.

19. Many are mentioned by Aage Brusendorff, *The Chaucer Tradition* (Oxford: Oxford University Press, 1925).

20. The text appears on sigs. Rrr, fol. 5r–Vvv, fol. 8v, the attribution on the title page.

21. Fols. 288v and 83r; the colophon on fol. 179r is a fairer description of the manuscript; "workes of John Lidgate which John Stow hath caused to be coppyed out of an owld booke somtyme wrytten by John Sherleye . . .," since not all the material is in Stow's own hand.

22. A. Erdmann and E. Ekwall, eds., *Lydgate's Siege of Thebes*, EETS, e.s., nos. 108, 125 (1911–30), 2.56, 61, 69–94.

23. Kingsford, *John Stow*, 2.111; cf. *Annales*, 1592, pp. 517–18, where Stow claims that his edition was "by viewe of diuers written copies, corrected by myself, the author of this

history, who at that time also corrected diuers works of the said master Geffrey Chaucers, neuer before imprinted . . . ."

24. Thomas Speght, ed., *The Workes of our Antient and Learned English Poet, Geffrey Chaucer, newly Printed.* (London, 1598; STC 5077) sig. a, fol. 4v.

25. Sig. c, fol. 2r; sig. b, fol. 8v; sig. c., fol. 5.

26. Kingsford, ed., *John Stow*, 2.24.

27. See Brusendorff, *The Chaucer Tradition*, pp. 207–36; also Eleanor P. Hammond, "Two British Museum Manuscripts, Harley 2251 and Adds. 34360," *Anglia* 28 (1905):1–28; Eleanor P. Hammond, "Ashmole 59 and Other Shirley Manuscripts," *Anglia* 30 (1907):320–48; Eleanor P. Hammond, "A Scribe of Chaucer," *MP* 27 (1929):27–33; A. I. Doyle, "More Light on John Shirley," *MÆ* 30 (1961):93–101; A. I. Doyle, "English Books in and out of Court," in V. J. Scattergood and J. W. Sherborne, eds., *English Court Culture in the Later Middle Ages* (London, 1983), pp. 175–78; R. F. Green, *Poets and Princepleasers* (Toronto, University of Toronto Press, 1980), pp. 130–33; the comments of C. Greenberg, "John Shirley and the English Book Trade," *Library* 6th ser., 4 (1982):369–80, need qualification.

28. This is not intended as a complete list of Stow's annotations; it covers only those manuscripts most interesting for his concern with Chaucer.

29. Brusendorff, *The Chaucer Tradition*, p. 295, n. 2. J. Norton-Smith, in his introduction to the facsimile edition, *Bodleian Library MS Fairfax 16* (London, 1979), p. xviii, does not attribute the addition to Stow.

30. For some bibliographical details and facsimiles of the most distinctive matter in the edition of 1561 see *Geoffrey Chaucer: The Works 1532, with supplementary material from the Editions of 1542, 1561, 1598 and 1602*, introduction by D. S. Brewer (Ilkley and London: Scolar Press, 1969; reprinted 1974, 1976). A useful outline of the prefatory material, and of differences among sixteenth-century editions of Chaucer, is in J. R. Hetherington, *Chaucer 1532–1602, Notes and Facsimile Texts* (Birmingham: Privately published, 1964; rev. ed., 1967), here p. 16. Charles Muscatine, *The Book of Geoffrey Chaucer* (San Francisco: Book Club of California, 1963), pp. 24–28, states that there is at least one copy where Wight's name is replaced by that of H. Bradsha[w]; this is recognized in the proof entry for the revised *STC*, which I am grateful to have been allowed to see, as 5076.3. A brief account appears in Pace and David, eds., *The Minor Poems, Part One*, pp. 32–33.

31. STC 5075 has on the title page no. 67 in R. B. McKerrow and F. S. Ferguson, *Title-Page Borders Used in England and Scotland, 1485–1640* (London, Oxford University Press, 1932); STC 5076 has Chaucer's arms on the title page with a small 1560 above the shield. The preliminary material is in Thynne's edition of 1532 (STC 5068), sig. A, fols. 2r–4v, and in STC 5075–76, opening sig., fols. 2r–4v.

32. I used as a check the last line of the right-hand column of each recto. There are some mistakes in the folio numbering; these mistakes are identical in the two issues.

33. Muscatine, *The Book of Geoffrey Chaucer*, p. 26, suggests that the order of the issues may be the reverse; the evidence is presumably the date 1560 above the shield in STC 5076.

34. An investigation of the typography of the poems that Stow added would suggest that the usual assumption is correct. Thus the error *me* appears in poem 21/40 and 41 (for the poem numbering see appendix) in the copies of STC 5075 in Newnham College (see Brewer's facsimile), British Library, pressmark 641 m. 10; and the Huntington Library, pressmark 84667; and in the doubtful copy (but from all signs STC 5075—it lacks everything up to sig. b, fol. 1r save one preliminary leaf) in Cambridge University Library, pressmark Syn 2.56.2; this is corrected in all copies of STC 5076 that I have seen. But the error *mockynge* for *makynge* in poem 23/4 is not in the British Library copy of STC 5075 or in any copy of STC 5076; *couerte* for *conuerte* in 9/74 is only in the Newnham copy and that in the British Library of STC 5075. On the other hand, in addition to all specified copies of STC 5075 having the error *nor selfe* for *our selfe* in 22/1146, this error also appears in Bodleian Library, pressmark C.1.7 Art., copy of STC 5076.

35. The precise details of this displacement can be seen in Brewer's facsimile, though there is no mention of it in the introduction.

36. Many of the portraits are in outline, and often in detail, traditional, but I assume that the most recent source is the most probable one. Those mentioned are in Pynson's edition (*STC* 5086) sig. M, fol. 6r; sig. D, fol. 5r; and sig. P, fol. 2r and 4r, respectively.

37. *STC* 5084, sig. a, fol 2v; sig. b, fol. 6r; sig. b, fol. 7v; sig. c, fol. 1r; and 11, fol. 3r and A, fol. 1r, respectively.

38. *STC* 5083, sig. B, fol. 3r.

39. *STC* 5086, sigs. H, fol. 5v and I, fol. 4, *STC* 5068 sig. I, fol. 3v.

40. Thynne, 1542, sigs. Y, fol. 5r–Z, fol. 6v; Stow, sigs. Q, fol. 8r–S, fol. 1r. For the early printing history of this text see A. Wawn, "Chaucer, *The Plowman's Tale* and Reformation Propaganda: The Testimonies of Thomas Godfray and *I Playne Piers*," *Bulletin of the John Rylands Library* 56 (1973):174–92.

41. Thynne, 1532, after Gower's *Balade to Kyng Henry the fourth*, ending there on sig. Vvv, fol. 1r, and before *The Cuckoo and the Nightingale*.

42. The poems are printed in Skeat, ed., *Complete Works of Chaucer*, 7.266–74, 285–90; and by H. N. MacCracken, ed., *John Lydgate: The Minor Poems*, vol. 2, *Secular Poems*, EETS, no. 192, (1934), pp. 410–18, and 839–44. For the text of the second see below.

43. (1550) sigs. R, fol. 3r–S, fol. 4v; for 1542 and Stow's edition see n. 40 above. Cf. Pace and David, eds., *The Minor Poems, Part One*, p. 31–32.

44. In works now accepted to be by Chaucer, references are given to F. N. Robinson, ed., *The Works of Geoffrey Chaucer*, 2d. ed. (Boston: Houghton Mifflin; London: Oxford University Press, 1957), though using the traditional lettered subdivisions for the groups of *Canterbury Tales*. Material not accepted to be by Chaucer is provided with references to a modern edition where this is reasonably accessible (mostly the editions in Skeat, ed., *Complete Works of Chaucer*, vol. 7); in other cases I have numbered the lines in Stow's edition, ignoring all headings.

45. See E. J. Dobson, *English Pronunciation, 1500–1700*, 2d ed. (Oxford: Oxford University Press, 1968), 1.235–37; 2.879–81.

46. This confirms earlier findings in Skeat, *Canon*, p. 117 and n., and more recently with regard to two short poems; see George B. Pace, "The Text of Chaucer's Purse," *SB* 1 (1948):111–12; H. Chewning, "The Text of the 'Envoy to Alison,' " *SB* 5 (1952):34–37. I am also indebted to Derek Pearsall for allowing me to see his conclusions about Stow's version of *The Nun's Priest's Tale* and telling me of his views on Stow's text of *The Assembly of Ladies*; in both cases Stow's text derived from the (1550) print of Thynne.

47. Skeat, ed., *Complete Works of Chaucer*, 7.xlix, 285–90; this text is used for the line numbering.

48. Edition of 1532, sig. Vvv, fols. 5v–6r; edition of 1542, sig. Tt, fols. 5r–6r, edition of (1550), sig. Qqq, fols. 5r–5v.

49. Skeat printed the poem from Thynne's edition of 1532, modified by comparison with Cambridge University Library Ff.1.6, fol. 147, and BL Harley 2251, fol. 151r. MacCracken, ed., *John Lydgate*, 2:839–44, printed it from Huntington El 26.A.13, fol. 20, collating this with Skeat's two manuscripts, Trinity College Cambridge R.3.20, Bodley 686, and BL Add. 29729. I am indebted to the Rector of the English College in Rome for a transcript of the version in manuscript 1405 (*olim* 1306); the text of this differs substantially from Stow's or Thynne's editions. The entry under *IMEV* 653 of Lambeth Palace 344, fol. 10v, is a mistake; the poem is Chaucer's genuine *Balade de Bon Conseyl (Truth)*.

50. Thus in line 24, A reads *for to* for T and Stow *on to*; line 85, A reads *ellis* for T and Stow *also*; line 87, A reads *is* for T and Stow *as*; line 98, A reads *wolde* for T and Stow *wol*; but in each case Thynne's text agrees with Stow's. Harley 2251 was also annotated by Stow, but its text of this poem differs considerably from the print, notably in lines 124–26.

51. Thynne, 1532, Gower's poem to Henry IV (*IMEV* 2587), sigs. Ttt, fol. 4v–Vvv, fol. 1r, and Scogan's *Moral Balade* (*IMEV* 2264), sig. Vvv, fols. 3r–4r; Stow, 1561, see above n. 48.

52. B. Y. Fletcher, "Printer's Copy for Stow's *Chaucer*," *SB* 31 (1978):184–201; I have retained Fletcher's numbering of the poems added by Stow.

53. Skeat, ed., *Complete Works of Chaucer*, 1:41, 7:lxxii, lxxx–lxxxiii; Skeat, *The Chaucer Canon*, p. 120; W. W. Greg, "Chaucer Attributions in MS.R.3.19 in the Library of Trinity College, Cambridge," *MLR* 8 (1913), 539–40; Brusendorff, *The Chaucer Tradition*, pp. 225–26.

54. That the manuscript had been used for setting up type was noted in passing by G. Bone, "Extant Manuscripts Printed from by W. de Worde with Notes on the Owner, Roger Thorney," *Library* 4th Ser., 12 (1931):303–304. Strangely George B. Pace, "Speght's Chaucer and MS. Gg.4.27," *SB* 21 (1968):225–35, esp. p. 230, ignored this case when he alleged that "we have no other instance [than Gg.4.27] in which the manuscript used for one of the Blackletter Chaucers has been identified."

55. Some of Fletcher's observations ("Printer's Copy") about marks in the manuscript presumed to derive from the printer, or from Stow as indications to the printer, seem overingenious (e.g., p. 191 on poem no. 11, the slash against the tenth stanza cannot be significant since there is a similar slash against the seventh, which is in the middle of a column in the print).

56. Fletcher's summary, "Printer's Copy," p. 201.

57. See M. R. James, *The Western Manuscripts in the Library of Trinity College, Cambridge* (Cambridge: The University Press, 1901), 2.69–74, no. 599, for a fairly complete list of the contents.

58. For the Chaucer poems see below; Lydgate attributions appear on fols. 68r (*IMEV* 4005), 157v (*IMEV* 2541), and 171r (*IMEV* 3983), and the Ashby attribution on fol. 41r (*IMEV* 437).

59. See references above, n.53.

60. BL Harley 2251, fol. 52r, and Additional 34360, fol. 76v.

61. *STC* 3175–78 and revised *STC* 17008–17013.

62. *IMEV* 1838. See Rossell H. Robbins, "A Love Epistle by 'Chaucer,' " *MLR* 49 (1954):289–92, who observes that stanzas 3, 4, 5, and 10 are the same as stanzas 3, 7, 11, and 15 of *The Craft of Lovers*; Robbins took the attributing hand to be before Stow.

63. The first two are unprinted; the third (*IMEV* 2625) has been printed several times though not from this manuscript (see, most accessibly, Lydgate, *Minor Poems*, 2.662–65). Some idea of the contents of the manuscript may be gained from K. G. Wilson, "Five Unpublished Secular Love Poems from MS Trinity College Cambridge 599," *Anglia* 72 (1955):400–18.

64. Fletcher, "Printer's Copy," p. 188; for the exemplar of no. 6 see further below. It is not entirely clear whether Stow knew Ashmole 59. Kingsford listed it among those that belonged to or were used by Stow (1.xcii), but his cross reference to his own 2.361 does not provide his evidence. There appear to be no notes in the manuscript in Stow's hand, but the Ashmole catalogue suggests that Stow obtained his copy of a brief historical text from this source.

65. Fletcher, "Printer's Copy," pp. 194–96. P. M. Clogan, "The Textual Reliability of Chaucer's Lyrics: *A Complaint to his Lady*," *M&H*, n.s., 5 (1974):185, states that the poem is attributed by Shirley to Chaucer in MS Harley 78, but the hand of the running titles from the beginning of Chaucer's *Pity* to the conclusion of these extra stanzas is not that of the main scribe.

66. Fletcher, "Printer's Copy," pp. 188–89; Fairfax, fol. 195v.

67. Fairfax, fols. 194v–95r, 199r–199*v: Fletcher, "Printer's Copy," pp. 189–90.

68. *Bodleian Library MS Fairfax 16*, intro. by John Norton-Smith, pp. xvi, xviii–xix and nn.

69. Speght sig. Ooo.1r–1v. The text appears in Fairfax on f. 188v, where a sixteenth-century hand (probably not Stow's) has added *Chaucers A.b.c.*

70. *Lydgate's Reson and Sensuallyte*, ed. E. Sieper, EETS ES 84 and 89 (1901-3), i. xl–xx; I

am grateful to Mr. Simon Mitchell for pointing out to me the difficulty of this text. The only other possible explanation seems to be that the anthology was compiled over a period of time after, as well as before, the writing of the 1558 colophon; this would also explain the oddity with regard to *The Siege of Thebes* (above p. 55–56). Further study of this complicated manuscript may elucidate the question.

71. George B. Pace, "The Chaucerian *Proverbs*," *SB* 18 (1965):42–48; Fletcher ("Printer's Copy," p. 188), however, rightly rejected Pace's use of *cher*, line 8, as evidence since this is a ghost form not found in any copy of Stow's edition known to him—it has disappeared from the variants cited in Pace and David, eds., *The Minor Poems, Part One*, p. 200.

72. See above, n. 27, and below in the table.

73. See James, *The Western Manuscripts*, pp. 75–82, for a list of the contents (his numbering 600). Many of the poems were ascribed by the original hand (works by Chaucer already printed before 1561, by Lydgate, by Hoccleve, and in French by the "lorde of Suffolk"), which is that of Shirley. Stow added a number of notes, including on p. 361 beside the verse containing Shirley's name a note about his tomb (cf. Kingsford, ed., *John Stow*, 2.23–24).

74. A. I. Doyle, "An Unrecognized Piece of *Piers the Ploughman's Creed* and other Work by its Scribe," *Speculum* 34 (1959):428; cf. Brusendorff, *The Chaucer Tradition*, p. 225 n. 6.

75. The other manuscript, Stow's Additional 34360, has an extra final stanza. But both manuscripts agree against Stow's edition in reading *truwly* line 54 (Stow *ruly*), and *so verrayly* line 113 (Stow *verely*); Harley has *þis*, line 108, against the print *thus*.

76. The main contents of the manuscript are in Latin and French; the English material, including Chaucer's *Lak of Stedfastnesse* and *Truth* in addition to the two here, all anonymous, occurring on fols. 183r–189v. With my doubt compare Pace and David, eds., *The Minor Poems, Part One*, p. 190n.5.

77. Bone, "Extant Manuscripts," pp. 303–304.

78. Fletcher's reading ("Printer's Copy," p. 191) *pperotent* results from a misreading of the abbreviated word; *OED* records the word from the fifteenth century.

79. A. S. G. Edwards and J. Hedley, "John Stowe, *The Craft of Lovers* and T.C.C. R.3.19," *SB* 28 (1975):265–68, argue that, while Stow's main exemplar was T, he adopted a few readings from BL Add. 34360, fols. 73v–77r, and Harley 2251, fols. 52r–54v. This is one of the seven instances they cite.

80. Poem 22/1146; copies of the issue with woodcuts, and at least one copy of that without (Bodleian C.1.7 Art.) read *nor selfe*, but this was corrected.

81. Some of Fletcher's additions to Bone's observations I cannot confirm; the smudges in T mentioned in Fletcher's description of poems 9 and 21, for example, are not of the same color as those discerned by Bone. The markings alleged in poem 22 need to be amplified with considerable faith before bearing the argument advanced from them.

82. Kingsford, ed., *John Stow*, 1.143; the attribution is in the text as well as the sidenote; Skeat, *Canon*, p. 126.

83. The stanza is the sixth of the poem as it appears in Fairfax, and the text in the *Survey* agrees, with a few modernizations, with this. The only other manuscript now known of the poem (*IMEV* 803) is Bodley 638, fols. 195–204; there are almost no textual differences in this stanza.

84. Fairfax, fol. 82v, "here lackethe 6 leves that are in Josephe hollands boke"; for Holland see R. A. Caldwell, "Joseph Holand, Collector and Antiquary," *MP* 40 (1943):295–301, and for further comments *The Poetical Works of Geoffrey Chaucer: A Facsimile of Cambridge University Library MS Gg.4.27*, intro. by M. B. Parkes and R. Beadle (Norman, Okla., 1979–80), 3:66.

85. See Norton-Smith's notes, Fairfax, p. xviii.

86. G. H. Kingsley, ed., *Francis Thynne's Animadversions upon Speght's first (1598) Edition of Chaucer's Works*, rev. F. J. Furnivall, EETS, no. 9 (1875), p. 5.

NOTES TO APPENDIX

1. Skeat, ed., *Complete Works of Chaucer*, 7.297 (hereafter Skeat); Skeat, *Canon*, pp. 117–18 (hereafter *Canon*); Hammond, *Chaucer*, pp. 545–55 (hereafter Hammond); Brusendorff, *The Chaucer Tradition*, pp. 225–26 (hereafter Brusendorff). Brusendorff did not mention items 1–3 or 8. In this and subsequent notes selective references only are given.

2. Skeat, 7.297; Hammond, pp. 427–28.

3. Skeat, 7.450; *Canon*, p. 125; Hammond, p. 446; Robbins, "The Chaucerian Apocrypha," 4.1066–67, 1291 (hereafter Robbins).

4. Skeat, 1.392–93; *Canon*, p. 118; Hammond, pp. 371–72; F. N. Robinson, ed., *The Works of Geoffrey Chaucer* (Boston: Houghton Mifflin, 1957), p. 536 (hereafter Robinson); Pace and David, eds., *The Minor Poems, Part One*, p. 69.

5. See N. Davis, "Chaucer's *Gentilesse*: A Forgotten Manuscript, with Some Proverbs," *RES*, n.s., 20 (1969):43–50; and A. I. Doyle and George B. Pace, "Further Texts of Chaucer's Minor Poems," *SB* 28 (1975):45–47.

6. Skeat, 1.407; *Canon*, p. 118; Hammond, pp. 449–50; Robinson, p. 543.

7. Pace and David, eds., *The Minor Poems, Part One*, pp. 196–200, include this fourth manuscript, though its text is severely curtailed and corrupted; it is printed by Doyle in *MÆ* 30 (1961):98n.41.

8. Skeat, 1.409–10; *Canon*, pp. 62–63; Hammond, pp. 440–41; Robinson, p. 540; Pace and David, eds., *The Minor Poems, Part One*, p. 190.

9. See Doyle and Pace, "Further Texts," pp. 47–49, 57–58.

10. Skeat, 1.41; *Canon*, p. 119; Hammond, pp. 421–22.

11. *Canon*, pp. 120–21; Hammond, p. 420; Robbins, pp. 1091–92, 1301.

12. *Canon*, p. 122; Hammond, p. 441; Robbins, pp. 1083, 1298.

13. *Canon*, p. 122; Hammond, p. 457; Robbins, pp. 1090, 1300.

14. *Canon*, p. 122; Hammond, p. 441; Robbins, pp. 1080–81, 1297.

15. Skeat, 7.448; *Canon*, pp. 122–23; Hammond, pp. 461–62; Robbins, pp. 1078, 1295–96.

16. *Canon*, p. 123; Hammond, p. 428; Robbins, pp. 1077, 1295.

17. *Canon*, p. 123; Hammond, p. 442; Robbins, pp. 1077, 1296.

18. *Canon*, p. 123; Hammond, p. 427; Robbins, pp. 1081–82, 1297.

19. See J. A. van Dorsten, "The Leyden 'Lydgate Manuscript,'" *Scriptorium* 14 (1960):315–25.

20. *Canon*, pp. 123–24; Hammond, p. 428; Robbins, pp. 1082, 1297.

21. *Canon*, p. 124; Hammond, p. 442; Robbins, pp. 1082–83, 1297–98.

22. Skeat, 1.41, 7.295–96; *Canon*, pp. 124–25; Hammond, pp. 412–13; Robbins, pp. 1083, 1298.

23. Skeat, 1.360–64; Hammond, pp. 411–12; Robinson, p. 528–29; it will be included in Pace and David, eds., *The Minor Poems, Part Two*.

24. Brusendorff, pp. 225–26, recognized that Stow's text of this poem must have been a Shirley manuscript, but thought that neither of the extant manuscripts (Harley 78, written by Shirley, Add. 34360, copied from another such) could have been Stow's exemplar.

25. *Canon*, pp. 119–20; Hammond, p. 415.

26. Skeat, 7.409–47; *Canon*, pp. 125, 127–35; Hammond, pp. 418–19; Robbins, pp. 1087–89, 1299–1300.

27. Skeat, 1.379; Hammond, p. 405; Robinson, p. 534; Pace and David, eds., *The Minor Poems, Part One*, p. 135.

Chapter 4

1. For accounts of the sixteenth-century prints of Chaucer's works, see *The Complete Works of Geoffrey Chaucer*, ed. W. W. Skeat, 6 vols. (Oxford: Oxford University Press, 1894), 1.27–46; Eleanor Prescott Hammond, *Chaucer: A Bibliographical Manual* (New York: Macmillan, 1908); Charles Muscatine, *The Book of Geoffrey Chaucer: An Account of the Publication of Geoffrey Chaucer's Works from the Fifteenth Century to Modern Times* (San Francisco: Book Club of California, 1963); John R. Hetherington, *Chaucer, 1532–1602, Notes and Facsimile Texts* (Birmingham: Privately published, 1964); D. S. Brewer, ed., *Geoffrey Chaucer, The Works, 1532* (facsimile, with supplementary material from the editions of 1542, 1561, 1598, and 1602) (London: Scolar Press, 1969); Derek Brewer, ed., *Chaucer: The Critical Heritage*, 2 vols. (London: Routledge and Kegan Paul, 1978), 1.33–36.

2. See Brewer, *Chaucer: The Critical Heritage*, 1.20, 98, 101; he suggests the existence of a "Peterhouse group" of Chaucerian enthusiasts.

3. For this and the subsequent two references, see Edward Arber, ed., *A Transcript of the Registers of the Company of Stationers of London, 1554–1640*, 5 vols. (London, 1875), 2.293, 395, 316.

4. STC nos. 5077, 5078, 5079 (A. W. Pollard and G. R. Redgrave, *A Short-Title Catalogue of Books Printed in England, Scotland, and Ireland, 1475–1640* [London: Biographical Society, 1926]). For technical description of the edition of 1598, see W. T. Lowndes, *The Bibliographer's Manual of English Literature*, ed. H. G. Bohn (London, 1864), p. 425; Caroline F. E. Spurgeon, *Five Hundred Years of Chaucer Criticism and Allusion, 1357–1900*, Chaucer Society, *Publications*, nos. 48–50, 52–56 (1908–17); in three vols. (Cambridge: The University Press, 1925), 1.147–48; and the works of Hammond (pp. 122–25), Muscatine (pp. 29–30), and Hetherington (pp. 5–7, 18–19), cited in n. 1 above.

5. See Muscatine, *The Book of Geoffrey Chaucer*, p. 29.

6. This is not Francis Beaumont the dramatist or his father of the same name but the unrelated Francis Beaumont who was at Peterhouse from 1565 to 1573 and who later became master of Charterhouse (d. 1624). See T. W. Baldwin, "The Three Francis Beaumonts," *MLN* 39 (1924):505–507; Ernest Kuhl, "Francis Beaumont and Speght," *TLS*, September 23, 1926, p. 632.

7. *Annales*, pp. 527–28, quoted in Spurgeon, *Chaucer Criticism and Allusion*, 1.165.

8. John Stow, *Survey of London*, ed C. L. Kingsford, 2 vols. (Oxford: Oxford University Press, 1908), 2.111.

9. There are further references in the "Life" to a text of the *Complaint to His Purse* in Stow's library (in the section "His Friends") and to "a booke of *Iohn Stowes* called Little Iohn" (in the concluding commendations).

10. For variations in the publisher's imprint, see above; and for additional detail on the title page, see Hammond, *Chaucer: A Bibliographical Manual*, pp. 122–23.

11. Brewer, *Chaucer: The Critical Heritage*, 1.35.

12. See William L. Alderson and Arnold C. Henderson, *Chaucer and Augustan Scholarship*, University of California Publications, English Studies, no. 35 (Berkeley, 1970), p. 2.

13. See Muscatine, *The Book of Geoffrey Chaucer*, p. 30.

14. Usually placed opposite the title page, but sometimes as the last leaf of the first quire of six; see Hetherington, *Chaucer, 1532–1602*, p. 7.

15. In his edition of Chaucer's works, (1.45–46), Skeat rather confusingly treats these as if they were introduced by Speght in 1602, but he knew better, as did Lounsbury (Thomas R. Lounsbury, *Studies in Chaucer: His Life and Writings*, 3 vols. (New York, 1892), 1.434), and that they were introduced in 1532.

16. See Hetherington, *Chaucer, 1532–1602*, p. 5; Brewer, ed., *The Works* (facsimile), Introduction.

17. There is a complete reprint of the "Life" in Hammond, *Chaucer: A Bibliographical Manual*, pp. 18ff., and valuable further comment in Lounsbury, *Studies*, 1.154–73; Spurgeon, *Chaucer Criticism and Allusion*, 1.ci–cviii.

18. He is described by Sir Anthony Wagner (*The Records and Collections of the College of Arms*, [London, 1952], p. 17) as "a critical scholar of the first rank."

19. This thesis is put forward, with some vigor, by Russell Krauss, *Chaucerian Problems: Especially the Petherton Forestership and the Question of Thomas Chaucer* (1932; reprint, New York: AMS Press, 1973), pp. 50–56.

20. Lounsbury, *Studies*, 1.172–73.

21. Edith Rickert, "Was Chaucer a Student at the Inner Temple?" *Manly Anniversary Studies in Language and Literature* (Chicago: University of Chicago Press, 1923), pp. 20–31; John M. Manly, *Some New Light on Chaucer* (New York: Holt, 1926), pp. 7–14.

22. For a judicious reconsideration of the whole matter, see D. S. Bland, "Chaucer and the Inns of Court: A Re-Examination," *ES* 33 (1952): 145–55. The editors of the *Chaucer Life-Records*, M. M. Crow and Clair C. Olson (Oxford: Oxford University Press, 1966), follow Bland in giving qualified support to the authenticity of Speght's comment.

23. Robert A. Caldwell, "Joseph Holand, Collector and Antiquary," *MP* 40 (1943):295–301, esp. p. 300.

24. For *The Nun's Priest's Tale*, see Derek Pearsall, ed., *The Nun's Priest's Tale*, vol. 2, pt. 9 in Paul Ruggiers and Donald C. Baker, gen. eds. *A Variorum Edition of the Works of Geoffrey Chaucer* (Norman: University of Oklahoma Press, 1983); for *The Assembly of Ladies*, see Derek A. Pearsall, ed., *The Floure and the Leafe and The Assembly of Ladies*, Nelson's Medieval and Renaissance Library (London and Edinburgh: Nelson, 1962).

25. Lounsbury, *Studies*, 1.275–76.

26. It is possible that Speght had done a small amount of collation with a bad manuscript. Francis Thynne, in his *Animadversions* of 1599 on Speght's edition of 1598 (ed. G. Kingsley and F. J. Furnivall, EETS, o.s., no. 9, [1865]), which we shall have occasion to revert to later, speaks as follows: "In those many written Bookes of Chaucer, whiche came to my fathers handes there were manye false copyes . . . of whiche written copies there came to me after my fathers death some fyve and twentye, whereof some had moore, and some fewer tales, and some but two, and some thre, whiche bookes beinge by me partly dispersed aboute xxvi yeres a-goo and partlye stoolen oute of my howse at Popler: I gave diuers of them to Stephen Batemanne, person of Newington, and to diuers other, whiche beinge copies vnperfecte, and some of them corrected by my fathers hande, yt may happen soome of them to coome to somme of your frendes handes; whiche I know yf I see agayne: and yf by anye suche written copies you have corrected Chaucer, you maye as well offende as seme to do good" (pp. 11–12). There may be some truth in this, and a veiled reference to Stow ("your frendes handes"), though Francis may simply be protecting his own and his father's privilege in the matter by casting doubt on anything used by Speght. The collation of Speght's edition of *The General Prologue* with Stow which has been made by Charles Moorman and which he has kindly made available to me does not suggest that Speght made systematic use of any extant manuscript. According to this collation, Speght introduces 109 variants in the 858 lines of *The General Prologue* as represented in Stow. There is no pattern of affiliation in these variants with other manuscripts or printed editions: some are "improvements"; some are merely intended as such. For some, such as the introduction of a substitute line at 219 ("More then a parish priest or a curate"), the substitution of *farled* for Stow's *fassed* at line 233, and the alteration in line 361 ("A goldsmith ther was and an haberdasher"), there is no obvious explanation. Many of these oddities are removed from Speght's second edition.

27. For their removal from the canon, see Skeat's comments in his six-volume edition of Chaucer's works, 1.43–6; also in *Chaucerian and Other Pieces*, published as a seventh volume to the edition (Oxford, 1897), pp. xiv–xv, lxii–lxix; and in *The Chaucer Canon* (Oxford, 1900), pp. 139–41.

28. For more extended discussion, see *The Floure and the Leafe*, ed. cit., pp. 2–4.

29. For full discussion of this poem, see Anthony Jenkins, ed., *The Isle of Ladies, or the Ile of Pleasaunce*, Garland Medieval Texts, no. 2 (New York and London: Garland, 1980).

30. In fact, the added couplet in manuscript Longleat 256 may have been copied in from Speght (Jenkins, ed. cit., p. 7).

31. See the comments in n. 26 above. Francis Thynne, in his *Animadversions*, speaks of the large number of manuscripts that passed through his father's hands, including one subscribed "examinatur Chaucer" (ed. cit., p. 6). From these he drew authentic items to augment the canon, "as you nowe haue donne soome," he says, addressing Speght, "of whiche I ame perswaded (and that not withoute reasone) the originall came from mee" (p. 7). This may be true, though the manuscripts concerned are not the Longleat text of *The Isle of Ladies* or, so far as one can see, the lost quire of the Longleat text of *The Floure and the Leafe*.

32. Jenkins, ed. cit., p. 6. The evident confusion in Francis's mind between the present poem, Lydgate's *Temple of Glass* and Chaucer's *House of Fame* hardly bears investigation.

33. See Alderson and Henderson, *Chaucer and Augustan Scholarship*, pp. 26–27.

34. Ibid., pp. 27–28.

35. Speght once acknowledges (for *yedding*) the existence of differences of opinion on the meaning of the word and twice leaves explanations unattempted (*hoppesteres, ruell bone*).

36. See *The Floure and the Leafe and The Assembly of Ladies*, ed. cit., p. 156.

37. See H. G. Wright, "Thomas Speght as a Lexicographer and Annotator of Chaucer's Works," *ES* 40 (1959):194–208, esp. p. 195.

38. See ibid., p. 198; *DNB*, 1.312–13; and above. See also Andrew G. Watson, "Thomas Allen of Oxford and His Manuscripts," in M. B. Parkes and Andrew G. Watson, eds., *Medieval Scribes, Manuscripts and Libraries: Essays presented to N. R. Ker* (London: Scolar Press, 1978), pp. 279–314.

39. Wright, "Thomas Speght," p. 203.

40. *The Canterbury Tales*, ed. Thomas Tyrwhitt (1775), quoted by Alderson and Henderson, *Chaucer and Augustan Scholarship*, p. 31.

41. The edition of the *Animadversions* cited above (n. 26) contains also a mass of information on Francis's life and other matters.

42. Muscatine, *The Book of Geoffrey Chaucer*, p. 31.

43. Harrison Ross Steeves, *Learned Societies and English Literary Scholarship* (New York: Columbia University Press, 1913), p. 16; May McKisack (*Medieval History in the Tudor Age* [Oxford: Oxford University Press, 1971], pp. 67–68) also speaks respectfully of Francis Thynne's abilities as a scholar.

44. Muscatine, *The Book of Geoffrey Chaucer*, p. 31.

45. Nos. 5080 and 5081 in the *Short-Title Catalogue*. For a technical description of the edition of 1602, see Lowndes (p. 425), Hammond (p. 125–27), Muscatine (pp. 31–35), and Hetherington (pp. 8, 20–21), cited in note 4 above. Hammond gives a succinct account of the changes from 1598 to 1602.

46. For the sources of evidence alluded to here, and in the following remarks on *The Nun's Priest's Tale*, see n. 24 above.

47. Thynne, *Animadversions*, pp. 59–62.

48. In *The Floure and the Leafe*, for instance, note the ineptness of the punctuation added at the end of lines 201, 224, 329, 355, 382, 400, 495, 502, 586.

49. See George B. Pace, "Speght's Chaucer and MS. Gg.4.27," *SB* 21 (1968):225–35. See also above. There is no evidence whatsoever, incidentally, that Gg.4.27 was used by Speght for any purpose other than the acquisition of a copy of the *ABC*.

50. For full discussion of the textual tradition of *Jack Upland*, see P. L. Heyworth, ed., *Jack Upland, Friar Daw's Reply and Upland's Rejoinder* (Oxford: Oxford University Press, 1968).

51. Thynne, *Animadversions*, pp. 75–76.

52. See R. A. Fraser, ed., *The Court of Love* (Durham, N.C.: Duke University Press, 1955).

53. For identification of this encyclopaedic compilation, see Wright, "Speght as Lexicographer," p. 195.

54. See above. In one of the 1602 additions to the address "To the Readers," Speght explains that he has deliberately abandoned the ambition of commenting on and annotating

Chaucer's works ("This course I began in the former Impression, but here of purpose have left it off"), as "a labour rather for a Commentor, for that it concerneth Matter, than for him that intendeth only the explaining of words."

55. This paragraph and the following are much indebted for their selection of information to Wright, "Speght as Lexicographer" (cited above, n. 37).

56. Hammond, *Chaucer: A Bibliographical Manual*, p. 507.

57. See Alderson and Henderson, *Chaucer and Augustan Scholarship*, pp. 47–48. For technical description of the edition of 1687, see the works by Lowndes, Hammond, Muscatine, and Hetherington cited in n. 4 above.

58. Alderson and Henderson, *Chaucer and Augustan Scholarship*, p. 48.

59. As indeed they were. See Hammond, *Chaucer: A Bibliographical Manual*, pp. 276–77, 312–13.

60. See Muscatine, *The Book of Geoffrey Chaucer*, pp. 33, 35; Alderson and Henderson, *Chaucer and Augustan Scholarship*, pp. 40–41; Wright, "Speght as Lexicographer," p. 208; Frederick Tupper, "Dryden and Speght's Chaucer," *MLN* 12 (1897):347–53; Brewer, *Chaucer: The Critical Heritage*, 1.20.

61. See Atcheson L. Hench, "Printer's Copy for Tyrwhitt's Chaucer," *SB* 3 (1950):265–66.

Chapter 5

1. Caroline F. E. Spurgeon, *Five Hundred Years of Chaucer Criticism and Allusion, 1357–1900* (Cambridge: Cambridge University Press, 1925), 1.334. Hereafter cited as Spurgeon. Miss Spurgeon's assignment to Timothy Thomas of this MS notation inserted in a British Museum copy of Urry is acceptable, but her dating, a tentative 1715, is almost certainly too early. Just when Timothy Thomas assumed the task of completing Urry's work is not known, but some period of time seems to have elapsed after Urry's death on March 18, 1715. If we may assume that Lintot was well informed, we should have to conclude that Thomas entered the picture some time between June 30, 1716, when Lintot's printed *Proposals* announced that Anthony Hall was to do the glossary to the edition, and October 5, 1717, when Hearne noted in his diary that "M^r. Tim Thomas, A.B. and Stud^t of X^t Church, does the Glossary to Chaucer since M^r. Urry's Death. He also takes care of the Ed." (Thomas Hearne, *Remarks and Collections*, Oxford: The English Historical Society at Clarendon Press, 1885–1921). Thomas himself confessed, "I was equally a stranger to Mr. *Urry* and his Undertaking, till some time after his Death; when a Person, whose Commands I was in all Duty bound to obey, put the Works of *Chaucer* into my hands, with his Instructions to assist in carrying on this Edition, and to prepare Matter for a *Glossary* to it" (Preface, sig. I2r). Thomas's note itself is a bit of academic doodling which optimistically calculates what he might expect to receive if he were granted a third, a fourth, or a fifth part of the Brome–Christ Church share in the receipts for the edition in return for his labor ("Correcting and Glossary").

2. John Dart, *Westmonasterium*, (London: James Cole et al., 1723), 1.87.

3. Spurgeon, 1.372; for corrected identification of both writer and addressee, see James T. Hillhouse, *The Grub-Street Journal* (Durham, N.C., 1928), p. 300. In the *Gentleman's Magazine* for June, 1758, Samuel Pegge similarly points out that a MS of *The Legend of Good Women* in his possession gives readings for F 59–62 "preferrable to what at present are read in Mr. Urry" (Spurgeon, 1.414).

4. John Walker, ed., *Letters Written by Eminent Persons*, (London: Longman, Hurst, Rees, Orme, Brown [etc.], 1813), 2.97; Spurgeon, 1.376.

5. Walker, ed., *Letters Written by Eminent Persons*, 2.95; Spurgeon, 1.375.

6. See Appendix to Alderson and Henderson, letters 3 and 5.

7. 1798 ed., Appendix to the Preface, 1.xiii.

8. Spurgeon, 1.363.

9. Advertisement to the Glossary, 2.521.

10. In a letter printed in the *Gentleman's Magazine* for June, 1783, Tyrwhitt lodged a strong public protest against Bell's unauthorized use of his text and apparatus and incidentally criticized "Mr. Bell's having printed the greatest part of Chaucer's works from Urry's edition; in which (as you know very well) there is scarce a line as the author wrote it" (Spurgeon, 1.474). Ideally, of course, a better text than Urry's was desirable, but on a more practical level, Tyrwhitt's objection neglects the fact that his own notes and glossary refer repeatedly to Chaucer via the line numbering of the Urry edition. After Anderson the collections of British poets gradually alter the basis of their Chaucerian texts: Alexander Chalmers (1810) uses Tyrwhitt for *CT* and "black-letter editions" for the remaining works; the Chiswick *British Poets* (1822) employs Tyrwhitt for *CT*, but goes back to Thynne (1532, 1542) for all except a few of the other works; Edward Moxon (1843) likewise depends on Tyrwhitt and black-letter texts; it is not until Robert Bell's Chaucer of 1854 that the whole text of Chaucer is again referred to manuscripts. For these and other nineteenth-century editions, see Eleanor P. Hammond, *Chaucer: A Bibliographical Manual* (New York: Macmillan, 1908), pp. 135ff. Hereafter cited as Hammond.

11. *Remarks and Collections*, 5.248; in Urry's list of members of the Oxford company—as recorded by Hearne, 5.248–49—we also find the names of Atterbury, Smalridge, Brome, and Edward Lloyd (identified with "Mus. Ashm.").

12. *Remarks and Collections*, 5.34, 279.

13. Ibid., 3.155.

14. Anton Bohm, *Literary Anecdotes* (Denver: Sans Souci Press, 1963), 1.199n.

15. *Remarks and Collections*, 3.273f. This and most of the subsequent entries in Hearne's diary concerned with Urry's activities are liberally quoted in Spurgeon, 1.315–45.

16. The absence of Oxford MSS in the list is in itself enough to raise a question about the list's completeness. Urry certainly knew about them, Hearne having described some of their points of interest in his 1709 letter to Bagford.

17. Spurgeon, 1.325.

18. *Literary Anecdotes*, 8.304.

19. Royster's additions to Bond in *SP* 25 (1928):336.

20. Printed at the end of Thomas's Preface, sig. m2^r.

21. The date on which Thomas received the charge is uncertain, though it was presumably not long before Hearne's diary entry for October 5, 1717. See note 1 above.

22. *Cider . . . with Notes . . . by Charles Dunster* (1791), p. 10n.; cited by Bowyer in *SP* 28 (1931):507.

23. John M. Manly and Edith Rickert, *The Text of the Canterbury Tales: Studied on the Basis of All Known Manuscripts* (Chicago: University of Chicago Press, 1940), 1.115. This Stow also contains a later collection of the Cholmondeley (now Delamere MS by Timothy Thomas. Tyrwhitt also seems to have used a black-letter Chaucer as the basis for his recording of MS variants, but, unlike Urry, he made the revised black-letter text serve as printer's copy. See Acheson L. Hench, "Printer's Copy for Tyrwhitt's Chaucer," *SB* 3 (1950):265–66. The British Museum catalogue, further, lists a copy of Speght (1602) with MS notes by Tyrwhitt. Harvard College Library possesses [12421.33*] Tyrwhitt's collations of a number of MSS which he used in devising his own text of *CT*. He interleaved a copy of the 1687 Speght edition and recorded MS variants, with brief identification, on the blank leaves, changing the printed text, presumably, only when, in his editorial judgment, it was warranted by MS authority and/or common sense. As F. J. Child observes in a MS accompanying these collations, "None of the Oxford MSS. are here collated. Considerable use must have been made of them: at least Tyrwhitt's printed text does not at all conform to what will be found here."

24. A minor typographical feature of the Urry edition serves to emphasize the likelihood that Urry employed the revised edition of Speght as his copy text. While the usage is not

explained in any of the introductory matter of the volume, proverbial sayings are in Urry's text sometimes set in italics, a device which recalls Speght's use of marginal symbols to call attention to Chaucer's proverbs in the 1602 edition. The Urry text employs such italics rather sparingly, but in certain parts of the work—in the text of *TC*, for example—the lines italicized are consistently the same as those which Speght designated as proverbial.

25. George B. Pace, "The Text of Chaucer's *Purse*," *SB* 1 (1948–49):105–21, says that Urry's text of that poem is "only a sophisticated version of Stow" (p. 112). The Urry text, however, can seldom be confidently identified as coming from a particular black-letter edition. The orthographical and other changes Urry introduced disguise the relationships, and except for such obvious cases as the poems first printed by Speght—e.g., *The Flower and the Leaf*, *Chaucer's Dreme* (i.e., *The Isle of Ladies*), and *Jack Upland*—Stow or Speght might have served almost equally well as "copy" text.

26. If Spurgeon's dating (1712?) of Maurice Johnson's *An Introduction to the Minute Books of the Spalding Society* is even roughly correct, it is obvious that Dart's life of Chaucer was known, to interested antiquaries at least, distinctly earlier than Urry's death. My own inspection of the Introduction (as it appears in *Literary Anecdotes* 6.37 ff.) suggests that it was either composed or revised later, and that no prepublication acquaintance with Dart's biography is necessarily entailed.

27. Thomas Tyrwhitt, ed., *The Canterbury Tales of Chaucer* (London: T. Payne, 1775), 1.xiii.

28. *Westmonasterium*, 1.88.

29. Thomas Morell, ed., *The Canterbury Tales of Chaucer* (London: Morell, 1737), Preface, p. xxiii.

30. Joseph Foster, *Alumni Oxoniensis*, (Nendeln, Lichtenstein: Kraus Reprints, 1968), 4.1474.

31. *Remarks and Collections*, 6.110. For other references to William Thomas and extracts from Hearnes's correspondence with him see the indices to vols. 6 and 7 of *Remarks and Collections*. The reference in 6.51, however, is not to our William Thomas. The presence of at least two other scholarly William Thomases in this period is confusing; ours is "of London" (list of subscribers to vol. 1 of Hall's *Trivet* [Oxford, 1719]), *not* the Cambridge antiquary who edited Dugdale's *Warwickshire* or the William Thomas who was Proctor of Wadham College in Oxford in 1734.

32. *Diary*, as quoted by James F. Royster in his addition to Bond, *SP* 25 (1928):337.

33. Wanley, *Diary*, quoted by Royster in ibid.; Thomas's collations in a printed Urry noted by Tyrwhitt, 1.xiiin.; for Sneyd Davies's letters to T. Thomas in 1738 and 1740, see Spurgeon, 1.383; and John Nichols, *Illustrations of the Literary History of the Eighteenth Century*, vol. 1 (1817), p. 631.

34. Letter to Bagford (1709), in *Robert of Gloucester's Chronicle*, 2.600ff.; Spurgeon, 1.306.

35. The list does not, for example, contain any reference to a MS owned by Thomas Rawlinson which was surely in Urry's hands in 1712 and about which Hearne was obliged to write to Brome in 1715–16 (Spurgeon, 1.342). Manly and Rickert (1.630–31) tentatively identify this MS as Rawlinson Poetry 149. As noted earlier, the list also strangely omits reference to the several MSS in the Bodleian and in the libraries of various Oxford colleges. The detail in which Hearne had treated some of these in his diary during 1709 and in his letter to Bagford would make it almost impossible for Urry to have been ignorant of them. On the basis of Manly and Rickert's descriptions of provenance, the following MSS can be located with certainty in Oxford collections during the period in which Urry worked on his text: Barlow 20, Bodley 686, Corpus Christi 198, Hatton Donat 1, Laud 600, Laud 739, Selden Arch. B.14 (present in T. Thomas's additions to Urry), and Trinity College Arch. 49. Perhaps New College D.314 was also present at this time. It was employed by Morell sometime before 1737 and is listed as a New College MS in his edition. Christ Church 142, though it may have been used by Urry, was not given to the college until later in the century.

36. This is MS Ashmole 781. The only other footnote which is conceivably to be attributed to Urry takes the form of a conjectured emendation to the text of *A Ballad in commendacion of our Ladie* (p. 538).

37. If *Gamelyn* and *The Plowman's Tale* be omitted from consideration, there are several presently known MSS of Manly and Rickert's type *b* (vol. 2, chart 2) which show Urry's order, but Urry's adoption of this scheme almost unquestionably springs from his respect for the tradition of printed texts, in which it had been current since Caxton's time.

38. Hammond, p. 129, is wrong in claiming that the links are added by Urry. Furthermore, the last five lines of the *CyT–PhyT* link, in both Speght and Urry, are practically identical with the lines which Tyrwhitt, on the authority of Harley 7335, accepts as a genuine link between *FrT* and *PhyT*. Robinson (p. 1010) seems to imply that the lines were first printed by Tyrwhitt.

39. Later Tyrwhitt (Introductory Discourse, ed. 1798, 1.88) drops *Gamelyn* from the canon because it does not appear in his MSS "of first authority" and because it is not Chaucerian in style and versification. It should be incidentally noted that the spurious couplet linking *CkT* and Gamelyn which Urry quotes appears in only three of his numbered MSS: VII, X, and XII. Laud 739, not in Urry's list but probably known to him, also carries the link, with one minor variation. [The MSS have been studied by Franklin R. Rogers, "The *Tale of Gamelyn* and the Editing of the *Canterbury Tales*," *JEGP* 58 (1959):49–59.—ACH.]

40. I.e., Urry I. In Urry's printed text (p. 107) the lines, enclosed within brackets, stand incomprehensibly between F 710 and F 711, but this position must be a compositor's error.

41. *Remarks and Collections*, 2.200; Letter to Bagford, *Robert of Gloucester's Chronicle*, 2.601–605 (Spurgeon, 1.307–308).

42. The 1721 edition takes over such a large number of Speght's headings and notes without changes—even perpetuating such "ghost" titles as the obviously misread "Balade of the village without paintyng"—that differences may easily go undetected. In addition to those subjected to comment in my text proper, the following changes should be a matter of record. In *TC* (1.400) the song of Troilus is qualified as "out of Petrarche" (p. 272). The headnote to *LGW* (p. 338) shows concern for order of composition ("This seems to have been written after the *Flower and the Leaf* "). On p. 413 a new heading is provided for the poem which we now recognize as *The Envoy to Bukton. The Complaint of Chaucer to His Purse*, which in 1602 and 1687 had been erroneously assigned to Occleve, is returned to Chaucer (p. 549). Other minor additions appear in notes on pp. 24, 31, and 439.

43. Hammond, p. 458; Spurgeon, 1.207. The *DNB* shows no James Erskine who can be identified as Earl of Kelly, although Kynaston's "Thomas" Erskine is clearly the first earl, who died in 1639. It remained for Tyrwhitt, after citing Urry's note, to take the last step in identifying the author as Robert Henryson (1798 ed., 2.531).

44. In his modernization of the work under the title *The Proclamation of Cupid* (1718), George Sewell felt it necessary to argue for Chaucer's authorship against the ascription to Occleve in "some Editions of *Chaucer*" (Spurgeon, 1.348). Tyrwhitt, it should be observed, uses the evidence of dates emphasized in the 1721 edition as one of his two grounds for rejecting the poem (2.531).

45. Dart strongly reiterates his rejection of *The Plowman's Tale* in *Westmonasterium* (1742), 1.86–87; see Spurgeon under 1723.

46. Thomas also points out Urry's use of the apostrophe to indicate what we would classify as cases of syncope or elision and to distinguish genitive singulars (*'is*) from plural endings in nouns. In the text proper Urry employs these devices only erratically, and the prominence which Thomas gives to the spelling of the genitive springs, conceivably, from his disagreement with Urry's view of the historical source of this case ending.

47. A typographical error, corrected in the "Errata" leaf of the edition.

48. Thomas R. Lounsbury, *Studies in Chaucer* (New York: Harper, 1892), 1.288.

49. Ibid., p. 286. Lounsbury also feels that Urry deserves credit for "noticing, in a vague

way, that there are distinct complete groups of the 'Canterbury Tales' " (p. 286). The edition, it is true, presents a novel system of abbreviated references to *CT* through continuous line-numbering within each of ten "Divisions," as they are called in the explanation of abbreviations prefixed to the Glossary, but only two of the 1721 "Divisions" agree with the textual fragments of *CT* recognized by modern editors, and it may well be Thomas rather than Urry who is responsible for the scheme.

50. Thomas's reliability as a judge of Chaucer's metrics is somewhat tarnished by Tyrwhitt's record (1798 ed., 2.467) of a MS note in a British Museum copy of Urry in which Thomas suggests that *The Tale of Melibee* was written in blank verse.

51. In grappling with Chaucer's metrics, Urry and Thomas, like Morell and Tyrwhitt later, were dealing with issues about which we are today far less dogmatically assured than Lounsbury was . . . . A wide variation in assumptions about syllabic final -*e* is apparent in studies such as Ruth Buchanan McJimsey's *Chaucer's Irregular -E* (New York, 1942), and the controversy between 1947 and 1949 (Southworth, "Chaucer's Final -*E*," *PMLA* 63 [1948]:1101–24; Southworth and Donaldson, "Chaucer's Final -*E* (Continued)," *PMLA* 64 [1949]:601–10). Indeed, Southworth in his *Verses of Cadence* (Oxford, 1954) maintains that Chaucer's rhythmic organization has been misconstrued ever since the seventeenth century and singles out Urry and Tyrwhitt as eighteeth-century proponents of an erroneous scansion which has propagated the "myth of the final -*e*." Proceeding from the far more secure basis of the fullest textual study to which Chaucer has thus far been subjected, Manly and Rickert may be allowed the last word both on final -*e* and on Chaucer's metrics in general. "[N]ot even the earliest and best [MSS] can be depended on to represent Chaucerian usage in the matter of the final -*e*," they claim (3.421), and "It is still uncertain whether Chaucer's versification should always have the regularity assumed for it by the scholars of the late 19C. Current theories of Chaucer's versification are based, not upon the text as found in the MSS, or as established by critical processes, but upon an artificial text made regular by all the devices at the disposal of the scholar" (2.40–41).

52. See Aage Brusendorff, *The Chaucer Tradition* (London: Oxford University Press, 1925), pp. 110–12.

53. John Walker, ed., *Letters Written by Eminent Persons*, 2.97; Spurgeon, 1.376. Both Morell (Preface, p. xxv) and Tyrwhitt (1798 ed., Appendix to the Preface, 1.xiii) emphasize the lack of "notice" or "distinction" of such emendations in their criticism of Urry. Another ground of attack was Urry's orthography. Some of the complaints are comprehensible. Morell and Tyrwhitt, for instance, refer specifically to the respelling of endings in a fashion not warranted by MS usage. Other comments on spelling from John Upton in 1751 (quoted by Mark Noble, *A Bibliographical History of England* [1806], 2.295) down to Lounsbury (*Studies*, 1.287) object to Urry's modernizing of Chaucerian forms, Upton going so far as to compare Urry with an "officious servant of the learned Dr. Woodward, who scoured off the rust from an old shield which his master had just purchased, making it more resemble the new-scoured cover of an old kettle, than the shield of an ancient heroe." This charge is hard to understand, for Urry's spellings are, if anything, more archaic than those of the 1687 Speght. A certain degree of normalization of orthography is present in Urry, but normalized spelling is, after all, a common feature of modern editions such as that of Skeat or, for a recent and radical case, that of E. Talbot Donaldson, ed., *Chaucer's Poetry: An Anthology for the Modern Reader* (New York: Ronald, 1958).

Chapter 6

1. All quotation of Tyrwhitt's edition of *The Canterbury Tales* is taken from the five-volume first edition of 1775–78. For the two-volume posthumous edition of 1798, see below, n. 28. A print of a portrait of Tyrwhitt is included in the edition of 1798; for other extant likenesses cf *Dictionary of British Portraiture*, vol. 2, E. Kilmurray, comp. [London,

1979], 2.212; and for the portrait of Tyrwhitt by an unknown artist in the National Portrait Gallery (cat. no. 2942), cf. K. K. Yung, comp., *National Portrait Gallery: Complete Illustrated Catalogue 1856–1979* (London, 1981), p. 580. For a full account of Tyrwhitt's publications see the article in DNB. On Tyrwhitt as a classical scholar, cf. J. E. Sandys, *A History of Classical Scholarship* (Cambridge, 1908), 2.419–20; and for the context of his work, cf. R. Pfeiffer, *History of Classical Scholarship from 1300–1850* (Oxford: Oxford University Press, 1976), Chaps. 11, 12; and C. O. Brink, "Studi classici e critica testuale in Inghilterra," *Annali della Scuola Normale Superiore di Pisa* 8 (1978):1071–1228, esp. pp. 1176–77. On the Rowley controversy, see L. F. Powell, "Thomas Tyrwhitt and the Rowley Poems," *RES* 7 (1931):314–26), for an account of how Tyrwhitt's attitude developed from implicit acceptance in his first edition of the Rowley poems (1777), to the Appendix added to the third (1778) edition "containing some observations upon the language of the poems attributed to Rowley, tending to prove, that they were written, not by any ancient author, but entirely by Thomas Chatterton"; and finally to Tyrwhitt's pamphlet rejoinder (in 1782) to some responses to this Appendix.

2. "It is so little a while since the world has been informed, that the Palamon and Arcite of Chaucer was taken from the *Theseida* of Boccace, that it would not have been surprizing if another century had elapsed without our knowing that our countryman had also borrowed his Troilus from the *Filostrato* of the same author" (4.85n.).

3. If this critic found the "great proportion of the verses were strictly conformable to the ordinary rules of Metre," then he would conclude this was "by art and design, and not by mere chance." If he found lines deficient, "he would not, I think, immediately condemn the old Bard, as having all at once forgotten the fundamental principles of his art. . . . If he were really (as I have supposed him) a sensible critic, he would be apt rather to expect patiently the solution of his difficulties from more correct manuscripts, or a more complete theory of his author's versification, than to cut the knot, by deciding peremptorily, that the work was composed without any regard to metrical rules" (4.89–91).

4. Recalling Urry's plan to print *ed* and *es* as *id* and *is* where they were to be pronounced, Tyrwhitt comments, "As such a distinction is entirely unsupported by the Mss. and must necessarily very much disfigure the orthography of the language, I cannot think that an Editor has a right to introduce it upon ever so plausible a pretence." And after dismissing his own idea of using apostrophes, he concludes, "But after all a reader, who cannot perform such operations for himself, had better not trouble his head about the Versification of Chaucer" (4.95n). Similarly, on Urry's marking of pronounced *e*'s with an accent: "It would be apt to mislead the ignorant reader (for whom only it can be intended), by making him suppose that the *e* so marked was really to be accented, whereas the true *e* feminine is always to be pronounced with an obscure evanescent sound, and is incapable of bearing any stress or accent" (4.95–96n).

5. These collation papers were bequeathed by F. J. Child, who—though recognizing Tyrwhitt's achievements in other respects—criticized by the more rigid editing ideas of his own time Tyrwhitt's choice of manuscript A, his pragmatic method of moving between his manuscript sources, and the fact that Tyrwhitt's edition consequently presents, to nineteenth-century ideas, "an artificial text." Cf. "Observations on the Language of Chaucer," *Memoirs of the American Academy of Arts and Sciences* 8 (1862):445–502.

6. Cf. A. L. Hench, "Printer's Copy for Tyrwhitt's Chaucer," *SB* 3 (1950):265–66. See also T. J. Monaghan, "Thomas Tyrwhitt (1730–86) and His Contribution to English Scholarship," (Ph.D. diss., Oxford University, 1947); Sister Mary Florence Burns, *A Textual Study of Thomas Tyrwhitt's Edition of the Canterbury Tales (1775–1778)*, (Ann Arbor, Mich.: University Microfilms, 1967); F. B. Thomas, "Thomas Tyrwhitt and *The Canterbury Tales*," *DA* 28 (1967):1088A.

7. Thus, commenting on vagaries in manuscript spelling, Tyrwhitt illustrates his own practice in one aspect of editorial uniformity: "There seems to be no reason for perpetuating varieties of this kind. . . . In this edition therefore, *Hir* is constantly put to signify *Their*; and *Hire* to signify *Her*" (4.109n.).

8. On manuscript A Tyrwhitt comments: "It is also unluckily very imperfect; beginning only at ver. 1204, and ending (with several intermediate breaks) at ver. 12610. in the *Pardoner's Tale*" (1.xxiii). But where A or C.1 is present Tyrwhitt makes most use of them. Where both are absent Tyrwhitt turns to C: his emendations on Speght in the first 18 lines of *The General Prologue*, which he analyzes metrically in his "Essay" (4. 106ff.), seem modeled on C. In using W and T, Tyrwhitt is properly cautious, e.g., "In Ms. T. it is *the Grekish See*; a reading, to which I should have had no objection, if I had found it confirmed by any better Ms." (4.193).

9. In Tyrwhitt's edition the verse lines are numbered through continuously from the start of *The General Prologue* to *The Parson's Prologue*, with page numbers for the prose tales. References are cited thus: *T* 17,368. Modern line equivalents refer to Robinson.

10. Samuel Johnson, *Johnson on Shakespeare*, ed. A. Sherbo, Yale Edition of the Works of Samuel Johnson (Hartford, Conn.: Yale University Press, 1968), 7.94–95.

11. The tale order in Tyrwhitt's edition is thus as follows: *The General Prologue, The Knight's Tale, The Miller's Prologue* and *Tale, The Reeve's Prologue* and *Tale, The Cook's Prologue* and *Tale, The Man of Law's Prologue* and *Tale, The Wife of Bath's Prologue* and *Tale, The Friar's Prologue* and *Tale, The Summoner's Prologue* and *Tale, The Clerk's Prologue* and *Tale, The Merchant's Prologue* and *Tale, The Squire's Prologue* and *Tale, The Franklin's Prologue* and *Tale, The Physician's Prologue* and *Tale, The Pardoner's Prologue* and *Tale, The Shipman's Prologue* and *Tale, The Prioress's Prologue* and *Tale, The Prologue to Sir Thopas, The Tale of Sir Thopas, The Prologue to Melibee, The Tale of Melibee, The Monk's Prologue* and *Tale, The Nun's Priest's Prologue* and *Tale, The Second Nun's Tale, The Canon's Yeoman's Prologue* and *Tale, The Manciple's Prologue* and *Tale, The Parson's Prologue* and *Tale, Chaucer's Retraction*.

12. In his notes (4.289), Tyrwhitt specifies which are here his "best Mss." (A, C.1, Ask. 1 and 2, HA, D, Bod.α, γ, δ) commenting that "the concurrence of the first five Mss. would alone have been more than sufficient to outweigh the authorities in favour of the other Prologue." Caxton's second edition also places *The Squire's Tale* after *The Merchant's Tale*.

13. Cf. Tyrwhitt's note (p. 295): "The authorities for giving this Prologue to the Frankelein, and for placing his tale next to the Squieres, are Mss. A. Ask. 1.2. HA. Bod. α. γ." Another note rejects as scribal the two-line "Third Part" of *The Squire's Tale* (i.e., F 671–72).

14. Cf. Tyrwhitt's note: "So Ms. B. δ. the *one* Ms . . . which countenances the giving of this Prologue to the Shipman," (4.311) and he goes on to list its position in some other manuscripts.

15. Tyrwhitt is very open to the possibilities that manuscripts misinterpreted Chaucer's unfinished work. *The Merchant's Tale*, lines 1305–1306 ("And if thou take a wyf unto thyn hoold, / Ful lightly maystow ben a cokewold"), are excluded from Tyrwhitt's text. His note lists variant lines from manuscripts and continues: "In Mss. Ask. 1. 2. E. H. B. θ. Nc. and both Caxton's Editt. they are entirely omitted, and so I believe they should be. If any one of these couplets should be allowed to be from the hand of Chaucer, it can only be considered as the opening of a new argument, which the author, for some reason or other, immediately abandoned, and consequently would have cancelled, if he had lived to publish his work" (4.283). Cf. Robinson, p. 893

16. Cf. Tyrwhitt's emendations of other garbled lines in Speght (SP):
The Franklin's Tale, line 1065:
> SP: This thing may ye lightly done for me
> T: Lord Phebus, this miracle doth for me (Tyrwhitt's line 11,377)

The Tale of Melibee, line 1300:
> SP: As to minister by my wit the doublenesse
> T: As minister of my wit, the doublenesse (Tyrwhitt's line 16,768)

The Physician's Tale, line 82:
> SP;   Keepeth well tho that he undertake...
> T: To teche hem vertue loke that ye ne slake (Tyrwhitt's line 12,016)

The Pardoner's Tale, lines 817–18:

SP: I woll well that the gold were ours two
        What should we doe, that it might be so . . . ?
T: He wote wel that the gold is with us tweye.
        What shuln we don? what shuln we to him seye? (Tyrwhitt's lines 12,751–52)

17. For other instances cf. Tyrwhitt's line 5527 (*MLT* B[1] 1107): "I am your doughter, your Custance, quod she," or Tyrwhitt's line 6797 (*WBT* D 1215): "For filthe, and elde also, so mote I the." In his notes Tyrwhitt explains that the second *your* in line 5527 and the *so* in line 6797 are added for the meter.

18. Cf. also Tyrwhitt's metrical perceptiveness in some notes: on his line 10,561 ("Tho speken they of Canacees ring") he notes that *Canacees* "should perhaps have had an accent on the first e . . . to shew that it is to be pronounced as of four syllables" (4.291). Or again on his line 761 ("And spake of mirthe amonges other thinges") he notes on *amonges*; "I have ventured to lengthen the common reading *among* by a syllable, as the metre requires it, and Chaucer uses the word so lengthened in other places" (4.215).

19. For other instances, cf. (*The Knight's Tale*):
Tyrwhitt's lines 2031–32:
    With thilke sharpe swerd over his hed
    Yhanging by a subtil twined thred.
Robinson's lines 2029–30:
    With the sharpe swerd over his heed
    Hangynge by a soutil twynes threed . . . .
Tyrwhitt notes: "*Thilke* is from conjecture only. The Mss. read—*the. Sharpe* is a Disyllable in other places. . . . In the next line I have also put *Yhanging* instead of *Hanging*" (4.225). Similarly with Tyrwhitt's line 3308 ("Of Cristes owen werkes for to werche"), Tyrwhitt notes "*Of* is added, from conjecture only" (4.239). And of Tyrwhitt's line 12,542 ("Yplaying atte hasard he hem fond"), Tyrwhitt notes: "I have added the prepositive *y* for the sake of the metre. *Atte* is a dissyllable" (4.309).

20. Cf. Tyrwhitt's note on *MkT* B[2] 2110: "Ver. 14116. the hevene on his nekke longe] This is the reading of the best Mss. and is agreable to Boethius, *loc.Lcit.* thus translated by Chaucer. 'And the last of his labors was, that *he susteined the heven upon his necke* unbowed.' The margin of Ms. C.1. explains *longe* to mean *diu.* The Editt. read, 'And bare *his hed* upon his *spere* long,' " (3.281–2).

21. Letter to Warton on his *Observations on Spenser's Fairy Queen, Boswell's Life of Johnson*, ed. G. B. Hill, rev. L. F. Powell (Oxford: Oxford University Press, 1934), 1.270.

22. Cf. Tyrwhitt's argument for emending the line "Hath in *the Ram* his halve cours yronne" (*GP* A 8) to read *the Bull*, as a solution to difficulties in the time of the pilgrimage discerned by Tyrwhitt (4.121ff.), though the proposed emendation is not carried out in the text. Even where Tyrwhitt is mistaken, however, he shows himself thinking closely and searchingly about the meaning of Chaucer's text in the light of his own reading of medieval works (referring in this case to the *Astrolabe*, Tyrwhitt characteristically comments, "The printed text of this Treatise is so monstrously incorrect, that it cannot be cited with any safety;" p. 122n.).

23. Tyrwhitt notices that Chaucer's Emelye is seen first by Palamon; that the rivals quarrel instantly (Boccaccio's account "without jealousy or rivalship, if not absolutely unnatural, is certainly very insipid and unpoetical"); that Emelye does not notice her lovers; that the rivals meet fiercely in the grove (*Teseida* is "too much in the style of Romance. Chaucer has made them converse more naturally"); and that Chaucer omits the personified prayers (4.135ff.).

24. Tyrwhitt's notes are full of varied instances of editorial shrewdness. He discovers the meaning of the term *askaunce* (*SumT* D 1745) by checking an instance in *Troilus* against the source line in *Filostrato* and thus producing a gloss (4.274). Tyrwhitt also notices (p. 312) that the reading *us* in *ShT* B[2] 12, suggests a female teller for the tale.

25. "The neglect of this precaution . . . has made Mr. Hearne's Glossaries to *Robert of Gloucester* and *Robert of Brunne* of very little use" (5.iii).

26. Tyrwhitt pointed out (5.xviiff.) that works printed in early editions are actually ascribed to other authors, including Henryson's *Testament of Cresseid, La Belle Dame sans Merci, The Letter to Cupid, Gower to King Henry IV,* and various pieces by Lydgate. These, of course, Tyrwhitt dismissed from a place in "Chaucer's works." He also removed from the canon such works as *Jack Upland, Gamelyn, The Tale of Beryn, The Plowman's Tale, The Assembly of Ladies,* and *The Lamentation of Mary Magdalen,* among other spuriously connected pieces.

27. Tyrwhitt's retention in the canon of some now-rejected works inevitably colors his account of Chaucer's life. Thus, *The Court of Love* was taken to show Chaucer's education at Cambridge, though Tyrwhitt is typically reasonable: "This is by no means a decisive proof that he was really educated at Cambridge; but it may be admitted, I think, as a strong argument that he was not educated at Oxford" (1.xxiv–xxv).

28. In 1798 a two-volume posthumous edition of Tyrwhitt's *Canterbury Tales* was published by the Clarendon Press, the Delegates' Preface declaring that they had in this acceded to a proposal from Tyrwhitt's nephew and "out of their own desire to shew every respect on the part of the University to Mr. Tyrwhitt's name and abilities." Moreover, the preface states:

"The Nephew and Executor of the Editor made an offer in the handsomest manner to the Delegates, of a copy of the work, which Mr. Tyrwhitt had reserved for his own use, and in which it was found that he had inserted several emendations and additions; having revised the punctuation and orthography of the Tales themselves, (though in this he seemed to have proceeded no further than the Manciple's Tale,) and in other parts of the work having written some things otherwise than as he first gave them to the world."

The edition of 1798 accordingly reflects these emendations and revisions, though the Preface admits they are not numerous ("For notwithstanding that the corrections alluded to are not numerous, wherever they occur, they are the more deliberate opinions of the Editor himself"). Differences between the edition of 1798 and that of 1775–78 are not extensive: a tidying up of misprints and the inclusion in the notes of material added in appendices in 1775 (cross reference to the Rowley poems as a medieval source—reflecting Tyrwhitt's earlier judgment—is excised). But a few "Additions and Corrections to the Essay, and Introductory Discourse" are added, characteristic of Tyrwhitt's consistent concern in his annotation to understand Chaucer in the context of his times and his sources ("I am obliged to Mr. Steevens for pointing out to me a story, which has a great resemblance in its principal incidents, to the *Freres Tale*"). In another additional note Tyrwhitt essentially maintains the view on Chaucer's meter that he had published in 1775 ("A learned person, whose favours I have already acknowledged . . . cannot acquiesce in this notion, 'that the greatest part of Chaucer's heroic verses, when properly written and pronounced, are verses of eleven syllables'; . . . I am sorry that by an unguarded expression I should have exposed myself to a controversy, which can only be decided by a careful examination of the final syllables of between thirty and forty thousand lines. It would answer my purpose as well to say '*a great part*' instead of '*the greatest part*')." As with these additional notes, changes in punctuation do not occur especially thickly or persistently in the edition of 1798, perhaps because Tyrwhitt's original attention to the punctuation of Chaucer had shown a sense and sensitivity that has been favorably compared with the practice of later editors: cf. Aage Brusendorff, *The Chaucer Tradition* (Oxford: Oxford University Press, 1925), pp. 477–78; and P. L. Heyworth, "The Punctuation of Middle English Texts," in P.L. Heyworth, ed., *Medieval Studies for J. A. W. Bennett Aetatis Suae LXX* (Oxford: Oxford University Press, 1981), pp. 139–57 ("Tyrwhitt's punctuation is full of good sense and is always intelligent"; p. 154, n. 12).

Chapter 7

1. *DNB*, 21.1047.
2. Ibid., p. 1045.
3. Ibid., p. 1048.
4. The choice of black letter probably indicates the editor's and publisher's attitude toward the material: it was "queynte Englysshe." It will be remembered that Blake preferred the older black-letter editions to the more recent and much better roman-type edition by Tyrwhitt. See Alice Miskimin, "The Illustrated Eighteenth-Century Chaucer," *MP* 77 (1979):26–55.
5. W. W. Skeat, ed., *The Vision of William Concerning Piers the Plowman*, 2 vols. (London: Oxford University Press, Humphrey Milford, 1886; reprint, 1924), 2.lxxviii. Skeat goes on (p. lxxviin.) to express his *"very great* obligations" (italics Skeat's) to Wright's work, but he also calls his readers' attention to more than 50 misprints in Wright's *Piers* (p. lxxviii). Wright used a similar approach to the mystery plays, though they present a different sort of editorial problem. See R. M. Lumiansky and David Mills, eds., *The Chester Mystery Cycle*, EETS (London: Oxford University Press, 1974), p. xxvii: "Wright printed A [Additional 10305] with some corrections from R [Harley 2103] and a few readings from H [Harley 2124]; he did not consider a full collation of the five cyclic manuscripts worth the effort."
6. Quoted by W. W. Skeat, *The Chaucer Canon* (Oxford: Clarendon Press, 1900; reprint, New York: Haskell House, 1965), p. 23, hereafter cited as *Canon*. Skeat's line-by-line annotation of Wright's remarks is reproduced below.
7. Thomas Wright, ed., *The Canterbury Tales of Geoffrey Chaucer*, 3 vols. (London: Percy Society, 1847–51), 1.xxxiii.
8. For a full account of Tyrwhitt's methods, see B. A. Windeatt's chapter in this volume, together with the section on his edition in the textual introduction to my edition of *The Miller's Tale* for the *Variorum Chaucer* (Norman: University of Oklahoma Press, 1983), pp. 80, 86–87, and 101–10.
9. Sir Paul Harvey, *The Oxford Companion to Classical Literature* (Oxford: Clarendon Press, 1946), p. 153.
10. J. M. Manly and Edith Rickert, *The Text of the Canterbury Tales*, 8 vols. (Chicago: University of Chicago Press, 1940), 1.219–30. See also the section on Ha[4] in the textual introduction to my edition of *The Miller's Tale* for the *Variorum Chaucer*, pp. 70–72.
11. Wright, 1.xxxv–xxxvii; for further evidence of Wright's impatience with collation, see n. 5 above.
12. Henry Bradshaw was tantalized by the engaging readings of Ha[4], but he is said to have abandoned his edition of *The Canterbury Tales* because he was unable to account for its divergences; see Eleanor Hammond, *Chaucer: A Bibliographical Manual* (New York: Macmillan, 1908), p. 178; and consult the chapter on Skeat by A. S. G. Edwards in this volume. Alfred Pollard thought that Ha[4] contained many readings that might represent Chaucer's own corrections upon a finished copy (Hammond, *Chaucer*, p. 178). Furnivall regretted not having included it in his Six-Text edition, and he later published a separate volume for the Chaucer Society which is an accurate diplomatic transcription (London: Trübner, 1885; see p. v). Skeat was of two minds about the manuscript. In two notes he says, "There is no doubt as to its early age and its frequent helpfulness in difficult passages. It offers readings which are better than those of the Six-Text, and should certainly be preferred." Compare this with "It is not the kind of MS. that should be greatly trusted. [Some of its readings are] due to a terrible blundering on the part of the scribe"; *The Complete Works of Geoffrey Chaucer*, 6 vols. (Oxford: Clarendon Press, 1894), 4.vii, 5.xx.
13. See below, the 1851 review of Wright's edition, for an early recognition of the quality of El. George Kane's essay on Manly-Rickert in this volume evaluates the relative merits of El and Hg.

14. See n. 12 above.

15. "Antiquarian Book Clubs," *Quarterly Review* 164 (1848):309–42. The author is identified in *DNB* 21.1048. The *DNB* article on Garnett, 7.885–86, says that he was a self-taught philologist and churchman who eventually became assistant keeper for printed books in the British Museum. At his death it was said, "Few men have left so fragrant a memory," and it was remarked that he displayed "playful wit at unmasking quackery." The tone of his review belies both the fragrance and the playfulness.

16. *Athenaeum* 23 (1851):294–95. None of the major descriptions of El mentions Stafford as a one-time owner of the manuscript. I am, however, grateful to Sara S. Hodson, assistant curator of literary manuscripts, Huntington Library, San Marino, Calif., for pointing out to me that George Granville Leveson-Gower, first marquis of Stafford, succeeded his maternal uncle, the last duke of Bridgewater, on March 8, 1803; in 1833 he was created duke of Sutherland. The second surviving and youngest son of Sutherland was Francis Leveson-Gower, first earl of Ellesmere. Thus it appears that the Bridgewater library, including El, passed from the duke of Bridgewater to Stafford and then to the earl of Ellesmere, who added to the library and from whose heirs Henry Huntington acquired the Bridgewater library in 1917. Until I made inquiries about the manuscript alluded to in the *Athenaeum* review of Wright's edition, the Huntington staff had not been aware of this early mention of El.

17. Hammond, *Chaucer*, pp. 142–43; Skeat, *Canon*, p. 26. The Crowell edition is not dated, but Hammond says that it was published in 1880.

18. Quoted in Skeat, *Canon*, pp. 22–23. Hammond, *Chaucer*, p. 211, says that Child was confident of the accuracy of Wright's text, but clearly that is not true.

19. Skeat, *Canon*, pp. 22–23, points out in a note that Child had no means of knowing that Wright's edition was in no sense a trustworthy reprint.

20. Ibid., pp. 28, 25.

21. In his chapter on Skeat in this volume Edwards says: "Thomas Wright's 1847–51 edition of *The Canterbury Tales* was notable as the first since Tyrwhitt to return to the manuscripts, albeit in a slapdash way. It is only with Richard Morris's 1866 revision of the 1845 Aldine Chaucer that there is the first serious attempt to use manuscript evidence as a basis for establishing texts." This is evidently true only of the Minor Poems; both the Aldine and the Morris revision simply reprint Tyrwhitt's text of *The Canterbury Tales*. See Hammond, *Chaucer*, p. 140.

Chapter 8

1. *Frederick James Furnivall: A Volume of Personal Record* (Oxford: Oxford University Press, 1911), with a brief biography by John Munro and many personal accounts and tributes by scholars who knew and worked with Furnivall, gives a good flavor of the man and his many-sided personality. K. M. Elisabeth Murray, in the biography of her grandfather, J. A. H. Murray, *Caught in the Web of Words* (New Haven, Conn.: Yale University Press, 1977), gives, passim, a portrait of Furnivall as he impinged upon the making of the *New English Dictionary*. Derek Brewer, in a brief but lucid and delightful address, presents the core of the man's personality and his passion for work in "Furnivall and the Old Chaucer Society," *Chaucer Newsletter* 1, no. 2 (Summer, 1979):1–6.

2. Chaucer Society (London: N. Trübner & Co., 1868), pp. 2–3.

3. Ibid., p. 3. Furnivall described himself in letters to Bradshaw as "something of an American," and he loathed the fashionable Englishman's contempt for the Yankee and particularly deplored the British attitude toward American English. See his prints of extracts from British newspapers in relation to this (*Temporary Prefaces*, p. 4).

4. *Temporary Prefaces*, p. 6.

5. K. M. Elisabeth Murray, in her life of her grandfather (see n. 1 above), tends to take the view of Murray, that Furnivall, while an excellent fellow in his way, was essentially an amateur who interfered too much in the *NED*. Murray's own assessment in *Frederick James Furnivall*, while quite impersonal in comparison with the warmth of most of the other tributes (suggesting that his granddaughter is right in her opinion) is nevertheless scrupulously detailed in describing Furnivall's originating role in the dictionary scheme and his contribution as the most voluminous compiler of slips of all who contributed to the *NED*. Skeat, on the other hand, in the same volume, does not mention the enormous help that Furnivall had been to him (other than very generally), but says downrightly that the *NED* was the brainchild of Furnivall, who had done much of the work before Murray even started, and that it is finally to Furnivall that the principal credit must go. Skeat, of course, was closely involved with the *NED* and on good terms with both men, but in view of his closer relation with Furnivall, and in view of Furnivall's role in assisting the career of the younger Skeat, some of this assessment must be discounted. The truth probably lies somewhere between the two views.

6. In the essay "Origin and Development of Our Plan," (1.1) Manly makes clear that the Furnivall prints pointed the way for the great Chicago work, which was enabled to go beyond the Chaucer Society achievement, to some extent at any rate, by the availability of cheap photographic reproduction, which was, of course, unavailable very much earlier. Who can doubt that if this method had been available to Furnivall *all* the *Canterbury Tales* manuscripts known to exist would have been printed? But the Manly-Rickert *Text*, of course, became a great *edition*, assembling and organizing the material which Furnivall, even had he had access to the new technology, would probably only have printed. He saw himself, as always, as preparing the ground for other scholars.

7. Donald C. Baker, "The Evolution of Henry Bradshaw's Idea of the Order of *The Canterbury Tales*," *Chaucer Newsletter* 3 (Winter, 1981):2–6.

8. For a survey, see Robert Pratt, "The Order of the *Canterbury Tales*," *PMLA* 66 (1951):1141–67. Pratt supported the Bradshaw order, and subsequently followed it in his edition. Other modern editors continue generally to follow the Ellesmere order.

9. The letters are nos. 607 and 608, box 2, Add. 2591, University Library, Cambridge. Every reasonable attempt has been made to reach any who might have a legal right in these letters, but in this I have been unsuccessful. Bradshaw, of course, never married. I thank the University Library, Cambridge, for making the correspondence available to me.

10. This letter is dated from the University Library, Cambridge August 16, 1867, and is no. 384a in box 2, Add. 2591, University Library, Cambridge.

11. J. Koch, *A Detailed Comparison of the Eight Manuscripts of Chaucer's Canterbury Tales* . . . , Chaucer Society (London: Kegan Paul, Trench, Trübner & Co., 1913 for 1907); Ewald Flügel, "A New Collation of the Ellesmere MS.," *Anglia* 30 (1907):401–12.

12. W. W. Skeat, *The Eight-Text Edition of the Canterbury Tales*, Chaucer Society (London: Kegan Paul, Trench, Trübner & Co., 1909 for 1905).

13. Ibid., p. 30.

14. W. W. Skeat, *The Evolution of the Canterbury Tales*, Chaucer Society (London: Kegan Paul, Trench, Trübner & Co., 1907 for 1903).

15. Skeat, *The Eight-Text Edition of the Canterbury Tales*, p. 55.

Chapter 9

1. I refer to Skeat's edition of *The Complete Works of Geoffrey Chaucer*, 6 vols. (Oxford: Clarendon Press, 1894), by this title throughout. All citations from this edition are by volume and page and are generally incorporated into the text without additional reference.

2. For authoritative assessments of these editions see Eleanor P. Hammond, *Chaucer: A Bibliographical Manual* (New York: Macmillan, 1908).

3. On Morris's edition, see ibid., p. 141.

4. I quote from the Introduction to Skeat's *A Student's Pastime* (Oxford: Clarendon Press, 1896), p. viii. This autobiographical memoir remains the fullest account of Skeat's life yet undertaken. On Cockayne, see the *DNB*.

5. Skeat, *A Student's Pastime*, p. xx.

6. Ibid., p. xxi.

7. Ibid., p. xxv.

8. This letter is now Cambridge University Library Add. 2591 (240).

9. Skeat, *A Student's Pastime*, p. xxv.

10. There is no bibliography of Skeat, though one is at present projected by Philip N. Cronenwett, of Dartmouth College Library. There are partial listings in *A Student's Pastime* and in the *DNB* article on Skeat.

11. Cambridge University Library Add. 2591 (240).

12. The standard biography of Bradshaw remains G. W. Prothero, *A Memoir of Henry Bradshaw* (1888); a new study of his life by David McKitterick is in progress. See also the very interesting article by J. C. T. Oates, "Young Henry Bradshaw," in D. E. Rhodes, ed., *Essays in Honor of Victor Scholderer* (Mainz, 1970), pp. 276–81.

13. The only portions of his work on Chaucer that were ever published were his privately printed editions of *The Legend of Good Women* and *The Complaint of Mars* (both of which appeared in 1864), *The Skeleton of Chaucer's Canterbury Tales* (1868) and a list of editions of Chaucer's works in Skeat's EETS edition of the *Astrolabe* (1872), p. xxvi.

14. Prothero, *Memoir of Bradshaw*, p. 109.

15. Ibid., p. 223.

16. Ibid.; Prothero's assertion that he reverted to this idea in March, 1866, is clearly in error.

17. Ibid., p. 224.

18. This letter is now Cambridge University Library Add. 2592 (244); it is dated November 10, 1870.

19. Bradshaw Papers, box 1, Cambridge University Library.

20. This is the interpretation that I place on a letter of Furnivall's printed in Prothero, *Memoir of Bradshaw*, p. 222; dated March, 1872, it is an attempt "to urge you to edit your Globe Chaucer at once, and do justice to your work. . . . if you go on refusing to set down and produce your results, you'll leave your friends to lament, when you die, the waste of power in you." I do not know what weight can be placed on an assertion of Aldis Wright's, reported in ibid., p. 225n., that it was Bradshaw's "inability to account for the wide divergences which distinguish [Harley 7334] of the *Canterbury Tales*" that led to his procrastination. One suspects that the reasons were more complex.

21. Skeat did not wish a biography and ordered that his papers were to be burned after his death. Apparently his family complied, and only scattered papers exist in the Skeat-Furnivall Library in King's College, London, and among the Henry Bradshaw Papers in Cambridge University Library. I have not had access to the Minutes of the Delegates of the Clarendon Press. The Letter Books of Oxford University Press have been of some assistance, but a number of potentially relevant volumes are missing. (I am most grateful to R. E. Vyse, assistant archivist, Bodleian Library, Oxford, for her assistance with the press's records.)

22. The draft table of contents appears in Cambridge University Library Add. 2592 (244), pp. 5–6.

23. The earliest record of this seventh volume that I have been able to find is a letter from C. E. Doble, assistant secretary to the Clarendon Press, of October 22, 1894, to Skeat, agreeing to publish a volume of about six hundred pages of works attributed to Chaucer (letter book 60, Oxford University Press Archives, Bodleian Library, Oxford).

24. Skeat had apparently suggested publication at monthly intervals. Doble countered by suggesting two-monthly ones, observing that "the demand on less opulent Chaucer students, of (perhaps) twelve and sixpence a month might be a little terrifying" (letter of December 18, 1893, letter book 59, Oxford University Press Archives).

25. Letter book 59, Oxford University Press Archives.

26. Letter of December 17, 1894, letter book 61, Oxford University Press Archives.

27. *Athenaeum*, April 28, 1894, p. 535.

28. *Quarterly Review* 180 (1895):548.

29. E. Flügel, "Skeat's Great Edition of Chaucer," *Dial*, February 16, 1895, p. 116.

30. *Nation*, 1895, p. 240.

31. For Skeat's (generally dismissive) views on the achievements of his predecessors, see 5.ix–xvii.

32. Skeat, *A Student's Pastime*, p. xxiii.

33. Ibid.

34. Ibid.

35. See her *Caught in the Web of Words* (New Haven, Conn., Yale University Press, 1977), for her account of Furnivall's relationship with her grandfather James Murray and the origins of the *New English Dictionary*.

36. See E. Flügel, "A New Collation of the Ellesmere MS.," *Anglia* 30 (1907):401–12, for a confirmation of the general accuracy of Furnivall's transcriptions. This is not to suggest that Skeat's treatment is as accurate as one would wish. There are unquestionably a number of cases where Skeat either silently departs from his base manuscript or invents readings. The most striking example of the latter is in *The Canterbury Tales*, where Skeat records a number of readings from Hengwrt after I 550, even though the manuscript breaks off there (see, e.g., I 595, 629, 634, 641). I have not attempted any full record of his suppression of departures from his base manuscript, but I have noticed enough instances to suggest that this was a general but not a pervasive feature of his text (I am thinking here of substantive changes, not simply orthographic ones which will be discussed below).

37. "The Campsall MS . . . has been printed in full, as written, for the Chaucer Society; and I have relied upon the accuracy of this well-edited print" (2.xviii-lxix).

38. "No real advance towards a better text was made until Dr. Furnivall brought out, for the Chaucer Society, his valuable and exact prints of the manuscripts themselves. This splendid and important work gives the texts *in extenso* of all the MSS. [which Skeat used]" (2.liv).

39. "I must here acknowledge my great debt to Dr. Furnivall, whose excellent, careful, and exact reproduction in print of the various MSS. leaves nothing to be desired and is a great boon to Chaucer scholars" (1.48).

40. In discussing his base manuscript, Cambridge University Library Ii.3.21, Skeat observes, "The English portion of it was edited by Dr. Furnivall for the Chaucer Society in 1886; and I have usually relied on this very useful edition" (2.xxxvii).

41. Letter of January 26, 1871, Bradshaw Papers, box 1.

42. Letter of February 8, 1871, Bradshaw Papers, box 1.

43. Furnivall's scheme of printing parallel texts wherever possible (discussed by Donald C. Baker in his chapter of this volume) was particularly helpful for collation. In his edition of *The Legend of Good Women* (1889), Skeat observes "how much we are indebted to the publications of the Chaucer Society. I have obtained my results [i.e., his emendations] by the easy process of collating the Parallel-Texts, all conveniently printed in full and side by side, so that the eye can take in two or three texts at a glance. It then becomes an easy task to collate the texts line by line and word by word" (p. li).

44. I quote from the original text of this letter in Cambridge University Library Add. 2592 (502); the complete text is printed with only trifling variations in Prothero, *Memoir of Bradshaw*, pp. 358–59.

45. See Skeat's discussion (1.1–16) for some account of his changing views; Hammond, *Chaucer*, p. 452; and Ronald Sutherland, ed., *The Romaunt of the Rose and Le Roman de La Rose* (Oxford: Basil Blackwell, 1967), pp. ix–xi.

46. "Few happier hits have been made than the convincing argument which we are glad to owe to Mr. Bradshaw, whose knowledge of Chaucer's text was believed by many scholars to be without parallel" (3.419).

47. He gives no credit to Bradshaw for this discovery either in his 1889 edition of the *Legend* or in the edition included in vol. 3 of the Charendon Chaucer. In vol. 6 he remarks, "The discovery that the Prologue exists in two separate forms, both of them being genuine, was really made by Mr. Henry Bradshaw, who was familiar with the Cambridge MS. [Gg.4.27] (which contains the earlier version) for some time before he disclosed the full significance of it" (6.xx).

48. *Athenaeum*, April 28, 1844, p. 535.

49. It is true that Skeat does give parenthetically the lineations of Tyrwhitt's and Wright's editions (both different), but they are already made very hard to use by his adoption of the "Bradshaw shift."

50. See the excellent discussion by Larry Benson, "The Order of the *Canterbury Tales*," *SAC* 3 (1981):77–120, especially pp. 113–16.

51. Cf. Walter W. Skeat, *The Evolution of the Canterbury Tales* (London: Kegan Paul, Trench, Trübner, 1907): "The wrong place is therefore mentioned first. The simplest, and I believe the only true way, is to admit the fact and leave it. I do not doubt that Chaucer could easily have set it right; but if we are to go by the evidence, it is obvious that he never even attempted it . . . instead of considering what Chaucer ought to have done, we have rather to consider what he actually did" (pp. 30, 31).

52. Hammond, *Chaucer*, pp. 145–46.

53. Both are collated for B 1163–90; Sloane is also cited in the readings for the colophons of *The General Prologue* and *The Physician's Tale* (4.25, 298).

54. At, e.g., B 47, B 4637–52, D 583, D 717, and also in a stanza rejected in Ellesmere in E (see 4.424).

55. E.g., I 610, 630, 640, 677, 700.

56. E.g., B 1995, B 4637–52, D 717.

57. This is also used at B 4637–52 and at D 2201.

58. At, e.g., I 588.

59. E.g. A 1049, B 606, B 4031.

60. E.g., A 18, A 24.

61. E.g., A 613, A 629, A 761, A 785, B 4371, B 4380, B 4386, C 478, C 479.

62. At B 1189: the emendation of *Phisylas* to *physices*.

63. B 497, B 882, B 2252, B 2253, C 871, D 1647, D 2289, E 2240, and F 620 are the only ones I have noted.

64. E.g., B 2623, B 2624, G 277, I 5, I 177, I 983. Skeat's use of square brackets is generally erratic. Most often but not invariably he uses them to indicate conjectural emendations. In his text of *The Book of the Duchess* (one which he heavily emends), there are a number of points where such emendations are not placed in square brackets, e.g. lines 107, 158–59, 204, 348, 366, 652, 1020, 1264, 1266. See also his text of *The Parliament of Fowls*, lines 318, 396. And elsewhere he does put readings that have manuscript authority in square brackets: e.g. *TC* I.496. It is instructive to compare Skeat's 1872 edition of the *Astrolabe* for the Chaucer Society with the text he printed in the Clarendon Chaucer (3.175–232). In the former he announces: "Whenever any change of even slight importance is made, notice is drawn to the alteration by the use of square brackets" (p. vii). In the Clarendon edition all the square brackets in the text are silently removed.

65. Cf., e.g., A 1031, where he rejects Ellesmere's elliptical "This Palamon and his felawe Arcite" for the more explicit "Dwellen this Palamoun and eek Arcite"; or D 1568, where Ellesmere's "The carl spak oon but he thoughte another" becomes "The carl spak oo thing, but he thoughte another."

66. Cf., e.g., *KnT* A 1091, where Skeat contrives to create an inept line "We moste endure it: this is the short and pleyn" where Ellesmere is the only manuscript to omit "it." There are numerous instances where Skeat allows the quantitative weight of manuscript testimony to change Ellesmere where readings seem indifferent or Ellesmere is superior; for example, B 553, D 1332 (where he creates a hypermetric line), F 158.

67. Cf., e.g., A 923, A 1063, A 1179, A 1838, C 807, D 49, D 220, D 2062, D 2190, E 829, E 1706.

68. Cf., e.g., F 491, F 1129, G 806, H 76—all points where Skeat believes Ellesmere to be defective.

69. This includes five points where Skeat silently emends: B 4047, 4302, 4362, 4445, 4561.

70. In addition to the five noted in note 68 above, these are B 4045, 4068, 4072, 4084, 4117, 4132, 4167, 4181, 4200, 4219, 4296, 4309, 4374, 4404, 4434, 4448, 4452, 4482, 4489, 4491, 4552, 4575, 4594, 4601, 4608, 4612, 4613.

71. At B 4047, 4079, 4117, 4121, 4168, 4274, 4275, 4302, 4339, 4362, 4374, 4382, 4445, 4504, 4516, 4576, 4631.

72. The readings he cites for Ellesmere do not appear in Furnivall's Six-Text edition at B 4168 and 4339.

73. R. K. Root, ed., *The Book of Troilus and Criseyde*, (Princeton, N.J.: Princeton, University Press, 1926), p. lxix.

74. See, for example, Kittredge's criticism of Skeat's treatment of this manuscript and his editing of *Troilus* in general in his review in *Nation*, November 1, 1894, p. 329.

75. On Skeat's neglect of this manuscript and the early printed editions see G. G. Macaulay, "Troilus and Cressida [*sic*] in Prof. Skeat's Edition," *Academy*, April 20, 1895, pp. 338–39; Macaulay disputes a number of Skeat's readings here.

76. See the demonstration by Flügel in his review of Skeat in *Dial* February 16, 1895, pp. 118–19; he concludes that Skeat's text is "certainly not a *final* one, and certainly lacks the first requirement of a good text—a full consideration and a patient registration of all the MS. material."

77. In a check of one passage in *The Canterbury Tales* (A 165–269) I noted ten instances where Skeat has suppressed final -*e*'s in Ellesmere: A 170, 172, 208, 218, 229, 231, 232, 235, 260, 262. It must be said that in only three of these instances (A 172, 218, 260) is the suppression silent.

78. For example, in *The Cook's Tale* (A 4365–4422) Skeat makes several silent phonetic adjustments which have metrical effect: A 4368, MS *felwe* is printed as *felawe*; 4419, MS *owene* is printed as *owne*; 4421, MS *contenance* is printed as *countenance*.

79. See for example Kittredge's strictures on the handling of the versification of *The Canterbury Tales* in his review in *Nation*, November 1, 1894, p. 330, where he is criticized for inconsistency and the misrepresentation of Chaucer's scansion.

80. Kittredge discusses Skeat's use of earlier material as printer's copy for the Clarendon Chaucer in his review in *Nation*, October 25, 1894, pp. 309–10; he concludes that the process of revision has been imperfect: "Much has been done, but much has been passed over, sometimes deliberately—the editor maintaining his old position—sometimes, we fear, hastily" (p. 310).

81. See, for example, the comments of G. C. Macaulay, " 'Troilus and Criseyde' in Prof. Skeat's Edition," *Academy*, April 6, 1895, pp. 297–98; and Kittredge in *Nation*, November 1, 1894, pp. 329–30: "The notes are rather scanty. . . . they are not well distributed, many places needing annotation having none, though others that require it less are provided for; and they are not seldom either quite wrong or of highly questionably correctness" (p. 330).

82. In his review in *Dial*, February 18, 1895, p. 120.

83. I owe this point to Malcolm Andrew, who has reached this opinion in comparing editions in connection with his work on the *Variorum Chaucer*.

84. On Bradshaw's development of rhyme tests see Prothero, *Memoir of Bradshaw*, pp. 351–53 (quoting in part information supplied by Skeat); and Skeat, *The Chaucer Canon* (Oxford: Clarendon Press, 1900), esp. pp. 45–55.

85. Skeat first discovered this in April, 1891, and printed it initially in *Athenaeum*, April 4, 1891, p. 440.

86. These are *Complaint to my Mortal Foe* (4.xxvii–xxviii) and *Complaint to my Lode Sterre* (4.xxix–xxxi).

87. See 1. 75–76 n. 4; he remarks: "I think this proves I know how to estimate internal evidence aright."

88. Cf., e.g., 1.80: "The critics who brush aside such a statement as this [the collocation of *Merciless Beaute* with Chaucer poems of undisputed authorship] should learn to look at MSS. for themselves. . . . To weigh the evidence of a MS., it must be personally inspected by such as have had some experience." Or again, defending *Against Women Unconstant*: "It would be decent, on the part of such critics as do not examine the MSS., to speak of my opinions in a less contemptuous way" (1.88n.1). It is unclear whom Skeat has in mind.

89. There is extant among the Bradshaw papers a letter from Skeat to Bradshaw of 22 May, 1877 which reads: "Dear Bradshaw, Re-Romaunt of the Rose.—Not Chaucer's because written (originally) in a Northern dialect. I have just noted some rimes which seem to me most conclusive: & send a note of some to see whether you have noted them too" (Cambridge University Library Add. 2592 [478]).

90. See n. 45 above for references to account for Skeat's changing views about the *Romaunt*.

91. I gratefully acknowledge the assistance of the following in the preparation of this article: Patricia Methven, archivist, King's College Library, University of London; David McKitterick, Cambridge University Library; and Ruth Vyse, assistant archivist, Bodleian Library, Oxford.

Chapter 10

1. This assessment comes from the fullest biography I have found, the obituary at *Speculum* 26 (1951):576–77. Root's editorial work on the *Troilus* is not limited simply to *The Book of Troilus and Criseyde* (Princeton, N.J.: Princeton University Press, 1926); hereafter cited as *Book*; one must also take into account *The Manuscripts of Chaucer's Troilus*, Chaucer Society, 1st ser., no. 98 (1914; New York: Johnson, 1967); and *The Textual Tradition of Chaucer's Troilus*, Chaucer Society, 1st ser., no. 99 (1916; New York: Johnson, 1967). Root also proofread and saw through the press a volume of *Specimen Extracts*, Chaucer Society, 1st ser., no. 89 (1914; New York: Johnson, 1967).

2. For Root's reception and use of McCormick's materials, see *The Textual Tradition*, pp. vii–viii (the volume is dedicated to Root's predecessor). For McCormick's biography, see *DNB, 1922–1930* (London: Oxford University Press, 1937), pp. 527–28. McCormick began work toward an edition at the turn of the 1890s; the need for such an endeavor was obvious, since no editor had ever surveyed the full evidence for the text (for the techniques of Urry and of earlier nineteenth-century editors, see elsewhere in this volume and Root, *Book*, pp. lxvii–lxix). McCormick, harried by the press of other duties, published almost none of his findings: neither Chaucer Society, 1st ser., no. 89, nor 2d ser., no. 42, each supposed to elucidate the manuscript relations, ever appeared. For McCormick's statement that a stemma cannot be constructed, see *An English Miscellany Presented to Dr. Furnivall* (Oxford: Clarendon Press, 1901), pp. 298–99.

3. For McCormick's view of the revisions, see the report of his paper read to the Philological Society on December 6, 1895, *Academy* 48 (1895):552; and his brief textual introduction in Alfred W. Pollard et al., *The Works of Geoffrey Chaucer* (London: Macmillan, 1898), pp. xli–xlii. McCormick's views are stated in opposition to Skeat's presentation of an eclectic γ text relying on Cp and Cl; see further, Root, *Book*, p. lxix.

4. Such is demonstrably the case with *Troilus*, particularly in Root's account. Seven of the sixteen manuscripts shift from one of Root's recensions to another: Gg H_2 H_3 H_4 H_5 J S_1. H_2 is a large fragment, completed to give a full text by three later scribes, and its change of recension likely reflects the two separate bouts of copying. But all the other texts except J persistently shift affiliations and must have conflated discrete textual traditions. And Ph shows after-the-fact conflation, supplying some α omissions on inserted sheets.

5. See J. H. G. Grattan, "The Text of *Piers Plowman*: Critical Lucubrations with Special Reference to the Independent Substitution of Similars," *SP* 44 (1947):593–604; and George Kane and E. Talbot Donaldson, eds., *Piers Plowman: The B Version* (London: Athlone, 1975), pp. 24, 32, 37, 47, 48, 63. This was a possibility of which Root was aware, though he thought most such variants trivial and recognizable; see, for example, *The Textual Tradition*, p. ix.

6. See such comments as *The Textual Tradition*, pp. 79, 125, 260. McCormick was wiser and stated categorically that all the texts were "contaminated"; see *An English Miscellany*, p. 298.

7. These readings are, following Root's lineation, 1.890–96 (absent from Root's βγ), 3.1401–14 (appear after line 1323 in Root's αγ), 3.1744–71 (absent from Root's α), 4.953–1085 (absent from Root's α), 5.1807–27 (absent from Root's α). A sixth possible example is 4.750–56 (appear after line 735 in α). For the note in J see the facsimile in *The Manuscripts*, p. 34; and Root's discussion, *The Textual Tradition*, pp. 217–19. Not all these examples have quite the pristine form Root claimed for them. Only H_2 actually omits 3.1744–71, though it has been added on a later inserted leaf in Ph. And no α manuscript actually omits 5.1807–27. The text is lacking in H_2H_4, *both β copies*, supplied on an inserted leaf in Ph, and present in the other extant α copies J H_3 (Gg lacks the leaves with these stanzas).

8. See B. A. Windeatt's compelling demonstration that these passages are integral portions of the poem in "The Text of the *Troilus*," in Mary Salu, ed., *Essays on Troilus and Criseyde* (Cambridge: Brewer, 1979), pp. 1–22, especially pp. 4–11. Windeatt's study, which summarizes the results of his Cambridge dissertation (see *Index of Theses Accepted* 25, no. 2 [1977]:6), is an important prolegomenon to any future text. One might further note that the omission of 1.890–96 probably reflects a simple eye-skip error: scribes who knew that the next block to be copied was a stanza beginning with "And" returned to their copy at line 897, rather than line 890.

9. *The Textual Tradition*, p. 53; see also further evocations of this view at pp. ix, 33, 36, 66, 69, 72–73, 126, 221, 248, 250–52.

10. For part of the activity of the Ph scribe, see G. H. Russell and Venetia Nathan, "A *Piers Plowman* Manuscript in the Huntington Library," *HLQ* 26 (1963):119–30. Root's theory rests in part on taking Ph readings as authorial and the center of the α tradition, a claim hard to sustain in the light of this scribe's independence and sophistication.

11. Thus Root almost forgets to identify α as a genetic group (or scribal version, which it is; see further, Windeatt, "The Text of the *Troilus*," pp. 14–15); only belatedly and offhandedly in *The Textual Tradition*, pp. 254–55, does he note this fact.

12. See Root's profession of confusion at *The Textual Tradition*, pp. 261–62. Only Charles A. Owen, Jr., with his customary seriousness about Victorian critical perspectives, has attempted to show a literary rationale for the revisions; see his articles "The Significance of Chaucer's Revision of *Troilus and Criseyde*," *MP* 55 (1957):1–5; "Mimetic Form in the Central Love Scene of *Troilus and Criseyde*," *MP* 67 (1969):125–32, esp. pp. 131–32; and "Minor Changes in Chaucer's *Troilus and Criseyde*," in Beryl Rowland, ed., *Chaucer and Middle English Studies in Honour of Rossell Hope Robbins* (London: Allen and Unwin, 1974), pp. 303–19. But see further Windeatt, "The Text of the *Troilus*," pp. 4–11.

13. The most thoroughgoing demonstration of the scribal nature of the β revisions appears, ironically, in an article designed to defend them: Daniel Cook, "The Revision of Chaucer's *Troilus*: The *Beta* Text," *ChauR* 9 (1974):51–72. What Cook describes as "the direction of the revision" (toward greater explicitness, away from ambiguous and complicated constructions) emphasizes precisely those features that most post-Kane editors would associate with scribal, rather than authorial, behavior. See further Windeatt, "The Text of the *Troilus*," pp. 16–17; F. N. Robinson's review of *Book, Speculum* 1 (1926):461–67, esp. pp. 463–64, and his further comments in *The Works of Geoffrey Chaucer*, 2d ed. (Boston: Houghton Mifflin, 1957), p. xl; J. R. H[ulbert]'s review, *MP* 24 (1926):243–44;

and Loretta Bulow's unpublished Yale dissertation, "Chaucer's Orchestration of the *Troilus*," *DAI* 31 (1970):2868A–69A.

14. *The Textual Tradition*, p. viii. The reference to "significant variation" under category (3) is designed to exclude many variants purely scribal; see further, Root's discussion, ibid., p. ix.

15. Quoted extensively by Joseph Bédier in "La Tradition manuscrite du *Lai de l'Ombre*" (Paris: Librairie Honoré Champion, 1929), pp. 22–28.

16. This and the next three paragraphs attempt an orderly summary of *The Textual Tradition*, chap. 2, pp. 33–83.

17. Root attempted to handle this problem by defining as scribal errors all α passages which do not resemble the Italian more nearly than β γ. But see further *The Textual Tradition*, pp. 111, 127 (on 2.1093) and Windeatt, "The Text of the *Troilus*," p. 12.

18. For Root's discussion of γ and the indefensible readings of J R H$_4$ in book 2, see *The Textual Tradition*, pp. 107–12, 127; for the notable γ variations in book 3, see pp. 129–42, 148, 181 (cf. pp. 173–74); and see n. 13 above.

19. See ibid., pp. 80; 42, 61 (1.143); 43–44, 62 (1.167); and 46–47, 62 (1.259) for the most compelling of the very few examples.

20. See Root's frequent discussions of "The Scattering Agreements of β Manuscripts," for example, in ibid., pp. 76–80, 174–80.

21. See "Publication Before Printing," *PMLA* 28 (1913):417–31. Root probably over-formalizes the process, especially with regard to the preparation of presentation copies; see Richard Firth Green's strictures at *Poets and Princepleasers: Literature and the English Court in the Later Middle Ages* (Toronto: University of Toronto Press, 1980), pp. 205–206.

22. On Adam and his fair copy, see especially *The Textual Tradition*, pp. 119, 125, 177, 180–81, 256–60.

23. See ibid., pp. 80, 94, 142, 236, 259–60.

24. See ibid., pp. 79–80, 174, 177, 255–56. Five copies are presupposed by Root's discussion of β and occur in his diagram of manuscript relations in ibid., p. 272. This conclusion underlies Root's belief that the shared readings of three β copies determine β and that the shared readings of two β copies a "possible β reading," an incongruous retention of genetic conceptions unlikely to be applicable in the situation Root describes.

25. See ibid., pp. 127–28. Root was forced here to hypothesize a further recension "not otherwise represented by any existing MS." (p. 128).

26. The problem of a base text, a form in which to present Chaucer's poem, shows Root at his worst and most out of touch with fact. For although Root required that the text reflect his β readings throughout, there was no surviving usable manuscript that did so—only the late copy R and the *editio princeps* Cx! For the base text Root had to rely on the discredited γ version (especially Cp and Cl); in the process he managed to ignore both the antiquity of these manuscripts (Cp probably pre-1420; Cl, 1399–1413) and the possibility that they were prepared for people likely to have had an intelligent interest in the text.

27. For retention of the nonrhyming manuscript forms where Chaucer's intent and usage is clear, see 3.510 and 1595 (though see also 3.352, where Root emends a rhyme). For the creation of implausible forms resulting from a refusal to acknowledge authorial final -*e*, see 4.1241, *slayn*; 4.1321, *erst*; 5.37, *hors*. For simple conservatism which destroys the meter, see 1.458, 2.220, 5.421. For retention of clearly scribal minor readings, with concomitant assertion that they are the readings of an authorial fair copy, see 1.363, *and*[1]; 3.17, *hem*; 3.1420, *that*.

28. Perhaps the most notable example of rejection concerns the extra stanza following 2.1750 in R: Root thought it genuine but banished it from the text. Other promising but rejected readings occur at 2.777, *why*; 3.529, *fremed*; 4.590, *curiously*; 5.115, *peyne*. In contrast, minority readings which cannot in Root's theory have been authorial are incorporated into the text at 2.248, *fremde*; 3.9, *wel*; 4.302, *wery*; 4.818, *martire*; in many of these cases Root uses the Italian to determine anteriority. See further, *Book*, pp. lxxxiii–lxxxiv.

29. See *The Textual Tradition*, pp. 271–72; and *Book*, pp. lxxxvii–lxxxix. In spite of my cavils, the evidence that Root chose to print still was the most extensive data collection available for any Middle English poem until the Manly-Rickert *Canterbury Tales*.

30. I have used the transcripts at Chaucer Society, 1st ser., nos. 44–65, pp. 114–16 (H$_2$); 1st ser., nos. 63–64, pp. 112–14 (Cl H$_1$ Gg); 1st ser., nos. 87–88, pp. 112–14 (J Cp H$_3$); 1st ser., no. 89, pp. 10–15 (Ph H$_4$ H$_5$ R S$_1$ Cx), 40–45 (A D S$_2$ Dig Th).

31. I give first the reading I would restore to the text, in the spelling of Cp, followed by Root's reading, in the spelling of J and with the sigla of those manuscripts providing it:

256   Al sey I nought thow wost wel what I meene] Ph H$_2$ J Gg H$_5$ H$_4$ Cx Thow woost (H$_5$ wotist) thiseluen what (H$_2$Cx what þat) I wolde meene (R Al seye I noght thow wost what I wolde mene). Root's α β reject the parenthetical clause with its appeal to decorousness and expand the second part over a full line; their archetype must have resembled R, with *wel* already altered to *wolde*. See *The Textual Tradition*, p. 131.

266   and] Ph H$_2$ J Gg H$_5$ so (H$_4$ Inouh to; R to; Cx *om. but* So as *at head of line*). The *and* coordinates *saue* with *kepe*, line 265 (J Gg H$_5$ Cx repeat this verb here, and hence wish to split the construction).

269   that man is vnbore] J Gg H$_5$ H$_4$ S$_1$ Cx neuere was ther (H$_5$ þat, Cx yit) wight. The *neuere* reflects scribal misconception of authorial *vnbore*, with resulting adjustment of word order to achieve meter and substitution of semantic similar *wight* for *man*. See ibid., p. 158.

277   vpon it wolde] Root Ph H$_2$ J H$_3$ S$_1$ Cx Th walde vpon it (Gg H$_5$ wolde on it [H$_5$ þat] gaure *and*; H$_4$ wolde on me pleyne *and*; R wolden on yt). A simple transposition which destroys the meter. See ibid., p. 178.

282   Зet eft I the biseche and fully seye] Root Ph H$_2$ J H$_4$ R Cx The preye ich eft althogh (Ph Cx thogh) thow shuldest dye. Root's α β scribes found Pandarus's statement pallid and "improved" it. The semantic similar *preyen* has been suggested by lines 285 and 287; *fully* may modify *go* 283, but all recorded versions of the line appear scribal. See ibid., p. 178; *Book*, p. 468.

293   Han euere thus prouerbed to vs Зonge] Root J H$_4$ R Cx Han writen or (Cx on) this (H$_4$ o.t. alwey) as yit men (J m.y.) teche vs yonge. The four mss. try to avoid the difficult verb *prouerbed* by the approximation *teche*; at least some scribes seem to have interpreted *euere* as *ere*. The major editorial problem in the line is not, however, the scribal rewriting but *thus* (cf. H$_3$ H$_1$ Th this, J R Cx this . . . yit, Ph H$_2$ Gg H$_5$ Cl A D S$_1$ yet, H$_4$ alwey . . . yit). See *The Textual Tradition*, p. 158.

301   Al seyde men soth] Ph H$_2$ J Gg H$_5$ H$_4$ R Cx Thogh men soth seide (Cx sey). Root's α β manuscripts reject a regular Chaucerian locution which requires inverted verb-subject order for a more prosaic and less metrical equivalent. See ibid., p. 131.

303   Hastow made many] Ph H$_2$ J H$_4$ R Cx Hath maade ful many. The change of verb form reflects misunderstanding of the subject (*O tonge*, line 302, taken as "one tongue" rather than correct apostrophe); *ful* is a typical scribal addition to repair the damage done the meter. See ibid., p. 178; *Book*, pp. 468–69.

310   graunte] Ph H$_2$ J H$_5$ R graunteth (Gg grauntede, S$_2$ Th graunt, Cx louyth). Scribes have substituted the indicative for the idiomatic subjunctive under influence of the subsequent indicative *seith*, line 311.

315   And a lyere] J Gg H$_5$ H$_4$ R H$_1$ Th And liere (Th lyer eke). The omission reflects scribal confusion over the meter: Chaucer's line was headless, with strong rhetorical stress on *And* and with *lyere* a monosyllable.

316   be nought] Ph H$_2$ J H$_3$ Gg H$_5$ H$_4$ R be(n) aught. The text, as Root prints it, nearly inverts the intended sense of the question: "Are they in any wise culpable?" rather than "Aren't they indeed culpable?" The α β version reflects inaccurate scribal word division.

319   Зet bihyghte hem neuere] H$_2$ J Gg H$_5$ H$_4$ R S$_1$ Cl neu*ere* yit behight them (Ph *om. line*; Cx neuer yit, *rest of line Cx's rewriting*). The scribes reduce Chaucer's doubly

emphatic version in order to provide the syntactically explicit *neuere yit*. See *The Textual Tradition*, p. 131.

Root rejected his α β manuscripts at line 262, *for t'abregge* (Ph H_2 J Gg H_5 Cx D *t(o) abregge*), and line 280, *forlost* (Ph H_2 J H_3 R S_1 Cx Th *fordon*); for the latter, see ibid., p. 178. In addition to these readings, he ignored line 255, *maken*, the ungrammatical reading of nearly all manuscripts (S_2 Dig *makes*, probably intended as plurals; H_4 *don these*): the text should, I think, read *maketh*. The form *maken* has been scribally generated on the mistaken assumption that its adjacent plural object *wommen* is in fact its subject. And line 304, *Seyde* (H_5 R Cx S_2 Dig *Sey*) needs at least a note to indicate that the construction is not "made her say" but "made (such a situation that) she said."

32. See *Book*, pp. li–lxxxix, for textual material, and pp. xx–li, for literary material.

33. See the notes to 3.715ff., 3.1419–20, 1.306–307, 3.404–406, 5.745–49, 4.622 for examples of Root's knowledge of the medieval background. As simply one example of the broad literary familiarity which Root brings to the poem, see the note to 2.22–25.

I wish to express my gratitude to Professors George Kane, Barry Windeatt, A. S. G. Edwards, and Donald C. Baker for their several suggestions now incorporated into this essay.

Chapter 11

1. The important reviews were those by Carleton Brown, *MLN* 55 (1940):606–21; Dorothy Everett, *RES* 18 (1942):93–109, and *YWES* 21 (1940):46–50; and R. K. Root, *SP* 38 (1941):1–13. Manly's apologist Germaine Dempster singled out Root's review as especially perceptive ("Manly's Conception of the Early History of the *Canterbury Tales*," *PMLA* 61 (1946):379–415); Brown's was in fact also penetrating. The language of all was gentle, but Root's hostility can by hindsight be detected.

2. The process is well described in G. Pasquali, *Storia della Tradizione e Critica del Testo*, 2d ed. (Florence: F. Le Monnier, 1952).

3. There is even resistance to the process, as if our poets had been careless of the form and meaning of their verse, and their medieval readers content with texts that sometimes made bad sense or bad verse. Some of the blame for this lies with George Saintsbury (see *A History of English Prosody*, [London, 1906], 1.167, 168), some with French textual critics two generations ago (on whom see J. Fourquet, *Le Paradoxe de Bédier*, University of Strasbourg Faculty of Letters Publications, fasc. 105 [Paris, 1946]). But the notion that textual criticism is frivolous or self-indulgent will always have an appeal for those who find its conditions intellectually too demanding.

4. John M. Manly and Edith Rickert, eds., *The Text of the Canterbury Tales Studied on the Basis of All Known Manuscripts* (Chicago and London: University of Chicago Press, 1940), 1.150. Parenthetical text and note references are to volume and page of this edition.

5. This is a trap for the inexperienced, but in fairness the suggestion of inconsistency between the account of collation in 2.10 and the description of the contents of the apparatus (5.v) is not real: it is quickly apparent that language variants do not figure in the latter. It was clearly impracticable to admit them.

6. Of course, when that process which, as a hypothesis, is by definition provisional, has been carried out, the archetypal text of the manuscript has to a large extent effectively been recovered. This is such an obvious consideration that I continue amazed at never having seen it expressed.

7. This was apparently the *Student's Chaucer* first issued in 1895 by the Clarendon Press and often reprinted. It was a confidently edited text: Skeat observed (p. 719) that "there are very few doubtful readings in the Canterbury Tales" and listed thirty-three (pp. 731, 732). He did not signal emendations.

8. Either they changed their views about this, or they did not have any clearly formed views. Compare 2.22, 23, 26 and 2.419. In the first place "individually trifling variants" are said to have classificatory value, to indicate "the original text-tradition" better than striking variants; in the second agreement between a number of such variants is ascribed to coincident variation.

9. Carleton Brown (*MLN*, pp. 609, 610) sensed involvement in "contradictions and discrepancies" here.

10. The system of symbols set out at 2.44, 45 makes this impracticable.

11. See note 36 below.

12. See above, p. 209 and n. 36 below.

13. Its greatest exponent in our time, Paul Maas, spent more than a generation refining its techniques, already well developed by classical editors. His essay *Textkritik* first appeared in 1927 in Gercke and Norden's *Einleitung in die Altertumswissenschaft*; he several times modified and supplemented it. The last impression appeared in 1960.

14. Dempster, "Manly's Conception of the Early History of the *Canterbury Tales*," p. 414.

15. This was noticed by Brown (*MLN*, p. 620) and by Everett (*RES*, pp. 108, 109).

16. A. E. Housman, *Selected Prose* (Cambridge: Cambridge University Press, 1961), p. 43.

17. Maas, sec. 13; cf. Housman, *Selected Prose*, pp. 35ff.

18. Much information about scribal habits was available in the 1930s. In particular, F. W. Hall's *Companion to Classical Texts* (Oxford: Oxford University Press, 1913) provided analysis of mechanical error; J. J. Griesbach, *Novvm Testamentvm Graece*, 2d ed. (London, 1796), B. F. Westcott and F. J. A. Hort, *The New Testament in the Original Greek* (Cambridge and London: Cambridge University Press, 1881), identified kinds of variation prompted by scribal response to the text being copied.

19. See below, p. 217ff.

20. As was suggested by E. T. Donaldson, *Chaucer's Poetry*, 2d ed. (New York: Ronald Press, 1975), p. 254.

21. *Procul recedant somnia Et noctium phantasmata; hostemque nostrum comprime Ne polluantur corpora.* The lines are from "Hymn for Compline," *Te lucis ante terminum*, F. J. E. Raby, ed., *The Oxford Book of Medieval Latin Verse* (Oxford: Oxford University Press, 1959), p. 48, See *Breviarium ad Usum Insignis Ecclesie Eboracensis, Surtees Society*, vol. 71 (London, 1880), col. 5. I am obliged to my colleague J. S. Wittig for pointing out their aptness here.

22. *RES*, p. 96.

23. 3.465, 466: notes to D 1693, 1695.

24. See *OED*, s.v. *As* conj. 9, *MED* s.v. *as* conj. 2a; *OED* s.v. *Be* v. 16, *MED* s.v. *ben* v. 8; also T. Mustanoja, *A Middle English Syntax* (Helsinki, 1960), p. 465.

25. *OED*, s.v. *That* conj. II.2, "Introducing a clause expressing the cause, ground or reason of what is stated in the principal clause." Compare, e.g., *Me is þe vvrs þat ich þe so*, E. G. Stanley, ed., *The Owl and the Nightingale* (London: Nelson, 1960), line 34; *Two dayes þer fastinde he yede þat non for his werk wolde him fede*, W. W. Skeat, ed., *The Lay of Havelok the Dane*, 2d ed., rev. K. Sisam (Oxford: Oxford University Press, 1973), lines 865, 866; and *To him heo hadde gret envie þat he so riche beo* (sc. *sholde beo*), C. d'Evelyn and A. J. Mills, eds., *The South English Legendary*, EETS, o.s. 235 (London, 1956), p. 282.

26. Likely usages would be *I hote*, *I bidde*, or imperative *do way* or *do so*. I cannot recall *I seie* in such a use.

27. See, for instance, 2.84, 102, 157, 201–202, 238–39.

28. F. N. Robinson, ed., *The Complete Works of Geoffrey Chaucer* (Cambridge, Mass.: Houghton Mifflin, 1933), p. xxxiii.

29. *Confessio Amantis* 5.4787, 4788 and 7716, 7717: *The English Works of John Gower*, vol. II, EETS, o.s. 82 (London, 1901), pp. 77, 163.

30. So Larry D. Benson, "The Order of *The Canterbury Tales*," *Studies in the Age of Chaucer*

2(1981):77–120, and Charles Owen, "The Alternative Reading of *The Canterbury Tales*: Chaucer's Text and the Early Manuscripts," *PMLA* 97 (1982):237–50.

31. Whether or not Chaucer knew this, it is a *sirventes* in the form *coblas unissonans*.

32. F. N. Robinson, *The Works of Geoffrey Chaucer*, 2d ed. (Boston: Houghton Mifflin, 1957), p. 712.

33. If I read the apparatus correctly, these are He Ne Cx^1 Tc^2 (the editors' group *b*), To (?)Ld^1 Ry^1 (in the editors' group *d**), Ha^2 (in the "*cd* line") and Se (in group *d**). In Se the lines are at the foot of the page in the main hand. The classifications are from the descriptions of the manuscripts. I have been unable to translate them meaningfully into the genetic scheme for *The Miller's Tale* (3.128).

34. There is a suggestion in the variants that the original of 1007, 1008 read *Wo was his herte . . . And with a sorweful chere*.

35. Cf. *OED*, s. vv. *Win* v. [1]7d and *Spur* sb. 3a.

36. For a start the Manly and Rickert collations, which survive, will have to be checked for correctness: we know nothing about the training of the "very large staff" who produced them, and not all fifteenth-century Chaucer manuscript hands are easy. If the check is favorable, the next step is to establish a norm for collection of variant groups by provisional determination of originality in the largest possible number of places. That sounds formidible, but should not be hard in most instances, as Skeat (*Student's Chaucer*, p. 719) observed. Only then comes the collection of the groups formed by agreement in variation from that text. This will be best done in the first instance separately for each formal section of the poem. Here the *codices deteriores*, copies of surviving copies, will identify themselves and are to be eliminated. Now at length the variant groups can be examined with respect to persistency and congruency, with allowance for the essential likelihood of convergent variation (by both coincidence and contamination) and taking into account that in genetic schemes it is possible for a single manuscript to have the status of a family. It may turn out that no significant classification is possible. If, on the other hand, a system of groupings sufficiently well defined to be recognizable as stemmatic should prove discernible, the result will have great value, for simply by its existence as a consonant hypothesis it will confirm the effectiveness of the first one, the provisional identification of originality. It will also enable identification of authorial revision to be undertaken with less danger of begging the question.

Chapter 12

1. Typed carbon single sheet of December 1, 1904, on Houghton Mifflin letterhead, closing (typescript) "Bliss Perry for Houghton, Mifflin & Co.," in the contractual files of Houghton Mifflin. See also Bliss Perry's autobiography, *And Gladly Teach* (Boston: Houghton Mifflin, 1935), pp. 185, 228, 236, and chap. 10 *passim*, as well as Ellen B. Ballou, *The Building of the House: Houghton Mifflin's Formative Years* (Boston: Houghton Mifflin, 1970).

2. Manuscript letter, single sheet, headed Longfellow Park, Cambridge, and signed "Fred N. Robinson," in the contractual files, Houghton Mifflin. My sincere thanks to Paul Kosiak and Dorothy Kirk, of Houghton Mifflin, for receiving my requests so courteously and giving me copies of the papers still surviving.

3. A two-page bibliography made available by Charles W. Dunn, of the Celtic Department, Harvard, admittedly incomplete, lists only two older English items other than the *Complete Works*. Dunn was named literary executor in Robinson's will. My thanks are due him for a very courteous reception and permission to use and copy the materials now uncatalogued in the Harvard Archives.

4. "Fred Norris Robinson: Memorial Minute Adopted by the Faculty of Arts and Sciences, Harvard University, April 11, 1967," reprint from *Harvard University Gazette* 62, no. 34 (May 13, 1967).

5. Two sheets (both sides) of typescript letter to me, headed "Harvard University Department of English" but reheaded "Belfast, Maine" and dated December 2, 1980, signed "Jere."

6. Ibid.

7. My sincere thanks are due to Francis Brooks, of Chestnut Hill, Mass., who entrusted to me a large selection of Robinson's papers in his possession.

8. Typed, signed one-page letter from Walter Clyde Curry, headed "Nashville," dated October 12, 1933.

9. One-sheet handwritten letter from Chester Greenough, headed "Cambridge," dated June 15, 1933.

10. Review, *Saturday Review of Literature* 10 (1934):311.

11. One-sheet handwritten letter from G. G. Coulton, signed, dated June 5, 1933; typed, signed two-sheet letter from Carleton Brown, headed "New York," dated May 17, 1933.

12. One-sheet handwritten letter from Karl Young, headed "New Haven," dated May 11, 1933.

13. None of these letters, all among the Robinson papers in the Pusey Library, Harvard Archives, were catalogued when I used them in April, 1981. The director and staff of the archives were most helpful in giving me room in which to work and assisting me in having Xerox reproductions made of the more important papers. Thanks are also due to the Graduate Council Research Fund, University of New Orleans, which assisted my travel.

14. Albert Marckwardt, Review, *EJ* 23, pp. 433–34.

15. Dorothy Everett, in *YWES* 14 (1935):103ff.; "A New Chaucer," *TLS*, February 22, 1934, p. 123. See also Everett's review in *MÆ* 7 (1938):204–13.

16. Hermann Heuer, Review, *Anglia Beiblatt* 45, pp. 201–204.

17. Alois Brandl, Review, *Herrigs Archiv* 164 (1934):266–68.

18. Everett in *YWES*, p. 104.

19. M. B. Ruud, Review, *MLN* 50 (1935):329–32.

20. J. S. P. Tatlock, Review, *Speculum* 9 (1934):459–64.

21. Ibid., pp. 459–60.

22. John A. Burrow, *Geoffrey Chaucer: A Critical Anthology* (Harmondsworth: Penguin, 1970).

23. F. W. Bateson, *A Guide to English Literature*, 2d ed. (Garden City, N.Y.: Doubleday, Anchor Books, 1968), p. 38.

24. Aage Brusendorff, *The Chaucer Tradition* (Oxford: Oxford University Press, 1925), pp. 93ff.; John Strong Perry Tatlock, *The Harleian MS 7334 and Revision of the Canterbury Tales* (London: Chaucer Society, 2d ser., no. 41, 1909), passim.

25. Joseph Bédier, ed., *Le Lai de l'ombre*, by Jean Renart (Paris: Société des Anciens Textes Français, no. 12, 1913), pp. vi–vii, xxiii—xlv. See also James Thorpe, *Principles of Textual Criticism* (San Marino, Calif.: Huntington Library, 1972), pp. 114–15.

26. André Morize, *Problems and Methods of Literary History* (Boston: Ginn and Co., ca. 1922, pp. 41–47.

27. Bédier, ed., *Le Lai de l'ombre*, p. xli.

28. See n. 24.

29. John M. Manly and Edith Rickert, eds., *The Text of the Canterbury Tales*, 8 vols. (Chicago: University of Chicago Press, 1940).

30. Walter W. Skeat, ed., *The Works of Geoffrey Chaucer and others: A Facsimile of the Edition of 1532* (London: A. Moring and Oxford University Press, 1905).

31. John Koch, ed., *Geoffrey Chaucers Kleinere Dichtungen* (Heidelberg: Carl Winter, 1928); Alfred W. Pollard, H. Frank Heath, et al., eds., *The Works of Geoffrey Chaucer*, Globe edition (London: Macmillan, 1898).

32. D. S. Brewer, ed., *The Parlement of Foulys* (London: Nelson, ca. 1960).

33. Mabel Day, Review of RB[1] in *RES* 11 (1935):346–47.

34. Charles Moorman, *Editing the Middle English Manuscript* (Jackson: University Press of Mississippi, 1975), p. 46, says that Manly and Rickert used Skeat's one-volume edition as copy text.

35. John S. P. Tatlock and Arthur G. Kennedy, *A Concordance to the Complete Works of Geoffrey Chaucer and to the Romaunt of the Rose* (Washington, D.C.: Carnegie Institution, 1927).

36. See lines H 46, 89, 99, 147, 157, 170, 185, 263, 268, 280, 290, 310.

37. It may be useful bibliographically to remark that Houghton Mifflin, without Robinson's knowledge, changed the title page of RB[1] shortly after World War II, and thereby the title was silently changed from *The Complete Works of Chaucer* to *The Poetical Works of Chaucer*, though the plates of the edition remained the same, and none of the prose was eliminated. The simultaneous publication in 1933 by Oxford University Press bears a different title page, of course, but the title remained as in the American first edition before the change. The second edition, published in 1957, bears the title *The Works of Chaucer* because *The Equatorie of the Planets*, ed. Derek Price and R. M. Wilson (1955), had been advanced as Chaucer's work, and Robinson did not wish to edit it again.

Index